ANNA JULIA COOPER

# The Portable
# Anna Julia Cooper

*Edited with an Introduction by*
SHIRLEY MOODY-TURNER

*General Editor:*
HENRY LOUIS GATES, JR.

PENGUIN BOOKS

PENGUIN BOOKS

An imprint of Penguin Random House LLC
penguinrandomhouse.com

LIBRARY OF CONGRESS CATALOGING-IN-PUBLICATION DATA
Names: Cooper, Anna J. (Anna Julia), 1858–1964, author. |
Moody-Turner, Shirley, editor, writer of introduction. | Gates, Henry Louis, Jr., editor.
Title: The portable Anna Julia Cooper / Anna Julia Cooper ; edited and with an
introduction by Shirley Moody-Turner ; general editor, Henry Louis Gates, Jr.
Description: [New York, New York] : Penguin Books, [2022] | Series: Penguin classics |
Includes bibliographical references.
Identifiers: LCCN 2021051069 (print) | LCCN 2021051070 (ebook) |
ISBN 9780143135067 (trade paperback) | ISBN 9780525506713 (ebook)
Subjects: LCSH: Cooper, Anna J. (Anna Julia), 1858–1964—Correspondence. |
African American women—Southern States—History—19th century—Sources. |
Southern States—Race relations—Sources.
Classification: LCC E185.86 .C5868 2022 (print) | LCC E185.86 (ebook) |
DDC 370.92—dc23/eng/20211108
LC record available at https://lccn.loc.gov/2021051069
LC ebook record available at https://lccn.loc.gov/2021051070

Printed in the United States of America
1st Printing

Set in Sabon LT Pro

# Contents

## THE PORTABLE ANNA JULIA COOPER

### PART I: MAJOR TEXT

### PART II: *ON EDUCATION*

## PART III:
## SCRAPBOOK, 1931–1940:
## NEWSPAPER AND OTHER WRITINGS

## PART IV: CORRESPONDENCES

### Anna Julia Cooper–W. E. B. Du Bois
### Correspondences, 1923–1932

# What Is an African
# American Classic?

I have long nurtured a deep and abiding affection for the Penguin Classics, at least since I was an undergraduate at Yale. I used to imagine that my attraction for these books—grouped together, as a set, in some independent bookstores when I was a student, and perhaps even in some today—stemmed from the fact that my first-grade classmates, for some reason that I can't recall, were required to dress as penguins in our annual all-school pageant, and perform a collective side-to-side motion that our misguided teacher thought she could choreograph into something meant to pass for a "dance." Piedmont, West Virginia, in 1956, was a very long way from Penguin Nation, wherever that was supposed to be! But penguins we were determined to be, and we did our level best to avoid wounding each other with our orange-colored cardboard beaks while stomping out of rhythm in our matching orange, veined webbed feet. The whole scene was madness, one never to be repeated at the Davis Free School. But I never stopped loving penguins. And I have never stopped loving the very audacity of the idea of the Penguin Classics, an affordable, accessible library of the most important and compelling texts in the history of civilization, their black-and-white spines and covers and uniform type giving each text a comfortable, familiar feel, as if we have encountered it, or its cousins, before. I think of the Penguin Classics as the very best and most compelling in human thought, an Alexandrian library in paperback, enclosed in black and white.

I still gravitate to the Penguin Classics when killing time in an airport bookstore, deferring the slow torture of the security lines. Sometimes I even purchase two or three, fantasizing that I can speed-read one of the shorter titles, then make a dent in the longer one, vainly attempting to fill the holes in the liberal arts education that our degrees suggest we have, over the course of a plane ride! Mark Twain once quipped that a classic is "something that everybody wants to have read and nobody wants to read," and perhaps that applies to my airport purchasing habits. For my generation, these titles in the Penguin Classics form the canon—the canon of the texts that a truly well-educated person should have read, and read carefully and closely, at least once. For years I rued the absence of texts by black authors in this series, and longed to be able to make even a small contribution to the diversification of this astonishingly universal list. I watched with great pleasure as titles by African American and African authors began to appear, some two dozen over the past several years. So when Elda Rotor approached me about editing a series of African American classics and collections for Penguin's Portable Series, I eagerly accepted.

Thinking about the titles appropriate for inclusion in these series led me, inevitably, to think about what, for me, constitutes a "classic." And thinking about this led me, in turn, to the wealth of reflections on what defines a work of literature or philosophy somehow speaking to the human condition beyond time and place, a work somehow endlessly compelling, generation upon generation, a work whose author we don't have to look like to identify with, to feel at one with, as we find ourselves transported through the magic of a textual time machine; a work that refracts the image of ourselves that we project onto it, regardless of our ethnicity, our gender, our time, our place. This is what centuries of scholars and writers have meant when they use the word *classic*, and—despite all that we know about the complex intersubjectivity of the production of meaning in the wondrous exchange between a reader and a text—it remains true that classic texts, even in the most conventional, conservative sense of the word *classic*, do exist, and these books will continue to be read long after the generation the text reflects and defines, the generation of readers contemporary with the text's author, is dead and gone. Classic texts speak from their authors' graves, in their names, in their voices. As Italo Calvino once remarked, "A classic is a book that has never finished saying what it has to say."

Faulkner put this idea in an interesting way: "The aim of every artist is to arrest motion, which is life, by artificial means, and hold it fixed so that a hundred years later, when a stranger looks at it, it moves again since it is life." That, I am certain, must be the desire of every writer. But what about the reader? What makes a book a classic to a reader? Here, perhaps, Hemingway said it best: "All good books are alike in that they are truer than if they had really happened and after you are finished reading one you will feel that all that happened to you, and afterward it belongs to you, the good and the bad, the ecstasy, the remorse and sorrow, the people and the places and how the weather was."

I have been reading black literature since I was fifteen, yanked into the dark discursive universe by an Episcopal priest at a church camp near my home in West Virginia in August 1965, during the terrifying days of the Watts Riots in Los Angeles. Eventually, by fits and starts, studying the literature written by black authors became my avocation; ultimately, it has become my vocation. And, in my own way, I have tried to be an evangelist for it, to a readership larger than my own people, people who, as it were, look like these texts. Here, I am reminded of something W. S. Merwin said about the books he most loved: "Perhaps a classic is a work that one imagines should be common knowledge, but more and more often isn't." I would say, of African and African American literature, that perhaps classic works by black writers are works that one imagines should be common knowledge among the broadest possible readership but that less and less are, as the teaching of reading to understand how words can create the worlds into which books can transport us yields to classroom instruction geared toward passing a state-authorized standardized exam. All literary texts suffer from this wrongheaded approach to teaching, mind you; but it especially affects texts by people of color, and texts by women—texts still struggling, despite enormous gains over the last twenty years, to gain a solid foothold in anthologies and syllabi. For every anthology, every syllabus, every publishing series such as the Penguin Classics constitutes a distinct "canon," an implicit definition of all that is essential for a truly educated person to read.

James Baldwin, who has pride of place in my personal canon

of African American authors since it was one of his books that that Episcopal priest gave me to read in that dreadful summer of 1965, argued that "the responsibility of a writer is to excavate the experience of the people who produced him." But surely Baldwin would have agreed with E. M. Forster that the books that we remember, the books that have truly influenced us, are those that "have gone a little further down our particular path than we have yet ourselves." Excavating the known is a worthy goal of the writer as cultural archeologist; yet, at the same time, so is unveiling the unknown, the unarticulated yet shared experience of the colorless things that make us human: "something we have always known (or thought we knew)," as Calvino puts it, "but without knowing that this author said it first." We might think of the difference between Forster and Baldwin, on the one hand, and Calvino, on the other, as the difference between an author representing what has happened (Forster, Baldwin) in the history of a people whose stories, whose very history itself, has long been suppressed, and what could have happened (Calvino) in the atemporal realm of art. This is an important distinction when thinking about the nature of an African American classic—rather, when thinking about the nature of the texts that constitute the African American literary tradition or, for that matter, the texts in any under-read tradition.

One of James Baldwin's most memorable essays, a subtle meditation on sexual preference, race, and gender, is entitled "Here Be Dragons." So much of traditional African American literature, even fiction and poetry—ostensibly at least once removed from direct statement—was meant to deal a fatal blow to the dragon of racism. For black writers since the eighteenth-century beginnings of the tradition, literature has been one more weapon—a very important weapon, mind you, but still one weapon among many—in the arsenal black people have drawn upon to fight against antiblack racism and for their equal rights before the law. Ted Joans, the black surrealist poet, called this sort of literature from the sixties' Black Arts Movement "hand grenade poems." Of what possible use are the niceties of figuration when one must slay a dragon? I can hear you say, give me the blunt weapon anytime! Problem is, it is more difficult than some writers seem to think to slay a dragon with a poem or a novel. Social problems persist; literature too tied to addressing those social problems tends to enter the historical archives, leaving the realm of the literary. Let me state bluntly what should be obvious: Writers are read for how they write, not what they write about.

Frederick Douglass—for this generation of readers one of the most widely read writers—reflected on this matter even in the midst of one of his most fiery speeches addressing the ironies of the sons and daughters of slaves celebrating the Fourth of July while slavery continued unabated. In his now-classic essay "What to the Slave Is the Fourth of July?" (1852), Douglass argued that an immediate, almost transparent form of discourse was demanded of black writers by the heated temper of the times, a discourse with an immediate end in mind: "At a time like this, scorching irony, not convincing argument, is needed . . . a fiery stream of biting ridicule, blasting reproach, withering sarcasm, and stern rebuke. For it is not light that is needed, but fire; it is not the gentle shower, but thunder. We need the storm, the whirlwind, and the earthquake." Above all else, Douglass concludes, the rhetoric of the literature created by African Americans must, of necessity, be a purposeful rhetoric, its ends targeted at attacking the evils that afflict black people: "The feeling of the nation must be quickened; the conscience of the nation must be roused; the propriety of the nation must be startled; the hypocrisy of the nation must be exposed; and its crimes against God and man must be proclaimed and denounced." And perhaps this was so; nevertheless, we read Douglass's writings today in literature classes not so much for their content but to understand, and marvel at, his sublime mastery of words, words—to paraphrase Calvino—that never finish saying what it is they have to say, not because of their "message" but because of the language in which that message is inextricably enfolded.

There are as many ways to define a classic in the African American tradition as there are in any other tradition, and these ways are legion. So many essays have been published entitled "What Is a Classic?" that they could fill several large anthologies. And while no one can say explicitly why generations of readers return to read certain texts, just about everyone can agree that making a best-seller list in one's lifetime is most

certainly not an index of fame or influence over time; the longevity of one's readership—of books about which one says, "I am
rereading," as Calvino puts it—on the other hand, most certainly is. So, the size of one's readership (through library use,
Internet access, and sales) cumulatively is an interesting factor to
consider; and because of series such as the Penguin Classics, we
can gain a sense, for our purposes, of those texts written by authors in previous generations that have sustained sales—mostly
for classroom use—long after their authors were dead.

There can be little doubt that *Narrative of the Life of Frederick
Douglass* (1845), *The Souls of Black Folk* (1903) by W. E. B. Du
Bois, and *Their Eyes Were Watching God* (1937) by Zora Neale
Hurston, are the three most classic of the black classics—again,
as measured by consumption—while Langston Hughes's poetry,
though not purchased as books in these large numbers, is ac-
cessed through the Internet as frequently as that of any other
American poet, and indeed profoundly more so than most.
Within Penguin's Portable Series list, the most popular individ-
ual titles, excluding Douglass's first slave narrative and Du Bois's
*Souls*, are:

*Up from Slavery* (1903), Booker T. Washington
*The Autobiography of an Ex-Colored Man* (1912),
    James Weldon Johnson
*God's Trombones* (1926), James Weldon Johnson
*Passing* (1929), Nella Larsen
*The Marrow of Tradition* (1898), Charles W. Chesnutt
*Incidents in the Life of a Slave Girl* (1861), Harriet Jacobs
*The Interesting Narrative* (1789), Olaudah Equiano
*The House Behind the Cedars* (1900), Charles W. Chesnutt
*My Bondage and My Freedom* (1855), Frederick Douglass
*Quicksand* (1928), Nella Larsen

These titles form a canon of classic African American literature, judged by classroom readership. If we add Jean Toomer's
novel *Cane* (1922), arguably the first work of African American modernism, along with Douglass's first narrative, Du Bois's
*The Souls*, and Hurston's *Their Eyes*, we would most certainly
have included many of the touchstones of black literature

published before 1940, when Richard Wright published *Native Son*.

Every teacher's syllabus constitutes a canon of sorts, and I teach these texts and a few others as the classics of the black canon. Why these particular texts? I can think of two reasons: First, these texts signify or riff upon each other, repeating, borrowing, and extending metaphors book to book, generation to generation. To take just a few examples, Equiano's eighteenth-century use of the trope of the talking book (an image found, remarkably, in five slave narratives published between 1770 and 1811) becomes, with Frederick Douglass, the representation of the quest for freedom as, necessarily, the quest for literacy, for a freedom larger than physical manumission; we might think of this as the representation of metaphysical manumission, of freedom and literacy—the literacy of great literature—inextricably intertwined. Douglass transformed the metaphor of the talking book into the trope of chiasmus, a repetition with a stinging reversal: "You have seen how a man becomes a slave, you will see how a slave becomes a man." Du Bois, with Douglass very much on his mind, transmuted chiasmus a half century later into the metaphor of duality or double consciousness, a necessary condition of living one's life, as he memorably put it, behind a "veil."

Du Bois's metaphor has a powerful legacy in twentieth-century black fiction: James Weldon Johnson, in *Ex-Colored Man*, literalizes the trope of double consciousness by depicting as his protagonist a man who, at will, can occupy two distinct racial spaces, one black, one white, and who moves seamlessly, if ruefully, between them; Toomer's *Cane* takes Du Bois's metaphor of duality for the inevitably split consciousness that every Negro must feel living in a country in which her or his status as a citizen is liminal at best, or has been erased at worst, and makes of this the metaphor for the human condition itself under modernity, a tellingly bold rhetorical gesture—one designed to make the Negro the metaphor of the human condition. And Hurston, in *Their Eyes*, extends Toomer's revision even further, depicting a character who can gain her voice only once she can name this condition of duality or double consciousness and then glide gracefully and lyrically between her two selves, an "inside" self and an "outside" one.

More recently, Alice Walker, in *The Color Purple*, signifies upon two aspects of the narrative strategy of *Their Eyes*: First, she revisits the theme of a young black woman finding her voice, depicting a protagonist who writes herself into being through letters addressed to God and to her sister, Nettie—letters that grow ever more sophisticated in their syntax and grammar and imagery as she comes to consciousness before our very eyes, letter to letter; and second, Walker riffs on Hurston's use of a vernacular-inflected free indirect discourse to show that black English has the capacity to serve as the medium for narrating a novel through the black dialect that forms a most pliable and expansive language in Celie's letters. Ralph Ellison makes Du Bois's metaphor of the veil a trope of blindness and life underground for his protagonist in *Invisible Man*, a protagonist who, as he types the story of his life from a hole underground, writes himself into being in the first person (in contradistinction to Richard Wright's protagonist, Bigger Thomas, whose reactive tale of fear and flight is told in the third person). Walker's novel also riffs on Ellison's claim for the revolutionary possibilities of writing the self into being, whereas Hurston's protagonist, Janie, speaks herself into being. Ellison himself signified multiply upon Richard Wright's *Native Son*, from the title to the use of the first-person bildungs-roman to chart the coming to consciousness of a sensitive protagonist moving from blindness and an inability to do little more than react to his environment, to the insight gained by wresting control of his identity from social forces and strong individuals that would circumscribe and confine his life choices. Toni Morrison, master supernaturalist and perhaps the greatest black novelist of all, trumps Ellison's trope of blindness by returning over and over to the possibilities and limits of insight within worlds confined or circumscribed not by supraforces (à la Wright) but by the confines of the imagination and the ironies of individual and family history, signifying upon Faulkner, Woolf, and García Márquez in the process. And Ishmael Reed, the father of black postmodernism and what we might think of as the hip-hop novel, the tradition's master parodist, signifies upon everybody and everything in the black literary tradition, from the slave narratives to the Harlem Renaissance to black nationalism and feminism.

This sort of literary signifying is what makes a literary tradition, well, a "tradition," rather than a simple list of books whose authors happen to have been born in the same country, share the same gender, or would be identified by their peers as belonging to this ethnic group or that. What makes these books special—"classic"—however, is something else. Each text has the uncanny capacity to take the seemingly mundane details of the day-to-day African American experience of its time and transmute those details and the characters' actions into something that transcends its ostensible subject's time and place, its specificity. These texts reveal the human universal through the African American particular: All true art, all classics, do this; this is what "art" is, a revelation of that which makes each of us sublimely human, rendered in the minute details of the actions and thoughts and feelings of a compelling character embedded in a time and place. But as soon as we find ourselves turning to a text for its anthropological or sociological data, we have left the realm of art; we have reduced the complexity of fiction or poetry to an essay, and this is not what imaginative literature is for. Richard Wright, at his best, did this, as did his signifying disciple Ralph Ellison; Louis Armstrong and Duke Ellington, Bessie Smith and Billie Holiday achieved this effect in music; Jacob Lawrence and Romare Bearden achieved it in the visual arts. And this is what Wole Soyinka does in his tragedies, what Toni Morrison does in her novels, what Derek Walcott did in his poetry. And while it is risky to name one's contemporaries in a list such as this, I think that Rita Dove and Jamaica Kincaid achieve this effect as well, as do Colson Whitehead and Edwidge Danticat, in a younger generation. (There are other writers whom I would include in this group had I the space.) By delving ever so deeply into the particularity of the African and African American experience, these authors manage, somehow, to come out the other side, making the race or the gender of their characters almost translucent, less important than the fact that they stand as aspects of ourselves beyond race or gender or time or place, precisely in the same magical way that Hamlet never remains for long stuck as a prince in a court in Denmark.

Each classic black text reveals to us, uncannily, subtly, how the Black Experience is inscribed, inextricably and indelibly, in the human experience, and how the human experience takes one of its myriad forms in blackface, as it were. Together, such texts also demonstrate, implicitly, that African American culture is one of the world's truly great and eternal cultures, as noble and as resplendent as any. And it is to publish such texts, written by African and African American authors, that Penguin has created this new series, which I have the pleasure of editing.

HENRY LOUIS GATES, JR.

# Introduction

To me life has always meant a big opportunity and I am
thankful that my work has always been the sort that beckoned
me on.

—Anna Julia Cooper

In March 1886, Anna Julia Cooper (1858–1964) addressed the
"colored clergy" of the Protestant Episcopal Church in Washington,
DC. Only twenty-eight years old at the time, she stood before
the convocation and asserted that the Black woman had not
yet received her "hearing at the bar." Her voice, Cooper contended,
had been left out of the social and political debates about
African Americans' rights and women's rights that preoccupied
the country in the turbulent years following Reconstruction. In
the clashes over Black political rights and freedom, the Black
woman was as yet the "mute and voiceless note." Now, however,
in the waning years of the nineteenth century, Cooper was calling
for a change.

Recognized as an iconic foremother of Black women's intellectual
history and activism, Anna Julia Cooper penned one of the
most forceful and enduring statements of Black feminist thought
to come out of the nineteenth century. *The Portable Anna Julia
Cooper* publishes Cooper's groundbreaking text, *A Voice from
the South, by a Black Woman of the South*, alongside several
previously unpublished poems, plays, journalism, and selected
correspondences, including almost thirty letters between Cooper
and W. E. B. Du Bois, that chart the emergence of Cooper's
voice as an educator, public intellectual, social theorist, cultural
critic, essayist, poet, and reformer. It locates Cooper's writings

in the context of key historical moments spanning from the Civil War to the Civil Rights movement. More than simply a collection of writings, however, this edition also documents the arduous path to voice and publication that Cooper, and so many of her contemporaries, trudged in order to steward their writings into print, or as Cooper stated, to claim their "hearing at the bar." In this way, *The Portable Anna Julia Cooper* introduces a new generation of readers to an educator, public intellectual, and community activist whose prescient insights and eloquent prose underlie some of the most important developments in modern American intellectual thought and African American social and political activism. At the same time, this edition makes visible the ways race and gender discrimination impacted publishing opportunities for Black women, asking readers to be attentive not only to the published documents and printed materials, but also to the gaps, silences, and fissures that often haunt the archives of Black women writers.

Born into slavery in Raleigh, North Carolina, in 1858, Anna Julia Haywood Cooper rose to prominence by century's end as one of the most influential voices on racial and gender equality in the US. Her mother, Hannah Stanley Haywood (1817–1899), was enslaved by the Haywood family in Raleigh, and Cooper's father was likely her mother's "owner," Fabius J. Haywood. Cooper, however, never recognized Fabius Haywood as such, writing in an autobiographical note, "I was born in Raleigh North Carolina. My mother was a slave & the finest woman I have ever known. Tho untutored she could read her Bible & write a little. . . . Presumably my father was her master, if so I owe him not a sou."[1] At age nine, Cooper followed the trajectory of many post-Emancipation African Americans in seeking educational opportunities and entered Saint Augustine Normal and Collegiate Institute in Raleigh. It was there that Cooper staged one of her earliest protests against the educational disparities she would go on to confront throughout her life. Founded in 1867 under the auspices of the Freedmen's Bureau and the Episcopal Church, Saint Augustine offered African Americans in Raleigh and surrounding areas access to both vocational training and liberal arts education. This access, however, was not without its gender disparities, and Cooper had to petition for admittance into Saint Augustine's courses in Greek and Latin. Cooper recalls of her time at Saint Augustine, "A boy . . . had only to declare a floating intention to study theology and he could get all the support, encouragement and stimulus he needed . . . While a self-supporting girl had to struggle on by teaching in the summer and working after school hours to keep up with her board bills, and actually to fight her way against positive discouragement to the higher education."[2] Through her protests, Cooper gained access to the courses, but she would be forced to wage a similar protest when she left Saint Augustine to attend Oberlin College in 1881. Upon arriving at Oberlin, Cooper found herself again shut out of the "gentlemen's courses," and she again petitioned for access to the classes. These early protests would be critical in shaping Cooper's intellectual and activist agenda as she worked to pursue advanced educational opportunities for herself and others. At age nineteen Cooper married George A. C. Cooper, a Greek teacher and theology student at Saint Augustine, but was widowed just two years later before leaving for Oberlin. She never remarried, though during her life she would assume responsibility for the care of at least two foster and five adopted children.

In 1892, Cooper published *A Voice from the South, by a Black Woman of the South* with Aldine Printing House in Xenia, Ohio. The book comprised essays and speeches likely written between 1886 and 1892, the year of the book's publication. Written in a moment of social and political backlash, *A Voice from the South* reflects Cooper's "clear-eyed" commentaries on a nation faced with the failures of Reconstruction and in the midst of the rapidly solidifying system of Jim Crow segregation. While African Americans, at the turn of the twentieth century, had made gains in literacy, education, entrepreneurship, and military service, they also experienced the spread and implementation of racial segregation, the rise of racial terror and lynching, disenfranchisement through poll taxes and other means, and the expansion of forced labor through debt peonage and the convict labor system—all experienced as the nation sought to represent itself as a beacon of social and technological advancement and a model of honor and justice for the world.

Indeed, by the last decade of the nineteenth century, many white Americans were ready to wash their hands of the "race problem" and to move forward into the new century, leaving sectional divisions behind them. In *A Voice from the South*, Cooper critiqued this reunionist politics and challenged the nation to live up to its professed ideals. She called out the politics of representation that created an inaccurate and demeaning picture of African Americans and erased their vital contributions to US social, political, cultural, and economic wealth. She chastised Black men for neglecting to address the racialized and sexualized violence faced by Black women, and argued for greater protections and opportunities to address these specific forms of oppression. She excoriated white women for abandoning a commitment to universal suffrage and casting their lot with white Southerners at the expense of their alliances with African American and other women of color. She argued that Black women, situated at the intersection of overlapping forms of oppression, possessed a unique and necessary perspective on both the "race problem" and the "woman question," but were often the neglected and overlooked factor in both. Finally, she joined her educational training in history, philosophy, rhetoric, and literature with her own lived experiences to outline a broad and inclusive approach to liberation, arguing, as she did, that "the cause of freedom is not the cause of a race or a sect, a party or a class—it is the cause of humankind, the very birthright of humanity."[3]

With the publication of *A Voice from the South* in 1892, Cooper articulated an intellectual framework that placed Black women at the center of the national discourse on race and gender, famously announcing, "Only the black woman can say . . . 'when and where I enter, in the quiet, undisputed dignity of my womanhood . . . then and there the whole *Negro race enters with me.*'"[4] Her call would be answered by her and her contemporaries, and she became part of an active and vocal cadre of Black women who, in the late 1890s, organized and moved to the forefront of their own national social and political reform movements. Denied more overt forms of political representation, women such as Mary Church Terrell, Josephine St. Pierre Ruffin, Fannie Barrier Williams, and Ida B. Wells-Barnett became literary and intellectual activists who used their essays, speeches, and conference proceedings to influence and inform public opinions about African Americans.[5] They joined their intellectual activism with social strategies developed in concert with local communities to address the range of issues facing Black communities. Alongside her writing and speeches, for instance, Cooper was active in founding several organizations created to address both the ideological and material conditions that left African Americans in general, and Black women in particular, vulnerable, imperiled, or invisible. She was a lifetime member of the Phyllis Wheatley YWCA and co-founded the Colored Settlement House, the first social services agency in Washington, DC, for African Americans. She was also a charter member of the Colored Women's League of Washington, DC, an organization that would join with the National Federation of Afro-American Women in 1896 to form the National Association of Colored Women (NACW), which at its height included over 50,000 members and was "the first major national organization to effectively coordinate local Black social and political concerns on a national scale."[6] As Cooper had announced in "Woman Versus the Indian" in 1892, this was the "age of organizations," and the intellectual framework she outlined in *A Voice from the South* laid a foundation for Black women in the late 1890s to claim a central place in the national conversation shaping public opinion about African Americans, and Black women in particular.

From there, Cooper went on to serve as the seventh principal of M Street (later Dunbar) High School. In 1902, when Cooper began her position as principal, it had been only six years since Plessy v. Ferguson had upheld racial segregation in public accommodations, including schools—and it would be another fifty-two years before Brown v. Board of Education would rule the segregation of public schools unconstitutional. Thus, almost the entirety of Cooper's career in public education took place under the shroud of legalized racial segregation. This was also the era that saw the ascendency of Booker T. Washington and his Tuskegee model for industrial education. Washington's accommodationist approach, which emphasized training African Americans for vocational and trade jobs, found enthusiastic support among white philanthropists and became the dominant, though not exclusive, model for Black education. Running counter to this current, Cooper, in her position as principal, continued and expanded M Street's tradition of encouraging higher education for her students.

As principal of M Street, Cooper succeeded in sending students to Harvard, Brown, Oberlin, Yale, Amherst, University of Pennsylvania, Dartmouth, and Radcliffe, as well as prestigious Black colleges and universities, such as Fisk, Atlanta, and Howard. In her 1934 history of Dunbar High School, fellow author, reformer, and longtime Washingtonian Mary Church Terrell credits Cooper with the transformation of education in Washington, DC. Cooper, she notes, instituted a liberal arts curriculum, began placing students at prestigious colleges and universities, and earned accreditation for M Street from such esteemed institutions as Harvard University. Cooper accomplished this in spite of resistance from the DC school board and the political machine that opposed liberal or classical education for African Americans, and she carried it out at great personal and professional cost. When, for example, the white director of Washington high schools, Percy Hughes, insisted Cooper teach "the colored curriculum," she refused, for at least the third time in her life, to accept for herself or her students an inferior program of study. Instead, she waged what she referred to as "the courageous revolt . . . against a lower 'colored' curriculum for the M Street High School." Despite her best efforts and the swell of support from the local community, in 1906 Cooper was removed from her post as principal of M Street when the board voted not to reappoint her. She was effectively exiled from her home in Washington, DC, and she was denied official recognition as the educational leader she was. As she explained in a letter written from Lincoln, Missouri, in 1909:

> I served as a principal of M Street High School [for five years]. In this work I had the satisfaction of believing that I was able to encourage the effort of higher development. I can only say that my labor in this direction met with appreciative recognition from the people I served. But they are lowly and for the most part voiceless. The dominant forces of our country are not yet tolerant of the higher steps for colored youth; so that while our course of study was for the time being saved, *my head was lost in the fray.*[7]

The M Street controversy, as it has come to be known, is often boiled down to a debate between the W. E. B. Du Bois versus Booker T. Washington models for Black education. This approach, however, diminishes Cooper's agency in what Cooper identified as one of the most significant contributions of her life's work, her "courageous revolt" against Jim Crow education in the nation's capital. It also elides the ways in which her gender made her even more vulnerable to attack and how racism and sexism at the individual and structural levels worked to forestall Black education and deny Black excellence. For instance, in 1904 Anna Julia Cooper penned a note, found among her papers at the Moorland-Spingarn Research Center, listing the names of fourteen M Street students who had earned placements at top universities and colleges or were entering professional fields. She identified the preparation and placement of the students at prestigious Black and white institutions as part of her "courageous revolt," even as she recounted the retribution she faced for daring to fight for higher education for African Americans.[8]

After spending four years, from 1906 to 1910, teaching at the Lincoln Institute in Jefferson City, Missouri, Cooper was called back to Washington, DC, and accepted a position as a teacher at M Street. Though she would never again serve as principal, she continued to advance higher education for her students and to advocate for recognition of their achievements. As Vivian May asserts, "Cooper held to her conviction that all forms of education . . . should be sites of liberation," and she advocated a critical pedagogy where students and teachers would "eschew models of learning based on rote memory, the uncritical reproduction of information and/or facile imitation."[9]

While working full time as a teacher, Cooper also continued to pursue her own education, but again, not without challenges and roadblocks. In 1925 she traveled to Paris, under duress of being fired from Dunbar High School, to complete her doctoral degree. Though she had started her advanced studies in 1914 at Columbia University, when her nephew's wife died and she adopted their five children, she put her graduate studies on hold. Then, because M Street would not give her leave, she was unable to fulfill the residency requirements to complete her degree at Columbia University. With the assistance of French scholar Abbé

Felix Klein (who had written a glowing review of M Street twenty years earlier), she transferred her credits to the University of Paris, Sorbonne, where she wrote a new doctoral thesis that "charted a transatlantic revolutionary consciousness" and centered the impacts of slavery and race on the eventual outcomes of the French and Haitian revolutions.[10] Cooper defended her dissertation, *L'Attitude de la France à l'égard de l'esclavage pendant la Révolution*, on March 23, 1925, becoming the fourth Black woman in the US to earn a PhD.

In 1930, after more than three decades of service, Cooper retired from Dunbar High School, only to accept the presidency at Frelinghuysen University. Established in 1906, Frelinghuysen was a group of community schools founded to provide continuing education for working Black adults in Washington, DC. As Leona Gabel explains, "Frelinghuysen was an effort to fill a serious need. . . . Out of the seven full-time universities in Washington, there was but one [Black] institution; and in a list of 88 part-time colleges and special schools, not one would admit African Americans."[11] When the DC Board of Education refused Frelinghuysen the right to grant bachelor's degrees, and funds became increasingly tight, Cooper appealed to the NAACP to support it. She felt it was the duty and responsibility of the community to do so. When they did not, she moved portions of the administrative and teaching services into her T Street home in the LeDroit Park neighborhood of Washington, DC.

For Cooper, education, her own and others, was a central part of her intellectual activism. In *A Voice from the South* and other writings, she theorized about the intersecting forms of oppression and saw education as a way not only to expand opportunities but also to awaken a critical consciousness through which one could transform self and society. Cooper viewed education as the vehicle to answer the innate longing of each individual for self-realization and as a basis for the highest expressions of freedom and self-determination. She believed that an awakening of the individual consciousness could give rise to individual and social transformation. She advocated for the ideological *and* material support for all people dispossessed from seats of power and privilege, but especially for Black girls and women. As an educator and community activist, she translated her principles into practice by protecting the rights to higher education for African Americans in Washing-ton, DC, and by creating a steady stream of Black students into colleges and universities (including the Ivy League). She also created community schools that put pressure on other institutions to create continuing education programs. Through these and other efforts, she modeled and inspired, at the very core of all her work, education in service to the common good.

## COOPER'S *A VOICE FROM THE SOUTH*, SHADOW WRITING, AND THE ARCHIVES

*A Voice from the South*, reprinted here in part 1, is a collection of eight essays and speeches introduced by a short preface that collectively constitute one of Cooper's most forceful statements on the pressing race and gender issues of the day. The essays include responses crafted for specific occasions such as "Womanhood: A Vital Element in the Regeneration and Progress of the Race," delivered in 1886 to a convocation of what Cooper referred to as the "colored clergy" of the Protestant Episcopal Church in Washington, DC, and "The Higher Education of Women" presented at the American Conference of Educators in 1890 and published in *Southland* magazine in 1891, as well as her "Woman Versus the Indian," Cooper's response to Anna Howard Shaw's speech by the same name in which Shaw positioned white women's suffrage in opposition to that of Native Americans and other people of color. It also includes essays likely written expressly for *A Voice*. As Karen Baker-Fletcher asserts, Cooper clearly collected and arranged her writings specifically for publication and utilized a musical metaphor to structure and frame the work. The first half of the writings fall under the heading "Soprano Obligato," referencing the part of a musical composition performed by a specific instrument and considered indispensable to the performance. Writings in this section focus more explicitly on the "Woman question" and Black women's critical contributions to those conversations. The essays in the second half of the book are introduced with the title "Tutti ad Libitum," referencing the part of a performance where the musical components come together in a manner marked by improvisation (or translated literally, "at liberty") and take up issues of race and culture more generally. Upon its publication in 1892, *A Voice from the South* was reviewed widely and favorably by both the Black and white press throughout the US and abroad and lauded for its contributions to both the "race problem" and "the woman questions."* While *A Voice from the South* established Cooper's place as a foremost spokesperson on issues of race and gender, it represents only a small portion of Cooper's larger oeuvre and longer publishing and writing career.

Indeed, just two years after *A Voice from the South* was published, a review in *Southern Workman* noted that Cooper had a second book on the way, but that book never materialized and instead we are left to imagine what that second book might have been. In editing this current edition, I have sought to be attentive to what Kevin Young refers to as African American shadow books, or "books" that for any number of reasons are never written, written and never published, or written and now lost. These books, Young explains, are part of a shadow tradition of an African American literature denied existence. By returning to Cooper's archive, we not only encounter existing writings anew, but find traces of books that might have been and learn to read for the mechanics at work in disappearing Black women's writings. This allows us to move beyond an approach in which one major text comes to stand in for the entirety of an author's work, eclipsing the range, productivity, and shifts that may have characterized the writer's longer career and intellectual output. Cooper lived another seven decades after the publication of *A Voice from the South*, and she worked, wrote, and taught for almost all of those seventy years. Her continued work and larger body of writing, produced between 1892 until the time of her death in 1964, is critical to our understanding of the depth and persistence of Cooper's commitment to recording, engaging, and promoting Black women's intellectual histories and to advocating for educational opportunities and social justice for Black communities at the local and national levels.

*The digital collections of the reviews are available through the Black Women's Organizing Archive at https://bwoaproject.org/cooper/

Found among her papers at the Moorland-Spingarn Research Center, for instance, is an outline Cooper drafted for a collection of her writings, simply titled *On Education*.[12] Assembled and published together for the first time in part 2 of this edition, the book Cooper outlined includes articles, essays, plays, and pageants. This range of eleven writings across various genres and forms comes together to represent Cooper's philosophy on education as a right for all people regardless of age, race, class, gender, or ability, and as rooted in a democratic ideal and Christian theology that elevated the most neglected and ignored in society to a place of respect and worthiness. In *On Education*, we learn what Cooper, looking back on her long career in education, viewed as her most important works and lasting contributions. We know from her correspondences with W. E. B. Du Bois, for instance, that she held Two Scenes from the *Aeneid* (the final selection in *On Education*) as one of her and her students' most significant achievements, not only in performing and transforming a classic of Western literary tradition in ways that recover and foreground the African elements of the epic poem,[13] but also in the costs endured and sacrifices made by her students and their families to marshal the material resources to support the impressive production. If *On Education* constitutes Cooper's unified statement distilled from her lifetime as a teacher, student, and scholar, what other lessons can we learn from this text, one of her many shadow books, as it were, about Cooper's courageous and transformative approach to African American education?

Alongside her work in education, Cooper throughout the 1930s and into the 1940s wrote extensively for the local newspapers of Washington, DC, penning over two dozen articles, notes, and reviews that address local and national current events and take up a range of topics, including educational approaches and theories, discriminatory labor laws and practices, representations of African Americans in the arts and literature, extralegal and state-sanctioned violence, civic and social imperatives, and charitable giving and community organizing. Though these articles are seldom considered as a collection, Cooper saved, collated, and cut and pasted them into a scrapbook, effectively creating another book in her oeuvre.* The twenty-nine articles, notes, and essays, reprinted as a collection in part 3, were cut and pasted into a published book, and the interaction of Cooper's articles with the base text of the book create an alternative narrative that suggests the innovation and inventiveness through which Cooper claimed a space for her writings and her voice.

Part 4 publishes together for the first time twenty-nine correspondences that took place between Anna Julia Cooper and W. E. B. Du Bois, introducing the letters, collectively, as an important contribution to Black intellectual history. The numerous exchanges between Cooper and Du Bois allow us to chart the long and dynamic relationship between these two intellectual giants. They document the degree to which Cooper and Du Bois debated, critiqued, supported, and challenged each other as they conferred on key convenings, publications, and issues affecting Black communities at the local, national, and international levels. They record Cooper's effort to usher into print her writings, and they document Cooper's expansive concept of Black publishing as part and parcel of an activist platform that could build and support Black arts and education, dispute and debate racist propaganda, shape positive images of African Americans, and expand the knowledge base of African American readers by introducing important international and domestic scholarship. They also speak to the hidden forces that often shaped access to the publishing industry, revealing how deeply circumscribed publication opportunities could be for Black women intellectual activists in the first half of the twentieth century.

Elsewhere in her additional correspondences, published in the second section of part 4, we learn how the mechanisms of race, gender, class, and age often dogged Cooper's efforts to publish and disseminate her works and to preserve and steward into print the works of other Black women. In one instance of intellectual gatekeeping, Ray Billington, professor at Smith College and then Northwestern University, dismisses Cooper's

---

*A digital reproduction of the scrapbook demonstrating the interplay between Cooper's pasted articles and the base text she used for her scrapbook is available through the Black Women's Organizing Archive at https://bwoaproject.org/cooper/

standing as a respected scholar and belittles her role as executor of the papers of educator, author, and longtime friend Charlotte Forten Grimké. These, and other correspondences, reveal the mechanisms, so often hidden from view, that worked to curtail or deny Black women's access to conventional publishing outlets. The selected correspondences in part 4 also, however, document Cooper's national and international circle of friends, family, and colleagues with whom she corresponded regularly throughout her life. From the letter to her mother in which she relates updates on their family and friends, to the heartfelt missive from Lula Love, in which Love addresses Cooper with the intimate and loving endearment "my dear Cookie" and inquires if the dress sent for Cooper's birthday was found fitting, Cooper's personal correspondences reveal that she enjoyed a vast network of friends, family, and colleagues who supported, admired, respected, and loved her. For a woman who generally guarded her private life, particularly after the attempts to publicly denigrate her character during the M Street controversy, these letters provide a sense of the rich and enduring nature of her personal and intimate relationships.

Part 5 contains additional writings composed over a forty-year period from her address before the Congress of Representative Women at the Chicago World's Fair in 1893 to writings published in the Hampton Institute school newspaper, *Southern Workman*— where she contributed essays on the founding of societies, advanced her theory on the vital role of folklore in shaping and animating a distinctive African American literature, and made a plea for just compensation and recognition for Black women "wage workers." Part 5 also showcases Cooper as a poet whose verse often took up religious themes and was composed in conventional forms but that constituted poetic acts of commemoration, memory, and resistance.

In one of the most distinctive documents in Cooper's archive, and published as the closing selection of this edition, Cooper responds to a survey sent by sociologist and Fisk University president Charles S. Johnson in which she is asked if she has a racial philosophy and if so, "can it be briefly stated." In providing her response, Cooper fills all the available lines allotted for the "brief" answer and then wraps around and covers the back side of the page.[14] Cooper's lengthy response to the question is symbolic of the ways in which her literary and intellectual productivity exceeded the protocols of conventional publishing outlets and refused to be limited by the imposed structures of the form. In stating her "racial philosophy," Cooper first calls into doubt the nature of the question and, indeed, of the survey itself, stating, "The extent then of the optimism in my philosophy is that (Statisticians and Social Science Research compilers to the contrary notwithstanding) the solution of our problem will be individual and not *en mass*; the habit of generalization and deductive logic has done its worst." She concludes by reiterating her commitment to service rendered through education and activism and by asserting her intertwined identities as an intellectual and an educator. "My 'racial philosophy,'" she concludes, "is not far removed from my general philosophy of life: that the greatest happiness comes from altruistic service, and this is in reach of all of whatever race and condition;" and it was, as Cooper stated, her lifelong work as a "teacher and trained thinker" that had prepared her for the task.

SHIRLEY MOODY-TURNER

## NOTES

1. *Sou* is a French term, no longer in use, for a coin. Cooper, Autobiographical Note, and in Anna Julia Cooper Papers, box 23-1, folder 1, Moorland-Spingarn Research Center, Howard University (reprinted in Part V-1, p. 471).
2. Anna Julia Cooper, "The Higher Education of Women," in *A Voice from the South, by a Black Woman of the South* (Xenia, Ohio: Aldine Printing House, 1892) (reprinted in Part I, p. 26).
3. Cooper, "Woman Versus the Indian," in *A Voice from the South* (reprinted in Part I, p. 44).
4. Cooper, "Womanhood: A Vital Element in the Regeneration and Progress of the Race," in *A Voice from the South* (reprinted in Part I, p. 6).
5. Elizabeth McHenry identifies these women as "literary activists," and Brittney Cooper identifies their work as "intellectual activism." See Elizabeth McHenry, "Reading, Writing and Reform in

the Woman's Era," in *Forgotten Readers: Recovering the Lost History of African American Literary Societies* (Durham: Duke University Press, 2002); and Brittney C. Cooper, *Beyond Respectability: The Intellectual Thought of Race Women* (Urbana: University of Illinois Press, 2017).

6. Cooper, *Beyond Respectability*, 51.

7. Louise Daniel Hutchinson, *Anna J. Cooper: A Voice from the South* (Washington, DC: Smithsonian Institution, 1981), 83.

8. See Anna Julia Cooper Papers, box 23-1, folder 7, Moorland-Spingarn Research Center, Howard University.

9. Vivian M. May, *Anna Julia Cooper, Visionary Black Feminist; A Critical Introduction* (New York: Routledge, 2007), 64.

10. May, *Anna Julia Cooper*, 2.

11. Leona C. Gabel, *From Slavery to the Sorbonne and Beyond: The Life and Writings of Anna J. Cooper* (Northampton, MA: Smith College Studies in History, 1982), 7.

12. *On Education* as it appears in Cooper's "Outline Note": I. From Servitude to Service: A Pageant; II. Christ's Church: A 20th Century Parable; III. Ethics of the Negro Question, Introduction by J. B. W. Friends General Conference; IV. Educational Programs; 1. Foreword; 2. The Negro's Dialect; 3. Loss of Speech Through Isolation; 4. The Higher Calling for the Teacher of Unprivileged Adults; 5. The Social Settlement: What It Is, and What It Does; V. The Tie That Used to Bind; VI. Christmas Bells: A One Act Play for Children; VII. A Night with Vergil, Two Scenes from the Aeneid Translated and Arranged for High School Students. See "Outline Note," Anna Julia Cooper Papers, box 23-4, folder 28, Moorland-Spingarn Research Center, Howard University.

13. For a detailed discussion of Cooper's dramaturgy, see Monica White Ndounou, "Drama for 'Neglected People': Recovering Anna Julia Cooper's Dramatic Theory and Criticism from the Shadows of W. E. B. Du Bois and Alain Locke," *Journal of Dramatic Theory and Criticism* 27, no. 1 (Fall 2012): 25–50.

14. See "Negro College Graduates Individual Occupational History," Anna Julia Cooper Papers, box 23-1, folder 1, Moorland-Spingarn Research Center, Howard University.

# Suggestions for Further Reading

Alexander, Elizabeth. "'We Must Be About Our Father's Business': Anna Julia Cooper and the In-Corporation of the Nineteenth-Century African-American Woman Intellectual." *Signs* 20, no. 2 (Winter 1995): 336–55.

Baker-Fletcher, Karen. *A Singing Something: Womanist Reflections on Anna Julia Cooper.* New York: Crossroad, 1994.

Carby, Hazel V. "'In the Quiet Undisputed Dignity of My Womanhood': Black Feminist Thought After Emancipation." In *Reconstructing Womanhood: The Emergence of the Afro-American Woman Novelist,* 95–120. New York: Oxford University Press, 1989.

Cooper, Anna Julia. *Slavery and the French and Haitian Revolutionists.* Translated by Frances Richardson Keller. Lanham, MD: Rowman and Littlefield, 2006.

Cooper, Brittney C. *Beyond Respectability: The Intellectual Thought of Race Women.* Urbana: University of Illinois Press, 2017.

Evans, Stephanie Y. "African American Women Scholars and International Research: Dr. Anna Julia Cooper's Legacy of Study Abroad." *Frontiers: The Interdisciplinary Journal of Study Abroad* 18, no. 1 (Fall 2009): 77–100.

Fox, Regis M. "'Wondering Under Which Head I Come': Sounding Anna Julia Cooper's Fin-de-Siècle Song," 83–113. In *Resistance Reimagined: Black Women's Critical Thought as Survival.* Gainesville: University Press of Florida, 2017.

Giddings, Paula. *When and Where I Enter: The Impact of Black Women on Race and Sex in America.* New York: William Morrow, 2007.

Gines, Kathryn T. "Anna Julia Cooper." In *Stanford Encyclopedia of Philosophy Archive.* Stanford University, 1997–. Article published March 31, 2015. Edited by Edward N. Zalta. http://plato.stanford.edu/archives/sum2015/entries/anna-julia-cooper.

Grant, Carl A., Kefferlyn D. Brown, and Anthony L. Brown. "A Great
    American Voice for Democracy: Anna Julia Cooper." In *Black In-
    tellectual Thought in Education: The Missing Traditions of Anna
    Julia Cooper, Carter G. Woodson, and Alain LeRoy Locke*, 29–
    75. New York: Routledge, 2015.

Greene, Nathifa. "Anna Julia Cooper's Analysis of the Haitian Revolu-
    tion." *CLR James Journal* 23, no. 1/2 (Fall 2017): 83–104.

Guy-Sheftall, Beverly. "Black Feminist Studies: The Case of Anna Julia
    Cooper." *African American Review* 43, no. 1 (Spring 2009):
    11–15.

Hutchinson, Louise Daniel. *Anna J. Cooper: A Voice from the South.*
    Washington, DC: Smithsonian Institution, 1981.

James, Joy. *Transcending the Talented Tenth: Black Leaders and
    American Intellectuals.* New York: Routledge, 1996.

Johnson, Karen. *Uplifting the Women and the Race: The Lives, Edu-
    cational Philosophies and Social Activism of Anna Julia Cooper
    and Nannie Helen Burroughs.* London: Routledge, 2000.

Lemert, Charles, and Esme Bhan, eds. *The Voice of Anna Julia Coo-
    per.* Lanham, MD: Rowman and Littlefield, 1998.

May, Vivian M. *Anna Julia Cooper: Visionary Black Feminist; A Crit-
    ical Introduction.* New York: Routledge, 2007.

Moody-Turner, Shirley. "'Dear Dr. Du Bois': Anna Julia Cooper,
    W. E. B. Du Bois, and the Gender Politics of Black Publishing."
    *MELUS* 40, no. 3 (Fall 2015): 47–68.

Moody-Turner, Shirley. "Recovering Folklore as a Site of Resistance:
    Anna Julia Cooper and the Hampton Folklore Society." In *Black
    Folklore and the Politics of Racial Representation*, 72–100. Jack-
    son: University Press of Mississippi, 2013.

Ndounou, Monica White. "Drama for 'Neglected People': Recovering
    Anna Julia Cooper's Dramatic Theory and Criticism from the
    Shadows of W. E. B. Du Bois and Alain Locke." *Journal of Dra-
    matic Theory and Criticism* 27, no. 1 (Fall 2012): 25–50.

Pellow, David. "Anna J. Cooper: The International Dimensions." *In
    Recovered Writers/Recovered Texts: Race, Class, and Gender in
    Black Women's Literature.* Edited by Dolan Hubbard, 60–74.
    Knoxville: University of Tennessee Press, 1997.

Staton-Taiwo, Sandra L. "The Effect of Cooper's *A Voice from the
    South* on W. E. B. Du Bois's Souls and Black Flame Trilogy." *Phi-
    losophia Africana* 7, no. 2 (August 2004): 59–80.

Washington, Mary Helen. "Anna Julia Cooper: The Black Feminist
    Voice of the 1890s." *Legacy* 4, no. 2 (Fall 1987): 3–15.

# Chronology

**1858**  Anna Julia Cooper is born into slavery on August 10 in Raleigh, North Carolina, and named Annie Julia Haywood by her mother, Hannah Stanley Haywood. Though she never identified him, Cooper's biological father was likely Dr. Fabius J. Haywood, her mother's enslaver.

**1863**  Emancipation Proclamation issued on January 1.

**1868**  Cooper enrolls in Saint Augustine Normal School and Collegiate Institute and begins peer teaching around age ten to supplement her tuition.

**1877**  Cooper earns high school diploma and marries George A. C. Cooper, a theology student and Greek teacher.

**1879**  George Cooper dies.

**1881**  Cooper enrolls at Oberlin College.

**1884**  Earns her BA in mathematics at Oberlin. Accepts chair of languages and science at Wilberforce University in Xenia, Ohio, where she teaches math, languages, and literature for one year.

**1886**  Cooper steps into national spotlight when she delivers "Womanhood: A Vital Element in the Regeneration and Progress of a Race" before the national convention of African American Episcopal clergymen.

**1887**  Cooper awarded MA in mathematics from Oberlin. She is recruited to teach math and science at the highly regarded Preparatory High School for Colored Youth, in Washington, DC, known customarily as the M Street High School because of its address, and later renamed Paul Laurence Dunbar High School in 1916 after poet Paul Laurence Dunbar.

1891    Cooper travels to Toronto as part of a cultural exchange program facilitated by Bethel Literary and Historical Association.

1892    Cooper publishes *A Voice from the South* to national and international acclaim.

1893    Cooper is invited along with Fannie Barrier Williams and Fanny Jackson Coppin to address The World's Congress of Representative Women in Chicago.

ca. 1894    Cooper serves as interim editor for the Folk-Lore and Ethnology column for *Southern Workman*.

1895    Cooper addresses the National Federation of Afro-American Women, the first US national conference of Black women, which would merge with the Colored Women's League to become the National Association of Colored Women (NACW) the following year. Cooper would serve as chair of the NACW committee to study Georgia's system of convict peonage and Florida's inequitable state school laws.

1896    Cooper travels to Nassau, British West Indies, to visit family of her late husband.

1900    Cooper tours several European cities accompanied by Lula and John Love, whose guardian she had become after the death of their parents.

1900    Cooper travels to London to attend and speak at the first Pan-African Congress and to serve as an elected member of its Executive Committee.

1901    Cooper is promoted to principal of the M Street High School (effective January 2, 1902). She advances a course of higher education for her students and is successful in sending M Street graduates to prestigious colleges and universities.

1906    Due to her efforts on behalf of liberal arts and higher education for DC's Black students, Cooper is ousted from her position as M Street principal. Despite a groundswell of support for her from the local community and educational leaders around the country, the DC Board of Education votes not to reappoint Cooper as principal. Cooper goes to the Lincoln Institute in Jefferson City, Missouri, where she is appointed professor of languages. She continues to fight for her reinstatement and back salary during the years afterward.

1910   Cooper returns to M Street High School to teach Latin.

1911–   Cooper spends summers in Paris, France, at La
1913    Guilde Internationale studying French literature, history, and phonetics.

1914   Cooper enrolls as a doctoral student at Columbia University.

1915   Cooper adopts her brother's five grandchildren.

1917   Cooper finishes her translation of *Le Pèlerinage de Charlemagne*.

1925   Cooper completes and defends her doctoral dissertation, *L'Attitude de la France à l'égard de l'esclavage pendant la Révolution*, at the age of sixty-six, becoming the fourth African American woman to earn a PhD in the United States and the first Black woman to earn a doctorate at the Sorbonne.

1930   Cooper retires from her teaching position at M Street High School (now known as Dunbar High School) and becomes president of Frelinghuysen University. Frelinghuysen served adult working African Americans in Washington, DC, who, for financial and other reasons, were unable to attend Howard University, the only other option for postsecondary education in the District. Throughout the 1930s, Cooper continues to write and publish short essays and op-eds in *Oberlin Alumnae Club Journal*, the NAACP's *The Crisis* magazine, and in the *Washington Tribune*.

1940   Cooper retires from presidency of Frelinghuysen University but continues teaching there into the mid-1940s and works at the registrar until around 1950.

ca. 1945   Cooper writes a short memoir about her own life, *The Third Step*.

1951   Cooper privately publishes her two-volume *The Life and Writings of the Grimké Family*, which includes *Personal Recollections of the Grimké Family* and *The Life and Writings of Charlotte Forten Grimké*.

1958   Cooper celebrates her one hundredth birthday.

1964   Cooper dies on February 27 at the age of 105 in Washington, DC.

# A Note on the Text

*The Portable Anna Julia Cooper* introduces Cooper's classic writings alongside those previously unpublished or lesser known. The writings here include selections of her poetry, plays, short stories, correspondences, notes, essays, and articles. They show-case the range of writings she produced while presenting a different way of reading Black women's work that can incorporate the diversity of written forms and genres where intellectual productivity takes place.

The majority of Cooper's extant papers were donated by Cooper's grandniece Regia Haywood Bronson to Howard University and are collected at the Moorland-Spingarn Research Center and now digitized and available via the Digital Howard website. Other writings, however, are scattered among various repositories and found in collections around the country, as is the case with the more than thirty correspondences between Cooper and W. E. B. Du Bois found in the W. E. B. Du Bois Papers at UMass Amherst Special Collections and University Archives and available via the Credo project.

This edition also introduces two additional "books" into Cooper's body of work: the newspaper articles that she collected in her 1931–1940 scrapbook and the work she outlined, but never published, for her collected writings on education. These two projects provide a sense of what Cooper saw as the writings and work she most wanted to preserve and share with the world. They also ask us to redefine what we consider scholarly publications and our very definition of what constitutes a "book."

This edition does not include Cooper's 1925 dissertation, *L'Attitude de la France à l'égard de l'esclavage pendant la Révolution* (*France's Attitudes Toward Slavery During the Revolution*),[1] or her other French writings and related documents, which deserve a dedicated edition of their own. Throughout the edition, with the exception of her poetry, line breaks and formatting have been normalized. Minor corrections to spelling, grammar, and typography have been made for the sake of clarity and consistency. Footnotes made within the edition denoted by asterisk are Cooper's; notes included at the end of the edition are the editor's. Selected digital images documenting the unique interplay between Cooper's written texts and the base documents or forms on which she occasionally produced her writings (as in the case of her 1931–1940 scrapbook [part 3] or her response to the 1930 racial attitudes survey [see chapter 128, "Racial Philosophy Response to Occupational History Survey"]) can be found at the Anna Julia Cooper Project in the Black Women's Organizing Archive (https://bwoaproject.org/cooper). Additional digital images are available at the Digital Howard Anna Julia Cooper Collection (https://dh.howard.edu/ajcooper). This edition represents a cumulative and iterative process upon which we hope future work will engage, expand, correct, and advance. In sum, *The Portable Anna Julia Cooper* presents readers with Cooper's classic 1892 text, *A Voice from the South*, while also introducing new sets of writings and new ways of reading on which to build future inquiries into the remarkable work of this courageous and prophetic thinker and educator.

# The Portable
# Anna Julia Cooper

# PART I

# MAJOR TEXT

Cooper is most well known for *A Voice from the South, by a Black Woman of the South*. Published in 1892 by the Aldine Printing House, it was widely reviewed in the Black and white press, both within the US and abroad. While Cooper wrote, published, and privately printed a wide-ranging body of writing in the US and France, none of her works would garner the same attention in contemporary reception or ongoing engagement as *A Voice from the South*. At the time of its publication, *A Voice from the South* established Cooper, who was already a well-known and respected educator, intellectual, and civil rights advocate, as a leading spokesperson for African American rights and especially racial and gender equality for Black women. In *A Voice from the South*, Cooper utilizes her characteristic wit, deep philosophical and historical knowledge, personal experiences, and keen social and political observations to advance a biting critique of US racial and gender politics. Her work spoke in poignant and pointed terms about the unique station of Black women in American life. She argued that because Black women stood at the intersections of interlocking forms of racial and gender oppression, the status and quality of their treatment would be the true measure of US society's ability to live up to its own professed ideals. She asserted that Black women offered a critical and necessary, but often neglected, perspective on the national conversations about race, rights, and equality. *A Voice from the South* is now widely recognized as one of the foundational texts of Black feminist thought.

# I

# A Voice from the South, by a Black Woman of the South

## (1892)

In *A Voice from the South, by a Black Woman of the South* (1892), Cooper offers a critical analysis of and meditation on the historical, social, and literary contexts of the late nineteenth century. Her book is split into two parts, which take their titles from components of musical productions. The first part, "Soprano Obligato," explores Black women's roles in society and argues for the necessity of educating Black women and fighting injustices, particularly at the intersections of racial inequality and gendered oppression. The second part, "Tutti ad Libitum," addresses concerns related to the Black community across gender lines (i.e., the "race problem") and calls for more accurate representations of African American life and contributions to US history and culture.

SOURCE: Anna Julia Cooper, *A Voice from the South, by a Black Woman of the South* (Xenia, Ohio: Aldine Printing House, 1892).

> "WITH REGRET
> I FORGET
> IF THE SONG BE LIVING YET,
>    YET REMEMBER, VAGUELY NOW,
>    IT WAS HONEST, ANYHOW."[1]

# OUR RAISON D'ÊTRE

In the clash and clatter of our American Conflict, it has been said that the South remains Silent. Like the Sphinx she inspires vociferous disputation, but herself takes little part in the noisy controversy. One muffled strain in the Silent South, a jarring chord and a vague and uncomprehended cadenza has been and still is the Negro. And of that muffled chord, the one mute and voiceless note has been the sadly expectant Black Woman,

> An infant crying in the night,
> An infant crying for the light;
> And with *no language—but a cry.*

The colored man's inheritance and apportionment is still the sombre crux, the perplexing *cul de sac* of the nation,—the dumb skeleton in the closet provoking ceaseless harangues, indeed, but little understood and seldom consulted. Attorneys for the plaintiff and attorneys for the defendant, with bungling *gaucherie* have analyzed and dissected, theorized and synthesized with sublime ignorance or pathetic misapprehension of counsel from the black client. One important witness has not yet been heard from. The summing up of the evidence deposed, and the charge to the jury have been made—but no word from the Black Woman.

It is because I believe the American people to be conscientiously committed to a fair trial and ungarbled evidence, and because I feel it essential to a perfect understanding and an equitable verdict that truth from *each* standpoint be presented at the bar,—that this little Voice has been added to the already full chorus. The "other side" has not been represented by one who "lives there." And not many can more sensibly realize and more accurately tell the weight and the fret of the "long dull pain" than the open-eyed but hitherto voiceless Black Woman of America.

The feverish agitation, the perfervid energy, the busy objectivity of the more turbulent life of our men serves, it may be, at once to cloud or color their vision somewhat, and as well to relieve the smart and deaden the pain for them. Their voice is in consequence not always temperate and calm, and at the same time radically corrective and sanatory. At any rate, as our Caucasian barristers are not to blame if they cannot *quite* put themselves in the dark man's place, neither should the dark man be wholly expected fully and adequately to reproduce the exact Voice of the Black Woman.

Delicately sensitive at every pore to social atmospheric conditions, her calorimeter may well be studied in the interest of accuracy and fairness in diagnosing what is often conceded to be a "puzzling" case. If these broken utterances can in any way help to a clearer vision and a truer pulse-beat in studying our Nation's Problem, this Voice by a Black Woman of the South will not have been raised in vain.

TAWAWA CHIMNEY CORNER,[1]
SEPT. 17, 1892.

# SOPRANO OBLIGATO

For they the *Royal-hearted Women* are
Who nobly love the noblest, yet have grace
For needy, suffering lives in lowliest place;
Carrying a choicer sunlight in their smile,
The heavenliest ray that pitieth the vile.

\*   \*   \*

Though I were happy, throned beside the king,
I should be tender to each little thing
With hurt warm breast, that had no speech to tell
Its inward pangs; and I would sooth it well
With tender touch and with a low, soft moan
For company.

—*George Eliot.*[1]

## Womanhood: A Vital Element in the Regeneration and Progress of a Race[*]

The two sources from which, perhaps, modern civilization has derived its noble and ennobling ideal of woman are Christianity and the Feudal System.

In Oriental countries woman has been uniformly devoted to a life of ignorance, infamy, and complete stagnation. The Chinese shoe of to-day does not more entirely dwarf, cramp, and destroy

[*]Read before the convocation of colored clergy of the Protestant Episcopal Church at Washington, D.C., 1886.

her physical powers, than have the customs, laws, and social instincts, which from remotest ages have governed our Sister of the East, enervated and blighted her mental and moral life.

Mahomet makes no account of woman whatever in his polity. The Koran, which, unlike our Bible, was a product and not a growth, tried to address itself to the needs of Arabian civilization as Mahomet with his circumscribed powers saw them. The Arab was a nomad. Home to him meant his present camping place. That deity who, according to our western ideals, makes and sanctifies the home, was to him a transient bauble to be toyed with so long as it gave pleasure and then to be thrown aside for a new one. As a personality, an individual soul, capable of eternal growth and unlimited development, and destined to mould and shape the civilization of the future to an incalculable extent, Mahomet did not know woman. There was no hereafter, no paradise for her. The heaven of the Mussulman is peopled and made gladsome not by the departed wife, or sister, or mother, but by *houri*—a figment of Mahomet's brain, partaking of the ethereal qualities of angels, yet imbued with all the vices and inanity of Oriental women. The harem here, and—"dust to dust" hereafter, this was the hope, the inspiration, the *summum bonum* of the Eastern woman's life! With what result on the life of the nation, the "Unspeakable Turk," the "sick man" of modern Europe can to-day exemplify.

Says a certain writer: "The private life of the Turk is vilest of the vile, unprogressive, unambitious, and inconceivably low." And yet Turkey is not without her great men. She has produced most brilliant minds; men skilled in all the intricacies of diplomacy and statesmanship; men whose intellects could grapple with the deep problems of empire and manipulate the subtle agencies which check-mate kings. But these minds were not the normal outgrowth of a healthy trunk. They seemed rather ephemeral excrescencies which shoot far out with all the vigor and promise, apparently, of strong branches; but soon alas fall into decay and ugliness because there is no soundness in the root, no life-giving sap, permeating, strengthening and perpetuating the whole. There is a worm at the core! The homelife is impure! and when we look for fruit, like apples of Sodom, it crumbles within our grasp into dust and ashes.

It is pleasing to turn from this effete and immobile civilization to a society still fresh and vigorous, whose seed is in itself, and whose very name is synonymous with all that is progressive, elevating and inspiring, viz., the European bud and the American flower of modern civilization.

And here let me say parenthetically that our satisfaction in American institutions rests not on the fruition we now enjoy, but springs rather from the possibilities and promise that are inherent in the system, though as yet, perhaps, far in the future.

"Happiness," says Madame de Stael, "consists not in perfections attained, but in a sense of progress, the result of our own endeavor under conspiring circumstances *toward* a goal which continually advances and broadens and deepens till it is swallowed up in the Infinite." Such conditions in embryo are all that we claim for the land of the West. We have not yet reached our ideal in American civilization. The pessimists even declare that we are not marching in that direction. But there can be no doubt that here in America is the arena in which the next triumph of civilization is to be won; and here too we find promise abundant and possibilities infinite.

Now let us see on what basis this hope for our country primarily and fundamentally rests. Can any one doubt that it is chiefly on the homelife and on the influence of good women in those homes? Says Macaulay: "You may judge a nation's rank in the scale of civilization from the way they treat their women." And Emerson,[1] "I have thought that a sufficient measure of civilization is the influence of good women." Now this high regard for woman, this germ of a prolific idea which in our own day is bearing such rich and varied fruit, was ingrafted into European civilization, we have said, from two sources, the Christian Church and the Feudal System. For although the Feudal System can in no sense be said to have originated the idea, yet there can be no doubt that the habits of life and modes of thought to which Feudalism gave rise, materially fostered and developed it; for they gave us chivalry, than which no institution has more sensibly magnified and elevated woman's position in society.

Tacitus dwells on the tender regard for woman entertained by these rugged barbarians before they left their northern homes to overrun Europe. Old Norse legends too, and primitive poems, all breathe the same spirit of love of home and veneration for the pure and noble influence there presiding—the wife, the sister, the mother.

And when later on we see the settled life of the Middle Ages "oozing out," as M. Guizot[2] expresses it, from the plundering and pillaging life of barbarism and crystallizing into the Feudal System, the tiger of the field is brought once more within the charmed circle of the goddesses of his castle, and his imagination weaves around them a halo whose reflection possibly has not yet altogether vanished.

It is true the spirit of Christianity had not yet put the seal of catholicity on this sentiment. Chivalry, according to Bascom,[3] was but the toning down and softening of a rough and lawless period. It gave a roseate glow to a bitter winter's day. Those who looked out from castle windows revelled in its "amethyst tints." But God's poor, the weak, the unlovely, the commonplace were still freezing and starving none the less in unpitied, unrelieved loneliness.

Respect for woman, the much lauded chivalry of the Middle Ages, meant what I fear it still means to some men in our own day—respect for the elect few among whom they expect to consort.

The idea of the radical amelioration of womankind, reverence for woman as woman regardless of rank, wealth, or culture, was to come from that rich and bounteous fountain from which flow all our liberal and universal ideas—the Gospel of Jesus Christ.

And yet the Christian Church at the time of which we have been speaking would seem to have been doing even less to protect and elevate woman than the little done by secular society. The Church as an organization committed a double offense against woman in the Middle Ages. Making of marriage a sacrament and at the same time insisting on the celibacy of the clergy and other religious orders, she gave an inferior if not an impure character to the marriage relation, especially fitted to reflect discredit on woman. Would this were all or the worst! but the Church by the licentiousness of its chosen servants invaded the household and established too often as vicious connections those relations which it forbade to assume openly and in good faith. "Thus," to use the words of our authority, "the religious corps became as numerous, as searching, and as unclean as the frogs of Egypt, which penetrated into all quarters, into the ovens and kneading troughs, leaving their filthy trail wherever they went." Says Chaucer with characteristic satire, speaking of the Friars:

> "Women may now go safely up and doun,
> In every bush, and under every tree,
> Ther is non other incubus but he,
> And he ne will don hem no dishonour."

Henry, Bishop of Liege, could unblushingly boast the birth of twenty-two children in fourteen years.*

It may help us under some of the perplexities which beset our way in "the one Catholic and Apostolic Church" to-day, to re-call some of the corruptions and incongruities against which the Bride of Christ has had to struggle in her past history and in spite of which she has kept, through many vicissitudes, the faith once delivered to the saints. Individuals, organizations, whole sections of the Church militant may outrage the Christ whom they profess, may ruthlessly trample under foot both the spirit and the letter of his precepts, yet not till we hear the voices audibly saying "Come let us depart hence," shall we cease to believe and cling to the promise, "*I am with you to the end of the world.*"

> "Yet saints their watch are keeping,
> The cry goes up 'How long!'
> And soon the night of weeping
> Shall be the morn of song."

However much then the facts of any particular period of history may seem to deny it, I for one do not doubt that the source of the vitalizing principle of woman's development and amelioration is the Christian Church, so far as that church is coincident with Christianity.

Christ gave ideals not formulae. The Gospel is a germ requiring millennia for its growth and ripening. It needs and at the

*Bascom.

same time helps to form around itself a soil enriched in civilization, and perfected in culture and insight without which the embryo can neither be unfolded or comprehended. With all the
strides our civilization has made from the first to the nineteenth
century, we can boast not an idea, not a principle of action, not
a progressive social force but was already mutely foreshadowed,
or directly enjoined in that simple tale of a meek and lowly life.
The quiet face of the Nazarene is ever seen a little way ahead,
never too far to come down to and touch the life of the lowest in
days the darkest, yet ever leading onward, still onward, the tottering childish feet of our strangely boastful civilization.

By laying down for woman the same code of morality, the
same standard of purity, as for man; by refusing to countenance
the shameless and equally guilty monsters who were gloating
over her fall,—graciously stooping in all the majesty of his own
spotlessness to wipe away the filth and grime of her guilty past
and bid her go in peace and sin no more; and again in the moments of his own careworn and footsore dejection, turning
trustfully and lovingly, away from the heartless snubbing and
sneers, away from the cruel malignity of mobs and prelates in
the dusty marts of Jerusalem to the ready sympathy, loving appreciation and unfaltering friendship of that quiet home at Beth-
any; and even at the last, by his dying bequest to the disciple
whom he loved, signifying the protection and tender regard to be
extended to that sorrowing mother and ever afterward to the sex
she represented;—throughout his life and in his death he has
given to men a rule and guide for the estimation of woman as an
equal, as a helper, as a friend, and as a sacred charge to be sheltered and cared for with a brother's love and sympathy, lessons
which nineteen centuries' gigantic strides in knowledge, arts,
and sciences, in social and ethical principles have not been able
to probe to their depth or to exhaust in practice.

It seems not too much to say then of the vitalizing, regenerating, and progressive influence of womanhood on the civilization
of today, that, while it was foreshadowed among Germanic nations in the far away dawn of their history as a narrow, sickly
and stunted growth, it yet owes its catholicity and power, the
deepening of its roots and broadening of its branches to Christianity.

The union of these two forces, the Barbaric and the Christian, was not long delayed after the Fall of the Empire. The Church, which fell with Rome, finding herself in danger of being swallowed up by barbarism, with characteristic vigor and fertility of resources, addressed herself immediately to the task of conquering her conquerers. The means chosen does credit to her power of penetration and adaptability, as well as to her profound, unerring, all-compassing diplomacy; and makes us even now wonder if aught human can successfully and ultimately withstand her far-seeing designs and brilliant policy, or gainsay her well-earned claim to the word *Catholic*.

She saw the barbarian, little more developed than a wild beast. She forbore to antagonize and mystify his warlike nature by a full blaze of the heartsearching and humanizing tenets of her great Head. She said little of the rule "If thy brother smite thee on one cheek, turn to him the other also;" but thought it sufficient for the needs of those times, to establish the so-called "Truce of God" under which men were bound to abstain from butchering one another for three days of each week and on Church festivals. In other words, she respected their individuality: non-resistance pure and simple being for them an utter impossibility, she contented herself with less radical measures calculated to lead up finally to the full measure of the benevolence of Christ.

Next she took advantage of the barbarian's sensuous love of gaudy display and put all her magnificent garments on. She could not capture him by physical force, she would dazzle him by gorgeous spectacles. It is said that Romanism gained more in pomp and ritual during this trying period of the Dark Ages than throughout all her former history.

The result was she carried her point. Once more Rome laid her ambitious hand on the temporal power, and allied with Charlemagne, aspired to rule the world through a civilization dominated by Christianity and permeated by the traditions and instincts of those sturdy barbarians.

Here was the confluence of the two streams we have been tracing, which, united now, stretch before us as a broad majestic river. In regard to woman it was the meeting of two noble and ennobling forces, two kindred ideas the resultant of which, we doubt not, is destined to be a potent force in the betterment of the world.

Now after our appeal to history comparing nations destitute of this force and so destitute also of the principle of progress, with other nations among whom the influence of woman is prominent coupled with a brisk, progressive, satisfying civilization,—if in addition we find this strong presumptive evidence corroborated by reason and experience, we may conclude that these two equally varying concomitants are linked as cause and effect; in other words, that the position of woman in society determines the vital elements of its regeneration and progress.

Now that this is so on *a priori* grounds all must admit. And this not because woman is better or stronger or wiser than man, but from the nature of the case, because it is she who must first form the man by directing the earliest impulses of his character.

Byron and Wordsworth were both geniuses and would have stamped themselves on the thought of their age under any circumstances; and yet we find the one a savor of life unto life, the other of death unto death. "Byron, like a rocket, shot his way upward with scorn and repulsion, flamed out in wild, explosive, brilliant excesses and disappeared in darkness made all the more palpable."*

Wordsworth lent of his gifts to reinforce that "power in the Universe which makes for righteousness" by taking the harp handed him from Heaven and using it to swell the strains of angelic choirs. Two locomotives equally mighty stand facing opposite tracks; the one to rush headlong to destruction with all its precious freight, the other to toil grandly and gloriously up the steep embattlements to Heaven and to God. Who—who can say what a world of consequences hung on the first placing and starting of these enormous forces!

Woman, Mother,—your responsibility is one that might make angels tremble and fear to take hold! To trifle with it, to ignore or mis-use it, is to treat lightly the most sacred and solemn trust ever confided by God to human kind. The training of children is a task on which an infinity of weal or woe depends. Who does not covet it? Yet who does not stand awe-struck before its momentous issues! It is a matter of small moment, it seems to me, whether that

*Bascom's *Eng. Lit.*, p. 253.

lovely girl in whose accomplishments you take such pride and delight, can enter the gay and crowded salon with the ease and elegance of this or that French or English gentlewoman, compared with the decision as to whether her individuality is going to reinforce the good or the evil elements of the world. The lace and the diamonds, the dance and the theater, gain a new significance when scanned in their bearings on such issues. Their influence on the individual personality, and through her on the society and civilization which she vitalizes and inspires—all this and more must be weighed in the balance before the jury can return a just and intelligent verdict as to the innocence or bane-fulness of these apparently simple amusements.

Now the fact of woman's influence on society being granted, what are its practical bearings on the work which brought together this conference of colored clergy and laymen in Washington? "We come not here to talk." Life is too busy, too pregnant with meaning and far reaching consequences to allow you to come this far for mere intellectual entertainment.

The vital agency of womanhood in the re-generation and progress of a race, as a general question, is conceded almost before it is fairly stated. I confess one of the difficulties for me in the subject assigned lay in its obviousness. The plea is taken away by the opposite attorney's granting the whole question.

"Woman's influence on social progress"—who in Christendom doubts or questions it? One may as well be called on to prove that the sun is the source of light and heat and energy to this many-sided little world.

Nor, on the other hand, could it have been intended that I should apply the position when taken and proven, to the needs and responsibilities of the women of our race in the South. For is it not written, "Cursed is he that cometh after the king?" and has not the King already preceded me in "The Black Woman of the South"?[*4]

They have had both Moses and the Prophets in Dr. Crummell and if they hear not him, neither would they be persuaded though one came up from the South.

I would beg, however, with the Doctor's permission, to add my

*Pamphlet published by Dr. Alex. Crummell.

plea for the *Colored Girls* of the South:—that large, bright, promising fatally beautiful class that stand shivering like a delicate
plantlet before the fury of tempestuous elements, so full of promise and possibilities, yet so sure of destruction; often without a
father to whom they dare apply the loving term, often without a
stronger brother to espouse their cause and defend their honor
with his life's blood; in the midst of pitfalls and snares, waylaid by
the lower classes of white men, with no shelter, no protection
nearer than the great blue vault above, which half conceals and
half reveals the one Care-Taker they know so little of. Oh, save
them, help them, shield, train, develop, teach, inspire them! Snatch
them, in God's name, as brands from the burning! There is material in them well worth your while, the hope in germ of a staunch,
helpful, regenerating womanhood on which, primarily, rests the
foundation stones of our future as a race.

It is absurd to quote statistics showing the Negro's bank account and rent rolls, to point to the hundreds of newspapers
edited by colored men and lists of lawyers, doctors, professors,
D. D's, LL D's, etc., etc., etc., while the source from which the
life-blood of the race is to flow is subject to taint and corruption
in the enemy's camp.

True progress is never made by spasms. Real progress is
growth. It must begin in the seed. Then, "first the blade, then the
ear, after that the full corn in the ear." There is something to encourage and inspire us in the advancement of individuals since
their emancipation from slavery. It at least proves that there is
nothing irretrievably wrong in the shape of the black man's
skull, and that under given circumstances his development,
downward or upward, will be similar to that of other average
human beings.

But there is no time to be wasted in mere felicitation. That the
Negro has his niche in the infinite purposes of the Eternal, no
one who has studied the history of the last fifty years in America
will deny. That much depends on his own right comprehension
of his responsibility and rising to the demands of the hour, it will
be good for him to see; and how best to use his present so that
the structure of the future shall be stronger and higher and
brighter and nobler and holier than that of the past, is a question
to be decided each day by every one of us.

The race is just twenty-one years removed from the conception and experience of a chattel, just at the age of ruddy manhood. It is well enough to pause a moment for retrospection, introspection, and prospection. We look back, not to become inflated with conceit because of the depths from which we have arisen, but that we may learn wisdom from experience. We look within that we may gather together once more our forces, and, by improved and more practical methods, address ourselves to the tasks before us. We look forward with hope and trust that the same God whose guiding hand led our fathers through and out of the gall and bitterness of oppression, will still lead and direct their children, to the honor of His name, and for their ultimate salvation.

But this survey of the failures or achievments of the past, the difficulties and embarrassments of the present, and the mingled hopes and fears for the future, must not degenerate into mere dreaming nor consume the time which belongs to the practical and effective handling of the crucial questions of the hour; and there can be no issue more vital and momentous than this of the womanhood of the race.

Here is the vulnerable point, not in the heel, but at the heart of the young Achilles; and here must the defenses be strengthened and the watch redoubled.

We are the heirs of a past which was not our fathers' moulding. "Every man the arbiter of his own destiny" was not true for the American Negro of the past: and it is no fault of his that he finds himself to-day the inheritor of a manhood and womanhood impoverished and debased by two centuries and more of compression and degradation.

But weaknesses and malformations, which to-day are attributable to a vicious schoolmaster and a pernicious system, will a century hence be rightly regarded as proofs of innate corruptness and radical incurability.

Now the fundamental agency under God in the regeneration, the re-training of the race, as well as the ground work and starting point of its progress upward, must be the *black woman*.

With all the wrongs and neglects of her past, with all the weakness, the debasement, the moral thralldom of her present, the black woman of to-day stands mute and wondering at the

Herculean task devolving upon her. But the cycles wait for her. No other hand can move the lever. She must be loosed from her bands and set to work.

Our meager and superficial results from past efforts prove their futility; and every attempt to elevate the Negro, whether undertaken by himself or through the philanthropy of others, cannot but prove abortive unless so directed as to utilize the indispensable agency of an elevated and trained womanhood.

A race cannot be purified from without. Preachers and teachers are helps, and stimulants and conditions as necessary as the gracious rain and sunshine are to plant growth. But what are rain and dew and sunshine and cloud if there be no life in the plant germ? We must go to the root and see that that is sound and healthy and vigorous; and not deceive ourselves with waxen flowers and painted leaves of mock chlorophyll.

We too often mistake individuals' honor for race development and so are ready to substitute pretty accomplishments for sound sense and earnest purpose.

A stream cannot rise higher than its source. The atmosphere of homes is no rarer and purer and sweeter than are the mothers in those homes. A race is but a total of families. The nation is the aggregate of its homes. As the whole is sum of all its parts, so the character of the parts will determine the characteristics of the whole. These are all axioms and so evident that it seems gratuitous to remark it; and yet, unless I am greatly mistaken, most of the unsatisfaction from our past results arises from just such a radical and palpable error, as much almost on our own part as on that of our benevolent white friends.

The Negro is constitutionally hopeful and proverbially irrepressible; and naturally stands in danger of being dazzled by the shimmer and tinsel of superficials. We often mistake foliage for fruit and overestimate or wrongly estimate brilliant results.

The late Martin R. Delany,[5] who was an unadulterated black man, used to say when honors of state fell upon him, that when he entered the council of kings the black race entered with him; meaning, I suppose, that there was no discounting his race identity and attributing his achievements to some admixture of Saxon blood. But our present record of eminent men, when placed beside the actual status of the race in America to-day, proves that no man can represent the race. Whatever the attainments of the individual may be, unless his home has moved on *pari passu*, he can never be regarded as identical with or representative of the whole.

Not by pointing to sun-bathed mountain tops do we prove that Phoebus warms the valleys. We must point to homes, average homes, homes of the rank and file of horny handed toiling men and women of the South (where the masses are) lighted and cheered by the good, the beautiful, and the true,—then and not till then will the whole plateau be lifted into the sunlight.

Only the BLACK WOMAN can say "when and where I enter, in the quiet, undisputed dignity of my womanhood, without violence and without suing or special patronage, then and there the whole *Negro race enters with me.*"[6] Is it not evident then that as individual workers for this race we must address ourselves with no half-hearted zeal to this feature of our mission. The need is felt and must be recognized by all. There is a call for workers, for missionaries, for men and women with the double consecration of a fundamental love of humanity and a desire for its melioration through the Gospel; but superadded to this we demand an intelligent and sympathetic comprehension of the interests and special needs of the Negro.

I see not why there should not be an organized effort for the protection and elevation of our girls such as the White Cross League in England. English women are strengthened and protected by more than twelve centuries of Christian influences, freedom and civilization; English girls are dispirited and crushed down by no such all-levelling prejudice as that supercilious caste spirit in America which cynically assumes "A Negro woman cannot be a lady." English womanhood is beset by no such snares and traps as betray the unprotected, untrained colored girl of the South, whose only crime and dire destruction often is her unconscious and marvelous beauty. Surely then if English indignation is aroused and English manhood thrilled under the leadership of a Bishop of the English church to build up bulwarks around their wronged sisters, Negro sentiment cannot remain callous and Negro effort nerveless in view of the imminent peril of the mothers of the next generation. "*I am my Sister's keeper!*" should be the hearty response of every man and woman of the race, and this conviction should purify and exalt the narrow, selfish and petty personal aims of life into a noble and sacred purpose.

We need men who can let their interest and gallantry extend outside the circle of their æsthetic appreciation; men who can be a father, a brother, a friend to every weak, struggling unshielded girl. We need women who are so sure of their own social footing that they need not fear leaning to lend a hand to a fallen or falling sister. We need men and women who do not exhaust their genius splitting hairs on aristocratic distinctions and thanking God they are not as others; but earnest, unselfish souls, who can go into the highways and byways, lifting up and leading, advising and encouraging with the truly catholic benevolence of the Gospel of Christ.

As Church workers we must confess our path of duty is less obvious; or rather our ability to adapt our machinery to our conception of the peculiar exigencies of this work as taught by experience and our own consciousness of the needs of the Negro, is as yet not demonstrable. Flexibility and aggressiveness are not such strong characteristics of the Church to-day as in the Dark Ages.

As a Mission field for the Church the Southern Negro is in some aspects most promising; in others, perplexing. Aliens neither in language and customs, nor in associations and sympathies, naturally of deeply rooted religious instincts and taking most readily and kindly to the worship and teachings of the Church, surely the task of proselytizing the American Negro is infinitely less formidable than that which confronted the Church in the Barbarians of Europe. Besides, this people already look to the Church as the hope of their race. Thinking colored men almost uniformly admit that the Protestant Episcopal Church with its quiet, chaste dignity and decorous solemnity, its instructive and elevating ritual, its bright chanting and joyous hymning, is eminently fitted to correct the peculiar faults of worship—the rank exuberance and often ludicrous demonstrativeness of their people. Yet, strange to say, the Church, claiming to be missionary and Catholic, urging that schism is sin and denominationalism inexcusable, has made in all these years almost no inroads upon this semi-civilized religionism.

Harvests from this over ripe field of home missions have been gathered in by Methodists, Baptists, and not least by

Congregationalists, who were unknown to the Freedmen before their emancipation.[7]

Our clergy numbers less than two dozen* priests of Negro blood and we have hardly more than one self-supporting colored congregation in the entire Southland. While the organization known as the A. M. E. Church has 14,063 ministers, itinerant and local, 4,069 self-supporting churches, 4,275 Sunday-schools, with property valued at $7,772,284, raising yearly for church purposes $1,427,000.

Stranger and more significant than all, the leading men of this race (I do not mean demagogues and politicians, but men of intellect, heart, and race devotion, men to whom the elevation of their people means more than personal ambition and sordid gain—and the men of that stamp have not all died yet) the Christian workers for the race, of younger and more cultured growth, are noticeably drifting into sectarian churches, many of them declaring all the time that they acknowledge the historic claims of the Church, believe her apostolicity, and would experience greater personal comfort, spiritual and intellectual, in her revered communion. It is a fact which any one may verify for himself, that representative colored men, professing that in their heart of hearts they are Episcopalians, are actually working in Methodist and Baptist pulpits; while the ranks of the Episcopal clergy are left to be filled largely by men who certainly suggest the propriety of a *"perpetual* Diaconate"* if they cannot be said to have created the necessity for it.

Now where is the trouble? Something must be wrong. What is it?

A certain Southern Bishop of our Church reviewing the situation, whether in Godly anxiety or in "Gothic antipathy" I know not, deprecates the fact that the colored people do not seem *drawn* to the Episcopal Church, and comes to the sage conclusion that the Church is not adapted to the rude untutored minds of the Freedmen, and that they may be left to go to the Methodists and Baptists whither their racial proclivities undeniably tend. How

---

*The published report of '91 shows 26 priests for the entire country, including one not engaged in work and one a professor in a non-sectarian school, since made Dean of an Episcopal Annex to Howard University known as King Hall.

the good Bishop can agree that all-foreseeing Wisdom, and Catholic Love would have framed his Church as typified in his seamless garment and unbroken body, and yet not leave it broad enough and deep enough and loving enough to seek and save and hold seven millions of God's poor, I cannot see.

But the doctors while discussing their scientifically conclusive diagnosis of the disease, will perhaps not think it presumptuous in the patient if he dares to suggest where at least the pain is. If this be allowed, a *Black woman of the South* would beg to point out two possible oversights in this southern work which may indicate in part both a cause and a remedy for some failure. The first is *not calculating for the Black man's personality*; not having respect, if I may so express it, to his manhood or deferring at all to his conceptions of the needs of his people. When colored persons have been employed it was too often as machines or as manikins. There has been no disposition, generally, to get the black man's ideal or to let his individuality work by its own gravity, as it were. A conference of earnest Christian men have met at regular intervals for some years past to discuss the best methods of promoting the welfare and development of colored people in this country. Yet, strange as it may seem, they have never invited a colored man or even intimated that one would be welcome to take part in their deliberations. Their remedial contrivances are purely theoretical or empirical, therefore, and the whole machinery devoid of soul.

The second important oversight in my judgment is closely allied to this and probably grows out of it, and that is not developing Negro womanhood as an essential fundamental for the elevation of the race, and utilizing this agency in extending the work of the Church.

Of the first I have possibly already presumed to say too much since it does not strictly come within the province of my subject. However, Macaulay somewhere criticises the Church of England as not knowing how to use fanatics, and declares that had Ignatius Loyola been in the Anglican instead of the Roman communion, the Jesuits would have been schismatics instead of Catholics; and if the religious awakenings of the Wesleys had been in Rome, she would have shaven their heads, tied ropes around their waists, and sent them out under her own banner and blessing. Whether this be true or not, there is certainly a vast amount of force potential for Negro evangelization rendered latent, or worse, antagonistic by the halting, uncertain, I had almost said, *trimming* policy of the Church in the South. This may sound both presumptuous and ungrateful. It is mortifying, I know, to benevolent wisdom, after having spent itself in the execution of well conned theories for the ideal development of a particular work, to hear perhaps the weakest and humblest element of that work asking "what doest thou?"

Yet so it will be in life. The "thus far and no farther" pattern cannot be fitted to any growth in God's kingdom. The universal law of development is "onward and upward." It is God-given and inviolable. From the unfolding of the germ in the acorn to reach the sturdy oak, to the growth of a human soul into the full knowledge and likeness of its Creator, the breadth and scope of the movement in each and all are too grand, too mysterious, too like God himself, to be encompassed and locked down in human molds.

After all the Southern slave owners were right: either the very alphabet of intellectual growth must be forbidden and the Negro dealt with absolutely as a chattel having neither rights nor sensibilities; or else the clamps and irons of mental and moral, as well as civil compression must be riven asunder and the truly enfranchised soul led to the entrance of that boundless vista through which it is to toil upwards to its beckoning God as the buried seed germ to meet the sun.

A perpetual colored diaconate, carefully and kindly superintended by the white clergy; congregations of shiny faced peasants with their clean white aprons and sunbonnets catechised at regular intervals and taught to recite the creed, the Lord's prayer and the ten commandments—duty towards God and duty towards neighbor, surely such well tended sheep ought to be grateful to their shepherds and content in that station of life to which it pleased God to call them. True, like the old professor lecturing to his solitary student, we make no provision here for irregularities. "Questions must be kept till after class," or dispensed with altogether. That some do ask questions and insist on answers, in class too, must be both impertinent and annoying. Let not our spiritual pastors and masters however be grieved at such self-assertion as merely signifies we have a destiny to fulfill and as men and women we must *be about our Father's business.*

It is a mistake to suppose that the Negro is prejudiced against a white ministry. Naturally there is not a more kindly and implicit follower of a white man's guidance than the average colored peasant. What would to others be an ordinary act of friendly or pastoral interest he would be more inclined to regard gratefully as a condescension. And he never forgets such kindness. Could the Negro be brought near to his white priest or bishop, he is not suspicious. He is not only willing but often longs to unburden his soul to this intelligent guide. There are no reservations when he is convinced that you are his friend. It is a saddening satire on American history and manners that it takes something to convince him.

That our people are not "drawn" to a church whose chief dignitaries they see only in the chancel, and whom they reverence as they would a painting or an angel, whose life never comes down to and touches theirs with the inspiration of an objective reality, may be "perplexing" truly (American caste and American Christianity both being facts) but it need not be surprising. There must be something of human nature in it, the same as that which brought about that "the Word was made flesh and dwelt among us" that He might "draw" us towards God.

Men are not "drawn" by abstractions. Only sympathy and love can draw, and until our Church in America realizes this and provides a clergy that can come in touch with our life and have a fellow feeling for our woes, without being imbedded and frozen up in their "Gothic antipathies," the good bishops are likely to continue "perplexed" by the sparsity of colored Episcopalians.

A colored priest of my acquaintance recently related to me, with tears in his eyes, how his reverend Father in God, the Bishop who had ordained him, had met him on the cars on his way to the diocesan convention and warned him, not unkindly, not to take a seat in the body of the convention with the white clergy. To avoid disturbance of their godly placidity he would of course please sit back and somewhat apart. I do not imagine that that clergyman had very much heart for the Christly (!) deliberations of that convention.

To return, however, it is not on this broader view of Church work, which I mentioned as a primary cause of its halting progress with the colored people, that I am to speak. My proper theme is the second oversight of which in my judgment our Christian propagandists have been guilty: or, the necessity of church training, protecting and uplifting our colored womanhood as indispensable to the evangelization of the race.

Apelles did not disdain even that criticism of his lofty art which came from an uncouth cobbler; and may I not hope that the writer's oneness with her subject both in feeling and in being may palliate undue obtrusiveness of opinions here. That the race cannot be effectually lifted up till its women are truly elevated we take as proven. It is not for us to dwell on the needs, the neglects, and the ways of succor, pertaining to the black woman of the South. The ground has been ably discussed and an admirable and practical plan proposed by the oldest Negro priest in America, advising and urging that special organizations such as Church Sisterhoods and industrial schools be devised to meet her pressing needs in the Southland. That some such movements are vital to the life of this people and the extension of the Church among them, is not hard to see. Yet the pamphlet fell still-born from the press. So far as I am informed the Church has made no motion towards carrying out Dr. Crummell's suggestion.

The denomination which comes next our own in opposing the proverbial emotionalism of Negro worship in the South, and which in consequence like ours receives the cold shoulder from the old heads, resting as we do under the charge of not "having religion" and not believing in conversion—the Congregationalists— have quietly gone to work on the young, have established industrial and training schools, and now almost every community in the South is yearly enriched by a fresh infusion of vigorous young hearts, cultivated heads, and helpful hands that have been trained at Fisk, at Hampton, in Atlanta University, and in Tuskegee, Alabama.

These young people are missionaries actual or virtual both here and in Africa. They have learned to love the methods and doctrines of the Church which trained and educated them; and so Congregationalism surely and steadily progresses.

Need I compare these well known facts with results shown by

the Church in the same field and during the same or even a longer time.

The institution of the Church in the South to which she mainly
looks for the training of her colored clergy and for the help of the
"Black Woman" and "Colored Girl" of the South, has graduated
since the year 1868, when the school was founded, *five young
women;* and while yearly numerous young men have been kept
and trained for the ministry by the charities of the Church, the
number of indigent females who have here been supported, sheltered and trained, is phenomenally small. Indeed, to my mind,
the attitude of the Church toward this feature of her work is as if
the solution of the problem of Negro missions depended solely on
sending a quota of deacons and priests into the field, girls being a
sort of *tertium quid* whose development may be promoted if they
can pay their way and fall in with the plans mapped out for the
training of the other sex. Now I would ask in all earnestness,
does not this force potential deserve by education and stimulus to
be made dynamic? Is it not a solemn duty incumbent on all colored churchmen to make it so? Will not the aid of the Church be
given to prepare our girls in head, heart, and hand for the duties
and responsibilities that await the intelligent wife, the Christian
mother, the earnest, virtuous, helpful woman, at once both the
lever and the fulcrum for uplifting the race.

As Negroes and churchmen we cannot be indifferent to these
questions. They touch us most vitally on both sides. We believe in
the Holy Catholic Church. We believe that however gigantic and
apparently remote the consummation, the Church will go on
conquering and to conquer till the kingdoms of this world, not
excepting the black man and the black woman of the South,
shall have become the kingdoms of the Lord and of his Christ.

That past work in this direction has been unsatisfactory we
must admit. That without a change of policy results in the future
will be as meagre, we greatly fear. Our life as a race is at stake.
The dearest interests of our hearts are in the scales. We must either break away from dear old landmarks and plunge out in any
line and every line that enables us to meet the pressing need of
our people, or we must ask the Church to allow and help us,

---

*Five have been graduated since '86, two in '91, two in '92.

untrammelled by the prejudices and theories of individuals, to work agressively under her direction as we alone can, with God's help, for the salvation of our people.

The time is ripe for action. Self-seeking and ambition must be laid on the altar. The battle is one of sacrifice and hardship, but our duty is plain. We have been recipients of missionary bounty in some sort for twenty-one years. Not even the senseless vegetable is content to be a mere reservoir. Receiving without giving is an anomaly in nature. Nature's cells are all little workshops for manufacturing sunbeams, the product to be *given out* to earth's inhabitants in warmth, energy, thought, action. Inanimate creation always pays back an equivalent.

Now, *How much owest thou my Lord?* Will his account be overdrawn if he call for singleness of purpose and self-sacrificing labor for your brethren? Having passed through your drill school, will you refuse a general's commission even if it entail responsibility, risk and anxiety, with possibly some adverse criticism? Is it too much to ask you to step forward and direct the work for your race along those lines which you know to be of first and vital importance?

Will you allow these words of Ralph Waldo Emerson? "In ordinary," says he, "we have a snappish criticism which watches and contradicts the opposite party. We want the will which advances and dictates [acts]. Nature has made up her mind that what cannot defend itself, shall not be defended. Complaining never so loud and with never so much reason, is of no use. What cannot stand must fall; *and the measure of our sincerity and therefore of the respect of men is the amount of health and wealth we will hazard in the defense of our right.*"

## The Higher Education of Women

In the very first year of our century, the year 1801, there appeared in Paris a book by Silvain Marechal, entitled "Shall Woman Learn the Alphabet." The book proposes a law prohibiting the alphabet to women, and quotes authorities weighty and various, to prove that the woman who knows the alphabet has already lost part of her womanliness. The author declares that woman can use the alphabet only as Moliere predicted they would, in spelling out the verb *amo*; that they have no occasion to peruse Ovid's *Ars Amoris*, since that is already the ground and limit of their intuitive furnishing; that Madame Guion would have been far more adorable had she remained a beautiful ignoramus as nature made her; that Ruth, Naomi, the Spartan woman, the Amazons, Penelope, Andromache, Lucretia, Joan of Arc, Petrarch's Laura, the daughters of Charlemagne, could not spell their names; while Sappho, Aspasia, Madame de Maintenon, and Madame de Stael could read altogether too well for their good; finally, that if women were once permitted to read Sophocles and work with logarithms, or to nibble at any side of the apple of knowledge, there would be an end forever to their sewing on buttons and embroidering slippers.[1]

Please remember this book was published at the *beginning* of the Nineteenth Century. At the end of its first third, (in the year 1833) one solitary college in America decided to admit women within its sacred precincts, and organized what was called a "Ladies' Course" as well as the regular B.A. or Gentlemen's course.[2]

It was felt to be an experiment—a rather dangerous experiment—and was adopted with fear and trembling by the good fathers, who looked as if they had been caught secretly mixing explosive compounds and were guiltily expecting every moment to see the foundations under them shaken and rent and their fair superstructure shattered into fragments.

But the girls came, and there was no upheaval. They performed their tasks modestly and intelligently. Once in a while one or two were found choosing the gentlemen's course. Still no collapse; and the dear, careful, scrupulous, frightened old professors were just getting their hearts out of their throats and preparing to draw one good free breath, when they found they would have to change the names of those courses; for there were as many ladies in the gentlemen's course as in the ladies', and a distinctively Ladies' Course, inferior in scope and aim to the regular classical course, did not and could not exist.

Other colleges gradually fell into line, and to-day there are one hundred and ninety-eight colleges for women, and two hundred and seven coeducational colleges and universities in the United States alone offering the degree of B. A. to women, and sending out yearly into the arteries of this nation a warm, rich flood of strong, brave, active, energetic, well-equipped, thoughtful women—women quick to see and eager to help the needs of this needy world—women who can think as well as feel, and who feel none the less because they think—women who are none the less tender and true for the parchment scroll they bear in their hands—women who have given a deeper, richer, nobler and grander meaning to the word "womanly" than any one-sided masculine definition could ever have suggested or inspired—women whom the world has long waited for in pain and anguish till there should be at last added to its forces and allowed to permeate its thought the complement of that masculine influence which has dominated it for fourteen centuries.

Since the idea of order and subordination succumbed to barbarian brawn and brutality in the fifth century, the civilized world has been like a child brought up by his father. It has needed the great mother heart to teach it to be pitiful, to love mercy, to succor the weak and care for the lowly.

Whence came this apotheosis of greed and cruelty? Whence this sneaking admiration we all have for bullies and prize-fighters? Whence the self-congratulation of "dominant" races, as if "dominant" meant "righteous" and carried with it a title to inherit the earth? Whence the scorn of so-called weak or unwarlike races and individuals, and the very comfortable assurance that it is their manifest destiny to be wiped out as vermin before this advancing civilization? As if the possession of the Christian graces of meekness, non-resistance and forgiveness, were incompatible with a civilization professedly based on Christianity, the religion of love! Just listen to this little bit of Barbarian brag:

"As for Far Orientals, they are not of those who will survive. Artistic attractive people that they are, their civilization is like their own tree flowers, beautiful blossoms destined never to bear fruit. If these people continue in their old course, their earthly career is closed. Just as surely as morning passes into afternoon, so surely are these races of the Far East, if unchanged, destined to disappear before the advancing nations of the West. Vanish, they will, off the face of the earth, and leave our planet the eventual possession of the dwellers where the day declines. Unless their newly imported ideas really take root, it is from this whole world that Japanese and Koreans, as well as Chinese, will inevitably be excluded. Their Nirvana is already being realized; already, it has wrapped Far Eastern Asia in its winding sheet." —*Soul of the Far East*— P. Lowell.

Delightful reflection for "the dwellers where day declines." A spectacle to make the gods laugh, truly, to see the scion of an upstart race by one sweep of his generalizing pen consigning to annihilation one-third the inhabitants of the globe—a people whose civilization was hoary headed before the parent elements that begot his race had advanced beyond nebulosity.

How like Longfellow's Iagoo, we Westerners are, to be sure! In the few hundred years, we have had to strut across our allotted territory and bask in the afternoon sun, we imagine we have exhausted the possibilities of humanity. Verily, we are the people, and after us there is none other. Our God is power; strength, our standard of excellence, inherited from barbarian ancestors through a long line of male progenitors, the Law Salic permitting no feminine modifications.

Says one, "The Chinaman is not popular with us, and we do not like the Negro. It is not that the eyes of the one are set bias, and the other is dark-skinned; but the Chinaman, the Negro is weak—*and Anglo Saxons don't like weakness.*"

The world of thought under the predominant man-influence, unmollified and unrestrained by its complementary force, would become like Daniel's fourth beast: "dreadful and terrible, and *strong* exceedingly;" "it had great iron teeth; it devoured and brake in pieces, and stamped the residue with the feet of it;" and the most independent of us find ourselves ready at times to fall down and worship this incarnation of power.

Mrs. Mary A. Livermore,[3] a woman whom I can mention only to admire, came near shaking my faith a few weeks ago in my theory of the thinking woman's mission to put in the tender and sympathetic chord in nature's grand symphony, and counteract, or better, harmonize the diapason of mere strength and might.

She was dwelling on the Anglo-Saxon genius for power and his contempt for weakness, and described a scene in San Francisco which she had witnessed.

The incorrigible animal known as the American small-boy, had pounced upon a simple, unoffending Chinaman, who was taking home his work, and had emptied the beautifully laundried contents of his basket into the ditch. "And," said she, "when that great man stood there and blubbered before that crowd of lawless urchins, to any one of whom he might have taught a lesson with his two fists, *I didn't much care.*

This is said like a man! It grates harshly. It smacks of the worship of the beast. It is contempt for weakness, and taken out of its setting it seems to contradict my theory. It either shows that one of the highest exponents of the Higher Education can be at times untrue to the instincts I have ascribed to the thinking woman and to the contribution she is to add to the civilized world, or else the influence she wields upon our civilization may be potent without being necessarily and always direct and conscious. The latter is the case. Her voice may strike a false note, but her whole being is musical with the vibrations of human suffering. Her tongue may parrot over the cold conceits that some man has taught her, but her heart is aglow with sympathy and loving kindness, and she cannot be true to her real self without giving out these elements into the forces of the world.

No one is in any danger of imagining Mark Antony "a plain blunt man," nor Cassius a sincere one—whatever the speeches they may make.

As individuals, we are constantly and inevitably, whether we are conscious of it or not, giving out our real selves into our several little worlds, inexorably adding our own true ray to the flood of starlight, quite independently of our professions and our masquerading; and so in the world of thought, the influence of thinking woman far transcends her feeble declamation and may seem at times even opposed to it.

A visitor in Oberlin once said to the lady principal, "Have you no rabble in Oberlin? How is it I see no police here, and yet the streets are as quiet and orderly as if there were an officer of the law standing on every corner."

Mrs. Johnston replied, "Oh, yes; there are vicious persons in Oberlin just as in other towns—*but our girls are our police.*"

With from five to ten hundred pure-minded young women threading the streets of the village every evening unattended, vice must slink away, like frost before the rising sun: and yet I venture to say there was not one in a hundred of those girls who would not have run from a street brawl as she would from a mouse, and who would not have declared she could never stand the sight of blood and pistols.

There is, then, a real and special influence of woman. An influence subtle and often involuntary, an influence so intimately interwoven in, so intricately interpenetrated by the masculine influence of the time that it is often difficult to extricate the delicate meshes and analyze and identify the closely clinging fibers. And yet, without this influence—so long as woman sat with bandaged eyes and manacled hands, fast bound in the clamps of ignorance and inaction, the world of thought moved in its orbit like the revolutions of the moon; with one face (the man's face) always out, so that the spectator could not distinguish whether it was disc or sphere.

Now I claim that it is the prevalence of the Higher Education among women, the making it a common everyday affair for women to reason and think and express their thought, the training and stimulus which enable and encourage women to administer to the world the bread it needs as well as the sugar it cries for; in short it is the transmitting the potential forces of her soul into dynamic factors that has given symmetry and completeness to the world's agencies. So only could it be consummated that Mercy, the lesson she teaches, and Truth, the task man has set himself, should meet together: that righteousness, or *rightness*, man's ideal,—and *peace*, its necessary 'other half,' should kiss each other.

We must thank the general enlightenment and independence of woman (which we may now regard as a *fait accompli*) that both these forces are now at work in the world, and it is fair to demand from them for the twentieth century a higher type of civilization than any attained in the nineteenth. Religion, science, art, economics, have all needed the feminine flavor; and literature, the expression of what is permanent and best in all of these, may be guaged at any time to measure the strength of the feminine ingredient. You will not find theology consigning infants to lakes of unquenchable fire long after women have had a chance to grasp, master, and wield its dogmas. You will not find science annihilating personality from the government of the Universe and making of God an ungovernable, unintelligible, blind, often destructive physical force; you will not find jurisprudence formulating as an axiom the absurdity that man and wife are one, and that one the man—that the married woman may not hold or bequeath her own property save as subject to her husband's direction; you will not find political economists declaring that the only possible adjustment between laborers and capitalists is that of selfishness and rapacity—that each must get all he can and keep all that he gets, while the world cries *laissez faire* and the lawyers explain, "it is the beautiful working of the law of supply and demand;" in fine, you will not find the law of love shut out from the affairs of men after the feminine half of the world's truth is completed.

Nay, put your ear now close to the pulse of the time. What is the key-note of the literature of these days? What is the banner cry of all the activities of the last half decade? What is the dominant seventh which is to add richness and tone to the final cadences of this century and lead by a grand modulation into the triumphant harmonies of the next? Is it not compassion for the poor and unfortunate, and, as Bellamy[4] has expressed it, "indignant outcry against the failure of the social machinery as it is, to ameliorate the miseries of men!" Even Christianity is being brought to the bar of humanity and tried by the standard of its ability to alleviate the world's suffering and lighten and brighten its woe. What else can be the meaning of Matthew Arnold's saddening protest, "We cannot do without Christianity," cried he, "and we cannot endure it as it is."

When went there by an age, when so much time and thought, so much money and labor were given to God's poor and God's invalids, the lowly and unlovely, the sinning as well as the suffering—homes for inebriates and homes for lunatics, shelter for the aged and shelter for babes, hospitals for the sick, props and braces for the falling, reformatory prisons and prison reformatories, all show that a "mothering" influence from some source is leavening the nation.

Now please understand me. I do not ask you to admit that these benefactions and virtues are the exclusive possession of women, or even that women are their chief and only advocates. It may be a man who formulates and makes them vocal. It may be, and often is, a man who weeps over the wrongs and struggles for the amelioration: but that man has imbibed those impulses from a mother rather than from a father and is simply materializing and giving back to the world in tangible form the ideal love and tenderness, devotion and care that have cherished and nourished the helpless period of his own existence.

All I claim is that there is a feminine as well as a masculine side to truth; that these are related not as inferior and superior, not as better and worse, not as weaker and stronger, but as complements—complements in one necessary and symmetric whole. That as the man is more noble in reason, so the woman is more quick in sympathy. That as he is indefatigable in pursuit of abstract truth, so is she in caring for the interests by the way—striving tenderly and lovingly that not one of the least of these 'little ones' should perish. That while we not unfrequently see women who reason, we say, with the coolness and precision of a man, and men as considerate of helplessness as a woman, still there is a general consensus of mankind that the one trait is essentially masculine and the other as peculiarly feminine. That both are needed to be worked into the training of children, in order that our boys may supplement their virility by tenderness and sensibility, and our girls may round out their gentleness by strength and self-reliance. That, as both are alike necessary in giving symmetry to the individual, so a nation or a race will degenerate into mere emotionalism on the one hand, or bullyism on the other, if dominated by either exclusively; lastly, and most emphatically, that the feminine factor can have its proper effect only through woman's development and education so that she may fitly and intelligently stamp her force on the forces of her day, and add her modicum to the riches of the world's thought.

> "For woman's cause is man's: they rise or sink
>   Together, dwarfed or godlike, bond or free:
>   For she that out of Lethe scales with man
>   The shining steps of nature, shares with man
>   His nights, his days, moves with him to one goal.
>   If she be small, slight-natured, miserable,
>   How shall men grow?
>   *   *   *   Let her make herself her own
>   To give or keep, to live and learn and be
>   All that not harms distinctive womanhood.
>   For woman is not undeveloped man
>   But diverse: could we make her as the man
>   Sweet love were slain; his dearest bond is this,
>   Not like to like, but like in difference.
>   Yet in the long years liker must they grow;
>   The man be more of woman, she of man;
>   He gain in sweetness and in moral height,
>   Nor lose the wrestling thews that throw the world;
>   She mental breadth, nor fail in childward care,
>   Nor lose the childlike in the larger mind;
>   Till at the last she set herself to man,
>   Like perfect music unto noble words."

Now you will argue, perhaps, and rightly, that higher education for women is not a modern idea, and that, if that is the means of setting free and invigorating the long desired feminine force in the world, it has already had a trial and should, in the past, have produced some of these glowing effects. Sappho, the bright, sweet singer of Lesbos, "the violet-crowned, pure, sweetly smiling Sappho" as Alcaeus calls her, chanted her lyrics and poured forth her soul nearly six centuries before Christ, in notes as full and free, as passionate and eloquent as did ever Archilochus or Anacreon.

Aspasia, that earliest queen of the drawing-room, a century later ministered to the intellectual entertainment of Socrates and the leading wits and philosophers of her time. Indeed, to her is attributed, by the best critics, the authorship of one of the most noted speeches ever delivered by Pericles.[5]

Later on, during the Renaissance period, women were professors in mathematics, physics, metaphysics, and the classic languages in Bologna, Pavia, Padua, and Brescia. Olympia Fulvia Morata,[6] of Ferrara, a most interesting character, whose magnificent library was destroyed in 1553 in the invasion of Schweinfurt by Albert of Brandenburg, had acquired a most extensive education. It is said that this wonderful girl gave lectures on classical subjects in her sixteenth year, and had even before that written several very remarkable Greek and Latin poems, and what is also to the point, she married a professor at Heidelberg, and became a *help-meet for him*.

It is true then that the higher education for women—in fact, the highest that the world has ever witnessed—belongs to the past; but we must remember that it was possible, down to the middle of our own century, only to a select few; and that the fashions and traditions of the times were before that all against it. There were not only no stimuli to encourage women to make the most of their powers and to welcome their development as a helpful agency in the progress of civilization, but their little aspirations, when they had any, were chilled and snubbed in embryo, and any attempt at thought was received as a monstrous usurpation of man's prerogative.

Lessing declared that "the woman who thinks is like the man who puts on rouge—ridiculous;" and Voltaire in his coarse, flippant way used to say, "Ideas are like beards—women and boys have none." Dr. Maginn remarked, "We like to hear a few words of sense from a woman sometimes, as we do from a parrot—they are so unexpected!" and even the pious Fenelon taught that virgin delicacy is almost as incompatible with learning as with vice.

That the average woman retired before these shafts of wit and ridicule and even gloried in her ignorance is not surprising. The Abbe Choisi, it is said, praised the Duchesse de Fontanges as being pretty as an angel and silly as a goose, and all the young ladies of the court strove to make up in folly what they lacked in charms. The ideal of the day was that "women must be pretty, dress prettily, flirt prettily, and not be too well informed;" that it was the *summum bonum* of her earthly hopes to have, as Thackeray puts it, "all the fellows battling to dance with her;" that she had no God-given destiny, no soul with unquenchable longings and inexhaustible possibilities—no work of her own to do and give to the world—no absolute and inherent value, no duty to self, transcending all pleasure-giving that may be demanded of a mere toy; but that her value was purely a relative one and to be estimated as are the fine arts—by the pleasure they give. "Woman, wine and song," as "the world's best gifts to man," were linked together in praise with as little thought of the first saying, "What doest thou," as that the wine and the song should declare, "We must be about our Father's business."

Men believed, or pretended to believe, that the great law of self development was obligatory on their half of the human family only; that while it was the chief end of man to glorify God and put his five talents to the exchangers, gaining thereby other five, it was, or ought to be, the sole end of woman to glorify man and wrap her one decently away in a napkin, retiring into "Hezekiah Smith's lady during her natural life and Hezekiah Smith's relict on her tombstone;" that higher education was incompatible with the shape of the female cerebrum, and that even if it could be acquired it must inevitably unsex woman destroying the lisping, clinging, tenderly helpless, and beautifully dependent creatures whom men would so heroically think for and so gallantly fight for, and giving in their stead a formidable race of blue stockings with corkscrew ringlets and other spinster propensities.

But these are eighteenth century ideas.

We have seen how the pendulum has swung across our present century. The men of our time have asked with Emerson, "that woman only show us how she can best be served;" and woman has replied: the chance of the seedling and of the animalcule is all I ask—the chance for growth and self development, the permission to be true to the aspirations of my soul without incurring the blight of your censure and ridicule.

"Audetque viris concurrere virgo."

In soul-culture woman at last dares to contend with men, and we may cite Grant Allen (who certainly cannot be suspected of advocating the unsexing of woman) as an example of the broadening effect of this contest on the ideas at least of the men of the day. He says in his *Plain Words on the Woman Question*, recently published:

"The position of woman was not [in the past a] position which could bear the test of nineteenth-century scrutiny. Their education was inadequate, their social status was humiliating, their political power was nil, their practical and personal grievances were innumerable; above all, their relations to the family—to their husbands, their children, their friends, their property—was simply insupportable."

And again: "As a body we 'Advanced men' are, I think, prepared to reconsider, and to reconsider fundamentally, without prejudice or misconception, the entire question of the relation betwen the sexes. We are ready to make any modifications in those relations which will satisfy the woman's just aspiration for personal independence, for intellectual and moral development, for physical culture, for political activity, and for a voice in the arrangement of her own affairs, both domestic and national."

Now this is magnanimous enough, surely; and quite a step from eighteenth century preaching, is it not? The higher education of Woman has certainly developed the men;—let us see what it has done for the women.

Matthew Arnold during his last visit to America in '82 or '83, lectured before a certain co-educational college in the West. After the lecture he remarked, with some surprise, to a lady professor, that the young women in his audience, he noticed, paid as close attention as the men, *all the way through*." This led, of course, to a spirited discussion of the higher education for women, during which he said to his enthusiastic interlocutor, eyeing her philosophically through his English eyeglass: "But—eh—don't you think it—eh—spoils their *chawnces*, you know!"

Now, as to the result to women, this is the most serious argument ever used against the higher education. If it interferes with marriage, classical training has a grave objection to weigh and answer.

For I agree with Mr. Allen at least on this one point, that there must be marrying and giving in marriage even till the end of time.

I grant you that intellectual development, with the self-reliance and capacity for earning a livelihood which it gives, renders woman less dependent on the marriage relation for physical support (which, by the way, does not always accompany it). Neither is she compelled to look to sexual love as the one sensation capable of giving tone and relish, movement and vim to the life she leads. Her horizon is extended. Her sympathies are broadened and deepened and multiplied. She is in closer touch with nature. Not a bud that opens, not a dew drop, not a ray of light, not a cloud-burst or a thunderbolt, but adds to the expansiveness and zest of her soul. And if the sun of an absorbing passion be gone down, still 'tis night that brings the stars. She has remaining the mellow, less obtrusive, but none the less enchanting and inspiring light of friendship, and into its charmed circle she may gather the best the world has known. She can commune with Socrates about the *daimon* he knew and to which she too can bear witness; she can revel in the majesty of Dante, the sweetness of Virgil, the simplicity of Homer, the strength of Milton. She can listen to the pulsing heart throbs of passionate Sappho's encaged soul, as she beats her bruised wings against her prison bars and struggles to flutter out into Heaven's æther, and the fires of her own soul cry back as she listens. "Yes; Sappho, I know it all; I know it all." Here, at last, can be communion without suspicion; friendship without misunderstanding; love without jealousy.

We must admit then that Byron's picture, whether a thing of beauty or not, has faded from the canvas of to-day.

"Man's love," he wrote, "is of man's life a thing apart,
  'Tis woman's whole existence.
  Man may range the court, camp, church, the vessel and the mart,
  Sword, gown, gain, glory offer in exchange.
  Pride, fame, ambition, to fill up his heart—
  And few there are whom these cannot estrange.
  Men have all these resources, we *but one*—
  *To love again and be again undone.*"

This may have been true when written. *It is not true to-day.* The old, subjective, stagnant, indolent and wretched life for woman has gone. She has as many resources as men, as many activities beckon her on. As large possibilities swell and inspire her heart.

Now, then, does it destroy or diminish her capacity for loving?

Her standards have undoubtedly gone up. The necessity of speculating in 'chawnces' has probably shifted. The question is not now with the woman "How shall I so cramp, stunt, simplify and nullify myself as to make me elegible to the honor of being swallowed up into some little man?" but the problem, I trow, now rests with the man as to how he can so develop his God-given powers as to reach the ideal of a generation of women who demand the noblest, grandest and best achievements of which he is capable; and this surely is the only fair and natural adjustment of the chances. Nature never meant that the ideals and standards of the world should be dwarfing and minimizing ones, and the men should thank us for requiring of them the richest fruits which they can grow. If it makes them work, all the better for them.

As to the adaptability of the educated woman to the marriage relation, I shall simply quote from that excellent symposium of learned women that appeared recently under Mrs. Armstrong's signature in answer to the "Plain Words" of Mr. Allen, already referred to. "Admitting no longer any question as to their intellectual equality with the men whom they meet, with the simplicity of conscious strength, they take their place beside the men who challenge them, and fearlessly face the result of their actions. They deny that their education in any way unfits them for the duty of wifehood and maternity or primarily renders these conditions any less attractive to them than to the domestic type of woman. On the contrary, they hold that their knowledge of physiology makes them better mothers and housekeepers; their knowledge of chemistry makes them better cooks; while from their training in other natural sciences and in mathematics, they obtain an accuracy and fair-mindedness which is of great value to them in dealing with their children or employees."

So much for their willingness. Now the apple may be good for food and pleasant to the eyes, and a fruit to be desired to make one wise. Nay, it may even assure you that it has no aversion whatever to being tasted. Still, if you do not like the flavor all these recommendations are nothing. Is the intellectual woman *desirable* in the matrimonial market?

This I cannot answer. I confess my ignorance. I am no judge of such things. I have been told that strong-minded women could be, when they thought it worth their while, quite endurable, and, judging from the number of female names I find in college catalogues among the alumnae with double patronymics, I surmise that quite a number of men are willing to put up with them.

Now I would that my task ended here. Having shown that a great want of the world in the past has been a feminine force; that that force can have its full effect only through the untrammelled development of woman; that such development, while it gives her to the world and to civilization, does not necessarily remove her from the home and fireside; finally, that while past centuries have witnessed sporadic instances of this higher growth, still it was reserved for the latter half of the nineteenth century to render it common and general enough to be effective; I might close with a glowing prediction of what the twentieth century may expect from this heritage of twin forces—the masculine battered and toil-worn as a grim veteran after centuries of warfare, but still strong, active, and vigorous, ready to help with his hard-won experience the young recruit rejoicing in her newly found freedom, who so confidently places her hand in his with mutual pledges to redeem the ages.

> "And so the twain upon the skirts of Time,
>   Sit side by side, full-summed in all their powers,
>   Dispensing harvest, sowing the To-be,
>   Self-reverent each and reverencing each."

Fain would I follow them, but duty is nearer home. The high ground of generalities is alluring but my pen is devoted to a special cause: and with a view to further enlightenment on the achievements of the century for THE HIGHER EDUCATION OF COLORED WOMEN, I wrote a few days ago to the colleges which admit women and asked how many colored women had completed the B. A. course in each during its entire history. These are the figures returned: Fisk leads the way with twelve; Oberlin next with five; Wilberforce, four; Ann Arbor and Wellesley three each, Livingstone two, Atlanta one, Howard, as yet, none.

I then asked the principal of the Washington High School how many out of a large number of female graduates from his school had chosen to go forward and take a collegiate course. He replied that but one had ever done so, and she was then in Cornell.* [7]

Others ask questions too, sometimes, and I was asked a few years ago by a white friend, "How is it that the men of your race seem to outstrip the women in mental attainment?" "Oh," I said, "so far as it is true, the men, I suppose, from the life they lead, gain more by contact; and so far as it is only apparent, I think the women are more quiet. They don't feel called to mount a barrel and harangue by the hour every time they imagine they have produced an idea."

But I am sure there is another reason which I did not at that time see fit to give. The atmosphere, the standards, the requirements of our little world do not afford any special stimulus to female development.

It seems hardly a gracious thing to say, but it strikes me as true, that while our men seem thoroughly abreast of the times on almost every other subject, when they strike the woman question they drop back into sixteenth century logic. They leave nothing to be desired generally in regard to gallantry and chivalry, but they actually do not seem sometimes to have outgrown that old contemporary of chivalry—the idea that women may stand on pedestals or live in doll houses, (if they happen to have them) but they must not furrow their brows with thought or attempt to help men tug at the great questions of the world. I fear the majority of colored men do not yet think it worth while that women aspire to higher education. Not many will subscribe to the "advanced" ideas of Grant Allen already quoted. The three R's, a little music and a good deal of dancing, a first rate dressmaker and a bottle of magnolia balm, are quite enough generally

* Graduated from Scientific Course, June, 1890, the first colored woman to graduate from Cornell.

to render charming any woman possessed of tact and the capacity for worshipping masculinity.

My readers will pardon my illustrating my point and also giving a reason for the fear that is in me, by a little bit of personal experience. When a child I was put into a school near home that professed to be normal and collegiate, i. e. to prepare teachers for colored youth, furnish candidates for the ministry, and offer collegiate training for those who should be ready for it. Well, I found after a while that I had a good deal of time on my hands. I had devoured what was put before me, and, like Oliver Twist, was looking around to ask for more. I constantly felt (as I suppose many an ambitious girl has felt) a thumping from within unanswered by any beckoning from without. Class after class was organized for these ministerial candidates (many of them men who had been preaching before I was born). Into every one of these classes I was expected to go, with the sole intent, I thought at the time, of enabling the dear old principal, as he looked from the vacant countenances of his sleepy old class over to where I sat, to get off his solitary pun—his never-failing pleasantry, especially in hot weather—which was, as he called out "Any one!" to the effect that "*any* one" then meant "*Annie* one."

Finally a Greek class was to be formed. My inspiring preceptor informed me that Greek had never been taught in the school, but that he was going to form a class *for the candidates for the ministry*, and if I liked I might join it. I replied—humbly I hope, as became a female of the human species—that I would like very much to study Greek, and that I was thankful for the opportunity, and so it went on. A boy, however meager his equipment and shallow his pretentions, had only to declare a floating intention to study theology and he could get all the support, encouragement and stimulus he needed, be absolved from work and invested beforehand with all the dignity of his far away office. While a self-supporting girl had to struggle on by teaching in the summer and working after school hours to keep up with her board bills, and actually to fight her way against positive discouragements to the higher education; till one such girl one day flared out and told the principal "the only mission opening before a girl in his school was to marry one of those candidates." He said he didn't know but it was. And when at last that same girl announced her desire and intention to go to college it was received with about the same incredulity and dismay as if a brass button on one of those candidate's coats had propounded a new method for squaring the circle or trisecting the arc.[8]

Now this is not fancy. It is a simple unvarnished photograph, and what I believe was not in those days exceptional in colored schools, and I ask the men and women who are teachers and co-workers for the highest interests of the race, that they give the girls a chance! We might as well expect to grow trees from leaves as hope to build up a civilization or a manhood without taking into consideration our women and the home life made by them, which must be the root and ground of the whole matter. Let us insist then on special encouragement for the education of our women and special care in their training. Let our girls feel that we expect something more of them than that they merely look pretty and appear well in society. Teach them that there is a race with special needs which they and only they can help; that the world needs and is already asking for their trained, efficient forces. Finally, if there is an ambitious girl with pluck and brain to take the higher education, encourage her to make the most of it. Let there be the same flourish of trumpets and clapping of hands as when a boy announces his determination to enter the lists; and then, as you know that she is physically the weaker of the two, don't stand from under and leave her to buffet the waves alone. Let her know that your heart is following her, that your hand, though she sees it not, is ready to support her. To be plain, I mean let money be raised and scholarships be founded in our colleges and universities for self-supporting, worthy young women, to offset and balance the aid that can always be found for boys who will take theology.

The earnest well trained Christian young woman, as a teacher, as a home-maker, as wife, mother, or silent influence even, is as potent a missionary agency among our people as is the theologian; and I claim that at the present stage of our development in the South she is even more important and necessary.

Let us then, here and now, recognize this force and resolve to make the most of it—not the boys less, but the girls more.

## "Woman Versus the Indian"

In the National Woman's Council convened at Washington in February 1891, among a number of thoughtful and suggestive papers read by eminent women, was one by the Rev. Anna Shaw, bearing the above title.

That Miss Shaw is broad and just and liberal in principal is proved beyond contradiction. Her noble generosity and womanly firmness are unimpeachable. The unwavering stand taken by herself and Miss Anthony in the subsequent color ripple in Wimodaughsis ought to be sufficient to allay forever any doubts as to the pure gold of these two women.

Of Wimodaughsis (which, being interpreted for the uninitiated, is a woman's culture club whose name is made up of the first few letters of the four words wives, mothers, daughters, and sisters) Miss Shaw is president, and a lady from the Blue Grass State *was* secretary.

Pandora's box is opened in the ideal harmony of this modern Eden without an Adam when a colored lady, a teacher in one of our schools, applies for admission to its privileges and opportunities.

The Kentucky secretary, a lady zealous in good works and one who, I can't help imagining, belongs to that estimable class who daily thank the Lord that He made the earth that they may have the job of superintending its rotations, and who really would like to help "elevate" the colored people (in her own way of course and so long as they understand their places) is filled with grief and horror that any persons of Negro extraction should aspire to learn type-writing or languages or to enjoy any other advantages offered in the sacred halls of Wimodaughsis. Indeed, she had not calculated that there were any wives, mothers, daughters, and sisters, except white ones; and she is really convinced that *Whimodaughsis* would sound just as well, and then it need mean just *white mothers, daughters and sisters*. In fact, so far as there is anything in a name, nothing would be lost by omitting for the sake of euphony, from this unique mosaic, the letters that represent wives. *Whiwimodaughsis* might be a little startling, and on the whole wives would better yield to white; since clearly all women are not wives, while surely all wives are daughters. The daughters therefore could represent the wives and this immaculate assembly for propagating liberal and progressive ideas and disseminating a broad and humanizing culture might be spared the painful possibility of the sight of a black man coming in the future to escort from an evening class this solitary cream-colored applicant. Accordingly the Kentucky secretary took the cream-colored applicant aside, and, with emotions befitting such an epoch-making crisis, told her, "as kindly as she could," that colored people were not admitted to the classes, at the same time refunding the money which said cream-colored applicant had paid for lessons in type-writing.

When this little incident came to the knowledge of Miss Shaw, she said firmly and emphatically, NO. As a minister of the gospel and as a Christian woman, she could not lend her influence to such unreasonable and uncharitable discrimination; and she must resign the honor of president of Wimodaughsis if persons were to be proscribed solely on account of their color.

To the honor of the board of managers, be it said, they sustained Miss Shaw; and the Kentucky secretary, and those whom she succeeded in inoculating with her prejudices, resigned.

'Twas only a ripple,—some bewailing of lost opportunity on the part of those who could not or would not seize God's opportunity for broadening and enlarging their own souls—and then the work flowed on as before.

Susan B. Anthony and Anna Shaw are evidently too noble to be held in thrall by the provincialisms of women who seem never to have breathed the atmosphere beyond the confines of their grandfathers' plantations. It is only from the broad plateau of light and love that one can see petty prejudice and narrow priggishness in their true perspective; and it is on this high ground, as I sincerely believe, these two grand women stand.

As leaders in the woman's movement of today, they have need of clearness of vision as well as firmness of soul in adjusting recalcitrant forces, and wheeling into line the thousand and one none-such, never-to-be-modified, won't-be-dictated-to banners of their somewhat mottled array.

The black woman and the southern woman, I imagine, often

get them into the predicament of the befuddled man who had to take singly across a stream a bag of corn, a fox and a goose. There was no one to help, and to leave the goose with the fox was death—with the corn, destruction. To re-christen the animals, the lion could not be induced to lie down with the lamb unless the lamb would take the inside berth.

The black woman appreciates the situation and can even sympathize with the actors in the serio-comic dilemma.

But, may it not be that, as women, the very lessons which seem hardest to master now, are possibly the ones most essential for our promotion to a higher grade of work?

We assume to be leaders of thought and guardians of society. Our country's manners and morals are under our tutoring. Our standards are law in our several little worlds. However tenaciously men may guard some prerogatives, they are our willing slaves in that sphere which they have always conceded to be woman's. Here, no one dares demur when her fiat has gone forth. The man would be mad who presumed, however inexplicable and past finding out any reason for her action might be, to attempt to open a door in her kingdom officially closed and regally sealed by her.

The American woman of to-day not only gives tone directly to her immediate world, but her tiniest pulsation ripples out and out, down and down, till the outermost circles and the deepest layers of society feel the vibrations. It is pre-eminently an age of organizations. The "leading woman," the preacher, the reformer, the organizer "enthuses" her lieutenants and captains, the literary women, the thinking women, the strong, earnest, irresistible women; these in turn touch their myriads of church clubs, social clubs, culture clubs, pleasure clubs and charitable clubs, till the same lecture has been duly administered to every married man in the land (not to speak of sons and brothers) from the President in the White House to the stone-splitter of the ditches. And so woman's lightest whisper is heard as in Dionysius' ear, by quick relays and endless reproductions, through every recess and cavern as well as on every hilltop and mountain in her vast domain. And her mandates are obeyed. When she says "thumbs up," woe to the luckless thumb that falters in its rising. They may be little things, the amenities of life, the little nothings which cost nothing and come to nothing, and yet can make a sentient being so comfortable or so miserable in this life, the oil of social machinery, which we call the courtesies of life, all are under the magic key of woman's permit.

The American woman then is responsible for American manners. Not merely the right ascension and declination of the satellites of her own drawing room; but the rising and the setting of the pestilential or life-giving orbs which seem to wander afar in space, all are governed almost wholly through her magnetic polarity. The atmosphere of street cars and parks and boulevards, of cafes and hotels and steamboats is charged and surcharged with her sentiments and restrictions. Shop girls and serving maids, cashiers and accountant clerks, scribblers and drummers, whether wage earner, salaried toiler, or proprietress, whether laboring to instruct minds, to save souls, to delight fancies, or to win bread,—the working women of America in whatever station or calling they may be found, are subjects, officers, or rulers of a strong centralized government, and bound together by a system of codes and countersigns, which, though unwritten, forms a network of perfect subordination and unquestioning obedience as marvelous as that of the Jesuits. At the head and center in this regime stands the Leading Woman in the principality. The one talis-manic word that plays along the wires from palace to cook-shop, from imperial Congress to the distant plain, is *Caste*. With all her vaunted independence, the American woman of to-day is as fearful of losing caste as a Brahmin in India. That is the law under which she lives, the precepts which she binds as frontlets between her eyes and writes on the door-posts of her homes, the lesson which she instils into her children with their first baby breakfasts, the injunction she lays upon husband and lover with direst penalties attached.

The queen of the drawing room is absolute ruler under this law. Her pose gives the cue. The microscopic angle at which her pencilled brows are elevated, signifies who may be recognized and who are beyond the pale. The delicate intimation is, quick as electricity, telegraphed down. Like the wonderful transformation in the House that Jack Built (or regions thereabouts) when the rat began to gnaw the rope, the rope to hang the butcher, the butcher to kill the ox, the ox to drink the water, the water to quench the fire, the fire to burn the stick, the stick to beat the dog, and the dog to worry the cat, and on, and on, and on,—when miladi causes the inner arch over her matchless orbs to ascend the merest trifle, *presto*! the Miss at the notions counter grows curt and pert, the dress goods clerk becomes indifferent and taciturn, hotel waiters and ticket dispensers look the other way, the Irish street laborer snarls and scowls, conductors, policemen and park superintendents jostle and push and threaten, and society suddenly seems transformed into a band of organized adders, snapping, and striking and hissing just because they like it on general principles. The tune set by the head singer, sung through all keys and registers, with all qualities of tone,—the smooth, flowing, and gentle, the creaking, whizzing, grating, screeching, growling—according to ability, taste, and temperament of the singers. Another application of like master, like man. In this case, like mistress, like nation.

It was the good fortune of the Black Woman of the South to spend some weeks, not long since, in a land over which floated the Union Jack. The Stars and Stripes were not the only familiar experiences missed. A uniform, matter-of-fact courtesy, a genial kindliness, quick perception of opportunities for rendering any little manly assistance, a readiness to give information to strangers,—a hospitable, thawing-out atmosphere everywhere—in shops and waiting rooms, on cars and in the streets, actually seemed to her chilled little soul to transform the commonest boor in the service of the public into one of nature's noblemen, and when the old whipped-cur feeling was taken up and analyzed she could hardly tell whether it consisted mostly of self pity for her own wounded sensibilities, or of shame for her country and mortification that her countrymen offered such an unfavorable contrast.

Some American girls, I noticed recently, in search of novelty and adventure, were taking an extended trip through our country unattended by gentleman friends; their wish was to write up for a periodical or lecture the ease and facility, the comfort and safety of American travel, even for the weak and unprotected, under our well-nigh perfect railroad systems and our gentlemanly and efficient corps of officials and public servants. I have some material I could furnish these young ladies, though possibly it might not be just on the side they wish to have illuminated. The Black Woman of the South has to do considerable travelling in this country, often unattended. She thinks she is quiet and unobtrusive in her manner, simple and inconspicuous in her dress, and can see no reason why in any chance assemblage of *ladies*, or even a promiscuous gathering of ordinarily well-bred and dignified individuals, she should be signaled out for any marked consideration. And yet she has seen these same "gentlemanly and efficient" railroad conductors, when their cars had stopped at stations having no raised platforms, making it necessary for passengers to take the long and trying leap from the car step to the ground or step on the narrow little stool placed under by the conductor, after standing at their posts and handing woman after woman from the steps to the stool, thence to the ground, or else relieving her of satchels and bags and enabling her to make the descent easily, deliberately fold their arms and turn round when the Black Woman's turn came to alight— bearing her satchel, and bearing besides another unnamable burden inside the heaving bosom and tightly compressed lips. The feeling of slighted womanhood is unlike every other emotion of the soul. Happily for the human family, it is unknown to many and indescribable to all. Its poignancy, compared with which even Juno's *spretae injuria formae* is earthly and vulgar, is holier than that of jealousy, deeper than indignation, tenderer than rage. Its first impulse of wrathful protest and proud self vindication is checked and shamed by the consciousness that self assertion would outrage still further the same delicate instinct. Were there a brutal attitude of hate or of ferocious attack, the feminine response of fear or repulsion is simple and spontaneous. But when the keen sting comes through the finer sensibilities, from a hand which, by all known traditions and ideals of propriety, should have been trained to reverence and respect them, the condemnation of man's inhumanity to woman is increased and embittered by the knowledge of personal identity with a race of beings so fallen.

I purposely forbear to mention instances of personal violence to colored women travelling in less civilized sections of our country, where women have been forcibly ejected from cars, thrown out of seats, their garments rudely torn, their person wantonly and cruelly injured. America is large and must for some time yet endure its out-of-the-way jungles of barbarism as Africa its uncultivated tracts of marsh and malaria. There are murderers and thieves and villains in both London and Paris. Humanity from the first has had its vultures and sharks, and representatives of the fraternity who prey upon mankind may be expected no less in America than elsewhere. That this virulence breaks out most readily and commonly against colored persons in this country, is due of course to the fact that they are, generally speaking, weak and can be imposed upon with impunity. Bullies are always cowards at heart and may be credited with a pretty safe instinct in scenting their prey. Besides, society, where it has not exactly said to its dogs "s-s-sik him!" has at least engaged to be looking in another direction or studying the rivers on Mars. It is not of the dogs and their doings, but of society holding the leash that I shall speak. It is those subtle exhalations of atmospheric odors for which woman is accountable, the indefinable, unplaceable aroma which seems to exude from the very pores in her finger tips like the delicate sachet so dexterously hidden and concealed in her linens; the essence of her teaching, guessed rather than read, so adroitly is the lettering and wording manipulated; it is the undertones of the picture laid finely on by woman's own practiced hand, the reflection of the lights and shadows on her own brow; it is, in a word, the reputation of our nation for general politeness and good manners and of our fellow citizens to be somewhat more than cads or snobs that shall engage our present study. There can be no true test of national courtesy without travel. Impressions and conclusions based on provincial traits and characteristics can thus be modified and generalized. Moreover, the weaker and less influential the experimenter, the more exact and scientific the deductions. Courtesy "for revenue only" is not politeness, but diplomacy. Any rough can assume civilty toward those of "his set," and does not hesitate to carry it even to servility toward those in whom he recognizes a possible patron or his master in power, wealth, rank, or influence. But, as the chemist prefers distilled $H_2 O$ in testing solutions to avoid complications and unwarranted reactions, so the Black Woman holds that her femineity linked with the impossibility of popular affinity or unexpected attraction through

position and influence in her case makes her a touchstone of
American courtesy exceptionally pure and singularly free from
extraneous modifiers. The man who is courteous to her is so, not
because of anything he hopes or fears or sees, but because *he is
a gentleman.*

I would eliminate also from the discussion all uncharitable reflections upon the orderly execution of laws existing in certain
states of this Union, requiring persons known to be colored to
ride in one car, and persons supposed to be white in another. A
good citizen may use his influence to have existing laws and statutes changed or modified, but a public servant must not be
blamed for obeying orders. A railroad conductor is not asked to
dictate measures, nor to make and pass laws. His bread and butter are conditioned on his managing his part of the machinery as
he is told to do. If, therefore, I found myself in that compartment
of a train designated by the sovereign law of the state for pre-
sumable Caucasians, and for colored persons only when traveling in the capacity of nurses and maids, should a conductor
inform me, as a gentleman might, that I had made a mistake,
and offer to show me the proper car for black ladies; I might
wonder at the expensive arrangements of the company and of
the state in providing special and separate accommodations for
the transportation of the various hues of humanity, but I certainly could not take it as a want of courtesy on the conductor's
part that he gave the information. It is true, public sentiment
precedes and begets all laws, good or bad; and on the ground I
have taken, our women are to be credited largely as teachers and
moulders of public sentiment. But when a law has passed and
received the sanction of the land, there is nothing for our officials to do but enforce it till repealed; and I for one, as a loyal
American citizen, will give those officials cheerful support and
ready sympathy in the discharge of their duty. But when a great
burly six feet of masculinity with sloping shoulders and unkempt
beard swaggers in, and, throwing a roll of tobacco into one corner of his jaw, growls out at me over the paper I am reading,
"Here gurl," (I am past thirty) "you better git out 'n dis kyar 'f
yer don't, I'll put yer out,"—my mental annotation is *Here's an
American citizen who has been badly trained. He is sadly lack-
ing in both 'sweetness' and 'light'*; and when in the same section

of our enlightened and progressive country, I see from the car window, working on private estates, convicts from the state penitentiary, among them squads of boys from fourteen to eighteen years of age in a chain-gang, their feet chained together and heavy blocks attached—not in 1850, but in 1890, '91 and '92, I make a note on the flyleaf of my memorandum, *The women in this section should organize a Society for the Prevention of Cruelty to Human Beings, and disseminate civilizing tracts, and send throughout the region apostles of anti-barbarism for the propagation of humane and enlightened ideas.* And when farther on in the same section our train stops at a dilapidated station, rendered yet more unsightly by dozens of loafers with their hands in their pockets while a productive soil and inviting climate beckon in vain to industry; and when, looking a little more closely, I see two dingy little rooms with "FOR LADIES" swinging over one and "FOR COLORED PEOPLE" over the other; while wondering under which head I come, I notice a little way off the only hotel proprietor of the place whittling a pine stick as he sits with one leg thrown across an empty goods box; and as my eye falls on a sample room next door which seems to be driving the only wide-awake and popular business of the commonwealth, I cannot help ejaculating under my breath, "What a field for the missionary woman." I know that if by any fatality I should be obliged to lie over at that station, and, driven by hunger, should be compelled to seek refreshments or the bare necessaries of life at the only public accommodation in the town, that same stick-whittler would coolly inform me, without looking up from his pine splinter, "We doan uccommo-date no niggers hyur." And yet we are so scandalized at Russia's barbarity and cruelty to the Jews! We pay a man a thousand dollars a night just to make us weep, by a recital of such heathenish inhumanity as is practiced on Selavonic soil.

A recent writer on Eastern nations says: "If we take through the earth's temperate zone, a belt of country whose northern and southern edges are determined by certain limiting isotherms, not more than half the width of the zone apart, we shall find that we have included in a relatively small extent of surface almost all the nations of note in the world, past or present. Now, if we examine this belt and compare the different parts of it with one another, we shall be struck by a remarkable fact. *The peoples inhabiting it grow steadily more personal as we go west.* So unmistakable is this gradation, that one is almost tempted to ascribe it to cosmical rather than to human causes. It is as marked as the change in color of the human complexion observable along any meridian, which ranges from black at the equator to blonde toward the pole. In like manner the sense of self grows more intense as we follow in the wake of the setting sun, and fades steadily as we advance into the dawn. America, Europe, the Levant, India, Japan, each is less personal than the one before. . . . *That politeness should be one of the most marked results of impersonality* may appear surprising, yet a slight examination will show it to be a fact. Considered *a priori*, the connection is not far to seek. Impersonality by lessening the interest in one's self, induces one to take an interest in others. Looked at *a posteriori*, we find that where the one trait exists the other is most developed, while an absence of the second seems to prevent the full growth of the first. This is true both in general and in detail. *Courtesy increases as we travel eastward round the world, coincidently with a decrease in the sense of self.* Asia is more courteous than Europe, Europe than America. Particular races show the same concomitance of characteristics. France, the most impersonal nation of Europe, is at the same time the most polite." And by inference, Americans, the most personal, are the least courteous nation on the globe.

The Black Woman had reached this same conclusion by an entirely different route; but it is gratifying to vanity, nevertheless, to find one's self sustained by both science and philosophy in a conviction, wrought in by hard experience, and yet too apparently audacious to be entertained even as a stealthy surmise. In fact the Black Woman was emboldened some time since by a well put and timely article from an Editor's Drawer on the "Mannerless Sex," to give the world the benefit of some of her experience with the "*Mannerless Race*"; but since Mr. Lowell shows so conclusively that the entire Land of the West is a *mannerless continent*, I have determined to plead with our women, the mannerless sex on this mannerless continent, to institute a reform by placing immediately in our national curricula a department for teaching GOOD MANNERS.

Now, am I right in holding the American Woman responsible? Is it true that the exponents of woman's advancement, the leaders in woman's thought, the preachers and teachers of all woman's reforms, can teach this nation to be courteous, to be pitiful, having compassion one of another, not rendering evil for inoffensiveness, and railing in proportion to the improbability of being struck back; but contrariwise, being *all* of one mind, to love as brethren?

I think so.

It may require some heroic measures, and like all revolutions will call for a determined front and a courageous, unwavering, stalwart heart on the part of the leaders of the reform.

The "*all*" will inevitably stick in the throat of the Southern woman. She must be allowed, please, to except the 'darkey' from the 'all'; it is too bitter a pill with black people in it. You must get the Revised Version to put it, "*love all white people* as brethren." She really could not enter any society on earth, or in heaven above, or in—the waters under the earth, on such unpalatable conditions.

The Black Woman has tried to understand the Southern woman's difficulties; to put herself in her place, and to be as fair, as charitable, and as free from prejudice in judging her antipathies, as she would have others in regard to her own. She has honestly weighed the apparently sincere excuse, "But you must remember that these people were once our slaves"; and that other, "But civility towards the Negroes will bring us on *social equality* with them."

These are the two bugbears; or rather, the two humbugbears: for, though each is founded on a most glaring fallacy, one would think they were words to conjure with, so potent and irresistible is their spell as an argument at the North as well as in the South.

One of the most singular facts about the unwritten history of this country is the consummate ability with which Southern influence, Southern ideas and Southern ideals, have from the very beginning even up to the present day, dictated to and domineered over the brain and sinew of this nation. Without wealth, without education, without inventions, arts, sciences, or industries, without well-nigh every one of the progressive ideas and impulses which have made this country great, prosperous and

happy, personally indolent and practically stupid, poor in everything but bluster and self-esteem, the Southerner has nevertheless with Italian finesse and exquisite skill, uniformly and
invariably, so manipulated Northern sentiment as to succeed
sooner or later in carrying his point and shaping the policy of
this government to suit his purposes. Indeed, the Southerner is a
magnificent manager of men, a born educator. For two hundred
and fifty years he trained to his hand a people whom he made
absolutely his own, in body, mind, and sensibility. He so insinu-
ated differences and distinctions among them, that their personal attachment for him was stronger than for their own
brethren and fellow sufferers. He made it a crime for two or
three of them to be gathered together in Christ's name without a
white man's supervision, and a felony for one to teach them to
read even the Word of Life; and yet they would defend his interest with their life blood; his smile was their happiness, a pat on
the shoulder from him their reward. The slightest difference
among themselves in condition, circumstances, opportunities,
became barriers of jealousy and disunion. He sowed his blood
broadcast among them, then pitted mulatto against black, bond
against free, house slave against plantation slave, even the slave
of one clan against like slave of another clan; till, wholly oblivi-
ous of their ability for mutual succor and defense, all became
centers of myriad systems of repellent forces, having but one sentiment in common, and that their entire subjection to that master hand.

And he not only managed the black man, he also hoodwinked
the white man, the tourist and investigator who visited his lordly
estates. The slaves were doing well, in fact couldn't be happier,—
plenty to eat, plenty to drink, comfortably housed and clothed—
they wouldn't be free if they could; in short, in his broad
brimmed plantation hat and easy aristocratic smoking gown, he
made you think him a veritable patriarch in the midst of a lazy,
well fed, good natured, over-indulged tenantry.

Then, too, the South represented blood—not red blood, but
blue blood. The difference is in the length of the stream and your
distance from its source. If your own father was a pirate, a robber, a murderer, his hands are dyed in red blood, and you don't
say very much about it. But if your great great great grandfather's

grandfather stole and pillaged and slew, and you can prove it, your blood has become blue and you are at great pains to establish the relationship. So the South had neither silver nor gold, but she had blood; and she paraded it with so much gusto that the substantial little Puritan maidens of the North, who had been making bread and canning currants and not thinking of blood the least bit, began to hunt up the records of the Mayflower to see if some of the passengers thereon could not claim the honor of having been one of William the Conqueror's brigands, when he killed the last of the Saxon kings and, red-handed, stole his crown and his lands. Thus the ideal from out the Southland brooded over the nation and we sing less lustily than of yore

> 'Kind hearts are more than coronets
> And simple faith than Norman blood.'

In politics, the two great forces, commerce and empire, which would otherwise have shaped the destiny of the country, have been made to pander and cater to Southern notions. "Cotton is King" meant the South must be allowed to dictate or there would be no fun. Every statesman from 1830 to 1860 exhausted his genius in persuasion and compromises to smooth out her ruffled temper and gratify her petulant demands. But like a sullen younger sister, the South has pouted and sulked and cried: "I won't play with you now; so there!" and the big brother at the North has coaxed and compromised and given in, and—ended by letting her have her way. Until 1860 she had as her pet an institution which it was death by the law to say anything about, except that it was divinely instituted, inaugurated by Noah, sanctioned by Abraham, approved by Paul, and just ideally perfect in every way. And when, to preserve the autonomy of the family arrangements, in '61, '62 and '63, it became necessary for the big brother to administer a little wholesome correction and set the obstreperous Miss vigorously down in her seat again, she assumed such an air of injured innocence, and melted away so lugubriously, the big brother has done nothing since but try to sweeten and pacify and laugh her back into a companionable frame of mind.

Father Lincoln did all he could to get her to repent of her

petulance and behave herself. He even promised she might keep her pet, so disagreeable to all the neighbors and hurtful even to herself, and might manage it at home to suit herself, if she would only listen to reason and be just tolerably nice. But, no—she was going to leave and set up for herself; she didn't propose to be meddled with; and so, of course, she had to be spanked. Just a little at first—didn't mean to hurt, merely to teach her who was who. But she grew so ugly, and kicked and fought and scratched so outrageously, and seemed so determined to smash up the whole business, the head of the family got red in the face, and said: "Well, now, he couldn't have any more of that foolishness. Arabella must just behave herself or take the consequences." And after the spanking, Arabella sniffed and whimpered and pouted, and the big brother bit his lip, looked half ashamed, and said: "Well, I didn't want to hurt you. You needn't feel so awfully bad about it, I only did it for your good. You know I wouldn't do anything to displease you if I could help it; but you would insist on making the row, and so I just had to. Now, there—there—let's be friends!" and he put his great strong arms about her and just dared anybody to refer to that little unpleasantness—he'd show them a thing or two. Still Arabella sulked,—till the rest of the family decided she might just keep her pets, and manage her own affairs and nobody should interfere.

So now, if one intimates that some clauses of the Constitution are a dead letter at the South and that only the name and support of that pet institution are changed while the fact and essence, minus the expense and responsibility, remain, he is quickly told to mind his own business and informed that he is waving the bloody shirt.

Even twenty-five years after the fourteenth and fifteenth amendments to our Constitution, a man who has been most unequivocal in his outspoken condemnation of the wrongs regularly and systematically heaped on the oppressed race in this country, and on all even most remotely connected with them—a man whom we had thought our staunchest friend and most noble champion and defender—after a two weeks' trip in Georgia and Florida immediately gives signs of the fatal inception of the virus. Not even the chance traveller from England or Scotland escapes. The arch-manipulator takes him under his special watch-care and training, uses up his stock arguments and gives object lessons with his choicest specimens of Negro depravity and worthlessness; takes him through what, in New York, would be called "the slums," and would predicate there nothing but the duty of enlightened Christians to send out their light and emulate their Master's aggressive labors of love; but in Georgia is denominated "our terrible problem, which people of the North so little understand, yet vouchsafe so much gratuitous advice about." With an injured air he shows the stupendous and atrocious mistake of reasoning about these people as if they were just ordinary human beings, and amenable to the tenets of the Gospel; and not long after the inoculation begins to work, you hear this old-time friend of the oppressed delivering himself something after this fashion: "Ah, well, the South must be left to manage the Negro. She is most directly concerned and must understand her problem better than outsiders. We must not meddle. We must be very careful not to widen the breaches. The Negro is not worth a feud between brothers and sisters."

Lately a great national and international movement characteristic of this age and country, a movement based on the inherent right of every soul to its own highest development, I mean the movement making for Woman's full, free, and complete emancipation, has, after much courting, obtained the gracious smile of the Southern woman—I beg her pardon—the Southern *lady*.

She represents blood, and of course could not be expected to leave that out; and firstly and foremostly she must not, in any organization she may deign to grace with her presence, be asked to associate with "these people who were once her slaves."

Now the Southern woman (I may be pardoned, being one myself) was never renowned for her reasoning powers, and it is not surprising that just a little picking will make her logic fall to pieces even here.

In the first place she imagines that because her grandfather had slaves who were black, all the blacks in the world of every shade and tint were once in the position of her slaves. This is as bad as the Irishman who was about to kill a peaceable Jew in the streets of Cork,—having just learned that Jews slew his Redeemer. The black race constitutes one-seventh the known population of the globe; and there are representatives of it here as elsewhere who were never in bondage at any time to any man,—whose blood is as blue and lineage as noble as any, even that of the white lady of the South. That her slaves were black and she despises her slaves, should no more argue antipathy to all dark people and peoples, than that Guiteau, an assassin, was white, and I hate assassins, should make me hate all persons more or less white. The objection shows a want of clear discrimination.

The second fallacy in the objection grows out of the use of an ambiguous middle, as the logicians would call it, or assigning a double signification to the term "*Social equality.*"

Civility to the Negro implies social equality. I am opposed to *associating* with dark persons on terms of social equality. Therefore, I abrogate civility to the Negro. This is like

> Light is opposed to darkness.
> Feathers are light.
> *Ergo*, Feathers are opposed to darkness.

The "social equality" implied by civility to the Negro is a very different thing from forced association with him socially. Indeed it seems to me that the mere application of a little cold common sense would show that uncongenial social environments could by no means be forced on any one. I do not, and cannot be made to associate with all dark persons, simply on the ground that I am dark; and I presume the Southern lady can imagine some whose faces are white, with whom she would no sooner think of chatting unreservedly than, were it possible, with a veritable 'darkey.' Such things must and will always be left to individual election. No law, human or divine, can legislate for or against them. Like seeks like; and I am sure with the Southern lady's antipathies at their present temperature, she might enter ten thousand organizations besprinkled with colored women without being any more deflected by them than by the proximity of a stone. The social equality scare then is all humbug, conscious or unconscious, I know not which. And were it not too bitter a thought to utter here, I might add that the overtures for forced association in the past history of these two races were not made by the manacled black man, nor by *the silent and suffering black woman!*

When I seek food in a public café or apply for first-class accommodations on a railway train, I do so because my physical necessities are identical with those of other human beings of like constitution and temperament, and crave satisfaction. I go because I want food, or I want comfort—not because I want association with those who frequent these places; and I can see no more "social equality" in buying lunch at the same restaurant, or riding in a common car, than there is in paying for dry goods at the same counter or walking on the same street.

The social equality which means forced or unbidden association would be as much deprecated and as strenuously opposed by the circle in which I move as by the most hide-bound Southerner in the land. Indeed I have been more than once annoyed by the inquisitive white interviewer, who, with spectacles on nose and pencil and note-book in hand, comes to get some "points" about "*your people.*" My "people" are just like other people— indeed, too like for their own good. They hate, they love, they attract and repel, they climb or they grovel, struggle or drift, aspire or despair, endure in hope or curse in vexation, exactly like all the rest of unregenerate humanity. Their likes and dislikes are as strong; their antipathies—and prejudices too I fear, are as pronounced as you will find anywhere; and the entrance to the inner sanctuary of their homes and hearts is as jealously guarded against profane intrusion.

What the dark man wants then is merely to live his own life, in his own world, with his own chosen companions, in whatever of comfort, luxury, or emoluments his talent or his money can in an impartial market secure. Has he wealth, he does not want to be forced into inconvenient or unsanitary sections of cities to buy a home and rear his family. Has he art, he does not want to be cabined and cribbed into emulation with the few who merely happen to have his complexion. His talent aspires to study without proscription the masters of all ages and to rub against the broadest and fullest movements of his own day.

Has he religion, he does not want to be made to feel that there is a white Christ and a black Christ, a white Heaven and a black Heaven, a white Gospel and a black Gospel,—but the one ideal of perfect manhood and womanhood, the one universal longing for development and growth, the one desire for being, and being better, the one great yearning, aspiring, outreaching, in all the heart-throbs of humanity in whatever race or clime.

A recent episode in the Corcoran art gallery at the American capital is to the point. A colored woman who had shown marked ability in drawing and coloring, was advised by her teacher, himself an artist of no mean rank, to apply for admission to the Corcoran school in order to study the models and to secure other advantages connected with the organization. She accordingly sent a written application accompanied by specimens of her drawings, the usual *modus operandi* in securing admission.

The drawings were examined by the best critics and pronounced excellent, and a ticket of admission was immediately issued together with a highly complimentary reference to her work.

The next day my friend, congratulating her country and herself that at least in the republic of art no caste existed, presented her ticket of admission *in propria persona*. There was a little preliminary side play in Delsarte pantomine,—aghast—incredulity—wonder; then the superintendent told her in plain unartistic English that of course he had not dreamed a colored person could do such work, and had he suspected the truth he would never have issued the ticket of admission; that, to be right frank, the ticket would have to be cancelled,—she could under no condition be admitted to the studio.

Can it be possible that even art in America is to be tainted by this shrivelling caste spirit? If so, what are we coming to? Can any one conceive a Shakespeare, a Michael Angelo, or a Beethoven putting away any fact of simple merit because the thought, or the suggestion, or the creation emanated from a soul with an unpleasing exterior?

What is it that makes the great English bard pre-eminent as the photographer of the human soul? Where did he learn the universal language, so that Parthians, Medes and Elamites, and the dwellers in Mesopotamia, in Egypt and Libya, in Crete and Arabia do hear every one in our own tongue the wonderful revelations of this myriad mind? How did he learn our language? Is it not that his own soul was infinitely receptive to Nature, the dear old nurse, in all her protean forms? Did he not catch and reveal her own secret by his sympathetic listening as she "would constantly sing a more wonderful song or tell a more marvellous tale" in the souls he met around him?

"Stand off! I am better than thou!" has never yet painted a true picture, nor written a thrilling song, nor given a pulsing, a soul-burning sermon. 'Tis only sympathy, another name for love,—that one poor word which, as George Eliot says, "expresses so much of human insight"—that can interpret either man or matter.

It was Shakespeare's own all-embracing sympathy, that infinite receptivity of his, and native, all-comprehending appreciation, which proved a key to unlock and open every soul that came within his radius. And *he received as much as he gave.* His own stores were infinitely enriched thereby. For it is decreed

> Man like the vine supported lives,
> The strength he gains is from th' embrace he gives.

It is only through clearing the eyes from bias and prejudice, and becoming one with the great all pervading soul of the universe that either art or science can

> "Read what is still unread
> In the manuscripts of God."

No true artist can allow himself to be narrowed and provincialized by deliberately shutting out any class of facts or subjects through prejudice against externals. And American art, American science, American literature can never be founded in truth, the universal beauty; can never learn to speak a language intelligible in all climes and for all ages, till this paralyzing grip of caste prejudice is loosened from its vitals, and the healthy sympathetic eye is taught to look out on the great universe as holding no favorites and no black beasts, but bearing in each plainest or loveliest feature the handwriting of its God.

And this is why, as it appears to me, woman in her lately acquired vantage ground for speaking an earnest helpful word, can do this country no deeper and truer and more lasting good than by bending all her energies to thus broadening, humanizing, and civilizing her native land.

"Except ye become as little children" is not a pious precept, but an inexorable law of the universe. God's kingdoms are all sealed to the seedy, moss-grown mind of self-satisfied maturity. Only the little child in spirit, the simple, receptive, educable mind can enter. Preconceived notions, blinding prejudices, and shrivelling antipathies must be wiped out, and the cultivable soul made a *tabula rasa* for whatever lesson great Nature has to teach.

This, too, is why I conceive the subject to have been unfortunately worded which was chosen by Miss Shaw at the Woman's Council and which stands at the head of this chapter.

Miss Shaw is one of the most powerful of our leaders, and we feel her voice should give no uncertain note. Woman should not, even by inference, or for the sake of argument, seem to disparage what is weak. For woman's cause is the cause of the weak; and when all the weak shall have received their due consideration, then woman will have her "rights," and the Indian will have his rights, and the Negro will have his rights, and all the strong will have learned at last to deal justly, to love mercy, and to walk humbly; and our fair land will have been taught the secret of universal courtesy which is after all nothing but the art, the science, and the religion of regarding one's neighbor as one's self, and to do for him as we would, were conditions swapped, that he do for us.

It cannot seem less than a blunder, whenever the exponents of a great reform or the harbingers of a noble advance in thought and effort allow themselves to seem distorted by a narrow view of their own aims and principles. All prejudices, whether of race, sect or sex, class pride and caste distinctions are the belittling inheritance and badge of snobs and prigs.

The philosophic mind sees that its own "rights" are the rights of humanity. That in the universe of God nothing trivial is or mean; and the recognition it seeks is not through the robber and wild beast adjustment of the survival of the bullies but through the universal application ultimately of the Golden Rule.

Not unfrequently has it happened that the impetus of a mighty thought wave has done the execution meant by its Creator in spite of the weak and distorted perception of its human embodi-ment. It is not strange if reformers, who, after all, but think God's thoughts after him, have often "builded more wisely than they knew;" and while fighting consciously for only a narrow gateway for themselves, have been driven forward by that irresistible "Power not ourselves which makes for right-eousness" to open a high road for humanity. It was so with our sixteenth century re-formers. The fathers of the Reformation had no idea that they were inciting an insurrection of the human mind against all dom-ination. None would have been more shocked than they at our nineteenth century deductions from their sixteenth century prem-ises. Emancipation of mind and freedom of thought would have been as appalling to them as it was distasteful to the pope. They were right, they argued, to rebel against Romish absolutism—because Romish preaching and Romish practicing were wrong. They denounced popes for hacking heretics and forthwith began themselves to roast witches. The Spanish Inquisition in the hands of Philip and Alva was an institution of the devil; wielded by the faithful, it would become quite another thing. The only "rights" they were broad enough consciously to fight for was the right to substitute the absolutism of their conceptions, their party, their 'ism' for an authority whose teaching they conceived to be cor-rupt and vicious. Persecution for a belief was wrong only when the persecutors were wrong and the persecuted right. The sacred prerogative of the individual to decide on matters of belief they did not dream of maintaining. Universal tolerance and its twin, universal charity, were not conceived yet. The broad foundation stone of all human rights, the great democratic principle "A man's a man, *and his own sovereign* for a' that" they did not dare enun-ciate. They were incapable of drawing up a Declaration of Inde-pendence for humanity. The Reformation to the Reformers meant one bundle of authoritative opinions vs. another bundle of au-thoritative opinions. Justification by faith, vs. justification by rit-ual. Submission to Calvin vs. submission to the Pope. English and Germans vs. the Italians.

To our eye, viewed through a vista of three centuries, it was the death wrestle of the principle of thought enslavement in the throt-tling grasp of personal freedom; it was the great Emancipation Day of human belief, man's intellectual Independence Day,

prefiguring and finally compelling the world-wide enfranchisement of his body and all its activities. Not Protestant vs. Catholic,
then; not Luther vs. Leo, not Dominicans vs. Augustinians, nor
Geneva vs. Rome;—but humanity rationally free, vs. the clamps
of tradition and superstition which had manacled and muzzled it.

The cause of freedom is not the cause of a race or a sect, a
party or a class,—it is the cause of human kind, the very birthright of humanity. Now unless we are greatly mistaken the Reform of our day, known as the Woman's Movement, is essentially
such an embodiment, if its pioneers could only realize it, of the
universal good. And specially important is it that there be no
confusion of ideas among its leaders as to its scope and univer-
sality. All mists must be cleared from the eyes of woman if she is
to be a teacher of morals and manners: the former strikes its
roots in the individual and its training and pruning may be accomplished by classes; but the latter is to lubricate the joints and
minimize the friction of society, and it is important and fundamental that there be no chromatic or other aberration when the
teacher is settling the point, "Who is my neighbor?"

It is not the intelligent woman vs. the ignorant woman; nor
the white woman vs. the black, the brown, and the red,—it is
not even the cause of woman vs. man. Nay, 'tis woman's stron-
gest vindication for speaking that *the world needs to hear her
voice*. It would be subversive of every human interest that the cry
of one-half the human family be stifled. Woman in stepping
from the pedestal of statue-like inactivity in the domestic shrine,
and daring to think and move and speak,—to undertake to help
shape, mold, and direct the thought of her age, is merely com-
pleting the circle of the world's vision. Hers is every interest that
has lacked an interpreter and a defender. Her cause is linked
with that of every agony that has been dumb—every wrong that
needs a voice.

It is no fault of man's that he has not been able to see truth from
her standpoint. It does credit both to his head and heart that no
greater mistakes have been committed or even wrongs perpetrated while she sat making tatting and snipping paper flowers.
Man's own innate chivalry and the mutual interdependence of
their interests have insured his treating her cause, in the main at
least, as his own. And he is pardonably surprised and even a little

chagrined, perhaps, to find his legislation not considered "perfectly lovely" in every respect. But in any case his work is only
impoverished by her remaining dumb. The world has had to
limp along with the wobbling gait and one-sided hesitancy of a
man with one eye. Suddenly the bandage is removed from the
other eye and the whole body is filled with light. It sees a circle
where before it saw a segment. The darkened eye restored, every
member rejoices with it.

What a travesty of its case for this eye to become plaintiff in a
suit, *Eye vs. Foot.* "There is that dull clod, the foot, allowed to
roam at will, free and untrammelled; while I, the source and medium of light, brilliant and beautiful, am fettered in darkness
and doomed to desuetude." The great burly black man, ignorant
and gross and depraved, is allowed to vote; while the franchise
is withheld from the intelligent and refined, the pure-minded
and lofty souled white woman. Even the untamed and untam-
able Indian of the prairie, who can answer nothing but 'ugh' to
great economic and civic questions is thought by some worthy to
wield the ballot which is still denied the Puritan maid and the
first lady of Virginia.

Is not this hitching our wagon to something much lower than
a star? Is not woman's cause broader, and deeper, and grander,
than a blue stocking debate or an aristocratic pink tea? Why
should woman become plaintiff in a suit versus the Indian, or the
Negro or any other race or class who have been crushed under
the iron heel of Anglo-Saxon power and selfishness? If the Indian has been wronged and cheated by the puissance of this
American government, it is woman's mission to plead with her
country to cease to do evil and to pay its honest debts. If the Negro has been deceitfully cajoled or inhumanly cuffed according
to selfish expediency or capricious antipathy, let it be woman's
mission to plead that he be met as a man and honestly given half
the road. If woman's own happiness has been ignored or misun-
derstood in our country's legislating for bread winners, for rum
sellers, for property holders, for the family relations, for any or
all the interests that touch her vitally, let her rest her plea, not on
Indian inferiority, nor on Negro depravity, but on the obligation
of legislators to do for her as they would have others do for them
were relations reversed. Let her try to teach her country that

every interest in this world is entitled at least to a respectful hearing, that every sentiency is worthy of its own gratification, that a helpless cause should not be trampled down, nor a bruised reed broken; and when the right of the individual is made sacred, when the image of God in human form, whether in marble or in clay, whether in alabaster or in ebony, is consecrated and inviolable, when men have been taught to look beneath the rags and grime, the pomp and pageantry of mere circumstance and have regard unto the celestial kernel uncontaminated at the core,—when race, color, sex, condition, are realized to be the accidents, not the substance of life, and consequently as not obscuring or modifying the inalienable title to life, liberty, and pursuit of happiness,—then is mastered the science of politeness, the art of courteous contact, which is naught but the practical application of the principal of benevolence, the back bone and marrow of all religion; then woman's lesson is taught and woman's cause is won—not the white woman nor the black woman nor the red woman, but the cause of every man or woman who has writhed silently under a mighty wrong. The pleading of the American woman for the right and the opportunity to employ the American method of influencing the disposal to be made of herself, her property, her children in civil, economic, or domestic relations is thus seen to be based on a principle as broad as the human race and as old as human society. Her wrongs are thus indissolubly linked with all undefended woe, all helpless suffering, and the plenitude of her "rights" will mean the final triumph of all right over might, the supremacy of the moral forces of reason and justice and love in the government of the nation.

God hasten the day.


## The Status of Woman in America


Just four hundred years ago an obscure dreamer and castle builder, prosaically poor and ridiculously insistent on the reality of his dreams, was enabled through the devotion of a noble woman to give to civilization a magnificent continent.

What the lofty purpose of Spain's pure-minded queen had brought to the birth, the untiring devotion of pioneer women nourished and developed. The dangers of wild beasts and of wilder men, the mysteries of unknown wastes and unexplored forests, the horrors of pestilence and famine, of exposure and loneliness, during all those years of discovery and settlement, were braved without a murmur by women who had been most delicately constituted and most tenderly nurtured.

And when the times of physical hardship and danger were past, when the work of clearing and opening up was over and the struggle for accumulation began, again woman's inspiration and help were needed and still was she loyally at hand. A Mary Lyon, demanding and making possible equal advantages of education for women as for men, and, in the face of discouragement and incredulity, bequeathing to women the opportunities of Holyoke.

A Dorothea Dix, insisting on the humane and rational treatment of the insane and bringing about a reform in the lunatic asylums of the country, making a great step forward in the tender regard for the weak by the strong throughout the world.

A Helen Hunt Jackson, convicting the nation of a century of dishonor in regard to the Indian.

A Lucretia Mott, gentle Quaker spirit, with sweet insistence, preaching the abolition of slavery and the institution, in its stead, of the brotherhood of man; her life and words breathing out in tender melody the injunction

> "Have love. Not love alone for one
> But man as man thy brother call;
> And scatter, like the circling sun,
> Thy charities *on all.*"

And at the most trying time of what we have called the Accumulative Period, when internecine war, originated through man's love of gain and his determination to subordinate national interests and black men's rights alike to considerations of personal profit and loss, was drenching our country with its own best blood, who shall recount the name and fame of the women on both sides the senseless strife,—those uncomplaining souls with

a great heart ache of their own, rigid features and pallid cheek
their ever effective flag of truce, on the battle field, in the camp,
in the hospital, binding up wounds, recording dying whispers for
absent loved ones, with tearful eyes pointing to man's last refuge, giving the last earthly hand clasp and performing the last
friendly office for strangers whom a great common sorrow had
made kin, while they knew that somewhere—somewhere a husband, a brother, a father, a son, was being tended by stranger
hands—or mayhap those familiar eyes were even then being
closed forever by just such another ministering angel of mercy
and love.

But why mention names? Time would fail to tell of the noble
army of women who shine like beacon lights in the otherwise
sordid wilderness of this accumulative period—prison reformers
and tenement cleansers, quiet un-noted workers in hospitals and
homes, among imbeciles, among outcasts—the sweetening, purifying antidotes for the poisons of man's acquisitiveness,—
mollifying and soothing with the tenderness of compassion and
love the wounds and bruises caused by his overreaching and av-
arice.

The desire for quick returns and large profits tempts capital
ofttimes into unsanitary, well nigh inhuman investments,—
tenement tinder boxes, stifling, stunting, sickening alleys and
pestiferous slums; regular rents, no waiting, large percentages,—
rich coffers coined out of the life-blood of human bodies and
souls. Men and women herded together like cattle, breathing in
malaria and typhus from an atmosphere seething with moral as
well as physical impurity, revelling in vice as their native habitat
and then, to drown the whisperings of their higher consciousness and effectually to hush the yearnings and accusations
within, flying to narcotics and opiates—rum, tobacco, opium,
binding hand and foot, body and soul, till the proper image of
God is transformed into a fit associate for demons,—a besotted,
enervated, idiotic wreck, or else a monster of wickedness terrible
and destructive.

These are some of the legitimate products of the unmitigated
tendencies of the wealth-producing period. But, thank Heaven,
side by side with the cold, mathematical, selfishly calculating,
so-called practical and unsentimental instinct of the business

man, there comes the sympathetic warmth and sunshine of good women, like the sweet and sweetening breezes of spring, cleansing, purifying, soothing, inspiring, lifting the drunkard from the gutter, the outcast from the pit. Who can estimate the influence of these "daughters of the king," these lend-a-hand forces, in counteracting the selfishness of an acquisitive age?

To-day America counts her millionaires by the thousand; questions of tariff and questions of currency are the most vital ones agitating the public mind. In this period, when material prosperity and well earned ease and luxury are assured facts from a national standpoint, woman's work and woman's influence are needed as never before; needed to bring a heart power into this money getting, dollar-worshipping civilization; needed to bring a moral force into the utilitarian motives and interests of the time; needed to stand for God and Home and Native Land *versus gain and greed and grasping selfishness.*

There can be no doubt that this fourth centenary of America's discovery which we celebrate at Chicago, strikes the keynote of another important transition in the history of this nation; and the prominence of woman in the management of its celebration is a fitting tribute to the part she is destined to play among the forces of the future. This is the first congressional recognition of woman in this country, and this Board of Lady Managers constitute the first women legally appointed by any government to act in a national capacity. This of itself marks the dawn of a new day.

Now the periods of discovery, of settlement, of developing resources and accumulating wealth have passed in rapid succession. Wealth in the nation as in the individual brings leisure, repose, reflection. The struggle with nature is over, the struggle with ideas begins. We stand then, it seems to me, in this last decade of the nineteenth century, just in the portals of a new and untried movement on a higher plain and in a grander strain than any the past has called forth. It does not require a prophet's eye to divine its trend and image its possibilities from the forces we see already at work around us; nor is it hard to guess what must be the status of woman's work under the new regime.

In the pioneer days her role was that of a camp-follower, an additional something to fight for and be burdened with, only repaying the anxiety and labor she called forth by her own incomparable gifts of sympathy and appreciative love; unable herself ordinarily to contend with the bear and the Indian, or to take active part in clearing the wilderness and constructing the home.

In the second or wealth producing period her work is abreast of man's, complementing and supplementing, counteracting excessive tendencies, and mollifying over rigorous proclivities.

In the era now about to dawn, her sentiments must strike the keynote and give the dominant tone. And this because of the nature of her contribution to the world.

Her kingdom is not over physical forces. Not by might, nor by power can she prevail. Her position must ever be inferior where strength of muscle creates leadership. If she follows the instincts of her nature, however, she must always stand for the conservation of those deeper moral forces which make for the happiness of homes and the righteousness of the country. In a reign of moral ideas she is easily queen.

There is to my mind no grander and surer prophecy of the new era and of woman's place in it, than the work already begun in the waning years of the nineteenth century by the W. C. T. U. in America, an organization which has even now reached not only national but international importance, and seems destined to permeate and purify the whole civilized world. It is the living embodiment of woman's activities and woman's ideas, and its extent and strength rightly prefigure her increasing power as a moral factor.

The colored woman of to-day occupies, one may say, a unique position in this country. In a period of itself transitional and unsettled, her status seems one of the least ascertainable and definitive of all the forces which make for our civilization. She is confronted by both a woman question and a race problem, and is as yet an unknown or an unacknowledged factor in both. While the women of the white race can with calm assurance enter upon the work they feel by nature appointed to do, while their men give loyal support and appreciative countenance to their efforts, recognizing in most avenues of usefulness the propriety and the need of woman's distinctive co-operation, the colored woman too often finds herself hampered and shamed by a less liberal sentiment and a more conservative attitude on the part of those for whose opinion she cares most. That this is not universally true I am glad to admit. There are to be found both intensely conservative white men and exceedingly liberal colored men. But as far as my experience goes the average man of our race is less frequently ready to admit the actual need among the sturdier forces of the world for woman's help or influence. That great social and economic questions await her interference, that she could throw any light on problems of national import, that her intermeddling could improve the management of school systems, or elevate the tone of public institutions, or humanize and sanctify the far reaching influence of prisons and reformatories and improve the treatment of lunatics and imbeciles,—that she has a word worth hearing on mooted questions in political economy, that she could contribute a suggestion on the relations of labor and capital, or offer a thought on honest money and honorable trade, I fear the majority of "Americans of the colored variety" are not yet prepared to concede. It may be that they do not yet see these questions in their right perspective, being absorbed in the immediate needs of their own political complications. A good deal depends on where we put the emphasis in this world; and our men are not perhaps to blame if they see everything colored by the light of those agitations in the midst of which they live and move and have their being. The part they have had to play in American history during the last twenty-five or thirty years has tended rather to exaggerate the importance of mere political advantage, as well as to set a fictitious valuation on those able to secure such advantage. It is the astute politician, the manager who can gain preferment for himself and his favorites, the demagogue known to stand in with the powers at the White House and consulted on the bestowal of government plums, whom we set in high places and denominate great. It is they who receive the hosannas of the multitude and are regarded as leaders of the people. The thinker and the doer, the man who solves the problem by enriching his country with an invention worth thousands or by a thought inestimable and precious is given neither bread nor a stone. He is too often left to die in obscurity and neglect even if spared in his life the bitterness of fanatical jealousies and detraction.

And yet politics, and surely American politics, is hardly a school for great minds. Sharpening rather than deepening, it develops the faculty of taking advantage of present emergencies rather than the insight to distinguish between the true and the false, the lasting and the ephemeral advantage. Highly cultivated selfishness rather than consecrated benevolence is its passport to success. Its votaries are never seers. At best they are but manipulators—often only jugglers. It is conducive neither to profound statesmanship nor to the higher type of manhood. Altruism is its *mauvais succes* and naturally enough it is indifferent to any factor which cannot be worked into its own immediate aims and purposes. As woman's influence as a political element is as yet nil in most of the commonwealths of our republic, it is not surprising that with those who place the emphasis on mere political capital she may yet seem almost a nonentity so far as it concerns the solution of great national or even racial perplexities.

There are those, however, who value the calm elevation of the thoughtful spectator who stands aloof from the heated scramble; and, above the turmoil and din of corruption and selfishness, can listen to the teachings of eternal truth and righteousness. There are even those who feel that the black man's unjust and unlawful exclusion temporarily from participation in the elective franchise in certain states is after all but a lesson "in the desert" fitted to develop in him insight and discrimination against the day of his own appointed time. One needs occasionally to stand aside from the hum and rush of human interests and passions to hear the voices of God. And it not unfrequently happens that the All-loving gives a great push to certain souls to thrust them out, as it were, from the distracting current for awhile to promote their discipline and growth, or to enrich them by communion and reflection. And similarly it may be woman's privilege from her peculiar coign of vantage as a quiet observer, to whisper just the needed suggestion or the almost forgotten truth. The colored woman, then, should not be ignored because her bark is resting in the silent waters of the sheltered cove. She is watching the movements of the contestants none the less and is all the better qualified, perhaps, to weigh and judge and advise because not herself in the excitement of the race. Her voice, too, has always been heard in clear, unfaltering tones, ringing the changes on those deeper interests which make for permanent good. She is always sound and orthodox on questions affecting the well-being of her race. You do not find the colored woman selling her birthright for a mess of pottage. Nay, even after reason has retired from the contest, she has been known to cling blindly with the instinct of a turtle dove to those principles and policies which to her mind promise hope and safety for children yet unborn. It is notorious that ignorant black women in the South have actually left their husbands' homes and repudiated their support for what was understood by the wife to be race disloyalty, or "voting away," as she expresses it, the privileges of herself and little ones.

It is largely our women in the South to-day who keep the black men solid in the Republican party. The latter as they increase in intelligence and power of discrimination would be more apt to divide on local issues at any rate. They begin to see that the Grand Old Party regards the Negro's cause as an outgrown issue, and on Southern soil at least finds a too intimate acquaintanceship with him a somewhat unsavory recommendation. Then, too, their political wits have been sharpened to appreciate the fact that it is good policy to cultivate one's neighbors and not depend too much on a distant friend to fight one's home battles. But the black woman can never forget—however lukewarm the party may to-day appear—that it was a Republican president who struck the manacles from her own wrists and gave the possibilities of manhood to her helpless little ones; and to her mind a Democratic Negro is a traitor and a time-server. Talk as much as you like of venality and manipulation in the South, there are not many men, I can tell you, who would dare face a wife quivering in every fiber with the consciousness that her husband is a coward who could be paid to desert her deepest and dearest interests.

Not unfelt, then, if unproclaimed has been the work and influence of the colored women of America. Our list of chieftains in the service, though not long, is not inferior in strength and excellence, I dare believe, to any similar list which this country can produce.

Among the pioneers, Frances Watkins Harper could sing with prophetic exaltation in the darkest days, when as yet there was not a rift in the clouds overhanging her people:

> "Yes, Ethiopia shall stretch
> Her bleeding hands abroad;
> Her cry of agony shall reach the burning throne of God.
> Redeemed from dust and freed from chains
>    Her sons shall lift their eyes,
> From cloud-capt hills and verdant plains
>    Shall shouts of triumph rise."

Among preachers of righteousness, an unanswerable silencer of cavilers and objectors, was Sojourner Truth, that unique and rugged genius who seemed carved out without hand or chisel from the solid mountain mass; and in pleasing contrast, Amanda Smith, sweetest of natural singers and pleaders in dulcet tones for the things of God and of His Christ.

Sarah Woodson Early and Martha Briggs, planting and watering in the school room, and giving off from their matchless and irresistible personality an impetus and inspiration which can never die so long as there lives and breathes a remote descendant of their disciples and friends.

Charlotte Fortin Grimke, the gentle spirit whose verses and life link her so beautifully with America's great Quaker poet and loving reformer.

Hallie Quinn Brown, charming reader, earnest, effective lecturer and devoted worker of unflagging zeal and unquestioned power.

Fannie Jackson Coppin, the teacher and organizer, pre-eminent among women of whatever country or race in constructive and executive force.

These women represent all shades of belief and as many departments of activity; but they have one thing in common—their sympathy with the oppressed race in America and the consecration of their several talents in whatever line to the work of its deliverance and development.

Fifty years ago woman's activity according to orthodox definitions was on a pretty clearly cut "sphere," including primarily the kitchen and the nursery, and rescued from the barrenness of prison bars by the womanly mania for adorning every discoverable bit of china or canvass with forlorn looking cranes balanced idiotically on one foot. The woman of to-day finds herself in the presence of responsibilities which ramify through the profoundest and most varied interests of her country and race. Not one of the issues of this plodding, toiling, sinning, repenting, falling, aspiring humanity can afford to shut her out, or can deny the reality of her influence. No plan for renovating society, no scheme for purifying politics, no reform in church or in state, no moral, social, or economic question, no movement upward or downward in the human plane is lost on her. A man once said when told his house was afire: "Go tell my wife; I never meddle with household affairs." But no woman can possibly put herself or her sex outside any of the interests that affect humanity. All departments in the new era are to be hers, in the sense that her interests are in all and through all; and it is incumbent on her to keep intelligently and sympathetically *en rapport* with all the great movements of her time, that she may know on which side to throw the weight of her influence. She stands now at the gateway of this new era of American civilization. In her hands must be moulded the strength, the wit, the statesmanship, the morality, all the psychic force, the social and economic intercourse of that era. To be alive at such an epoch is a privilege, to be a woman then is sublime.

In this last decade of our century, changes of such moment are in progress, such new and alluring vistas are opening out before us, such original and radical suggestions for the adjustment of labor and capital, of government and the governed, of the family, the church and the state, that to be a possible factor though an infinitesimal in such a movement is pregnant with hope and weighty with responsibility. To be a woman in such an age carries with it a privilege and an opportunity never implied before. But to be a woman of the Negro race in America, and to be able to grasp the deep significance of the possibilities of the crisis, is to have a heritage, it seems to me, unique in the ages. In the first place, the race is young and full of the elasticity and hopefulness of youth. All its achievements are before it. It does not look on the masterly triumphs of nineteenth century civilization with that *blasé* world-weary look which characterizes the old washed out and worn out races which have already, so to speak, seen their best days.

Said a European writer recently: "Except the Sclavonic, the Negro is the only original and distinctive genius which has yet to come to growth—and the feeling is to cherish and develop it."

Everything to this race is new and strange and inspiring. There is a quickening of its pulses and a glowing of its self-consciousness. Aha, I can rival that! I can aspire to that! I can honor my name and vindicate my race! Something like this, it strikes me, is the enthusiasm which stirs the genius of young Africa in America; and the memory of past oppression and the fact of present attempted repression only serve to gather momentum for its irrepressible powers. Then again, a race in such a stage of growth is peculiarly sensitive to impressions. Not the photographer's sensitized plate is more delicately impressionable to outer influences than is this high strung people here on the threshold of a career.

What a responsibility then to have the sole management of the primal lights and shadows! Such is the colored woman's office. She must stamp weal or woe on the coming history of this people. May she see her opportunity and vindicate her high prerogative.

# TUTTI AD LIBITUM

A *People* is but the attempt of many
To rise to the completer life of one.

*   *   *

The common *Problem*, yours, mine, every one's
Is—not to fancy what were fair in life
Provided it could be,—but, finding first
What may be, then find how to make it fair
Up to our means; a very different thing!

—*Robert Browning*

The greatest question in the world is how to give every man a
man's share in what goes on in life—we want a freeman's share,
and that is to think and speak and act about what concerns us
all, and see whether these fine gentlemen who undertake to
govern us are doing the best they can for us.—*Felix Holt.*

## Has America a Race Problem;[1]
## If So, How Can It Best Be Solved?

There are two kinds of peace in this world. The one produced by
suppression, which is the passivity of death; the other brought
about by a proper adjustment of living, acting forces. A nation or
an individual may be at peace because all opponents have been
killed or crushed; or, nation as well as individual may have
found the secret of true harmony in the determination to live
and let live.

A harmless looking man was once asked how many there were in his family.

"Ten," he replied grimly; "my wife's a one and I a zero." In that family there was harmony, to be sure, but it was the harmony of a despotism—it was the quiet of a muzzled mouth, the smoldering peace of a volcano crusted over.

Now I need not say that peace produced by suppression is neither natural nor desirable. Despotism is not one of the ideas that man has copied from nature. All through God's universe we see eternal harmony and symmetry as the unvarying result of the equilibrium of opposing forces. Fair play in an equal fight is the law written in Nature's book. And the solitary bully with his foot on the breast of his last antagonist has no warrant in any fact of God.

The beautiful curves described by planets and suns in their courses are the resultant of conflicting forces. Could the centrifugal force for one instant triumph, or should the centripetal grow weary and give up the struggle, immeasurable disaster would ensue—earth, moon, sun would go spinning off at a tangent or must fall helplessly into its master sphere. The acid counterbalances and keeps in order the alkali; the negative, the positive electrode. A proper equilibrium between a most inflammable explosive and the supporter of combustion, gives us water, the bland fluid that we cannot dispense with. Nay, the very air we breathe, which seems so calm, so peaceful, is rendered innocuous only by the constant conflict of opposing gases. Were the fiery, never-resting, all-corroding oxygen to gain the mastery we should be burnt to cinders in a trice. With the sluggish, inert nitrogen triumphant, we should die of inanition.

These facts are only a suggestion of what must be patent to every student of history. Progressive peace in a nation is the result of conflict; and conflict, such as is healthy, stimulating, and progressive, is produced through the co-existence of radically opposing or racially different elements. Bellamy's ox-like men pictured in *Looking Backward*, taking their daily modicum of provender from the grandmotherly government, with nothing to struggle for, no wrong to put down, no reform to push through, no rights to vindicate and uphold, are nice folks to read about; but they are not natural; they are not progressive. God's world is not governed that way. The child can never gain strength save by resistance, and there can be no resistance if all movement is in one direction and all opposition made forever an impossibility.

I confess I can see no deeper reason than this for the specializing of racial types in the world. Whatever our theory with reference to the origin of species and the unity of mankind, we cannot help admitting the fact that no sooner does a family of the human race take up its abode in some little nook between mountains, or on some plain walled in by their own hands, no sooner do they begin in earnest to live their own life, think their own thoughts, and trace out their own arts, than they begin also to crystallize some idea different from and generally opposed to that of other tribes or families.

Each race has its badge, its exponent, its message, branded in its forehead by the great Master's hand which is its own peculiar keynote, and its contribution to the harmony of nations.

Left entirely alone,—out of contact, that is with other races and their opposing ideas and conflicting tendencies, this cult is abnormally developed and there is unity without variety, a predominance of one tone at the expense of moderation and harmony, and finally a sameness, a monotonous dullness which means stagnation,—death.

It is this of which M. Guizot complains in Asiatic types of civilization; and in each case he mentions I note that there was but one race, one free force predominating.

In Lect. II. Hist. of Civ. he says:

"In Egypt the theocratic principle took possession of society and showed itself in its manners, its monuments and in all that has come down to us of Egyptian civilization. In India the same phenomenon occurs—a repetition of the almost exclusively prevailing influence of theocracy. In other regions the domination of a conquering caste; where such is the case the principle of force takes entire possession of society. In another place we discover society under the entire influence of the democratic principle. Such was the case in the commercial republics which covered the coasts of Asia Minor and Syria, in Ionia and Phoenicia. In a word whenever we contemplate the civilization of the ancients, we find them all impressed with *one ever prevailing character of unity*, visible in their institutions, their ideas and manners; *one sole influence seems to govern and determine all things. . . .* In one nation, as in Greece, the unity of the social principle led to a development of wonderful rapidity; no other people ever ran so brilliant a career in so short a time. But Greece had hardly become glorious before she appeared worn out. Her decline was as sudden as her rise had been rapid. It seems as if the principle which called Greek civilization into life was exhausted. No other came to invigorate it or supply its place. In India and Egypt where again only one principle of civilization prevailed (*one race predominant you see*) society became stationary. Simplicity produced monotony. Society continued to exist, but there was no progression. It remained torpid and inactive."

Now I beg you to note that in none of these systems was a RACE PROBLEM possible. The dominant race had settled that matter forever. Asiatic society was fixed in cast iron molds. Virtually there was but one race inspiring and molding the thought, the art, the literature, the government. It was against this shrivelling caste prejudice and intolerance that the zealous Buddha set his face like a flint. And I do not think it was all blasphemy in Renan when he said Jesus Christ was first of democrats, i. e., a believer in the royalty of the individual, a preacher of the brotherhood of man through the fatherhood of God, a teacher who proved that the lines on which worlds are said to revolve are *imaginary*, that for all the distinctions of blue blood and black blood and red blood—*a man's a man for a' that.* Buddha and the Christ, each in his own way, wrought to rend asunder the clamps and bands of caste, and to thaw out the ice of race tyranny and exclusiveness. The Brahmin, who was Aryan, spurned a suggestion even, from the Sudra, who belonged to the hated and proscribed Turanian race. With a Pariah he could not eat or drink. They were to him outcasts and unclean. Association with them meant contamination; the hint of their social equality was blasphemous. Respectful consideration for their rights and feelings was almost a physical no less than a moral impossibility.

No more could the Helots among the Greeks have been said to contribute anything to the movement of their times. The dominant race had them effectually under its heel. It was the tyranny and exclusiveness of these nations, therefore, which brought about their immobility and resulted finally in the barrenness of their one idea. From this came the poverty and decay underlying their civilization, from this the transitory, ephemeral character of its brilliancy.

To quote Guizot again: "Society belonged to *one exclusive* power which could bear with no other. Every principle of a different tendency was proscribed. The governing principle would nowhere suffer by its side the manifestation and influence of a rival principle. This character of unity in their civilization is equally impressed upon their literature and intellectual productions. Those monuments of Hindoo literature lately introduced into Europe seem all struck from the same die. They all seem the result of one same fact, the expression of one idea. Religious and moral treatises, historical traditions, dramatic poetry, epics, all bear the same physiognomy. The same character of unity and monotony shines out in these works of mind and fancy, as we discover in their life and institutions." Not even Greece with all its classic treasures is made an exception from these limitations produced by exclusiveness.

But the course of empire moves one degree westward. Europe becomes the theater of the leading exponents of civilization, and here we have a *Race Problem*,—if, indeed, the confused jumble of races, the clash and conflict, the din and devastation of those stormy years can be referred to by so quiet and so dignified a term as "problem." Complex and appalling it surely was. Goths and Huns, Vandals and Danes, Angles, Saxons, Jutes—could any prophet foresee that a vestige of law and order, of civilization and refinement would remain after this clumsy horde of wild barbarians had swept over Europe?

"Where is somebody'll give me some white for all this yellow?" cries one with his hands full of the gold from one of those magnificent monuments of antiquity which he and his tribe had just pillaged and demolished. Says the historian: "Their history is like a history of kites and crows." Tacitus writes: "To shout, to drink, to caper about, to feel their veins heated and swollen with wine, to hear and see around them the riot of the orgy, this was the first need of the barbarians. The heavy human brute gluts himself with sensations and with noise."

Taine describes them as follows:

"Huge white bodies, cool-blooded, with fierce blue eyes, reddish flaxen hair; ravenous stomachs, filled with meat and cheese, heated by strong drinks. Brutal drunken pirates and robbers, they dashed to sea in their two-sailed barks, landed anywhere, killed everything; and, having sacrificed in honor of their gods the tithe of all their prisoners, leaving behind the red light of their burning, went farther on to begin again."

A certain litany of the time reads: "From the fury of the Jutes, Good Lord deliver us." "Elgiva, the wife of one of their kings," says a chronicler of the time, "they hamstrung and subjected to the death she deserved;" and their heroes are frequently represented as tearing out the heart of their human victim and eating it while it still quivered with life.

A historian of the time, quoted by Taine, says it was the custom to buy men and women in all parts of England and to carry them to Ireland for sale. The buyers usually made the women pregnant and took them to market in that condition to ensure a better price. "You might have seen," continues the historian, "long files of young people of both sexes and of great beauty, bound with ropes and daily exposed for sale. They sold as slaves in this manner, their nearest relatives and even their own children."

What could civilization hope to do with such a swarm of sensuous, bloodthirsty vipers? Assimilation was horrible to contemplate. They will drag us to their level, quoth the culture of the times. Deportation was out of the question; and there was no need to talk of their emigrating. The fact is, the barbarians were in no hurry about moving. They didn't even care to colonize. They had come to stay. And Europe had to grapple with her race problem till time and God should solve it.

And how was it solved, and what kind of civilization resulted?

Once more let us go to Guizot. "Take ever so rapid a glance," says he, "at modern Europe and it strikes you at once as diversified, confused, and stormy. All the principles of social organization are found existing together within it; powers temporal, and powers spiritual, the theocratic, monarchic, aristocratic, and democratic elements, all classes of society *in a state of continual struggle* without any one having sufficient force to master the others and take sole possession of society." Then as to the result of this conflict of forces: "Incomparably more rich and diversified than the ancient, European civilization has within it the promise of *perpetual progress*. It has now endured more than fifteen centuries and in all that time has been in a state of progression, not so rapidly as the Greek nor yet so ephemeral. While in other civilizations the exclusive domination of a principle (*or race*) led to tyranny, in Europe the diversity of social elements (*growing out of the contact of different races*) the incapability of any one to exclude the rest, gave birth to the LIBERTY which now prevails. This inability of the various principles to exterminate one another compelled each to endure the others and made it necessary for them in order to live in common to enter into a sort of mutual understanding. Each consented to have only that part of civilization which equitably fell to its share. Thus, while everywhere else the predominance of one principle produced tyranny, the variety and warfare of the elements of European civilization gave birth to *reciprocity and liberty*."

There is no need to quote further. This is enough to show that the law holds good in sociology as in the world of matter, *that equilibrium, not repression among conflicting forces is the condition of natural harmony, of permanent progress, and of universal freedom.* That exclusiveness and selfishness in a family, in a community, or in a nation is suicidal to progress. Caste and prejudice mean immobility. One race predominance means death. The community that closes its gates against foreign talent can never hope to advance beyond a certain point. Resolve to keep out foreigners and you keep out progress. Home talent develops its one idea and then dies. Like the century plant it produces its one flower, brilliant and beautiful it may be, but it lasts only for a night. Its forces have exhausted themselves in that one effort. Nothing remains but to wither and to rot.

It was the Chinese wall that made China in 1800 A.D. the same as China in the days of Confucius. Its women have not even yet learned that they need not bandage their feet if they do not relish it. The world has rolled on, but within that wall the thoughts, the fashions, the art, the tradition, and the beliefs are those of a thousand years ago. Until very recently, the Chinese were wholly out of the current of human progress. They were like gray headed infants—a man of eighty years with the concepts and imaginings of a babe of eight months. A civilization measured by thousands of years with a development that might be comprised within as many days—arrested development due to exclusive living.

But European civilization, rich as it was compared to Asiatic types, was still not the consummation of the ideal of human possibilities. One more degree westward the hand on the dial points. In Europe there was conflict, but the elements crystallized out in isolated nodules, so to speak. Italy has her dominant principle, Spain hers, France hers, England hers, and so on. The proximity is close enough for interaction and mutual restraint, though the acting forces are at different points. To preserve the balance of power, which is nothing more than the equilibrium of warring elements, England can be trusted to keep an eye on her beloved step-relation-in-law, Russia,—and Germany no doubt can be relied on to look after France and some others. It is not, however, till the scene changes and America is made the theater of action, that the interplay of forces narrowed down to a single platform.

Hither came Cavalier and Roundhead, Baptist and Papist, Quaker, Ritualist, Freethinker and Mormon, the conservative Tory, the liberal Whig, and the radical Independent,—the Spaniard, the Frenchman, the Englishman, the Italian, the Chinaman, the African, Swedes, Russians, Huns, Bohemians, Gypsies, Irish, Jews. Here surely was a seething caldron of conflicting elements. Religious intolerance and political hatred, race prejudice and caste pride—

> "Double, double, toil and trouble;
> Fire burn and cauldron bubble."

Conflict, Conflict, Conflict.

America for Americans! This is the white man's country! The Chinese must go, shrieks the exclusionist. Exclude the Italians! Colonize the blacks in Mexico or deport them to Africa. Lynch, suppress, drive out, kill out! America for Americans!

"*Who are Americans?*" comes rolling back from ten million throats. Who are to do the packing and delivering of the goods?

Who are the homefolks and who are the strangers? Who are the absolute and original tenants in fee-simple?

The red men used to be owners of the soil,—but they are about to be pushed over into the Pacific Ocean. They, perhaps, have the best right to call themselves "Americans" by law of primogeniture. They are at least the oldest inhabitants of whom we can at present identify any traces. If early settlers from abroad merely are meant and it is only a question of squatters' rights— why, the May-flower, a pretty venerable institution, landed in the year of Grace 1620, and the first delegation from Africa just one year ahead of that,—in 1619. The first settlers seem to have been almost as much mixed as we are on this point; and it does not seem at all easy to decide just what individuals we mean when we yell "America for the Americans." At least the cleavage cannot be made by hues and noses, if we are to seek for the genuine F. F. V.'s as the inhabitants best entitled to the honor of that name.

The fact is this nation was foreordained to conflict from its incipiency. Its elements were predestined from their birth to an irrepressible clash followed by the stable equilibrium of opposition. Exclusive possession belongs to none. There never was a point in its history when it did. There was never a time since America became a nation when there were not more than one race, more than one party, more than one belief contending for supremacy. Hence no one is or can be supreme. All interests must be consulted, all claims conciliated. Where a hundred free forces are lustily clamoring for recognition and each wrestling mightily for the mastery, individual tyrannies must inevitably be chiselled down, individual bigotries worn smooth and malleable, individual prejudices either obliterated or concealed. America is not from choice more than of necessity republic in form and democratic in administration. The will of the majority must rule simply because no class, no family, no individual has ever been able to prove sufficient political legitimacy to impose their yoke on the country. All attempts at establishing oligarchy must be made by wheedling and cajoling, pretending that not supremacy but service is sought. The nearest approach to outspoken self-assertion is in the conciliatory tones of candid compromise. "I will let you enjoy that if you will not hinder me in the pursuit of this" has been the American sovereign's home policy since his first Declaration of Independence was inscribed as his policy abroad. Compromise and concession, liberality and toleration were the conditions of the nation's birth and are the *sine qua non* of its continued existence. A general amnesty and universal reciprocity are the only *modus vivendi* in a nation whose every citizen is his own king, his own priest and his own pope.

De Tocqueville, years ago, predicted that republicanism must fail in America. But if republicanism fails, America fails, and somehow I can not think this colossal stage was erected for a tragedy. I must confess to being an optimist on the subject of my country. It is true we are too busy making history, and have been for some years past, to be able to write history yet, or to understand and interpret it. Our range of vision is too short for us to focus and imagine our conflicts. Indeed Von Holtz, the clearest headed of calm spectators, says he doubts if the history of American conflict can be written yet even by a disinterested foreigner. The clashing of arms and the din of battle, the smoke of cannon and the heat of combat, are not yet cleared away sufficiently for us to have the judicial vision of historians. Our jottings are like newspaper reports written in the saddle, mid prancing steeds and roaring artillery.

But of one thing we may be sure: the God of battles is in the conflicts of history. The evolution of civilization is His care, eternal progress His delight. As the European was higher and grander than the Asiatic, so will American civilization be broader and deeper and closer to the purposes of the Eternal than any the world has yet seen. This the last page is to mark the climax of history, the bright consummate flower unfolding *charity toward all and malice toward none,*—the final triumph of universal reciprocity born of universal conflict with forces that cannot be exterminated. Here at last is an arena in which every agony has a voice and free speech. Not a spot where no wrong can exist, but where each feeblest interest can cry with Themistocles, *"Strike, but hear me!"* Here you will not see as in Germany women hitched to a cart with donkeys; not perhaps because men are more chivalrous here than there, but because woman can speak. Here labor will not be starved and ground to powder, because the laboring man can make himself heard. Here races that are weakest can, *if they so elect*, make themselves felt.

The supremacy of one race,—the despotism of a class or the tyranny of an individual can not ultimately prevail on a continent held in equilibrium by such conflicting forces and by so many and such strong fibred races as there are struggling on this soil. Never in America shall one man dare to say as Germany's somewhat bumptious emperor is fond of proclaiming: "There is only one master in the country and I am he. I shall suffer no other beside me. Only to God and my conscience am I accountable." The strength of the opposition tones down and polishes off all such ugly excrescencies as that. "I am the State," will never be proclaimed above a whisper on a platform where there is within arm's length another just as strong, possibly stronger, who holds, or would like to hold that identical proposition with reference to himself. In this arena then is to be the last death struggle of political tyranny, of religious bigotry, and intellectual intolerance, of caste illiberality and class exclusiveness. And the last monster that shall be throttled forever methinks is race prejudice. Men will here learn that a race, as a family, may be true to itself without seeking to exterminate all others. That for the note of the feeblest there is room, nay a positive need, in the harmonies of God. That the principles of true democracy are founded in universal reciprocity, and that "A man's a man" was written when God first stamped His own image and superscription on His child and breathed into his nostrils the breath of life. And I confess I can pray for no nobler destiny for my country than that it may be the stage, however far distant in the future, whereon these ideas and principles shall ultimately mature; and culminating here at whatever cost of production shall go forth hence to dominate the world.

Methought I saw a mighty conflagration, plunging and heaving, surging and seething, smoking and rolling over this American continent. Strong men and wise men stand helpless in mute consternation. Empty headed babblers add the din of their bray to the crashing and crackling of the flames. But the hungry flood rolls on. The air is black with smoke and cinders. The sky is red with lurid light. Forked tongues of fiery flame dart up and lick the pale stars, and seem to laugh at men's feebleness and frenzy. As I look on I think of Schiller's sublime characterization of fire:

"Frightful becomes this God-power, when it snatches itself free from fetters and stalks majestically forth on its own career—the free daughter of Nature." Ingenuity is busy with newly patented snuffers all warranted to extinguish the flame. The street gamin with a hooked wire pulls out a few nuggets that chanced to be lying on the outskirts where they were cooked by the heat; and gleefully cries "What a nice fire to roast my chestnuts," and like little Jack Horner, "what a nice boy am I!"

Meantime this expedient, that expedient, the other expedient is suggested by thinkers and theorizers hoping to stifle the angry, roaring, devouring demon and allay the mad destruction.

> "Wehe wenn sie losgelassen,
> Wachsend ohne Widerstand,
> Durch die volkbelebten Gassen
> Walzt den ungeheuren Brand!"

But the strength of the Omnipotent is in it. The hand of God is leading it on. It matters not whether you and I in mad desperation cast our quivering bodies into it as our funeral pyre; or whether, like the street urchins, we pull wires to secure the advantage of the passing moment. We can neither help it nor hinder; only

> "Let thy gold be cast in the furnace,
> Thy red gold, precious and bright.
> Do not fear the hungry fire
> With its caverns of burning light."

If it takes the dearest idol, the pet theory or the darling 'ism', the pride, the selfishness, the prejudices, the exclusiveness, the bigotry and intolerance, the conceit of self, of race, or of family superiority,—nay, if it singe from thee thy personal gratifications in thy distinction by birth, by blood, by sex—everything,—and leave thee nothing but thy naked manhood, solitary and unadorned,—let them go—let them go!

> "And thy gold shall return more precious,
> Free from every spot and stain,
> For gold must be tried by fire."

And the heart of nations must be tried by pain; and their polish, their true culture must be wrought in through conflict,

Has America a Race Problem?

Yes.

What are you going to do about it?

Let it alone and mind my own business. It is God's problem and He will solve it in time. It is deeper than Gehenna. What can you or I do!

Are there then no duties and special lines of thought growing out of the present conditions of this problem?

Certainly there are. *Imprimis*; let every element of the conflict see that it represent a positive force so as to preserve a proper equipoise in the conflict. No shirking, no skulking, no masquerading in another's uniform. Stand by your guns. And be ready for the charge. The day is coming, and now is, when America must ask each citizen not "who was your grandfather and what the color of his cuticle," but "*What can you do?*" Be ready each individual element,—each race, each class, each family, each man to reply "*I engage to undertake an honest man's share.*"

God and time will work the problem. You and I are only to stand for the quantities *at their best*, which he means us to represent.

Above all, for the love of humanity stop the mouth of those learned theorizers, the expedient mongers, who come out annually with their new and improved method of getting the answer and clearing the slate: amalgamation, deportation, colonization and all the other ations that were ever devised or dreamt of. If Alexander wants to be a god, let him; but don't have Alexander hawking his patent plan for universal deification. If all could or would follow Alexander's plan, just the niche in the divine cosmos meant for man would be vacant. And we think that men have a part to play in this great drama no less than gods, and so if a few are determined to be white—amen, so be it; but don't let them argue as if there were no part to be played in life by black men and black women, and as if to become white were the sole specific and panacea for all the ills that flesh is heir to—the universal solvent for all America's irritations. And again, if an American family of whatever condition or hue takes a notion to reside in Africa or in Mexico, or in the isles of the sea, it is most un-American for any power on this continent to seek to gainsay or obstruct their departure; but on the other hand, no power or element of power on this continent, least of all a self-constituted tribunal of "recent arrivals," possesses the right to begin figuring before-hand to calculate what it would require *to send* ten millions of citizens, whose ancestors have wrought here from the planting of the nation, to the same places at so much per head—at least till some one has consulted those heads.

We would not deprecate the fact, then, that America has a Race Problem. It is guaranty of the perpetuity and progress of her institutions, and insures the breadth of her culture, and the symmetry of her development. More than all, let us not disparage the factor which the Negro is appointed to contribute to that problem. America needs the Negro for ballast if for nothing else. His tropical warmth and spontaneous emotionalism may form no unseemly counterpart to the cold and calculating Anglo-Saxon. And then his instinct for law and order, his inborn respect for authority, his inaptitude for rioting and anarchy, his gentleness and cheerfulness as a laborer, and his deep-rooted faith in God will prove indispensable and invaluable elements in a nation menaced as America is by anarchy, socialism, communism, and skepticism poured in with all the jail birds from the continents of Europe and Asia. I believe with our own Dr. Crummell[2] that "the Almighty does not preserve, rescue, and build up a lowly people merely for ignoble ends." And the historian of American civilization will yet congratulate this country that she has had a Race Problem and that descendants of the black race furnished one of its largest factors.


## One Phase of American Literature


For nations as for individuals, a product, to be worthy the term literature, must contain something characteristic and *sui generis*.

So long as America remained a mere English colony, drawing all her life and inspiration from the mother country, it may well be questioned whether there was such a thing as American literature. "Who ever reads an American book?" it was scornfully asked in the eighteenth century. Imitation is the worst of suicides; it cuts the nerve of originality and condemns to mediocrity: and 'twas not till the pen of our writers was dipped in the life blood of their own nation and pictured out its own peculiar heart throbs and agonies that the world cared to listen. The nightingale and the skylark had to give place to the mocking bird, the bobolink and the whippoorwill, the heather and the blue bells of Britain, to our own golden-rod and daisy; the insular and monarchic customs and habits of thought of old England must develop into the broader, looser, freer swing of democratic America, before her contributions to the world of thought could claim the distinction of individuality and gain an appreciative hearing.

And so our writers have succeeded in becoming national and representative in proportion as they have from year to year entered more and more fully, and more and more sympathetically, into the distinctive life of their nation, and endeavored to reflect and picture its homeliest pulsations and its elemental components. And so in all the arts, as men have gradually come to realize that

> "Nothing useless is or low
> Each thing in its place is best,"

and have wrought into their products, lovingly and impartially and reverently, every type, every tint, every tone that they felt or saw or heard, just to that degree have their expressions, whether by pen or brush or rhythmic cadence, adequately and simply given voice to the thought of Nature around them. No man can prophesy with another's parable. For each of us truth means merely the re-presentation of the sensations and experiences of our personal environment, colored and vivified—fused into consistency and crystallized into individuality in the crucible of our own feelings and imaginations. The mind of genius is merely the brook, picturing back its own tree and bush and bit of sky and cloud ensparkled by individual salts and sands and rippling motion. And paradoxical as it may seem, instead of making us narrow and provincial, this trueness to one's habitat, this appreciative eye and ear for the tints and voices of one's own little wood serves but to usher us into the eternal galleries and choruses of God. It is only through the unclouded perception of our tiny "part" that we can come to harmonize with the "stupendous whole," and in order to this our sympathies must be finely attuned and quick to vibrate under the touch of the commonplace and vulgar no less than at the hand of the elegent and refined. Nothing natural can be wholly unworthy; and we do so at our peril, if, what God has cleansed we presume to call common or unclean. Nature's language is not writ in cipher. Her notes are always simple and sensuous, and the very meanest recesses and commonest byways are fairly deafening with her sermons and songs. It is only when we ourselves are out of tune through our pretentiousness and self-sufficiency, or are blinded and rendered insensate by reason of our foreign and unnatural "cultivation" that we miss her meanings and inadequately construe her multiform lessons.

For two hundred and fifty years there was in the American commonwealth a great *silent* factor. Though in themselves simple and unique their offices were those of the barest utility. Imported merely to be hewers of wood and drawers of water, no artist for many a generation thought them worthy the sympathetic study of a model. No Shakespeare arose to distil from their unmatched personality and unparalleled situations the exalted poesy and crude grandeur of an immortal Caliban. Distinct in color, original in temperament, simple and unconventionalized in thought and action their spiritual development and impressionability under their novel environment would have furnished, it might seem, as interesting a study in psychology for the poetic pen, as would the gorges of the Yosemite to the inspired pencil. Full of vitality and natural elasticity, the severest persecution and oppression could not kill them out or even sour their temper. With massive brawn and indefatigable endurance they wrought under burning suns and chilling blasts, in swamps and marshes,—they cleared the forests, tunneled mountains, threaded the land with railroads, planted, picked and ginned the cotton, produced the rice and the sugar for the markets of the world. Without money and without price they poured their hearts' best blood into the enriching and developing of this country. *They wrought but were silent.*

The most talked about of all the forces in this diversified civilization, they seemed the great American fact, the one objective reality, on which scholars sharpened their wits, at which orators and statesmen fired their eloquence, and from which, after so long a time, authors, with varied success and truthfulness have begun at last to draw subjects and models. Full of imagination and emotion, their sensuous pictures of the "New Jerusalem," "the golden slippers," "the long white robe," "the pearly gates," etc., etc., seem fairly to steam with tropical luxuriance and naive abandon. The paroxysms of religious fervor into which this simple-minded, child-like race were thrown by the contemplation of Heaven and rest and freedom, would have melted into sympathy and tender pity if not into love, a race less cold and unresponsive than the one with which they were thrown in closest contact. There was something truly poetic in their weird moanings, their fitful gleams of hope and trust, flickering amidst the darkness of their wailing helplessness, their strange sad songs, the half coherent ebullitions of souls in pain, which become, the more they are studied, at once the wonder and the despair of musical critics and imitators. And if one had the insight and the simplicity to gather together, to digest and assimilate these original lispings of an unsophisticated people while they were yet close—so close—to nature and to nature's God, there is material here, one might almost believe, as rich, as unhackneyed, as original and distinctive as ever inspired a Homer, or a Cædmon or other simple genius of a people's infancy and lisping childhood.

In the days of their bitterest persecution, their patient endurance and Christian manliness inspired *Uncle Tom's Cabin,* which revolutionized the thought of the world on the subject of slavery and at once placed its author in the front rank of the writers of her country and age. Here at last was a work which England could not parallel. Here was a work indigenous to American soil and characteristic of the country—a work which American forces alone could have produced. The subject was at once seen to be fresh and interesting to the world as well as national and peculiar to America; and so it has since been eagerly cultivated by later writers with widely varying degrees of fitness and success.

By a rough classification, authors may be separated into two groups: first, those in whom the artistic or poetic instinct is uppermost—those who write to please—or rather who write because *they* please; who simply paint what they see, as naturally, as instinctively, and as irresistibly as the bird sings—with no thought of an audience—singing because it loves to sing,—singing because God, nature, truth sings through it. For such writers, to be true to themselves and true to Nature is the only canon. They cannot warp a character or distort a fact in order to prove a point. They have nothing to prove. All who care to, may listen while they make the woods resound with their glad sweet carolling; and the listeners may draw their own conclusions as to the meaning of the cadences of this minor strain, or that hushed and almost awful note of rage or despair. And the myriad-minded multitude attribute their myriad-fold impressions to the myriad-minded soul by which they have severally been enchanted, each in his own way according to what he brings to the witching auditorium. But the singer sings on with his hat before his face, unmindful, it may be unconscious, of the varied strains reproduced from him in the multitudinous echoes of the crowd. Such was Shakespeare, such was George Eliot, such was Robert Browning. Such, in America, was Poe, was Bryant, was Longfellow; and such, in his own degree perhaps, is Mr. Howells.[1]

In the second group belong the preachers,—whether of righteousness or unrighteousness,—all who have an idea to propagate, no matter in what form their talent enables them to clothe it, whether poem, novel, or sermon,—all those writers with a purpose or a lesson, who catch you by the buttonhole and pommel you over the shoulder till you are forced to give assent in order to escape their vociferations; or they may lure you into listening with the soft music of the siren's tongue—no matter what the expedient to catch and hold your attention, they mean to fetter you with their one idea, whatever it is, and make you, if possible, ride their hobby. In this group I would place Milton in much of his writing, Carlyle in all of his, often our own Whittier, the great reformer-poet, and Lowell; together with such novelists as E. P. Roe, Bellamy, Tourgee[2] and some others.

Now in my judgment writings of the first class will be the ones to withstand the ravages of time. 'Isms' have their day and pass away. New necessities arise with new conditions and the emphasis has to be shifted to suit the times. No finite mind can grasp and give out the whole circle of truth. We do well if we can illuminate just the tiny arc which we occupy and should be glad that the next generation will not need the lessons we try so assiduously to hammer into this. In the evolution of society, as the great soul of humanity builds it "more lofty chambers," the old shell and slough of didactic teaching must be left behind and forgotten. The world for instance has outgrown, I suspect, those passages of *Paradise Lost* in which Milton makes the Almighty Father propound the theology of a seventeenth century Presbyterian. But a passage like the one in which Eve with guileless innocence describes her first sensations on awaking into the world is as perennial as man.

> "That day I oft remember, when from sleep
> I first awaked and found myself reposed
> Under a shade on flowers, much wondering where
> And what I was, whence thither brought and how.
> Not distant far from thence a murmuring sound
> Of waters issued from a cave, and spread
> Into a liquid plain, then stood unmoved
> Pure as the expanse of Heaven;
>                           I thither went
> With unexperienced thought and laid me down
> On the green bank, to look into the clear
> Smooth lake that to me seemed another sky.
> As I bent down to look, just opposite
> A shape within the watery gleam appeared,
> Bending to look on me; I started back,
> It started back; but pleased I soon returned,
> Pleased it returned as soon with answering looks
> Of sympathy and love; there I had fixed
> Mine eyes till now,—and pined with vain desire,
> Had not a voice thus warned me.
>                           'What thou seest,
> What there thou seest, fair creature, is thyself;
> With thee it came and goes; but follow me,

> And I will bring thee where no shadow stays
> Thy coming and thy soft embraces.'
>             What could I do but follow straight
> Invisibly thus led?
> Till I espied thee, fair indeed and tall,
> Under a plantain; yet methought less fair,
> Less winning soft, less amiably mild
> Than that smooth watery image; back I turned
> Thou following criedst aloud, 'Return, fair Eve,
> Whom fliest thou? whom thou fliest, of him thou art.
> Part of my soul, I seek thee, and thee claim
> My other half.'"

This will never cease to throb and thrill as long as man is man and woman is woman.

Now owing to the problematical position at present occupied by descendants of Africans in the American social polity,—growing, I presume, out of the continued indecision in the mind of the more powerful descendants of the Saxons as to whether it is expedient to apply the maxims of their religion to their civil and political relationships,—most of the writers who have hitherto attempted a portrayal of life and customs among the darker race have belonged to our class II: they have all, more or less, had a point to prove or a mission to accomplish, and thus their art has been almost uniformly perverted to serve their ends; and, to add to their disadvantage, most, if not all the writers on this line have been but partially acquainted with the life they wished to delineate and through sheer ignorance ofttimes, as well as from design occasionally, have not been able to put themselves in the darker man's place. The art of "thinking one's self imaginatively into the experiences of others" is not given to all, and it is impossible to acquire it without a background and a substratum of sympathetic knowledge. Without this power our portraits are but death's heads or caricatures and no amount of cudgeling can put into them the movement and reality of life. Not many have had Mrs. Stowe's power because not many have studied with Mrs. Stowe's humility and love. They forget that underneath the black man's form and behavior there is the great bed-rock of humanity, the key to which is the same that unlocks every tribe and kindred of the nations of earth. Some have taken up the subject with a view to establishing evidences of ready formulated theories and preconceptions; and, blinded by their prejudices and antipathies, have altogether abjured all candid and careful study. Others with flippant indifference have performed a few psychological experiments on their cooks and coachmen, and with astounding egotism, and powers of generalization positively bewildering, forthwith aspire to enlighten the world with dissertations on racial traits of the Negro. A few with really kind intentions and a sincere desire for information have approached the subject as a clumsy microscopist, not quite at home with his instrument, might study a new order of beetle or bug. Not having focused closely enough to obtain a clear-cut view, they begin by telling you that all colored people look exactly alike and end by noting down every chance contortion or idiosyncrasy as a race characteristic. Some of their conclusions remind one of the enterprising German on a tour of research and self improvement through Great Britain, who recommended his favorite sauer kraut both to an Irishman, whom he found sick with fever, and to a Scotchman, who had a cold. On going that way subsequently and finding the Scotchman well and the Irishman dead, he writes: *Mem.—Sauer kraut good for the Scotch but death to the Irish.*

This criticism is not altered by our grateful remembrance of those who have heroically taken their pens to champion the black man's cause. But even here we may remark that a painter may be irreproachable in motive and as benevolent as an angel in intention, nevertheless we have a right to compare his copy with the original and point out in what respects it falls short or is overdrawn; and he should thank us for doing so.

It is in no captious spirit, therefore, that we note a few contributions to this phase of American literature which have been made during the present decade; we shall try to estimate their weight, their tendency, their truthfulness and their lessons, if any, for ourselves.

Foremost among the champions of the black man's cause through the medium of fiction must be mentioned Albion W. Tourgee. No man deserves more the esteem and appreciation of the colored people of this country for his brave words. For ten years he has stood almost alone as the enthusiastic advocate, not of charity and dole to the Negro, but of justice. The volumes he has written upon the subject have probably been read by from five to ten millions of the American people. Look over his list consecrated to one phase or another of the subject: "A Fool's Errand," "A Royal Gentleman," "Bricks without Straw," "An Appeal to Cæsar," "Hot Ploughshares," "Pactolus Prime,"—over three thousand pages—enough almost for a life work, besides an almost interminable quantity published in periodicals.

Mr. Tourgee essays to paint life with the coloring of fiction, and yet, we must say, we do not think him a novelist primarily; that is, novel making with him seems to be a mere incident, a convenient vehicle through which to convey those burning thoughts which he is constantly trying to impress upon the people of America, whether in lecture, stump speech, newspaper column or magazine article. His power is not that already referred to of thinking himself imaginatively into the experiences of others. He does not create many men of many minds. All his offspring are little Tourgees—they preach his sermons and pray his prayers.

In "Pactolus Prime," for example, one of his latest, his hero, a colored bootblack in a large hotel, is none other than the powerful, impassioned, convinced and convincing lecturer, Judge Tourgee himself, done over in ebony. His caustic wit, his sledge hammer logic, his incisive criticism, his righteous indignation, all reflect the irresistible arguments of the great pleader for the Negro; and all the incidents are arranged to enable this bootblack to impress on senators and judges, lawyers, and divines, his plea for justice to the Negro, along with the blacking and shine which he skillfully puts on their aristocratic toes. And so with all the types which Mr. Tourgee presents—worthy or pitiful ones always—they uniformly preach or teach, convict or convert. Artistic criticism aside, it is mainly as a contribution to polemic literature in favor of the colored man that most of Tourgee's works will be judged; and we know of no one who can more nearly put himself in the Negro's place in resenting his wrongs and pleading for his rights. In presenting truth from the colored American's standpoint Mr. Tourgee excels, we think, in fervency and frequency of utterance any living writer, white or colored. Mr. Cable[3] is brave and just. He wishes to see justice done in the Freedman's case in equity, and we honor and revere him for his earnest manly efforts towards that end. But Mr. Cable does not forget (I see no reason why he should, of course) that he is a white man, a Southerner and an ex-soldier in the Confederate army. To use his own words, he writes, "with an admiration and affection for the South, that for justice and sincerity yield to none; in a spirit of faithful sonship to a Southern state." Of course this but proves his sincerity, illustrates his candor, and adds weight to the axiomatic justice of a cause which demands such support from a thoroughly disinterested party, or rather a party whose interest and sympathy and affection must be all on the side he criticises and condemns. The passion of the partisan and the bias of the aggrieved can never be charged against him. Mr. Cable's is the impartiality of the judge who condemns his own son or cuts off his own arm. His attitude is judicial, convincing, irreproachable throughout.

Not only the Christian conscience of the South, but also its enlightened self-interest is unquestionably on the side of justice and mainly dealing toward the black man; and one can not help feeling that a cause which thus enlists the support and advocacy of the "better self" of a nation must ultimately be invincible: and Mr. Cable, in my judgment, embodies and represents that Christian conscience and enlightened self-interest of the hitherto silent South; he vocalizes and inspires its better self. To him the dishonesty and inhumanity there practiced against the black race is a blot on the scutcheon of that fair land and doomed to bring in its wake untold confusion, disaster, and disgrace. From his calm elevation he sees the impending evil, and with loving solicitude urges his countrymen to flee the wrath to come. Mr. Tourgee, on the other hand, speaks with all the eloquence and passion of the aggrieved party himself. With his whip of fine cords he pitilessly scourges the inconsistencies, the weaknesses and pettiness of the black man's persecutors. The fire is burning within him, he cannot but speak. He has said himself that he deserves no credit for speaking and writing on this subject, for it has taken hold of him and possesses him to the exclusion of almost everything else. Necessity is laid upon him. Not more bound was Saul of Tarsus to consecrate his fiery eloquence to the cause of the persecuted Nazarene than is this white man to throw all the weight of his powerful soul into the plea for justice and Christianity in this

American anomaly and huge inconsistency. Not many colored men would have attempted Tourgee's brave defense of Reconstruction and the alleged corruption of Negro supremacy, more properly termed the period of white sullenness and desertion of duty. Not many would have dared, fearlessly as he did, to arraign this country for an enormous pecuniary debt to the colored man for the two hundred and forty-seven years of unpaid labor of his ancestors. Not many could so determinedly have held up the glass of the real Christianity before these believers in a white Christ and these preachers of the gospel, "Suffer the little *white* children to come unto me." We all see the glaring inconsistency and feel the burning shame. We appreciate the incongruity and the indignity of having to stand forever hat in hand as beggars, or be shoved aside as intruders in a country whose resources have been opened up by the unrequited toil of our forefathers. We know that our bill is a true one—that the debt is as real as to any pensioners of our government. But the principles of patience and forbearance, of meekness and charity, have become so ingrained in the Negro character that there is hardly enough self-assertion left to ask as our right that a part of the country's surplus wealth be *loaned* for the education of our children; even though we know that our present poverty is due to the fact that the toil of the last quarter century enriched these coffers, but left us the heirs of crippled, deformed, frost-bitten, horny-handed and empty handed mothers and fathers. Oh, the shame of it!

A coward during the war gets a few scratches and bruises—often in *fleeing from the enemy*—and his heirs are handsomely pensioned by his *grateful* country! But these poor wretches stood every man to his post for two hundred and fifty years, digging trenches, building roads, tunneling mountains, clearing away forests, cultivating the soil in the cotton fields and rice swamps till fingers dropped off, toes were frozen, knees twisted, arms stiff and useless—and when their sons and heirs, with the burdens of helpless parents to support, wish to secure enough education to enable them to make a start in life, *their* grateful country sagely deliberates as to the feasibility of sending them to another undeveloped jungle to show off their talent for unlimited pioneer work in strange climes! The Indian, during the entire occupancy of this

country by white men, has stood proudly aloof from all their efforts at development, and presented an unbroken front of hostility to the introduction and spread of civilization. The Negro,
though brought into the country by force and compelled under
the lash to lend his brawn and sturdy sinews to promote its material growth and prosperity, nevertheless with perfect amiability
of temper and adaptability of mental structure has quietly and
unhesitatingly accepted its standards and fallen in line with its
creeds. He adjusts himself just as readily and as appreciatively, it
would seem, to the higher and stricter requirements of freedom
and citizenship; and although from beginning to end, nettled and
goaded under unprecedented provocation, he has never once
shown any general disposition to arise in his might and deluge
this country with blood or desolate it with burning, as he might
have done. It is no argument to charge weakness as the cause of
his peaceful submission and to sneer at the "inferiority" of a race
who would allow themselves to be made slaves—unrevenged. It
*may* be nobler to perish redhanded, to kill as many as your battle
axe holds out to hack and then fall with an exultant yell and savage grin of fiendish delight on the hugh pile of bloody corpses,—
expiring with the solace and unction of having ten thousand
wounds all in front. I don't know. I sometimes think it depends
on where you plant your standard and who wears the white
plume which your eye inadvertently seeks. If Napoleon is the
ideal of mankind, I suppose 'tis only noble to be strong; and true
greatness may consist in an adamantine determination never to
serve. The greatest race with which I am even partially acquainted, proudly boasts that it has never met another race save
as either enemy or victim. They seem to set great store by this fact
and I judge it must be immensely noble according to their ideals.
But somehow it seems to me that those nations and races who
choose the Nazarene for their plumed knight would find some
little jarring and variance between such notions and His ideals.
There could not be at all times perfect unanimity between Leader
and host. A good many of his sayings, it seems to me, would have
to be explained away; not a few of his injunctions quietly ignored, and I am not sure but the great bulk of his principles and
precepts must after all lie like leaden lumps, an undigested and
unassimilable mass on an uneasy overburdened stomach. I find it

rather hard to understand these things, and somehow I feel at times as if I have taken hold of the wrong ideal. But then, I suppose, it must be because I have not enough of the spirit that comes with the blood of those grand old *sea kings* (I believe you call them) who shot out in their trusty barks speeding over unknown seas and, like a death-dealing genius, with the piercing eye and bloodthirsty heart of hawk or vulture killed and harried, burned and caroused. This is doubtless all very glorious and noble, and the seed of it must be an excellent thing to have in one's blood. But I haven't it. I frankly admit my limitations. I am hardly capable of appreciating to the full such grand intrepidity,—due of course to the fact that the stock from which I am sprung did not attain that royal kink in its blood ages ago. My tribe has to own kinship with a very tame and unsanguinary individual who, a long time ago when blue blood was distilling in the stirring fiery world outside, had no more heroic and daring a thing to do than help a pale sorrow-marked man as he was toiling up a certain hill at Jerusalem bearing his own cross whereon he was soon to be ignominiously nailed. This Cyrenian fellow was used to bearing burdens and he didn't mind giving a lift over a hard place now and then, with no idea of doing anything grand or memorable, or that even so much as his name would be known thereby. And then, too, by a rather strange coincidence this unwarlike and insignificant kinsman of ours had his home in a country (the fatherland of all the family) which had afforded kindly shelter to that same mysterious Stranger, when, a babe and persecuted by bloody power and heartless jealousy, He had to flee the land of his birth. And somehow this same country has in its day done so much fostering and sheltering of that kind—has watched and hovered over the cradles of religions and given refuge and comfort to the persecuted, the world weary, the storm tossed benefactors of mankind so often that she has come to represent nothing stronger or more imposing than the "eternal womanly" among the nations, and to accept as her mission and ideal, *loving service* to mankind.

With such antecedents then the black race in America should not be upbraided for having no taste for blood and carnage. It is the fault of their constitution that they prefer the judicial awards of peace and have an eternal patience to abide the bloodless triumph of right. It is no argument, therefore, when I point to the record of their physical supremacy—when the homes and helpless ones of this country were absolutely at the black man's mercy and not a town laid waste, not a building burned, and *not a woman insulted*—it is no argument, I say, for you to retort: *"He was a coward; he didn't dare!"* The facts simply do not show this to have been the case.

Now the tardy conscience of the nation wakes up one bright morning and is overwhelmed with blushes and stammering confusion because convicted of dishonorable and unkind treatment of *the Indian*; and there is a wonderful Scurrying around among the keepers of the keys to get out more blankets and send out a few primers for the *"wards."* While the black man, a faithful son and indefeasible heir,—who can truthfully say, "Lo, these many years do I serve thee, neither transgressed I at any time thy commandment, and yet thou never gavest me a kid that I might make merry with my friends,"—is snubbed and chilled and made unwelcome at every merry-making of the family. And when appropriations for education are talked of, the section for which he has wrought and suffered most, actually defeats the needed and desired assistance for fear they may not be able to prevent his getting a fair and equitable share in the distribution.

Oh, the shame of it!

In "Pactolus Prime" Mr. Tourgee has succeeded incomparably, we think, in photographing and vocalizing the feelings of the colored American in regard to the Christian profession and the pagan practice of the dominant forces in the American government. And as an impassioned denunciation of the heartless and godless spirit of caste founded on color, as a scathing rebuke to weak-eyed Christians who cannot read the golden rule across the color line, as an unanswerable arraignment of unparalleled ingratitude and limping justice in the policy of this country towards the weaker of its two children, that served it so long and so faithfully, the book is destined to live and to furnish an invaluable contribution to this already plethoric department of American literature.

Mr. Cable and Mr. Tourgee represent possibly the most eminent as well as the most prolific among the writers on this subject belonging to the didactic or polemic class. A host of others there are—lesser lights, or of more intermittent coruscations—who have contributed on either side the debate single treatises, numerous magazine articles or newspaper editorials, advocating some one theory some another on the so-called *race problem*. In this group belongs the author of "An Appeal to Pharoah," advocating the deportation absurdity; also the writings of H. W. Grady;[4] "In Plain Black and White," "The Brother in Black," "The South Investigated," "A Defense of the Negro Pace," "The Prosperity of the South Dependent on the Elevation of the Negro," "The Old South and the New," "Black and White," etc., etc., among which are included articles from the pen of colored men themselves, such as Mr. Douglass, Dr. Crummell, Dr. Arnett,[5] Dr. Blyden,[6] Dr. Scarborough,[7] Dr. Price,[8] Mr. Fortune,[9] and others. These are champions of the forces on either side. They stand ever at the forefront dealing desperate blows right and left, now fist and skull, now broad-sword and battle-axe, now with the flash and boom of artillery; while the little fellows run out ever and anon from the ranks and deliver a telling blow between the eyes of an antagonist. All are wrought up to a high tension, some are blinded with passion, others appalled with dread,—all sincerely feel the reality of their own vision and earnestly hope to compel their world to see with their eyes. Such works, full of the fever and heat of debate belong to the turmoil and turbulence of the time. A hundred years from now they may be interesting history, throwing light on a feature of these days which, let us hope, will then be hardly intelligible to an American citizen not over fifty years old.

Among our artists for art's sweet sake, Mr. Howells has recently tried his hand also at painting the Negro, attempting merely a side light in half tones, on his life and manners; and I think the unanimous verdict of the subject is that, in this single department at least, Mr. Howells does not know what he is talking about. And yet I do not think we should quarrel with *An Imperative Duty* because it lacks the earnestness and bias of a special pleader. Mr. Howells merely meant to press the button and give one picture from American life involving racial complications. The kodak does no more; it cannot preach sermons or solve problems.

Besides, the portrayal of Negro characteristics was by no means the main object of the story, which was rather meant, I judge, to be a thumb nail sketch containing a psychological study of a morbidly sensitive conscience hectoring over a weak and vacillating will and fevered into increased despotism by reading into its own life and consciousness the analyses and terrible retributions of fiction,—a product of the Puritan's uncompromising sense of "*right though the heavens fall,*" irritated and kept sore by being unequally yoked with indecision and cowardice. Of such strokes Mr. Howells is undoubtedly master. It is true there is little point and no force of character about the beautiful and irresponsible young heroine; but as that is an attainment of so many of Mr. Howells' models, it is perhaps not to be considered as illustrating any racial characteristics. I cannot help sharing, however, the indignation of those who resent the picture in the colored church,—"evidently," Mr. Howells assures us, "representing *the best colored society*"; where the horrified young prig, Rhoda Aldgate, meets nothing but the frog-like countenances and cat-fish mouths, the musky exhalations and the "bress de Lawd, Honey," of an uncultivated people. It is just here that Mr. Howells fails—and fails because he gives only a half truth, and that a partisan half truth. One feels that he had no business to attempt a subject of which he knew so little, or for which he cared so little. There is one thing I would like to say to my white fellow countrymen, and especially to those who dabble in ink and affect to discuss the Negro; and yet I hesitate because I feel it is a fact which persons of the finer sensibilities and more delicate perceptions must know instinctively: namely, that it is an insult to humanity and a sin against God to publish any such sweeping generalizations of a race on such meager and superficial information. We meet it at every turn—this obtrusive and offensive vulgarity, this gratuitous sizing up of the Negro and conclusively writing down his equation, sometimes even among his ardent friends and bravest defenders. Were I not afraid of falling myself into the same error that I am condemning, I would say it seems an *Anglo Saxon characteristic* to have such overweening confidence in his own power of induction that there is no equation which he would acknowledge to be indeterminate, however many unknown quantities it may possess.

Here is an extract from Dr. Mayo, a thoroughly earnest man and sincerely friendly, as I believe, to the colored people.

"Among these women are as many grades of native, intellectual, moral and executive force as among the white people. The plantations of the Gulf, the Atlantic coast and the Mississippi bottoms swarm with negro women who seem hardly lifted above the brutes. I know a group of young colored women, many of them accomplished teachers, who bear themselves as gently and with as varied womanly charms as any score of ladies in the land. The one abyss of perdition *to this class* is the slough of unchastity in which, *as a race* they still flounder, half conscious that it is a slough—the double inheritance of savage Africa and slavery."

Now there may be one side of a truth here, yet who but a self-confident Anglo Saxon would dare make such a broad unblushing statement about a people *as a race?* Some developments brought to light recently through the scientific Christianity and investigating curiosity of Dr. Parkhurst may lead one to suspect the need of missionary teaching to "elevate" the white race; and yet I have too much respect for the autonomy of races, too much reverence for the collective view of God's handiwork to speak of any such condition, however general, as characterizing *the race.* The colored people do not object to the adequate and truthful portrayal of types of their race in whatever degree of the scale of civilization, or of social and moral development, is consonant with actual facts or possibilities. As Mr. Howells himself says, "A man can be anything along the vast range from angel to devil, and without living either the good thing or the bad thing in which his fancy dramatizes him, he can perceive it"—and I would add, can appreciate and even enjoy its delineation by the artist. The average Englishman takes no exception to the humorous caricatures of Dickens or to the satires and cynicisms of Thackeray. The Quilps and the Bernsteins are but strongly developed negatives of our universal human nature on the dark side. We recognize them as genre sketches,—and with the Agneses and Esthers and Aunt Lamberts as foils and correctives, we can appreciate them accordingly: while we do not believe ourselves to be the original of the portrait, there is enough sympathy and fellow feeling for the character to prevent our human relationship from being outraged and insulted. But were Dickens to introduce an average scion of his countrymen to a whole congregation of *Quilps*, at the same time sagely informing him that these represented *the best there was* of English life and morals, I strongly suspect the charming author would be lifted out on the toe of said average Englishman's boot, in case there shouldn't happen to be a good horsewhip handy.

Our grievance then is not that we are not painted as angels of light or as goody-goody Sunday-school developments; but we do claim that a man whose acquaintanceship is so slight that he cannot even discern diversities of individuality, has no right or authority to hawk "the only true and authentic" pictures of a race of human beings. Mr. Howells' point of view is precisely that of a white man who sees colored people at long range or only in certain capacities. His conclusions about the colored man are identical with the impressions that will be received and carried abroad by foreigners from all parts of the globe, who shall attend our Columbian Exposition for instance, and who, through the impartiality and generosity of our white countrymen, will see colored persons only as bootblacks and hotel waiters, grinning from ear to ear and bowing and curtseying for the extra tips. In the same way Mr. Howells has met colored persons in hotels or on the commons promenading and sparking, or else acting as menials and lazzaroni. He has not seen, and therefore cannot be convinced that there exists a quiet, self-respecting, dignified class of easy life and manners (save only where it crosses the roughness of their white fellow countrymen's barbarity) of cultivated tastes and habits, and with no more in common with the class of his acquaintance than the accident of complexion,—beyond a sympathy with their wrongs, or a resentment at being socially and morally classified with them, according as the principle of altruism or of self love is dominant in the individual.

I respectfully submit that there is hardly a colored church in any considerable city in this country, which could be said in any sense to represent *the best colored society*, in which Rhoda Aldgate could not have seen, when she opened her eyes, persons as quietly and as becomingly dressed, as cultivated in tone and as refined in manner, as herself; persons, too, as sensitive to rough contact and as horribly alive as she could be (though they had known it from childhood) to the galling distinctions in this country which insist on *levelling down* all individuals more or less related to the

Africans. So far from the cringing deference which Mr. Howells paints as exhibited to "the young white lady," in nine cases out of ten the congregation would have supposed intuitively that she was a quadroon, so far from the unusual was her appearance and complexion. In not a few such colored churches would she have found young women of aspiration and intellectual activity with whom she could affiliate without nausea and from whom she could learn a good many lessons—and, sadly I say it, even more outside the churches whom bitterness at racial inconsistency of white Christians had soured into a silent disbelief of all religion. In either class she would have found no trouble in reaching a heart which could enter into all the agony of her own trial and bitter grief. Nor am I so sure, if she had followed her first gushing impulse to go South and "elevate" the race with whom she had discovered her relationship, that she would have found even them so ready to receive her condescending patronage.

There are numerous other inadvertent misrepresentations in the book—such as supposing that colored people voluntarily and deliberately prefer to keep to themselves in all public places and that from choice "they have their own neighborhoods, their own churches, their own amusements, their own resorts,"—the intimation that there is a "*black* voice," a black character, easy, irresponsible and fond of what is soft and pleasant, a black ideal of art and a black barbaric taste in color, a black affinity—so that in some occult and dreadful way one, only one-sixteenth related and totally foreign by education and environment, can still feel that one-sixteenth race calling her more loudly than the fifteen-sixteenths. I wish to do Mr. Howells the justice to admit, however, that one feels his blunders to be wholly unintentional and due to the fact that he has studied his subject merely from the outside. With all his matchless powers as a novelist, not even he can yet "think himself imaginatively" into the colored man's place.

To my mind the quaintest and truest little bit of portraiture from low-life that I have read in a long time is the little story that appeared last winter in the Harpers, of the "*Widder Johnsing and how she caught the preacher.*" It is told with naive impersonality and appreciative humor, and is quite equal, I think, both in subject and treatment to the best of Mrs. Stowe's New England

dialect stories. It is idyllic in its charming simplicity and naturalness, and delightfully fresh in its sparkling wit and delicious humor. We do not resent such pictures as this of our lowly
folk—such a homely and honest

> "Pomegranate, which, if cut deep down the middle,
> Shows a heart within blood tinctured of a *veined humanity*,"

is always sweet to the taste and dear to the heart, however plain
and humble the setting.

A longer and more elaborate work, *Harold,* published ano-
nymously, comes properly in our group second, the didactic
novel. It gives the picture of a black Englishman cultured and refined, brought in painful contact with American,—or rather *un-
American,* color prejudice. The point of the book seems to be to
show that education for the black man is a curse, since it increases
his sensitiveness to the indignities he must suffer in consequence of
white barbarity. The author makes Harold, after a futile struggle
against American inequalities, disappear into the jungles of Africa,
"there to wed a dusky savage," at the last cursing the day he had
ever suspected a broader light or known a higher aspiration; a conclusion which, to my mind, is a most illogical one. If the cultivated
black man cannot endure the white man's barbarity—the cure, it
seems to me, would be to cultivate the white man. Civilize both,
then each will know what is due from man to man, and that reduces at once to a minimum the friction of their contact.

In the same rank as *Harold* belongs that improbability of im-
probabilities, *Doctor Huguet,* by the arch-sensationalist, Ignatius
Donelly. As its purpose is evidently good, I shall not undertake to
review the book. Suffice it to say the plot hinges on the exchange
of soul between the body of a black chicken-thief and that of a
cultivated white gentleman, and sets forth the indignities and
wrongs to which the cultured soul, with all its past of refinement
and learning, has to submit in consequence of its change of cuticle. The book is an able protest against that snobbishness which
elevates complexion into a touchstone of aristocracy and makes
the pigment cells of a man's skin his badge of nobility regardless
of the foulness or purity of the soul within; the only adverse criticism from the colored man's point of view being the selection of a

chicken thief as his typical black man; but on the principle of antitheses this may have been artistically necessary.

I shall pass next to what I consider the most significant contribution to this subject for the last ten years—a poem by Maurice Thompson[10] in the New York *Independent* for January 21, 1892, entitled *A Voodoo Prophecy*. From beginning to end it is full of ghoulish imagery and fine poetic madness. Here are a few stanzas of it:

> "I am the prophet of the dusky race,
>     The poet of wild Africa.    Behold,
> The midnight vision brooding in my face!
>                 Come near me,
>                 And hear me,
>     While from my lips the words of Fate are told.
>
> A black and terrible memory masters me,
>     The shadow and the substance of deep wrong;
> You know the past, hear now what is to be:
>                 From the midnight land,
>                 Over sea and sand,
>     From the green jungle, hear my Voodoo-song:
>
> A tropic heat is in my bubbling veins,
>     Quintessence of all savagery is mine,
> The lust of ages ripens in my reins,
>                 And burns
>                 And yearns,
>     Like venom-sap within a noxious vine.
>
> Was I a heathen?    Ay, I was—am still
>     A fetich worshipper; but I was free
> To loiter or to wander at my will,
>                 To leap and dance,
>                 To hurl my lance,
>     And breathe the air of savage liberty.
>
> You drew me to a higher life, you say;
>     Ah, drove me, with the lash of slavery!

Am I unmindful?   Every cursed day
          Of pain
          And chain
Roars like a torrent in my memory.

You make my manhood whole with 'equal rights!'
     Poor empty words!   Dream you I honor them?—
I who have stood on Freedom's wildest heights?
          My Africa,
          I see the day
     When none dare touch thy garment's lowest hem.

You cannot make me love you with your whine
     Of fine repentance.   Veil your pallid face
In presence of the shame that mantles mine;
          Stand
          At command
     Of the black prophet of the Negro race!

I hate you, and I live to nurse my hate,
     Remembering when you plied the slaver's trade
In my dear land . . . How patiently I wait
          The day,
          Not far away,
     When all your pride shall shrivel up and fade.

Yea, all your whiteness darken under me!
     Darken and be jaundiced, and your blood
Take in dread humors from my savagery,
          Until
          Your will
     Lapse into mine and seal my masterhood.

You, seed of Abel, proud of your descent,
     And arrogant, because your cheeks are fair,
Within my loins an inky curse is pent,
          To flood
          Your blood
     And stain your skin and crisp your golden hair.

As you have done by me, so will I do
   By all the generations of your race;
Your snowy limbs, your blood's patrician blue
       Shall be
       Tainted by me,
   And I will set my seal upon your face!

Yea, I will dash my blackness down your veins,
   And through your nerves my sensuousness I'll fling
Your lips, your eyes, shall bear the musty stains
       Of Congo kisses,
       While shrieks and hisses
   Shall blend into the savage songs I sing!

Your temples will I break, your fountains fill,
   Your cities raze, your fields to deserts turn;
My heathen fires shall shine on every hill,
       And wild beasts roam,
       Where stands your home;—
Even the wind your hated dust shall spurn.

I will absorb your very life in me,
   And mold you to the shape of my desire;
Back through the cycles of all cruelty
       I will swing you,
       And wring you,
   And roast you in my passions' hottest fire.

You, North and South, you, East and West,
   Shall drink the cup your fathers gave to me;
My back still burns, I bare my bleeding breast,
       I set my face,
       My limbs I brace,
To make the long, strong fight for mastery.

My serpent fetich lolls its withered lip
   And bares its shining fangs at thought of this:
I scarce can hold the monster in my grip.
       So strong is he,

> So eagerly
> He leaps to meet my precious prophecies.
>
> Hark for the coming of my countless host,
> Watch for my banner over land and sea.
> The ancient power of vengeance is not lost!
> Lo! on the sky
> The fire-clouds fly,
> And strangely moans the windy, weltering sea."

Now this would be poetry if it were only truthful. Simple and sensuous it surely is, but it lacks the third requisite—truth. The Negro is utterly incapable of such vindictiveness. Such concentrated venom might be distilled in the cold Saxon, writhing and chafing under oppression and repression such as the Negro in America has suffered and is suffering. But the black man is in real life only too glad to accept the olive branch of reconciliation. He merely asks to be let alone. To be allowed to pursue his destiny as a free man and an American citizen, to rear and educate his children in peace, to engage in art, science, trades or industries according to his ability,—and *to go to the wall if he fail.* He is willing, if I understand him, to let bygones be bygones. He does not even demand satisfaction for the centuries of his ancestors' unpaid labor. He asks neither pension, nor dole nor back salaries; but is willing to start from the bottom, all helpless and unprovided for as he is, with absolutely nothing as his stock in trade, with no capital, in a country developed, enriched, and made to blossom through his father's "sweat and toil,"—with none of the accumulations of ancestors' labors, with no education or moral training for the duties and responsibilities of freedom; nay, with every power, mental, moral, and physical, emasculated by a debasing slavery—he is willing, even glad to take his place in the lists alongside his oppressors, who have had every advantage, to be tried with them by their own standards, and to ask no quarter from them or high Heaven to palliate or excuse the ignominy of a defeat.

The Voodoo Prophecy has no interest then as a picture of the black, but merely as a revelation of the white man. Maurice Thompson in penning this portrait of the Negro, has, unconsciously it may be, laid bare his own soul—its secret dread and horrible fear. And this, it seems to me, is the key to the Southern situation, the explanation of the apparent heartlessness and cruelty of some, and the stolid indifference to atrocity on the part of others, before which so many of us have stood paralyzed in dumb dismay. The Southerner is not a cold-blooded villain. Those of us who have studied the genus in its native habitat can testify that his impulses are generous and kindly, and that while the South presents a solid phalanx of iron resistance to the Negro's advancement, still as individuals to individuals they are warm-hearted and often even tender. And just here is the difference between the Southerner and his more philosophical, less sentimental Northern brother. The latter in an abstract metaphysical way rather wants you to have all the rights that belong to you. He thinks it better for the country, better for him that justice, universal justice be done. But he doesn't care to have the blacks, in the concrete, too near him. He doesn't know them and doesn't want to know them. He really can't understand how the Southerner could have let those little cubs get so close to him as they did in the old days—nursing from the same bottle and feeding at the same breast.

To the Southerner, on the other hand, race antipathy and color-phobia *as such* does not exist. Personally, there is hardly a man of them but knows, and has known from childhood, some black fellow whom he loves as dearly as if he were white, whom he regards as indispensable to his own pleasures, and for whom he would break every commandment in the decalogue to save him from any general disaster. But our Bourbon seems utterly incapable of generalizing his few ideas. He would die for A or B, but suddenly becomes utterly impervious to every principle of logic when you ask for the simple golden rule to be applied to the class of which A or B is one. Another fact strikes me as curious. A Southern white man's regard for his black friend varies in inverse ratio to the real distance between them in education and refinement. Puck expresses it—"I can get on a great deal better with a nigger than I can with a Negro." And Mr. Douglass puts it: "Let a colored man be out at elbows and toes and half way into the gutter and there is no prejudice against him; but let him respect himself and be a man and Southern whites can't abide to ride in the same car with him."

Why this anomaly? Is it pride? Ordinarily, congeniality increases with similarity in taste and manners. Is it antipathy to color? It does not exist. The explanation is the white man's dread dimly shadowed out in this Voodoo Prophecy of Maurice Thompson, and fed and inspired by such books as *Minden Armais* and a few wild theorizers who have nothing better to do with their time than spend it advocating the fusion of races as a plausible and expedient policy. Now I believe there are two ideas which master the Southern white man and incense him against the black race. On this point he is a monomaniac. In the face of this feeling he would not admit he was convinced of the axioms of Geometry. The one is personal and present, the fear of Negro political domination. The other is for his posterity—the future horror of being lost as a race in this virile and vigorous black race. Relieve him of this nightmare and he becomes "as gentle as the sucking dove." With that dread delusion maddening him he would drive his sword to the hilt in the tender breast of his darling child, did he fancy that through her the curse would come.

Now argument is almost supersensible with a monomaniac. What is most needed is a sedative for the excited nerves, and then a mental tonic to stimulate the power of clear perception and truthful cerebration. The Southern patient needs to be brought to see, by the careful and cautious injection of cold facts and by the presentation of well selected object lessons that so far as concerns his first named horror of black supremacy politically, the usual safeguards of democracy are in the hands of intelligence and wealth in the South as elsewhere. The weapons of fair argument and persuasion, the precautionary bulwark of education and justice, the unimpeachable supremacy and insuperable advantage of intelligence and discipline over mere numbers—are all in his reach. It is to his interest to help make the black peasant an intelligent and self-respecting citizen. No section can thrive under the incubus of an illiterate, impoverished, cheerless and hopeless peasantry. Let the South once address herself in good faith to the improvement of the condition of her laboring classes, let her give but a tithe of the care and attention which are bestowed in the

North on its mercurial and inflammable importations, let her show but the disposition in her relative poverty merely to utter the benediction, *Be ye warmed and fed and educated*, even while she herself has not the wherewithal to emulate the Pullman villages and the Carnegie munificence, let her but give him a fair wage and an honest reckoning and a kindly God-speed,—and she will find herself in possession of the most tractable laborer, the most faithful and reliable henchman, the most invaluable co-operator and friendly vassal of which this or any country can boast.

So far as regards the really less sane idea that amicable relations subsisting between the races may promote their ultimate blending and loss of identity, it hardly seems necessary to refute it. Blending of races in the aggregate is simply an unthinkable thought, and the union of individuals can never fall out by accident or haphazard. There must be the deliberate wish and intention on each side; and the average black man in this country is as anxious to preserve his identity and transmit his type as is the average white man. In any case, hybridity is in no sense dependent on sectional or national amity. Oppression and outrage are not the means to chain the affections. Cupid, who knows no bolt or bars, is more wont to be stimulated with romantic sympathy towards a forbidden object unjustly persecuted. The sensible course is to remove those silly and unjust barriers which protect nothing and merely call attention to the possibilities of law-breaking, and depend instead on religion and common sense to guide, control and direct in the paths of purity and right reason.

The froth and foam, the sticks and debris at the watertop may have an uncertain movement, but as deep calleth unto deep the mighty ocean swell is always true to the tides; and whatever the fluctuations along the ragged edge between the races, the home instinct is sufficiently strong with each to hold the great mass true to its attractions. If Maurice Thompson's nightmare vision is sincere on his part, then, it has no objective reality; 'tis merely a hideous phantasm bred of his own fevered and jaundiced senses; if he does not believe in it himself, it was most unkind and uncalled for to publish abroad such inflaming and irritating fabrications.

After this cursory glance at a few contributions which have

peculiarly emphasized one phase of our literature during the last decade or two, I am brought to the conclusion that an authentic portrait, at once æsthetic and true to life, presenting the black man as a free American citizen, not the humble slave of *Uncle Tom's Cabin*—but the *man*, divinely struggling and aspiring yet tragically warped and distorted by the adverse winds of circumstance, has not yet been painted. It is my opinion that the canvas awaits the brush of the colored man himself. It is a pathetic—a fearful arraignment of America's conditions of life, that instead of that enrichment from the years and days, the summers and springs under which, as Browning says,

"The flowers turn double and the leaves turn flowers,"—

the black man's native and original flowers have in this country been all hardened and sharpened into thorns and spurs. In literature we have no artists for art's sake. Albery A. Whitman in *"Twasinta's Seminole"* and *"Not a Man and Yet a Man"*[11] is almost the only poet who has attempted a more sustained note than the lyrics of Mrs. Harper,[12] and even that note is almost a wail.

The fact is, a sense of freedom in mind as well as in body is necessary to the appreciative and inspiring pursuit of the beautiful. A bird cannot warble out his fullest and most joyous notes while the wires of his cage are pricking and cramping him at every heart beat. His tones become only the shrill and poignant protest of rage and despair. And so the black man's vexations and chafing environment, even since his physical emancipation has given him speech, has goaded him into the eloquence and fire of oratory rather than the genial warmth and cheery glow of either poetry or romance. And pity 'tis, 'tis true. A race that has produced for America the only folk-lore and folk songs of native growth, a race which has grown the most original and unique assemblage of fable and myth to be found on the continent, a race which has suggested and inspired almost the only distinctive American note which could chain the attention and charm the ear of the outside world—has as yet found no mouthpiece of its own to unify and perpetuate its wondrous whisperings—no painter-poet to distil in the alembic of his own imagination the gorgeous dyes, the luxuriant juices of this rich and tropical vegetation. It was the glory of Chaucer that he justified the English language to itself—that he took the homely and hitherto despised Saxon elements and ideas, and lovingly wove them into an artistic product which even Norman conceit and uppishness might be glad to acknowledge and imitate. The only man who is doing the same for Negro folk-lore is one not to the manner born. Joel Chandler Harris has made himself rich and famous by simply standing around among the black railroad hands and cotton pickers of the South and compiling the simple and dramatic dialogues which fall from their lips. What I hope to see before I die is a black man honestly and appreciatively portraying both the Negro as he is, and the white man, occasionally, as seen from the Negro's standpoint.

There is an old proverb "The devil is always painted *black*— by white painters." And what is needed, perhaps, to reverse the picture of the lordly man slaying the lion, is for the lion to turn painter.

Then too we need the calm clear judgment of ourselves and of others born of a disenchantment similar to that of a little girl I know in the South, who was once being laboriously held up over the shoulders of a surging throng to catch her first glimpse of a real live president. "Why Nunny," she cried half reproachfully, as she strained her little neck to see—*"It's nuffin but a man!"*

When we have been sized up and written down by others, we need not feel that the last word is said and the oracles sealed. "It's nuffin but a man." And there are many gifts the giftie may gie us, far better than seeing ourselves as others see us—and one is that of Bion's maxim *"Know Thyself."* Keep true to your own ideals. Be not ashamed of what is homely and your own. Speak out and speak honestly. Be true to yourself and to the message God and Nature meant you to deliver. The young David cannot fight in Saul's unwieldy armor. Let him simply therefore gird his loins, take up his own parable and tell this would-be great American nation *"A chile's amang ye takin' notes;"* and when men act the part of cowards or wild beasts, this great silent but open-eyed constituency has a standard by which they are being tried. Know thyself, and know those around at their true weight of solid intrinsic manhood without being dazzled by the fact that littleness of soul is often gilded with wealth, power and intellect.

There can be no nobility but that of soul, and no catalogue of adventitious circumstances can wipe out the stain or palliate the meanness of inflicting one ruthless, cruel wrong. 'Tis not only safer, but nobler, grander, diviner,

> "To be that which we destroy
> Than, by destruction, dwell in doubtful joy."

With this platform to stand on we can with clear eye weigh what is written and estimate what is done and ourselves paint what is true with the calm spirit of those who know their cause is right and who believe there is a God who judgeth the nations.


## What Are We Worth?


I once heard Henry Ward Beecher make this remark: "Were Africa and the Africans to sink to-morrow, how much poorer would the world be? A little less gold and ivory, a little less coffee, a considerable ripple, perhaps, where the Atlantic and Indian Oceans would come together—that is all; not a poem, not an invention, not a piece of art would be missed from the world."[1]

This is not a flattering statement; but then we do not want flattery if seeing ourselves as others see us is to help us in fulfilling the higher order, "know thyself." The world is often called cold and hard. I don't know much about that; but of one thing I am sure, it is intensely practical. Waves of sentiment or prejudice may blur its old eyes for a little while but you are sure to have your bill presented first or last with the inexorable "How much owest thou?" What have you produced, what consumed? What is your real value in the world's economy? What do you give to the world over and above what you have cost? What would be missed had you never lived? What are you worth? What of actual value would go down with you if you were sunk into the ocean or buried by an earthquake to-morrow? Show up your cash account and your balance sheet. In the final reckoning do you belong on the debit or the credit side of the account?

according to a fair and square, an impartial and practical reckoning. It is by this standard that society estimates individuals; and by this standard finally and inevitably the world will measure and judge nations and races.

It may not be unprofitable then for us to address ourselves to the task of casting up our account and carefully overhauling our books. It may be well to remember at the outset that the operation is purely a mathematical one and allows no room for sentiment. The good housewife's pet chicken which she took when first hatched, fed from her own hand and fondled on her bosom as lovingly as if it were a babe, is worth no more (for all the affection and care lavished on it) when sold in the shambles: and that never-to-be-forgotten black hen that stole into the parlor, flew upon the mantel looking for a nest among those handsome curios, smashed the sèvers vases and picked the buds from the lovely tea rose—so exasperatingly that the good woman could never again endure the sight of her—this ill-fated bird is worth no less. There are sections of this country in which the very name of the Negro, even in homeopathic doses, stirs up such a storm of feeling that men fairly grow wild and are unfit to discuss the simplest principles of life and conduct where the colored man is concerned; and you would think it necessary for the Ethiopian actually to change his skin before there can be any harmonious living or lucid thinking: there are a few nooks and crannies, on the other hand, in another quarter of the same country, in which that name embodies an idealized theory and a benevolent sentiment; and the black man (the blacker the better) is the petted nursling, the haloed idea, the foregone conclusion. In these Arcadias, it is as good capital as pushing selfishness and aspiring mediocrity need ask, to be advertised as one of the oppressed race and probably born a slave.

But after all sentiment, whether adverse or favorable, is ephemeral. Ever shifting and unreliable, it can never be counted in estimating values. The sentiments of youth are out-grown in age, and we like to-day what we despised or were indifferent to yesterday. Nine-tenths of the mis-called color prejudice or race prejudice in this country is mere sentiment governed by the association of ideas. It is not color prejudice at all. The color of a man's face *per se* has no more to do with his worthiness and companionableness than the color of his eyes or the shades of his hair. You admire the one or think the other more beautiful to rest the gaze upon. But every one with brains knows and must admit that he must look deeper than this for the man. Mrs. Livermore once said in my hearing: "It is not that the Negro is black; Spaniards, Portuguese, East Indians, enter our parlors, sup at our tables, and, if they have a sufficiently long bank account, they may marry our daughters: but the Negro is weak—and we don't like weakness."

Now this dislike it is useless to inveigh against and folly to rail at. We share it ourselves and often carry it to a more unjustifiable extent. For as a rule the narrower the mind and the more circumscribed the experience, the greater will be the exaggeration of accidents over substance, and of circumstance over soul. It does no good to argue with the poor sea-sick wretch who, even on land after the voyage, is nauseated by the sight of clear spring water. In vain you show the unreason of the feeling. This, you explain, is a different time, a different place, a different stage of progress in the circulation of waters. That was salt, this is fresh, and so on. You might as well be presenting syllogisms to Etna. "Yes, my dear Fellow," he cries, "You talk admirably; but you don't know how I feel. You don't know how sick I was on that nasty ship!" And so your rhetoric cannot annihilate the association of ideas, He feels; *you know*. But he will outgrow his feeling,—and you are content to wait.

Just as impervious to reason is the man who is dominated by the sentiment of race prejudice. You can only consign him to the fatherly hand of Time; and pray that your own mental sight be not thus obscured and your judgment warped in your endeavors to be just and true.

Sentiment and cant, then, both being ruled out, let us try to study our subject as the world finally reckons it—not certain crevices and crannies of the earth, but the cool, practical, business-like world. What are we worth? not in Georgia nor in Massachusetts; not to our brothers and sisters and cousins and aunts, every one of whom would unhesitatingly declare us worth a great gold-lump; nor to the exasperated neighbor over the way who would be just as ready, perhaps, to write us down a most unmitigated nuisance. But what do we represent to the world? What is our market value. Are we a positive and additive quantity or a negative factor in the world's elements. What have we cost and what do we come to?

The calculation may be made in the same way and on the same principle that we would estimate the value of any commodity on the market. Men are not very unlike watches. We might estimate first the cost of material—is it gold or silver or alloy, solid or plated, jewelled or sham paste. Settle the relative value of your raw material, and next you want to calculate how much this value has been enhanced by labor, the delicacy and fineness, the honesty and thoroughness of the workmanship; then the utility and beauty of the product and its adaptability to the end and purpose of its manufacture; and lastly is there a demand in the market for such an article. Does it meet a want, *will it go* and *go right*? Is it durable and reliable. How often do you have to wind it before it runs down, how often repair it. Does it keep good time and require but little watching and looking after. And there is no radical difference, after all, between the world's way of estimating men and our usual way of valuing watches. In both the fundamental item is the question of material, and then the refining and enhancement of that material through labor, and so on through the list.

What then can we say for our raw material?

Again I must preface an apology for anything unpalatable in our menu. I promised, you remember, to leave out the sentiment— you may stir it in afterwards, mixing thoroughly according to taste. We must discuss facts, candidly and bluntly, without rhetoric or cant if we would have a clear light on our problem.

Now whatever notions we may indulge on the theory of evolution and the laws of atavism or heredity, all concede that no individual character receives its raw material newly created and independent of the rock from whence it was hewn. No life is bound up within the period of its conscious existence. No personality dates its origin from its birthday. The elements that are twisted into the cord did not begin their formation when first the tiny thread became visible in the great warp and filling of humanity. When first we saw the light many of the threads undoubtedly were spun and the color and fineness of the weft determined. The materials that go to make the man, the probabilities of his character and activities, the conditions and circumstances of his growth, and his quantum of resistance and mastery are the resultant of forces which have been accumulating and gathering momentum for generations. So that, as one tersely expresses it, in order to reform a man, you must begin with his great grandmother.

A few years ago a certain social scientist was struck by a remarkable coincidence in the name of a number of convicts in the State prison of New York. There were found thirty-five or forty men, of the same name with but slight modification in the spelling, all convicted of crimes similar in character. Looking into the matter, he traced them every one back to one woman of inferior character who had come from England in one of the first colonial ships. *And that woman had been a convict and charged with pretty nearly the same crime.*

Rightly to estimate our material, then, it is necessary to go back of the twenty or thirty years during which we have been in possession, and find out the nature of the soil in which it has been forming and growing.

There is or used to be in England a system of entail by which a lot of land was fixed to a family and its posterity forever, passing always on the death of the father to his eldest son. A man may misuse or abuse, he may impoverish, mortgage, sterilize, eliminate every element of value—but he can never sell. He may cut down every tree, burn every fence and house, abstract by careless tillage, or by no tillage, every nutritive element from the soil, encumber it to two or three times its value and destroy forever its beauty and fertility—but he can never rid himself of it. That land with all its encumbrances and liabilities, its barrenness and squalidness, its poverty and its degradation is inexorably, inevitably, inalienably his and like a shattered and debased personality it haunts him wherever he goes. An heir coming into an estate is thus often poorer than if he had no inheritance. He is chained to a life long possession of debt, toil, responsibility, often disgrace. Happier were it for him if he could begin life with nothing—an isolated but free man with no capital but his possibilities, with no past and no pedigree. And so it often is with men. These bodies of ours often come to us mortgaged to their full value by the extravagance, self-indulgence, sensuality of some ancestor. Some man, generations back, has encumbered his estate for strong drink, his descendants coming into that estate have the mortgage to pay off, principal and interest. Another cut down the fences of character by debauchery and vice,—and these have to ward off attacks of the enemy without bulwarks or embattlements. They have burnt their houses of purity and integrity, have rendered the soil poor and unproductive by extravagance and folly,—and the children have to shiver amid the storms of passion and feed on husks till they can build for themselves a shelter and fertilize their farms. Not very valuable estates, you will say. Well, no,—nothing to boast of, perhaps. But an energetic heir can often pay off some of the liabilities and leave the estate to his children less involved than when he received it. At least he can arrest the work of destruction and see to it that no further encumbrances are added through his folly and mismanagement.

In estimating the value of our material, therefore, it is plain that we must look into the deeds of our estates and ferret out their history. The task is an individual one, as likewise its application. Certainly the original timber as it came from the African forests was good enough. No race of heathen are more noted for honesty and chastity than are the tribes of Africa. For one of their women to violate the laws of purity is a crime punishable with death; and so strictly honest are they, it is said, that they are wont to leave their commodities at the place of exchange and go about their business. The buyer coming up takes what he wishes to purchase and leaves its equivalent in barter or money. A returned missionary tells the story that certain European traders, when at a loss as to the safe keeping of their wares, were told by a native chief, "Oh just lay them down there. *They are perfectly safe, there are no Christians here.*"

Whatever may be said of its beauty, then, the black side of the stream with us is pretty pure, and has no cause to blush for its honesty and integrity. From the nature of the case the infusions of white blood that have come in many instances to the black race in this country are not the best that race afforded. And if anything further is needed to account for racial irregularities— the warping and shrinking, the knotting and cracking of the sturdy old timber, the two hundred and fifty years of training here are quite sufficient to explain all. I have often thought, since coming in closer contact with the Puritan element in America, what a different planing and shaping this timber might have received under their hands!

As I compare the Puritan's sound, substantial, sanctified common sense with the Feudal froth and foam of the South; the Puritan's liberal, democratic, ethical and at the same time calculating, economical, stick-to-ative and go-ahead-ative spirit,—with the free and easy lavishness, the aristocratic notions of caste and class distinctions, the pliable consciences and unbending social bars amid which I was reared;—I have wished that it might have been ordered that as my race had to serve a term of bondage it might have been under the discipline of the successors of Cromwell and Milton, rather than under the training and example of the luxurious cavaliers. There is no doubt that the past two hundred and fifty years of working up the material we now inherit, has depreciated rather than enhanced its value. We find in it the foolish ideas of aristocracy founded on anything else than a moral claim; we find the contempt for manual labor and the horror of horny palms, the love of lavish expenditure and costly display, and—alas, that we must own it—the laxness of morals and easy-going consciences inherited and imitated from the old English gentry of the reigns of Charles and Anne. But to know our faults is one step toward correcting them, and there are, I trust, no flaws in this first element of value, *material*, which may not be planed and scraped and sand-papered out by diligent and strenuous effort. One thing is certain, the flaws that are simply ingrained in the timber are not our responsibility. A man is to be praised primarily not for having inherited fine tools and faultless materials but for making the most of the stuff he has, and doing his best in spite of disadvantages and poor material. The individual is responsible, not for what he has not, but for what he has; and the vital part for us after all depends on the use we make of our material.

Many a passable article has by diligent workmanship been made even from inferior material. And this brings us to our second item of value—Labor.

This is a most important item. It would seem sometimes that it is labor that creates all value. A gold mine is worth no more than common clay till it is worked. The simple element of labor bestowed on iron, the cheapest and commonest of metals, multiplies its value four hundred thousand times, making it worth sixty-five times its weight in gold, *e. g.*:

| | |
|---|---|
| A pound of good iron is worth about. . . | 4 cts. |
| A pound of inch screws. . . . . . . . . . . . . | $1.00 |
| A pound of steel wire from. . . . . . . . . . | $3.00 to $7.00 |
| A pound of sewing needles. . . . . . . . . . | $14.00 |
| A pound of fish hooks from. . . . . . . . . . | $20.00 to $50.00 |
| A pound of jewel screws for watches. . . . | $3,500.00 |
| A pound of hair springs for watches. . . . | $16,000.00 |
| While a pound of fine gold in standard coin is worth only about. . . . . . . . . . | $248.00 |

Now it is the same fundamental material in the hair springs valued at $16,000.00 which was sold in the rough at 4 cts. per pound. It is labor that has thus enhanced its value. Now let us see if there is a parallel rise of value in the material of which men are made.

No animal, the scientists tell us, is in infancy so utterly helpless, so completely destitute of the means of independent existence, so entirely worthless in itself as the world estimates values, as is man. The chick just out of the shell can pick up its own food and run away from approaching danger. Touch a snapping turtle just a moment after its birth, and it will bite at you. Cut off its head and it will still bite. Break open the egg of the young and the vivacious little creature will, even in the embryo, try to fight for its rights and maintain its independence. But the human babe can for weeks and months, do nothing but cry and feed and fear. It is a constant drain on the capital of its parents, both physically and mentally. It is to be fed, and worked for, and sheltered and protected. It cannot even defend itself against a draft of wind.

What is it worth? Unsentimentally and honestly,—it is worth just as much as a leak is worth to a ship, or what the mistletoe is worth to the oak. He is a parasite, a thief, a destroyer of values. He thrives at another's expense, and filches from that other every atom of his own existence. The infatuated mother, it is true, would not sell him, she will tell you, for his weight in gold; but that is sentiment —not business. Besides, there is no danger of her having the chance to make such a bargain. No one will ever tempt her with any such offer. The world knows too well what an outlay of time and money and labor must be made before he is worth even his weight in ashes. His present worth no one would accept even as a gift—and it is only the prospect of future development of worth that could induce any one, save that mother, to take up the burden. What an expenditure of toil and care, of heart power and brain power, what planning, what working, what feeding, what enriching, what sowing and sinking of values before one can tell whether the harvest is worth the output. Yet, how gladly does the mother pour out her strength and vitality, her energy, her life that the little bankrupt may store up capital for its own use. How anxiously does she hang over the lumpish little organism to catch the first awakening of a soul. And when the chubby little hands begin to swing consciously before the snapping eyes, and the great toe is caught and tugged towards the open mouth, when the little pink fists for the first time linger caressingly on her cheek and breast, and the wide open eyes say distinctly "I know you, I love you,"—how she strains him to her bosom as her whole soul goes out to this newly found intelligence in the impassioned cry of Carlyle: "*Whence— and Oh Heavens, whither!*"

> "How poor, how rich, how abject, how august,
> How complicate, how wonderful is man!"

It is labor, development, training, careful, patient, painful, diligent toil that must span the gulf between this vegetating life germ (now worth nothing but toil and care and trouble, and living purely at the expense of another)—and that future consummation in which "the elements are so mixed that Nature can stand up and say to all the world, '*This is a man.*'"

It is a heavy investment, requires a large outlay of money on long time and large risk, no end of labor, skill, pains. Education is the word that covers it all—the working up of this raw material and fitting it into the world's work to supply the world's need—the manufacture of men and women for the markets of the world. But there is no other labor which so creates value. The value of the well developed man has been enhanced far more by the labor bestowed than is the iron in the watch springs. The value of the raw material was far below zero to begin with; but this "quintessence of dust" has become, *through labor*, "the beauty of the world, the paragon of animals,—noble in reason and infinite in faculty!"

What a piece of work, indeed!

Education, then, is the safest and richest investment possible to man. It pays the largest dividends and gives the grandest possible product to the world—a man. The demand is always greater than the supply—and the world pays well for what it prizes.

Now what sort of workmanship are we putting on our raw material. What are we doing for education? The man-factories among our people make, I think, a fairly good showing. Figures are encouraging things to deal with, and too they represent something tangible in casting up our accounts. There are now 25,530 colored schools in the United States with 1,353,352 pupils; the colored people hold in landed property for churches and schools $25,000,000. 2,500,000 colored children have learned to read and most of these to write also. 22,956 colored men and women are teaching in these schools. There are sixty-six academies and high schools and one hundred and fifty schools for advanced education taught by colored teachers, together with seven colleges administered by colored presidents and faculties. There are now one thousand college bred Negro ministers in the country, 250 lawyers, 749 physicians; while, according to Dr. Rankin, there are 247 colored students preparing themselves in the universities of Europe.

The African Methodists alone, representing the unassisted effort of the colored people for self-development, have founded thirty-eight institutes and colleges, with landed property valued at $502,650, and 134 teachers supported entirely by the self denying effort of the colored people themselves.

This looks like an attempt, to say the least, to do the best we can with our material. One feels there has not been much shirking here; the workmanship may be crude sometimes, when measured by more finished standards,—but they have done what

they could; in their poverty and inexperience, through self de-
nial and perseverance, they are struggling upward toward the
light.

There is another item to be taken into account in estimating
the value of a product, to which we must give just a thought in
passing, *i. e.*, the necessary waste of material in the making.

The Sultan of Turkey once sent to China to procure a *fac sim-
ile* of some elegant plates he had had, all of which were now broken but one and that, unfortunately, was cracked. He sent this
one as a pattern and requested that the set be renewed exactly
like the former ones. He was surprised on receiving the plates to
note the fabulous sum charged for them,—but the Celestial explained that the cost was greatly increased by having *to put in
the crack*,—so many had been lost in the making.

The anecdote is not my own, but it suggests a thought that
may be useful to us and I borrow it for that purpose. They tell us
that the waste of material is greater in making colored men and
women than in the case of others—that a larger percentage of
our children die under twenty-one years of age, especially in
large cities, and that a larger number who reach that age and beyond, are to be classed among the world's invalids and paupers.
According to the census of 1880 the average death rate throughout the country was, among the whites 14.74 per 1000; among
colored 17.28 per 1000: the highest among whites being in New
Mexico, 22.04, lowest in Arizona, 7.91 per 1000. Among colored, the mortality ranges from 35.25 in the District of Columbia where it is the highest, to 1.89 in Arizona, the lowest.

For 1889 the relative death-rate of the two races in the District
of Columbia was: whites, 15.96 per 1000; colored, 30.48, about
double. In 1888 they stood 18+ to 30+; in 1886 and '87, about 17
to 31; in '85 and '86, 17 to 32. Especially noticeable is the difference in the mortality of children. This is simply alarming. The
report for 1889 shows that out of the 5,152 deaths occurring in
the District of Columbia during that year, 634 were white infants under one year old, while 834, an excess of 200, within the
same limits were colored. Yet the white population of the District outnumbers the colored two to one. The Health Commissioner, in his report for that year, says: "This material difference
in mortality may be charged to a great extent to the massing of

colored people in alleys and unhealthy parts of the city and to their unsanitary surroundings: while there is no doubt that a very large proportion of these children die in consequence of being fed improper and unhealthy food, especially cheap and badly prepared condensed milk, and cow's milk which has been allowed to stand to the point of acidity after having been kept in vessels badly or unskillfully cleaned." And he adds, "if the general statistics of infant mortality seem astounding to the public, the cause can most frequently be found in the reprehensible custom of committing little impoverished waifs to hired nurses and foul feeding bottles rather than allow them the food that nature has provided."

Now all this unquestionably represents a most wanton and flagrant *waste* of valuable material. By sapping out the possibilities of a healthy and vigorous existence it is deliberately and flagitiously breeding and multiplying paupers, criminals, idiots, drunkards, imbeciles and lunatics to infest and tax the commonwealth. The number spoiled in the making necessarily adds to the cost of those who survive. It is like the Sultan's cracked dinner-plates. It is no use to go into hysterics and explode in Ciceronian philippics[2] against life insurance companies for refusing to insure or charging a higher premium for colored policies. With them it is simply a question of dollars and cents. What are you worth? What are your chances, and what does it cost to take your risks in the aggregate? If thirty-five colored persons out of every thousand are, from any cause whatever, lost in the making, the remaining nine hundred and sixty-five will have to share the loss among them. This is an unavoidable law. No man can dissociate himself from his kind. The colored gentleman who keeps his horses, fares sumptuously, and lives in luxury is made to feel the death gasps of every squalid denizen of the alley and poor-house. It is God's own precaution to temper our self-seeking by binding our sympathies and interests indissolubly with the helpless and the wretched.

What our men of means need to do, then, is to devote their money, their enlightened interest, their careful attention to the improvement of sanitation among the poor. Let some of those who can command real estate in healthful localities build sweet and clean and wholesome tenements *on streets* and rent them at reasonable rates to the worthy poor who are at present forced into association with the vileness and foulness of alleys and filthy courts by the unfeeling discrimination of white dealers. Let some colored capitalists buy up a few of those immense estates in the South, divide them into single farms with neat, cheery, well-ventilated, healthsome cottages to be rented to the colored tenants who are toiling all these weary years in the one-room log hut, like their own cheerless mules—just to fodder themselves.

In cities, low priced houses on streets are almost uniformly kept for the white poor. I know of numerous houses in Washington the rent of which is no dearer than colored people are paying in alleys—but the advertisement says, "not rented to colored people." If the presence of a colored tenant in a neighborhood causes property to depreciate, it may be a question of sentiment,—it must be a question of business. The former it is superfluous to inveigh against or even to take cognizance of. It is possibly subject to enlightenment, and probably a sickness not unto death. But the practical reason underlying it is directly our concern and should command our energetic consideration. It is largely a question of what are we worth—and as such, subject to our immediate responsibility and amendment. If improvement is possible, if it is in our power to render ourselves *valuable* to a community or neighborhood, it should be the work of the earnest and able men and women among us, the moral physicians and reformers, to devise and apply a remedy. Sure it is that the burden rests on all till the deliverance comes. The richest and most highly favored cannot afford to be indifferent or to rest quietly complacent.

In rural districts, the relative mortality of colored people is not so excessive, still the poverty and destitution, the apparent dearth of accumulation notwithstanding ceaseless drudging toil is something phenomenal in labor statistics. I confess I have felt little enthusiasm for the labor riots which seem epidemic at the North. Carnegie's men at Homestead, for instance, were among the best paid workmen in the country, receiving many of them $240 per month, living luxuriously, dictating their own terms as to who should work with them, how many hours, and what special labor they will perform. Their employers are forced to hire so many and such men—for these laboring despots insist on an exact division of labor, no one must be called on to work outside his specialty. Then they must share profits, but be excused from all concern in losses—a patent adjustable sliding scale for wages which slides up beautifully, but never down! If the Northern laboring man has not become a tyrant, I would like to know what tyranny is.

But I wonder how many know that there are throughout the Southland able bodied, hard working men, toiling year in and year out, from sunrise to dusk, for fifty cents per day, out of which they must feed and shelter and clothe themselves and their families! That they often have to take their wage in tickets convertible into meat, meal and molasses at the village grocery, owned by the same ubiquitous employer! That there are tenants holding leases on farms who toil sixteen hours to the day and work every chick and child in their posession, not sparing even the drudging wife—to find at the end of the harvesting season and the squaring up of accounts that their accumulations have been like gathering water in a sieve.

Do you ask the cause of their persistent poverty? It is not found in the explanation often vouchsafed by the white landlord—that the Negro is indolent, improvident and vicious. Taking them man for man and dollar for dollar, I think you will find the Negro, in ninety-nine cases out of a hundred, not a whit behind the Anglo-Saxon of equal chances. It is a fact which every candid man who rides through the rural districts in the South will admit, that in progressive aspirations and industry the Negro is ahead of the white man of his chances. Indeed it would not be hard to show that the white man *of his chances* does not exist. The "Crackers" and "poor-whites" were never slaves, were never oppressed or discriminated against. Their time, their earnings, their activities have always been at their own disposal; and pauperism in their case can be attributed to nothing but stagnation,—moral, mental, and physical immobility: while in the case of the Negro, poverty can at least be partially accounted for by the hard conditions of life and labor,—the past oppression and continued repression which form the vital air in which the Negro lives and moves and has his being.

One often hears in the North an earnest plea from some

lecturer for "our working girls" (of course this means white working girls). And recently I listened to one who went into pious agonies at the thought of the future mothers of Americans having to stand all day at shop counters; and then advertised with applause a philanthropic firm who were giving their girls a trip to Europe for rest and recreation! I am always glad to hear of the establishment of reading rooms and social entertainments to brighten the lot of any women who are toiling for bread—whether they are white women or black women. But how many have ever given a thought to the pinched and down-trodden colored women bending over wash-tubs and ironing boards—with children to feed and house rent to pay, wood to buy, soap and starch to furnish—lugging home weekly great baskets of clothes for families who pay them for a month's laundrying barely enough to purchase a substantial pair of shoes!

Will you call it narrowness and selfishness, then, that I find it impossible to catch the fire of sympathy and enthusiasm for most of these labor movements at the North?

I hear these foreigners, who would boycott an employer if he hired a colored workman, complain of wrong and oppression, of low wages and long hours, clamoring for eight-hour systems and insisting on their right to have sixteen of the twenty-four hours for rest and self-culture, for recreation and social intercourse with families and friends—ah, come with me, I feel like saying, I can show you workingmen's wrong and workingmen's toil which, could it speak, would send up a wail that might be heard from the Potomac to the Rio Grande; and *should it unite and act*, would shake this country from Carolina to California.

But no man careth for their souls. The labor interests of the colored man in this country are as yet dumb and limp. The unorganized mass has found neither tongue nor nerve. In the free and liberal North, thanks to the amalgamated associations and labor unions of immigrant laborers, who cannot even speak English,—the colored man is relegated to the occupations of waiter and barber, unless he has a taste for school teaching or politics. A body of men who still need an interpreter to communicate with their employer, will threaten to cut the nerve and paralyze the progress of an industry that gives work to an American-born citizen, or one which takes measures to instruct any apprentice not supported by the labor monopoly. A skilled mechanic, a friend of mine, secured a job in one of our cities and was seen by union men at work on his house. He was immediately ordered in murderous English to take down his scaffolding and leave the town. Refusing to do so, before night he was attacked by a force that overwhelmed him and he was obliged to leave. Such crushing opposition is not alone against colored persons. These amalgamated and other unions hold and are determined to continue holding an impenetrable monopoly on the labor market, assuming supreme censorship as regards the knowledge and practice of their trade.

In the South, on the other hand, where the colored man virtually holds the labor market, he is too uncertain and unorganized to demand anything like a fair share of the products of his toil. And yet the man who thinks, must see that our labor interests lie at the foundation of our material prosperity. The growth of the colored man in this country must for a long time yet be estimated on his value and productiveness as a laborer. In adding up the account the aggregate of the great toiling mass largely overbalances the few who have acquired means and leisure. The nation judges us as workingmen, and poor indeed is that man or race of men who are compelled to toil all the weary years ministering to no higher want than that of bread. To feed is not the chief function of this material that has fallen to our care to be developed and perfected. It is an enormous waste of values to harness the whole man in the narrow furrow, plowing for bread. There are other hungerings in man besides the eternal all-subduing hungering of his despotic stomach. There is the hunger of the eye for beauty, the hunger of the ear for concords, the hungering of the mind for development and growth, of the soul for communion and love, for a higher, richer, fuller living—a more abundant life! And every man owes it to himself to *let nothing in him starve* for lack of the proper food. "What is man," says Shakespeare, "if his chief good and market of his time be but to sleep and feed!" Yet such slavery as that is the settled lot of four-fifths the laboring men of the Southland. This, I contend, is an enormous, a profligate waste of the richest possibilities and the divinest aptitudes. And we owe it to humanity, we owe it pre-eminently to those of our own household, to enlarge and enrich, so far as in us lies, the opportunity and grasp of every soul we can emancipate. Surely there is no greater boon we can bestow on our fellow-man in this life, none that could more truly command his deepest gratitude and love, than to disclose to his soul its possibilities and mend its opportunities,—to place its rootlets in the generous loam, turn its leaves towards the gracious dews and warm sunlight of heaven and let it grow, let it mature in foliage, flower and fruit for GOD AND THE RACE! Philanthropy will devise means—an object is not far to seek.

Closely akin to the value that may be said to have been wasted through the inclemency and barrenness of circumstance, through the sickness, sin and death that wait on poverty and squalor, a large item of worth has undoubtedly been destroyed by mistaken and unscientific manufacture—foolhardy educators rashly attempting to put in some theoretically desirable *crack*—the classical crack, or the professional crack, or the artistic-æsthetic-accomplishments crack—into material better fitted for household pottery and common every-day stone and iron ware. I want nothing I may say to be construed into an attack on classical training or on art development and culture. I believe in allowing every longing of the human soul to attain its utmost reach and grasp. But the effort must be a fizzle which seeks to hammer souls into preconstructed molds and grooves which they have never longed for and cannot be made to take comfort in. The power of appreciation is the measure of an individual's aptitudes; and if a boy hates Greek and Latin and spends all his time whittling out steamboats, it is rather foolish to try to force him into the classics. There may be a locomotive in him, but there is certainly no foreshadowing evidence of either the teacher or preacher. It is a waste of forces to strain his incompetence, and smother his proficiencies. If his hand is far more cunning and clever than his brain, see what he can best do, and give him a chance according to his fitness; try him at a trade.

Industrial training has been hitherto neglected or despised among us, due, I think, as I have said elsewhere, to two causes: first, a mistaken estimate of labor arising from its association with slavery and from its having been despised by the only class in the South thought worthy of imitation; and secondly, the fact that the Negro's ability to work had never been called in question, while his ability to learn Latin and construe Greek syntax needed to be proved to sneering critics. "Scale the heights!" was the cry. "Go to college, study Latin, preach, teach, orate, wear spectacles and a beaver!"

Stung by such imputations as that of Calhoun that if a Negro could prove his ability to master the Greek subjunctive he might vindicate his title to manhood, the newly liberated race first shot forward along this line with an energy and success which astonished its most sanguine friends.

This may not have been most wise. It certainly was quite natural; and the result is we find ourselves in almost as ludicrous a plight as the African in the story, who, after a sermon from his missionary pleading for the habiliments of civilization, complacently donned a Gladstone hat leaving the rest of his body in its primitive simplicity of attire. Like him we began at the wrong end. Wealth must pave the way for learning. Intellect, whether of races or individuals, cannot soar to the consummation of those sublime products which immortalize genius, while the general mind is assaulted and burdened with "what shall we eat, what shall we drink, and wherewithal shall we be clothed." Work must first create wealth, and wealth leisure, before the untrammeled intellect of the Negro, or any other race, can truly vindicate its capabilities. Something has been done intellectually we all know. That one black man has written a Greek grammar is enough to answer Calhoun's sneer; but it is leisure, the natural outgrowth of work and wealth, which must furnish room, opportunity, possibility for the highest endeavor and most brilliant achievement. Labor must be the solid foundation stone—the *sine qua non* of our material value; and the only effective preparation for success in this, as it seems to me, lies in the establishment of industrial and technical schools for teaching our colored youth trades. This necessity is obvious for several reasons. First, a colored child, in most cases, can secure a trade in no other way. We had master mechanics while the Negro was a chattel, and the ingenuity of brain and hand served to enrich the coffers of his owner. But to-day skilled labor is steadily drifting into the hands of white workmen—mostly foreigners. Here it is cornered. The white engineer holds a tight monopoly both of the labor market and of the science of his craft. Nothing would induce him to take a colored apprentice or even to work beside a colored workman. Unless then trades are to fall among the lost arts for us as a people, they must be engrafted on those benevolent institutions for Negro training established throughout the land. The youth must be taught to use his trigonometry in surveying his own and his neighbor's farm; to employ his geology and chemistry in finding out the nature of the soil, the constituents drafted from it by each year's crop and the best way to meet the demand by the use of suitable renewers; to apply his mechanics and physics to the construction and handling of machinery—to the intelligent management of iron works and water works and steam works and electric works: One mind in a family or in a town may show a penchant for art, for literature, for the learned professions, or more bookish lore. You will know it when it is there. No need to probe for it. It is a light that cannot be hid under a bushel—and I would try to enable that mind to go the full length of its desires. Let it follow its bent and develop its talent as far as possible: and the whole community might well be glad to contribute its labor and money for the sustenance and cultivation of this brain. Just as earth gives its raw material, its carbons, hydrogen, and oxygen, for the tree which is to elaborate them into foliage, flower and fruit, so the baser elements, bread and money furnished the true brain worker come back to us with compound interest in the rich thought, the invention, the poem, the painting, the statue. Only let us recognize our assignment and not squander our portion in over fond experiments. James Russell Lowell says, "As we cannot make a silk purse out of a sow's ear, no more can we perform the opposite experiment without having a fine lot of spoiled silk on our hands."

With most of us, however, the material, such as it is, has been already delivered. The working of it up is also well under way. The gold, the silver, the wood, the hay, the stubble, whatever there was at hand has all gone in. Now can the world use it? Is there a demand for it, does it perform the functions for which it was made, and is its usefulness greater than the cost of its production? Does it pay expenses and have anything over.

The world in putting these crucial questions to men and women, or to races and nations, classifies them under two heads—as consumers or producers. The man who consumes as much as he produces is simply *nil*. It is no matter to the world economically speaking whether he is in it or out of it. He is merely one more to count in taking the census. The man who consumes more than he produces is a destroyer of the world's wealth and should be estimated precisely as the housekeeper estimates moths and mice. These are the world's parasites, the shirks, the lazy lubbers who hang around rum shops and enter into mutual relationships with lamp posts to bear each the other's burdens, moralizing all the while (wondrous moralists and orators they often are!) and insisting that the world owes them a living! To be sure the world owes them nothing of the kind. The world would consider it a happy riddance from bad rubbish if they would pay up their debt and move over to Mars. Every day they live their unproductive bodies sink and destroy a regular portion of the world's values. At the very lowest estimate, a boy who has reached the age of twenty, has already burned up between three and four thousand dollars of the world's possessions. This is on the very closest and most economical count; I charge him nothing for fuel or lights, allowing him to have warmed by fires that would have burned for others and estimating the cost simply of what he has eaten and worn, *i. e.* the amount which he has actually sunk of the world's wealth. I put his board at the moderate sum of ten dollars per month, and charge him the phenomenally small amount of thirty dollars a year for clothing and incidentals. This in twenty years gives him a debt of three thousand dollars, which no honest man should be willing to leave the world without settling. The world does not owe them a living then—the world only waits for them to square up and change their residence. It is only they who produce more than they consume, that the world owes, or even acknowledges as having any practical value.

Now to which class do we belong? The question must in the first place be an individual one for every man of whatever race: Am I giving to the world an equivalent of what it has given and is giving me? Have I a margin on the outside of consumption for surplus production? We owe it to the world to give out at least as much as we have taken in, but if we aim to be accounted a positive value we must leave it a little richer than we found it. The boy who dies at twenty leaving three thousand dollars in bank to help another, has just paid expenses. If he lives longer it increases his debit and should be balanced by a corresponding increase on the credit side. The life that serves to develop another, the mother who toils to educate her boy, the father who invests his stored-up capital in education, giving to the world the energies and usefulness of his children trained into a well disciplined manhood and womanhood has paid his debt in the very richest coin,—a coin which is always legal tender, a priceless gift, the most precious payment we can make for what we have received. And we may be sure, if we can give no more than a symmetric life, an inspiring thought, a spark caught from a noble endeavor, its value will not be lost.

Previous to 1793 America was able to produce unlimited quantities of cotton, but unable to free the fibre from the seeds. Eli Whitney came to the rescue of the strangled industry and perfected a machine which did the work needed. The deliverance which he wrought was complete. The following year America's exports of cotton to England were increased from not one pound in previous years to 1,600,000 pounds. He gave dollars.

Just before the battle of Quebec Wolf repeated and enjoyed Gray's Elegy saying he valued that gem more highly than the capture of the city before which he was encamped. The next day the city was taken and Wolf was laid to rest. But the world is in debt to both the poet and the soldier—a boundless debt, to the one for an eternal thought-gem, to the other for immortal heroism and devoted patriotism.

Once there lived among men One whom sorrowing millions for centuries since have joyed to call friend—One whose "come unto me ye that are heavy laden" has given solace and comfort to myriads of the human race. *He gave a life.*

We must as individuals compare our cost with what we are able to give. The worth of a race or a nation can be but the aggregate worth of its men and women. While we need not indulge in offensive boasting, it may not be out of place in a land where there is some adverse criticism and not a little unreasonable prejudice, quietly to take account of stock and see if we really represent a value in this great American commonwealth. The average American is never too prejudiced, I think, to have a keen appreciation for the utilities; and he is certainly not behind the rest of the world in his clear perception of the purchasing power of a dollar. Beginning here, then, I find that, exclusive of the billions of wealth *given* by them to enrich another race prior to the passage of the Thirteenth Amendment, the colored people of America to-day hold in their own right $264,000,000 of taxable property; and this is over and above the $50,000,000 which collapsed in the Freedman's Savings Bank when that gigantic iniquity paralyzed the hope and shocked the faith of an inexperienced and unfinancial people.

One would like to be able to give reliable statistics of the agricultural and mechanical products of the colored laborer, but so far I have not been able to obtain them. It is a modest estimate, I am sure, to ascribe fully two-thirds of the 6,940,000 bales of cotton produced in 1888 to Negro cultivation. The reports give estimates only in bulk as to the products of a state or county. Our efficient and capable census enumerators never draw the color line on labor products. You have no trouble in turning to the page that shows exactly what percentage of colored people are illiterate, or just how many have been condemned by the courts; no use taking the trouble to specify whether it was for the larceny of a ginger cake, or for robbing a bank of a cool half million and skipping off to Canada: it's all crime of course, and crime statistics and illiteracy statistics must be accurately detailed—and colored.

Similar commendable handling meets the colored producer from the managers of our Big American Show at Chicago which we are all so nervously anxious shall put the best foot foremost in bowing to the crowned heads and the gracious lords and ladies from over the waters. To allow any invention or mechanism, art or farm product to be accredited a black man would be drawing the color line! And our immaculate American could never be guilty of anything so vile as drawing a color line!!!

I am unable to say accurately, then, just how many bales of cotton, pounds of tobacco, barrels of molasses and bushels of corn and wheat are given to the world through Negro industry. The same difficulty is met in securing authentic information concerning their inventions and patents. The records of the Patent Office at Washington do not show whether a patentee is white or colored. And all inventions and original suggestions made by a colored man before emancipation were necessarily accredited to some white individual, a slave not being able to take the oath administered to the applicant for a patent. Prof. Wright, however, by si...ply collecting through personal inquiry the number of colored patentees which could be remembered and identified by examiners and attorneys practicing before the Patent Office authorities, published upwards of fifty in the A. M. E. Review for April, 1886. Doubtless this number was far within the truth, and many new patents have been taken out since his count was made. Almost daily in my walk I pass an ordinary looking black man, who, I am told, is considering an offer of $30,000 for his patent rights on a corn planter, which, by the way, has been chosen as part of the Ohio exhibit for the Columbian Exposition. He has secured as many as half a dozen patents within a few years and is carrying around a "new machine" in his head every day.

Granville Wood, of Cincinnati, has given valuable returns to the world as an electrician; and there is no estimating the money in the outright gift of this people through unremunerated toil. The Negro does not always show a margin over and above consumption; but this does not necessarily in his case prove that he is not a producer. During the agitations for adverse legislation against the Chinese, the charge was alleged that they spent nothing in the country. They hoarded their earnings, lived on nothing, and finally returned to China to live in luxury and to circulate the wealth amassed in this country. A similar complaint can never be lodged against the Negro. Poor fellow, he generally lives pretty well up to his income. He labors for little and spends it all. He has never yet gained the full consent of his mind to "take his gruel a little thinner" till his little pile has grown a bit. He does not like to seem short. And had he the wage of a thousand a year his big-heartedness would immediately put him under the painful necessity of having it do the entertainment of five thousand. He must eat, and is miserable if he can't dress; and seems on the whole internally fitted every way to the style and pattern of a millionaire, rather than to the plain, plodding, stingy old path of common sense and economy. This is a flaw in the *material* of the creature. The grain just naturally runs that way. If our basal question of economics were put to him: "*What do you give—are you adding something every year to the world's stored up capital?*" His ingenuous answer would be, as the ghost of a smile flits across his mobile lips—"Yea, Lord; I give back *all*. I am even now living on the prospects of next year's income. I give my labor at accommodation rates, and forthwith reconvert my wages into the general circulation. Funds, somehow, don't seem to stick to me. I have no talents, or smaller coins either, hid in a napkin." It will be well for him to learn, however, that it is not what we make but what we save that constitutes wealth. The hod-carrier who toils for $1.50 a day, spending the dollar and laying up the half, is richer than the congressman with an annual income of $5000 and annual duns of $8000. What he most urgently needs to learn is systematic saving. He works hard enough generally—but does not seem able to retrench expenses—to cut off the luxuries which people of greater income and larger foresight, seeing to be costly and unnecessary would deny themselves. He wants to set to work vigorously to widen the margin outside the expenditures. He cannot be too deeply impressed with the fact that tobacco and liquors—even leaving out their moral aspects —are too costly to be indulged in by any who are not living on the interest of capital ready in store. A man living on his earnings should eschew luxuries, if he wishes to produce wealth. But when those luxuries deteriorate manhood, they impoverish and destroy the most precious commodity we can offer the world.

For after all, the highest gifts are not measurable in dollars and cents. Beyond and above the class who run an account with the world and merely manage honestly to pay *in kind* for what they receive, there is a noble army—the Shakespeares and Miltons, the Newtons, Galileos and Darwins,—Watts, Morse, Howe, Lincoln, Garrison, John Brown—a part of the world's roll of honor—whose price of board and keep dwindles into nothingness when compared with what the world owes them; men who have taken of the world's bread and paid for it in immortal thoughts, invaluable inventions, new facilities, heroic deeds of loving self-sacrifice; men who dignify the world for their having lived in it and to whom the world will ever bow in grateful worship as its heroes and benefactors. It may not be ours to stamp our genius in enduring characters—but we can give what we are *at its best*.

Visiting the slave market in Boston one day in 1761, Mrs. John Wheatley was attracted by the modest demeanor and intelligent countenance of a delicate looking black girl just from the slave ship. She was quite nude save for a piece of coarse carpet she had tied about her loins, and the only picture she could give of her native home was that she remembered her mother in the early morning every day pouring out water before the rising sun. The benevolent Mrs. Wheatley expended some labor in polishing up this crude gem, and in 1773 the gifted Phillis gave to the world a small octavo volume of one hundred and twenty precious pages, published in London and dedicated to the Countess of Huntingdon.[3] In 1776, for some lines she had sent him, she received from the greatest American the following tribute dated at Cambridge:

MISS PHILLIS:— ... I thank you most sincerely for your polite notice of me in the elegant lines you enclosed; and however undeserving I may be of such encomium and panegyric, the style and manner exhibit a striking proof of your poetical talents; in honor of which and as a tribute justly due to you, I would have published the poem had I not been apprehensive that, while I only meant to give the world this new instance of your genius, I might have incurred the imputation of vanity. This and nothing else determined me not to give it place in the public prints. If you should ever come to Cambridge or near headquarters, I shall be happy to see a person so favored by the Muses, and to whom nature has been so liberal and beneficent in her dispensations. I am, with great respect,

YOUR OBEDIENT HUMBLE SERVANT,
GEORGE WASHINGTON.

That girl paid her debts *in song.*

In South Carolina there are two brothers, colored men, who own and conduct one of the most extensive and successful farms in this country for floriculture. Their system of irrigating and fertilizing is the most scientific in the state, and by their original and improved methods of grafting and cultivating they have produced a new and rich variety of the rose called *Loiseaux*, from their name. Their roses are famous throughout Europe and are specially prized by the French for striking and marvellous beauty. The Loiseaux brothers send out the incense of their grateful returns to the world in the *sweet fragrance of roses.*

Some years ago a poor and lowly orphan girl stood with strange emotions before a statue of Benjamin Franklin in Boston. Her bosom heaved and her eyes filled as she whispered between her clenched teeth, "Oh, how I would like to make a stone man?" Wm. Lloyd Garrison became her providence and enlarged her opportunity; *she paid for it* in giving to the world the *Madonna with the Christ and adoring Angels,* now in the collection of the Marquis of Bute. From her studio in Rome Edmonia Lewis,[4] the colored sculptress, continues to increase the debt of the world to her by her graceful thoughts in the chaste marble.

On May 27, 1863, a mixed body of troops in blue stood eagerly expectant before a rebel stronghold. On the extreme right of the line, a post of honor and of danger, were stationed the Negro troops, the first and third regiments of the Louisiana Native Guards.[5] On going into action, says an eye witness, they were 1080 strong, and formed into four lines, Lieut.-Colonel Bassett, 1st Louisiana, forming the first line, and Lieut.-Colonel Henry Finnegas the second. Before any impression had been made upon the earth works of the enemy, and in full face of the batteries belching forth their sixty-two pounders, the order to charge was given,—and the black regiment rushed forward to encounter grape, canister, shell and musketry, having no artillery but two small howitzers—which seemed mere pop-guns to their adversaries—and with no reserve whatever. The terrible fire from the rebel guns upon the unprotected masses mowed them down like grass. Colonel Bassett being driven back, Colonel Finnegas took his place, and his men being similarly cut to pieces, Bassett reformed and recommenced. And thus these brave fellows went on from 7 o'clock in the morning till 3:30 p. m., under the most hideous carnage that men ever had to withstand. During this time they rallied and were ordered to make six distinct charges, losing thirty-seven killed, one hundred and fifty-five wounded, and one hundred and sixteen missing, "the majority, if not all of these," adds a correspondent of the *New York Times,* who was an eye witness of the fight, "being in all probability now lying dead on the gory field without the rights of sepulture! *for when, by flag of truce our forces in other directions were permitted to reclaim their dead, the benefit, through some neglect, was not extended to these black regiments.*"

"The deeds of heroism," he continues, "performed by these colored men were such as the proudest white men might emulate. Their colors are torn to pieces by shot, and literally bespattered by blood and brains. The color-sergeant of the 1st La. on being mortally wounded, hugged the colors to his breast when a struggle ensued between the two color-corporals on each side of him as to who should bear the sacred standard—and during this generous contention one of the corporals was wounded. One black lieutenant mounted the enemy's works three or four times, and in one charge the assaulting party came within fifty paces of them. If only ordinarily supported by artillery and reserve, no one can convince us that they would not have opened a passage through the enemy's works. Captain Callioux, of the 1st La., a man so black that he prided himself on his blackness, died the death of a hero leading on his men in the thickest of the fight. One poor wounded fellow came along with his arm shattered by a shell, jauntily swinging it with the other, as he said to a friend of mine: 'Massa, guess I can fight no more.' I was with one of the captains looking after the wounded, when we met one limping along toward the front. Being asked where he was going, he said, 'I been shot in de leg, cap'n, an' dey wants me to go to de hospital—but I reckon I c'n gib 'em some mo' yit.'"

Says Major-General Banks in the report from Headquarters of the Army of the Gulf, before Port Hudson, May 30, 1863, writing to Major-General Halleck, General-in-Chief at Washington: "The position occupied by the Negro troops was one of importance and called for the utmost steadiness and bravery in those to whom it was confided. It gives me pleasure to report that they answered every expectation. Their conduct was heroic. No troops could be more determined or more daring."

> "'Charge!' Trump and drum awoke,
> Onward the bondmen broke;
> Bayonet and sabre-stroke
> Vainly opposed their rush.
> Through the wild battle's crush,

With but one thought aflush,
Driving their lords like chaff,
In the guns' mouths they laugh;
Or at the slippery brands
Leaping with open hands,
Down they bear man and horse,
Down in their awful course;
Trampling with bloody heel
Over the crashing steel,
All their eyes forward bent,
Rushed the black regiment.

'Freedom!' their battle-cry—
'Freedom! or leave to die!'
Ah! and they meant the word,
Not as with us 'tis heard,
Not a mere party-shout:
*They gave their spirits out.*
Trusted the end to God,
And on the gory sod
Rolled in triumphant blood!"

And thus they paid *their debt.* "They gave—*their spirits out!*"
In the heart of what is known as the "Black Belt" of Alabama
and within easy reach of the great cotton plantations of Georgia,
Mississippi, and Florida, a devoted young colored man ten years
ago started a school with about thirty Negro children assembled
in a comical looking shanty at Tuskegee.[6] His devotion was contagious and his work grew; an abandoned farm of 100 acres was
secured and that gradually grew to 640 acres, largely wood-land,
on which a busy and prosperous school is located; and besides a
supply farm was added, of heavy rich land, 800 acres, from which
grain and sugar cane are main products. Since 1881, 2,947 students have been taught here, of whom 102 have graduated, while
200 more have received enough training to fit them to do good
work as teachers, intelligent farmers, and mechanics. The latest
enrollment shows girls, 247; boys, 264. Of the 102 graduates, 70
per cent are teachers, ministers and farmers. They usually combine teaching and farming. Three are printers (learned the trades

at school), one is a tinner, one a blacksmith, one a wheel-wright, three are merchants, three are carpenters, others in the professions or filling miscellaneous positions.

That man is paying his debt by giving to this country *living, working, consecrated men and women!*

Now each can give something. It may not be a poem, or marble bust, or fragrant flower even; it may not be ours to place our lives on the altar of country as a loving sacrifice, or even to devote our living activities so extensively as B. T. Washington[7] to supplying the world's need for strong and willing helpers. But we can at least *give ourselves.* Each can be *one* of those strong willing helpers—even though nature has denied him the talent of endlessly multiplying his force. And nothing less can honorably cancel our debt. Each is under a most sacred obligation not to squander the material committed to him, not to sap its strength in folly and vice, and to see at the least that he delivers a product worthy the labor and cost which have been expended on him. A sound manhood, a true womanhood is a fruit which the lowliest can grow. And it is a commodity of which the supply never exceeds the demand. There is no danger of the market being glutted. The world will always want *men.* The worth of one is infinite. To this value all other values are merely relative. Our money, our schools, our governments, our free institutions, our systems of religion and forms of creeds are all first and last to be judged by this standard: what sort of men and women do they grow? How are men and women being shaped and molded by this system of training, under this or that form of government, by this or that standard of moral action? You propose a new theory of education; *what sort of men does it turn out?* Does your system make boys and girls superficial and mechanical? Is it a producing of average percentages or a rounding out of manhood,—a sound, thorough, and practical development,—or a scramble for standing and marks?

We have a notion here in America that our political institutions,—the possibilities of a liberal and progressive democracy, founded on universal suffrage and in some hoped-for, providential way *compelling* universal education and devotion,— our peculiar American attainments are richly worth all they have cost in blood and anguish. But our form of government, divinely ordered as we dream it to be, must be brought to the bar to be tested by this standard. It is nothing worth of itself— independently of whether it furnishes a good atmosphere in which to cultivate men. Is it developing a self respecting freedom, a sound manliness on the part of *the individual*—or does it put into the power of the wealthy few the opportunity and the temptation to corrupt the many? If our vaunted *"rule of the people"* does not breed nobler men and women than monarchies have done—it must and will inevitably give place to something better.

I care not for the theoretical symmetry and impregnable logic of your moral code, I care not for the hoary respectability and traditional mysticisms of your theological institutions, I care not for the beauty and solemnity of your rituals and religious ceremonies, I care not even for the reasonableness and unimpeachable fairness of your social ethics,—if it does not turn out better, nobler, truer men and women,—if it does not add to the world's stock of valuable souls,—if it does not give us a sounder, healthier, more reliable product from this great factory of *men*—I will have none of it. I shall not try to test your logic, but weigh your results—and that test is the *measure of the stature of the fullness of a man.* You need not formulate and establish the credibility and authenticity of Christian Evidences, when you can demonstrate and prove the present value of CHRISTIAN MEN. And this test for systems of belief, for schools of thought, and for theories of conduct, is also the ultimate and inevitable test of nations, of races and of individuals. What sort of men do you turn out? *How* are you supplying the great demands of the world's market? What is your true value? This, we may be sure, will be the final test by which the colored man in America will one-day be judged in the cool, calm, unimpassioned, unprejudiced second thought of the American people.

Let us then quietly commend ourselves to this higher court— this final tribunal. Short sighted idiosyncracies are but transient phenomena. It is futile to combat them, and unphilosophical to be depressed by them. To allow such things to overwhelm us, or even to absorb undue thought, is an admission of weakness. As sure as time *is—these mists will clear away.* And the world— our world, will surely and unerringly see us as we are. Our only care need be the intrinsic worth of our contributions. If we represent the ignorance and poverty, the vice and destructiveness, the vagabondism and parasitism in the world's economy, no amount of philanthropy and benevolent sentiment can win for us esteem: and if we contribute a positive value in those things the world prizes, no amount of negrophobia can ultimately prevent its recognition. And our great "problem" after all is to be solved not by brooding over it, and orating about it, but by *living into it.*

## The Gain from a Belief

A solitary figure stands in the market-place, watching as from some lonely tower the busy throng that hurry past him. A strange contrast his cold, intellectual eye to the eager, strained, hungry faces that surge by in their never ending quest of wealth, fame, glory, bread.

Mark his pallid cheek and haggard brow, and the fitful gleam of those restless eyes like two lone camp-fires on a deserted plain.

Why does that smile, half cynical, half sad, flit across his countenance as he contemplates these mighty heart-throbs of human passions and woes, human hopes and human fears? Is it pity—is it contempt—is it hate for this struggling, working, believing humanity which curls those lips and settles upon that hitherto indifferent brow?

Who is he?

Earth's skepticism looking on at the protean antics of earth's enthusiasms. Speculative unbelief, curiously and sneeringly watching the humdrum, common-place, bread-and-butter toil of unspeculative belief. Lofty, unimpassioned agnosticism, *that thinks*—face to face with hobbling, blundering, unscientific faith, *that works.*

Dare we approach?

"Sir: I perceive you are not drawn into the whirl-pool of hurrying desires that sweep over earth's restless sons. Your philosophy,

I presume, lifts you above the toils and anxieties the ambitions and aspirations of the common herd. Pardon me, but do you not feel called to devote those superior powers of yours to the uplifting of your less favored brethren? May not you pour the oil of human kindness and love on these troubled waters? May not your wisdom shape and direct the channel of this tortuous stream, building up here, and clearing out there, till this torrent become once more a smiling river, reflecting Heaven's pure love in its silvery bosom, and again this fruitful valley blossom with righteousness and peace? Does not your soul burn within you as you look on this seething mass of struggling, starving, sinning souls? Are you not inspired to lift up despairing, sinking, grovelling man,—to wipe the grime and tears from his marred countenance, and bid him Look aloft and be strong, Repent and be saved, Trust God and live!"

Ah! the coldness of the look he turned on me! Methought 'twould freeze my soul. "Poor fool!" it seemed to say; and yet I could not but think I discovered a trace of sadness as he replied:—

"What is man?—A curiously fashioned clock; a locomotive, capable of sensations;—a perfected brute. Man is a plant that grows and thinks; the form and place of his growth and the product of his thought are as little dependent on his will or effort as are the bark, leaves, and fruit of a tree on its choice. Food, soil, climate,—these make up the man,—the whole man, his life, his soul (if he have one). Man's so-called moral sense is a mere dance of molecules; his spiritual nature, a pious invention. Remorse is a blunder, repentance is vain, self-improvement or reformation an impossibility. The laws of matter determine the laws of intellect, and these shape man's nature and destiny and are as inevitable and uncontrollable as are the laws of gravitation and chemical affinity. You would-be reformers know not the stupendous non-sense you are talking. Man is as little responsible for vice or crime as for fever or an earthquake. Those in whom the cerebrum shows a particular formation, will make their holidays in gambling, betting, drinking, horseracing—their more serious pursuits in stealing, ravening, murdering. They are not immoral any more than a tiger is immoral; they are simply *un*moral. They need to be restrained, probably, as pests of society, or submitted to treatment as lunatics. Their fellows in whom the white and gray matter of the brain cells are a little differently correlated, will in their merry moods sing psalms and make it their habitual activity to reach out after the Unknown in various ways, trying to satisfy the vague and restless longings of what they call their souls by punishing themselves and pampering the poor. I have neither blame nor praise. Each class simply believe and do as they must. And as for God—science finds him not. If there be a God—He is unknown and unknowable. The finite mind of man cannot conceive the Infinite and Eternal. And if such a being exists, he cannot be concerned about the miserable wretches of earth. Searching after him is vain. Man has simply projected his own personality into space and worshipped it as a God—a person—himself. My utmost knowledge is limited to a series of sensations within, aware of itself; and a possibility of sensations without, both governed by unbending laws within the limits of experience and a reasonable distance beyond."

"And beyond that Beyond" I ask breathlessly—"beyond that Beyond?"

I am sure I detected just then a tremor as of a chill running through that fragile frame and the eye, at first thoughtful and coldly scornful only, is now unmistakably shaded with sadness. "Beyond that Beyond?" he repeated slowly,—beyond that Beyond, *if* there be such,—*spaces of darkness and eternal silence!*

Whether this prolonged throb of consciousness exist after its external possibilities have been dissolved—I cannot tell. That is to me —a horrible plunge—*in the dark!* I stand at the confluence of two eternities and three immensities. I see, with Pascal, only infinities in all directions which envelop me like an atom—like a shadow which endures for a moment and—will never return! All that I know is that I must die, but what I know the very least of is that very death—which I cannot avoid! *The eternal silence* of these infinite spaces maddens me!"

Sick at heart, I turn away and ask myself what is this system which, in the words of Richter, makes the universe an automaton, and man's future—a coffin! Is this the cold region to which thought, as it moves in its orbit, has brought us in the nineteenth century? Is this the germ of the "Philosophy of the future"—the exponent of our "advanced ideas," the "new light" of which our age so uproariously boasts? Nay rather is not this *monstruum*

*horrendum* of our day but a renewal of the empiricism and skepticism of the days of Voltaire? Here was undoubtedly the nucleus
of the cloud no bigger than a man's hand, which went on increasing in bulk and blackness till it seemed destined to enshroud
earth and heaven in the gloom of hell.

David Hume, who, though seventeen years younger than Voltaire, died in 1776 just two years before the great French skeptic,
taught skepticism in England on purely metaphysical grounds.
Hume knew little or nothing about natural science; but held that
what we call mind consists merely of successive perceptions, and
that we can have no knowledge of anything but phenomena. His
system afterwards passes through France, is borrowed and fil-
tered through the brain of a half crazy French schoolmaster,
Auguste Conte, who thus becomes the founder of the Contist
school of Positivism or Nescience or Agnosticism[1] as it is variously called. The adherents of his school admit neither revelation, nor a God, nor the immortality of the soul. Conte held,
among other things, that two hours a day should be spent in the
worship of Collective Humanity to be symbolized by some of
the *sexe aimant*. On general principles it is not quite clear which
is the *sexe aimant*. But as Conte proceeds to mention one's wife,
mother, and daughter as fitting objects of religious adoration
because they represent the present, past and future of
Humanity—one is left to infer that he considered the female the
*loving sex* and the ones to be worshipped; though he does not set
forth who were to be objects of woman's own adoring worship.
In this ecclesiastical system which Prof. Huxley wittily denomi-
nates *Romanism minus Christianity*, Conte made himself High
Pontiff, and his inamorata, the widow of a galley slave, was chief
saint. This man was founder of the system which the agnostic
prefers to the teachings of Jesus! However, had this been all, the
positivist would have been as harmless as any other lunatic. But
he goes a step farther and sets up his system as the philosophy of
*natural science*, originating in and proved by pure observation
and investigation of physical phenomena; and scoffs at as presumptuous and unwarrantable all facts that cannot be discerned
through the senses. In this last position he is followed by John
Stuart Mill, Herbert Spencer,[2] G. H. Lewes, and a noble army of
physicists, naturalists, physiologists, and geologists. Says one:

"We have no knowledge of anything but phenomena, and the essential nature of phenomena and their ultimate causes are unknown and inscrutable to us." Says another: "All phenomena without exception are governed by invariable laws with which no volitions natural or supernatural interfere." And another: "Final causes are unknown to us and the search after them is fruitless, a mere chase of a favorite will-o-the-wisp. We know nothing about any supposed purposes for which organs 'were made.' Birds fly because they have wings, a true naturalist will never say—he can never know they have wings *in order that* they may fly."

And Mr. Ingersoll, the American exponent of positivism, in his "Why I Am an Agnostic," winds up a glittering succession of epigrammatic inconsistencies with these words: "Let us be honest with ourselves. In the presence of countless mysteries, standing beneath the boundless heaven sown thick with constellations, knowing that each grain of sand, each leaf, each blade of grass, asks of every mind the answerless question; knowing that the simplest thing defies solution; feeling that we deal with the superficial and the relative and that we are forever eluded by the real, the absolute,—let us admit the limitations of our minds, and let us have the courage and the candor to say: we do not know."

It is no part of my purpose to enter into argument against the agnostics. Had I the wish, I lack the ability. It is enough for me to know that they have been met by foemen worthy their steel and that they are by no means invincible.

"The average man," says Mr. Ingersoll, "does not reason—he feels." And surely 'twere presumption for an average woman to attempt more. For my part I am content to 'feel.' The brave Switzer who sees the awful avalanche stealing down the mountain side threatening death and destruction to all he holds dear, hardly needs any very correct ratiocination on the mechanical and chemical properties of ice. He *feels* there is danger nigh and there is just time for him to sound the tocsin of alarm and shout to his dear ones 'fly!'

For me it is enough to know that by this system God and Love are shut out; prayer becomes a mummery; the human will but fixed evolutions of law; the precepts and sanctions of morality a lie; the sense of responsibility a disease. The desire for reformation and for propagating conviction is thus a fire consuming its tender. Agnosticism has nothing to impart. Its sermons are the exhortations of one who convinces you he stands on nothing and urges you to stand there too. If your creed is that nothing is sure, there is certainly no spur to proselytize. As in an icicle the agnostic abides alone. The vital principle is taken out of all endeavor for improving himself or bettering his fellows. All hope in the grand possibilities of life are blasted. The inspiration of beginning now a growth which is to mature in endless development through eternity is removed from our efforts at self culture. The sublime conception of life as the seed-time of character for the growing of a congenial inner-self to be forever a constant conscious presence is changed into the base alternative conclusion, *Let us eat and drink for to-morrow we die.*

To my mind the essence of the poison is just here. As far as the metaphysical grounds for skepticism are concerned, they are as harmless to the masses as if they were entombed in Greek or Hebrew. Many of the terms, it is true, are often committed to memory and paraded pretty much in the spirit of the college sophomore who affects gold-bowed spectacles and stooping shoulders—it is scholarly, you know. But the real reasons for and against agnosticism rest on psychological and scientific facts too abstruse for the laity to appreciate. There is much subtle sophistry in the oracular utterances of a popular speaker like Mr. Ingersoll, which catch the fancy and charm the imagination of the many. His brilliant blasphemies like the winged seed of the thistle are borne on the slightest breath of wind and find lodgment in the shallowest of soils; while the refutation of them, undertaken in a serious and logical vein is often too conclusive to convince: that is, it is too different in kind to reach the same class of minds that have been inoculated with the poison germs.

My own object, however, is neither to argue nor to refute argument here. I want to utter just this one truth:—The great, the fundamental need of any nation, any race, is for heroism, devotion, sacrifice; and there cannot be heroism, devotion, or sacrifice in a primarily skeptical spirit. A great man said of France, when she was being lacerated with the frantic stripes of her hysterical children,—*France needs a religion!* And the need of

France during her trying Revolution is the need of every crisis and conflict in the evolution of nations and races. At such times most of all, do men need to be anchored to what they *feel* to be eternal verities. And nothing else at any time can propel men into those sublime efforts of altruism which constitute the moral heroes of humanity. The demand for heroism, devotion and sacrifice founded on such a faith is particularly urgent in a race at almost the embryonic stage of character-building. The Hour is *now*;—where is the man? He must *believe* in the infinite possibilities of devoted self-sacrifice and in the eternal grandeur of a human idea heroically espoused. It is the enthusiasms, the faiths of the world that have heated the crucibles in which were formed its reformations and its impulses toward a higher growth. And I do not mean by faith the holding of correct views and unimpeachable opinions on mooted questions, merely; nor do I understand it to be the ability to forge cast-iron formulas and dub them TRUTH. For while I do not deny that absolute and eternal truth *is*,—still truth must be infinite, and as incapable as infinite space, of being encompassed and confined by one age or nation, sect or country—much less by one little creature's finite brain.

To me, faith means *treating the truth as true*. Jesus *believed* in the infinite possibilities of an individual soul. His faith was a triumphant realization of the eternal development of *the best* in man—an optimistic vision of the human aptitude for endless expansion and perfectibility. This truth to him placed a sublime valuation on each individual sentiency—a value magnified infinitely by reason of its immortal destiny. He could not lay hold of this truth and let pass an opportunity to lift men into nobler living and firmer building. He could not lay hold of this truth and allow his own benevolence to be narrowed and distorted by the trickeries of circumstance or the colorings of prejudice.

Life must be something more than dilettante speculation. And religion (ought to be if it isn't) a great deal more than mere gratification of the instinct for worship linked with the straight-teaching of irreproachable credos. Religion must be *life made true*; and life is action, growth, development—begun now and ending never. And a life made true cannot confine itself—it must reach out and twine around every pulsing interest within reach of its uplifting tendrils. If then you *believe* that intemperance is a growing vice among a people within touch of your sympathies; if you see that, whereas the "Lord had shut them in," so that from inheritance there are but few cases of alcoholized blood,— yet that there is danger of their becoming under their changed circumstances a generation of inebriates—if you believe this, then this is your truth. Take up your parable and in earnestness and faith *give it out* by precept and by example.

Do you *believe* that the God of history often chooses the weak things of earth to confound the mighty, and that the Negro race in America has a veritable destiny in His eternal purposes,— then don't spend your time discussing the 'Negro Problem' amid the clouds of your fine havanna, ensconced in your friend's well-cushioned arm-chair and with your patent leather boot-tips elevated to the opposite mantel. Do those poor "cowards in the South" need a leader—then get up and lead them! Let go your purse-strings and begin to *live* your creed. Or is it your modicum of truth that God hath made of one blood all nations of the earth; and that all interests which specialize and contract the broad, liberal, cosmopolitan idea of universal brotherhood and equality are narrow and pernicious, then treat that truth as true. Don't inveigh against lines of longitude drawn by others when at the same time you are applying your genius to devising lines of latitude which are neither race lines, nor character lines, nor intelligence lines—but certain social-appearance circlets assorting your "universal brotherhood" by shapes of noses and texture of hair. If you object to imaginary lines—don't draw them! Leave only the real lines of nature and character. And so whatever the vision, the revelation, the idea, vouchsafed *you*,

> Think it truly and thy thoughts shall the soul's famine feed. *Speak*
> it truly and each word of thine shall be a fruitful seed; *Live* it truly
> and thy life shall be a grand and holy creed!

Macaulay has left us in his masterly description of Ignatius Loyola a vivid picture of the power of a belief and its independence of material surroundings.

'On the road from the Theatine convent in Venice might have been seen once a poor crippled Spaniard, wearily but as fast as his injured limbs can carry him making his way toward Rome.

His face is pinched, his body shrunken, from long fast and vigil. He enters the City of the Cæsars without money, without patrons, without influence! but there burns a light in his eye that reeks not of despair. In a frequented portion of a busy street he stops and mounts a stone, and from this rude rostrum begins to address the passers by in barbarous Latin. Lo, there is contagion in the man! He has actually imparted of his spirit to that mottled audience! And now the same fire burns in a hundred eyes, that shone erewhile from his. Men become his willing slaves to do his bidding even unto the ends of the earth. With what courage, what zeal, what utter self-abnegation, with what blind devotion to their ends regardless of means do they preach, teach, write, act! Behind the thrones of kings, at the bedside of paupers, under every disguise in every land, mid pestilence and famine, in prisons oft, in perils by land and perils by sea, the Jesuit, undaunted, pursues his way.'

Do you seek to know the secret charm of Ignatius Loyola, the hidden spring of the Jesuit's courage and unfaltering purpose? It is these magic words, "*I believe.*" That is power. That is the stamping attribute in every impressive personality, that is the fire to the engine and the moter force in every battery. That is the live coal from the altar which at once unseals the lips of the dumb—and that alone which makes a man a positive and not a negative quantity in the world's arithmetic. With this potent talisman man no longer "abideth alone." He cannot stand apart, a cold spectator of earth's pulsing struggles. The flame must burst forth. The idea, the doctrine, the device for betterment must be imparted. "*I believe,*"—this was strength and power to Paul, to Mohammed, to the Saxon Monk and the Spanish Zealot,—and they must be our strength if our lives are to be worth the living. They mean as much today as they did in the breast of Luther or of Loyola. Who cheats me of this robs me of both shield and spear. Without them I have no inspiration to better myself, no inclination to help another.

It is small service to humanity, it seems to me, to open men's eyes to the fact that the world rests on nothing. Better the turtle of the myths, than a *perhaps*. If "fooled they must be, though wisest of the wise," let us help to make them the fools of virtue. You may have learned that the pole star is twelve degrees from the pole and forbear to direct your course by it—preferring your needle taken from earth and fashioned by man's device. The slave brother, however, from the land of oppression once saw the celestial beacon and dreamed not that it ever deviated from due North.[3] He *believed* that *somewhere* under its beckoning light, lay a far away country where a man's a man. He sets out with his heavenly guide before his face—would you tell him he is pursuing a wandering light? Is he the poorer for his ignorant hope? Are you the richer for your enlightened suspicion?

Yes, I believe there is existence beyond our present experience; that that existence is conscious and culturable; and that there is a noble work here and now in helping men to live *into* it.

> "Not in Utopia,—subterraneous fields,—
>    Or some secreted island, Heaven knows where!
>    But in this very world, which is the world
>    Of all of us—the place where in the end
>    We find our happiness, or not at all!"

There are nations still in darkness to whom we owe a light. The world is to be moved one generation forward—whether by us, by blind force, by fate, or by God! If thou believest, all things are possible; and *as* thou believest, so be it unto thee.

# PART II

# ON EDUCATION

This section collates and reproduces for the first time a project Cooper organized as a selection of her key works and writings on education. Published here in the order in which Cooper outlined them, *On Education* includes a compilation of various forms and genres of writing, from plays and pageants to short fiction and essays, in which she argues for and demonstrates her educational philosophy and practice. Cooper's outline organizes the writings into seven parts with the first and last three featuring a single writing and part 4 including five essays ("Foreword," "The Negro's Dialect," "Loss of Speech Through Isolation," "The Higher Calling for the Teacher of Underprivileged Adults," and *The Colored Social Settlement*) under the title "Educational Programs" (see "Introduction," note 12). Taken as a whole, the writings in this section represent the kinds of scholarly and pedagogical interventions Cooper sought to make and include examples of educational programs that engage students in the retelling and performance of historical narratives that center Blacks' contributions to US and world history. They include essays, speeches, and reflections that articulate Cooper's belief in the need for a democratically rooted, Christian education that would recognize access to higher education as a human right and extend it to all people regardless of their race, gender, ability, age, color, class, or station in life. Throughout the selections, Cooper advances her biting critiques of what she identified as an exclusionary, mechanistic, and corporatized approach to education and instead asserts the importance of community self-determination, equal access, and a holistic pedagogical approach that focused on educating the entire person. They also showcase Cooper's vibrant, experimental, and multifaceted approach to education. In the book she outlined, she selected writings that illustrated her willingness to break from conventional modes of education and to use fun, humor, play, and experiential learning to engage her students. The writings she proposed to collect in *On Education* represent works spanning from the early 1900s such as "The Ethics of the Negro Question" (1902) through at least the 1930s, some of which she continued to seek publication outlets for as late as 1958 (see "Letter to Afro-American," in part 4, Additional Correspondences).

# 2

# *From Servitude to Service:*
# *A Pageant*

*(ca. 1940)*

This musical stage production is split into three epi-
sodes wherein Cooper presents various phases of the
founding and development of the United States. A litany of nationally recognized figures in the arts, literature, political organizing, and education, many of
whom were prominent African Americans, appear in
the pageant singing hymns, sorrow songs, poems, and
proclamations as they celebrate African Americans'
foundational contributions toward achieving American
ideals of fairness, justice, and "true Democracy"
for all.

SOURCE: Anna Julia Cooper Papers (Box 23-4, Folder 43),
Moorland-Spingarn Research Center, Howard University.

The contribution from the Negro peoples
to American History

# A PAGEANT IN THREE EPISODES AND FOURTEEN SCENES

*by Anna J. Cooper, Frelinghuysen University*

---

# EPISODE I.
# THE FORMATIVE PERIOD OF THE NATION.

### Exiles

SCENE 1. The Landing at Jamestown:[1] Dutch Traders, 20 Africans, English Settlers.
Overture: **Deep River,** Harry Burleigh
Dance of Ethiopia: **Thaba Nabandji,** S. Coleridge Taylor
Sorrow Songs:[2]
"My Way is Cloudy."
"I'm rolling thro an unfriendly world."
"Roll Jordon roll."
"Standin' in the need of prayer."

*Enter Spirit of Religion who points the way to consolation.*

SOLO—"Steal away to Jesus"
Accompaniment, moans by Exiles
CHORUS, Exiles:
"Everytime I feel the Spirit."
"Nobody knows the trouble I see."
"Swing low Sweet Chariot" (all kneeling)

SCENE 2. Phyllis Wheatley and George Washington

SCENE 3. Benjamin Banneker and Thomas Jefferson

SCENE 4. Crispus Attucks and the English Red Coats.

SCENE 5. Absalom Jones and Richard Allen, founders of African Methodism.

"How firm a foundation" (full chorus strong male voices).

**Interlude.** (In lighter vein).

(a) Juba Dance, Nathaniel Dett
(b) Hoe the corn, Dunbar-Taylor
(c) Banjo pickers and a buck dance
(d) Cotton pickers drill, 12 graceful brown girls with baskets of cotton.
(e) Swanee River
(f) **Southland,** Rosamond Johnson.

# EPISODE II.
# THE CLASH OF IDEALS AND CIVIL CONFLICT.[3]

### The Crux

SCENE 1. Columbia declaims: Battle Hymn of the Republic.
"Glory, Glory Halleluja" (in muffled chorus).
(Narka Lee as Columbia).

SCENE 2. Frederick Douglass, "the Moses of his people."
CHORUS: "Go down Moses"

SCENE 3. John Brown on way to scaffold with colored matron.
"We're coming, Father Abraham."

SCENE 4. G.A.R. Civil War Veterans: Sergeant Carney Color bearer.
"The Flag never touched the ground."
Sojourner Truth—Harriet Tubman.

SCENE 5. Abraham Lincoln signing the Emancipation Proclamation.
Jubilee Singers:
"The Year of Jubilee."
"Didn't my Lord deliver Daniel?" Coleridge-Taylor.
"Children we shall be free."

General B. F. Butler's (1818–1893) tribute to Negro soldiers.
Star Spangled Banner. Salute and pledge.


# EPISODE III.
## COMMUNITY SERVICE.

### A National Asset

In the struggle for true Democracy and the Better America
   Movement.
   A dance of Emancipated Service.

SCENE 1. Home Coming of the boys in Khaki: Pickens'
Marseillaise.

SCENE 2. Patriots and Heroes: Gold Stars in our Service
Flag.
   Major Walker, Lt. Kenneth Lewis, Colonel Young, Major
      Brooks.
   "In Flanders Field."
   "Bow Your Head, Columbia," E. Lee Williams

SCENE 3. The Church: Surpliced choir with crucifer.
   "O God our help in ages past."
   ANTHEM— "'Twere vain O God," Hill-Johnson.

SCENE 4. Father Time, leading a procession of children from
Schools.
   His long cloak symbolizes the Constitution, Amendment
      XIV, visible.
   Children carry banners such as "100% Americans," "Not
      hyphenated," "Genuine F. F. V's.,"[4] "300 years on the
      soil," "Our father's blood seals our patriotism."
   ANTHEM: **Don't be weary traveller,** Nathaniel Dett.
   Father Time: Declaims:
   "I believe the Negro citizens of America should be guaran-
      teed the enjoyment of all their rights; that they have
      earned their full measure of citizenship bestowed; that
      their sacrifices in blood on battlefields of the Republic
      have entitled them to all of freedom and opportunity, all

of sympathy and aid that the American spirit of fairness and justice demands."

SOLO: **Invictus,** Dr. C. Sumner Wormley.

Procession: **Educators.** G. F. T. Cook, Booker T. Washington, Fannie Jackson Coppin, Reason, Clark, Peterson, Garnet, Crumwell.

"Lift Every Voice and Sing." Full chorus. All stanzas. High school cadets, athletes, collegians, Fisk, Atlanta, Howard, Hampton, Tuskegee, scientists, inventors, laborers, stevedores, farmers, porters, riviters, Red Cross, blue triangle, red triangle, community service, Paul Lawrence Dunbar, S. Coleridge-Taylor, Jas. Reese Europe, Layton, Grant, Burleigh, Dett, Tyler, White, Cook, Tanner, May Howard Jackson, Meta Warrick Fuller, etc., etc., artists, painters, sculptors, musicians, seeking the note of inspiration in the common consciousness of race.

Ensemble with special characters in foreground.

Music by Burleigh:

Artists: Come sing us a song of hoeing the corn.
And picking the cotton in bowls;
Where the sweet scuppernong scents the dewy morn
And the mocking bird note trills and trolls.
Oh sing once again the wild plaintive strain
Of the land of the westward sun;
Songs born of the soil from its children of toil,
Where singing and laughter were one.

Refrain: "We're rolling thru an unfriendly world. Nobody knows the trouble, Nobody cares but Jesus, Swing low sweet chariot, swing lower, come, carry me home."

Artists: Nay, is't not your home, O children of song, this land o' the sun o' the West?
Where new comer's roam finding surcease from wrong and a haven of freedom and rest.
Lo, the land of your birth, of your toil, tears and mirth, where your fore-fathers' brawn wrought of yore,
Where brave Attucks died and thousands beside on battlefields red with their gore.
Those graves of your sires, these blest altar fires, those hearth stones enshrined in your hearts;

Can you leave them for aye, will you wander away, while
  the tear of old home longing starts?
Sweet Land, Liberty! Land of the noble free! Just God, do
  not mock! Mote it be!
Sons, gird up anew! Pray, fight, LIVE it true! Till brotherhood resigns from sea to sea.

FINALE: Full Chorus: **America,** All stanzas.

# 3

# Christ's Church:
# A Twentieth-Century Parable

*(no date)*

This contemporary retelling of the parable of the Good Samaritan features a man who is robbed and beaten on his way from the countryside into the city. In his ensuing desperation, he finds Christ's church ostensibly to be a welcoming refuge. Cooper, however, reveals the hypocrisy behind the church's pageantry, showing that the Black man is not truly welcomed at all.

SOURCE: Anna Julia Cooper Papers, box 23-4, folder 31, Moorland-Spingarn Research Center, Howard University.

A certain poor man in mean apparel went down from the rural districts to the city. It is needless to add that he fell among thieves who stripped him of whatever of worth he happened still to possess, leaving him naked and half dead. When he came to himself and looked around he saw a vision of the Good Samaritan gleaming in the brilliant red and gold of a fine old Gothic window nearby. A countenance of ineffable tenderness glowed in the mellow lights of the skillfully wrought glass. The face was sad— oh, so sad—but the sadness was that of infinite pity and love, not of self-centered wretchedness and self-wrought ruin and woe. The hand is extended in benign benediction and kingly hospitality; upon the brow majestic sweetness sits enthroned. The figure breathed, the lips framed a bounteous, a royal *welcome*. The hungry outcast could have sworn he saw the eyes light up as they rested on him. He had known better days, and when younger, much cleaner and far happier, had heard his dear old mother tell about the Good Samaritan.[1]

At any rate he thinks this may be a good house for him to knock at for a little human sympathy and help. He crawls up the white marble steps and stops a moment on the threshold to listen. Strains of delicious music were issuing from within, and groups of well dressed people with subdued, reverential mien, carrying in their hands dainty little books like gilded toys, filed past and were lost in the voluptuousness of soft carpets and elegant cushions beyond. At the door on either side stood, in immaculate shirt front and richest broadcloth a bowing and smiling personage who seemed a sort of master of ceremonies at some grand reception of the elite.

The poor devil at the door was entirely overcome by the splendor of what he saw. His eyes glowed like coals. His fingers fumbled awkwardly at a button on his tattered coat, and he tried hard to gulp down a tear that was choking him. Just then a sweet, rippling sound rose and floated out on the chill air. It was a woman's voice of wonderful pathos and power accompanied by the grand old chords of the organ.

"Come," she was singing. "Come unto me and I will give you rest.

> "*Come, ye that are heavy laden. Come, ye that labor.*
> "*Come, and ye shall find rest unto your souls. Come! Come!*"

The wretch gathered himself up with fresh courage and crept over to one of the elegant gentlemen at the door to see what relief there was in this most generous invitation for all his need and misery. He thought he noticed a start and a look of repulsion on the part of the man at the door, but concluded that he must have been mistaken, for, just then a full chorus came in a grand swell through the open door with the words:

> "For I, like you, have been a man of sorrows;
> "I, like you, have made companionship with grief.
> "Of all your sorrows I have been partaker!
> "Come unto me, come! and you shall find relief. *Shall find relief!*"

The stranger twitched at his shabby old hat and caught his breath. Surely this was just the place that he ought to seek. Such generosity, such munificence, such a heartiness of welcome, as if he, *he* were really wanted and sought for. No questions asked apparently; just, "ye that are heavy laden," kept rippling over the arches and reverberating under the vaulted ceiling, "Ye that are heavy laden. Come! Come!"

"Eh, will you kindly tell me what this is?" asked the bewildered stranger of the magnificent doorkeeper.

"Why this is Christ's Church," was the quick reply with a grand air.

"*Christ's?* Oh, yes;" that NAME, he had heard it before. He rather thought his mother must have known and loved that Name. It had seemed to comfort and gladden her a deal, too, just to whisper it softly to herself sometimes. What recollections of the old days it brought up!

"Ah, yes; Christ's House! *Is He in?*"

—Well, it seems that He was not in!

The stranger, after certain difficult explanations, which proved unaccountably hard for him to take in, was finally made to understand that the gentle folk who were entertained weekly at this house, felt very kindly toward "his class" of people and were glad to do what they could for them in a certain chapel on a certain street in the city; but here the seats were all taken, except a very few in the organ loft. He might go around to the side door. He would see the staircase and find a seat in the gallery.

"We are exceedingly glad to see any of 'your people' go to church,—but really—"

Just then the minister from the pulpit announced in a fine, orotund voice: "The text for our consideration this morning is—

"*I was a stranger and ye took me not in.*"[2]

But you see, the stranger at the door was—Black!

And, of course, that settles it.

# 4

# "The Ethics of the Negro Question"

*(1902)*

Delivered at the Friends General Conference in Asbury
Park, New Jersey, on September 5, 1902, Cooper
thanks the Quakers for their long history of antislavery
work and addresses the status of Black Americans at
the dawn of the twentieth century. She praises the nation's ideals and values and calls upon all Americans to
live up to such promises in their actions and attitudes
toward Black citizens. She calls for a program of
"Christian Education," rooted in fairness and kindness
as the nation's Black community builds itself up following the horrors of slavery and the ongoing realities of
racial prejudice and extralegal violence.

SOURCE: Anna Julia Cooper Papers, box 23-4, folder 32,
Moorland-Spingarn Research Center, Howard University.

Where there is no vision, the people perish.
PROVERBS 29:18.

A nation's greatness is not dependent upon the things it makes
and uses. Things without thots are mere vulgarities. America
can boast her expanse of territory, her gilded domes, her paving
stones of silver dollars; but the question of deepest moment in
this nation today is its span of the circle of brotherhood, the
moral stature of its men and its women, the elevation at which it
receives its "vision" into the firmament of eternal truth.

I walked not long since thro the national library at Washington. I confess that my heart swelled and my soul was satisfied; for however overpowering to a subdued individual taste the loud scream of color in the grand hall way may be, one cannot but feel that the magnificence of that pile, the loftiness of sentiment and grandeur of execution here adequately and artistically express the best in American life and aspiration. I have often sat silent in the gallery under the great dome contemplating the massive pillars that support the encircling arches and musing on the texts traced above the head of each heroic figure: Science, holding in her hand instrument for the study of Astronomy, proclaims "The heavens declare the glory of God and the firmament showeth His handiwork." "Law bears the equal scales with the text: "Of Law there can be no less acknowledged than that her voice is the harmony of the world." Religion stands with firm feet and fearless mien, unequivocally summing up the whole matter: "What doth the Lord require of thee but to do justly, to love mercy and to walk humbly with the God."

Surely if American civilization should one day have to be guessed from a few broken columns and mutilated statues like the present grandeur of Egypt, Greece and Rome, the antiquarian or the historian who shall in future ages, dig from the dust of centuries this single masterpiece, this artistic expression of a people's aspiration and achievement, will yield ready homage to the greatness of the nation which planned and executed such a monument of architectural genius. "Surely here was a Nation" they must conclude, "whose God was the Lord! A nation whose vision was direct from the Mount of God!"

Whether such an estimate is just, it is our deepest concern to examine. Where there is no vision, the people perish. A nation cannot long survive the shattering of its own ideals. Its doom is already sounded when it begins to write one law on its walls and lives another in its halls. Weighed in the balance and found wanting was not more terribly signed and sealed for the trembling Belshazzar than for us by these handwritings on our walls if they have lost their hold on the thot and conduct of the people.

The civilizations that have flowered and failed in the past did not harvest their fruit and die of old age. A worm was eating at the core even in the heyday of their splendor and magnificence so soon as the grand truths which they professed had ceased to vitalize and vivify their national life.

Rome's religion was pagan, it is true, but for all that it was because Rome had departed from the integrity of her own ideals and was laughing in her sleeve at the gods of her fathers that she found herself emasculated and effete before the virile hordes that plundered and finally superseded her Thor and Woden had not become to the barbarians a figure to paint a wall or adorn a fountain. Let America beware how she writes on her walls to be seen of men the lofty sentiment *"Give instruction to those who cannot procure it for themselves,"* while she tips a wink at those communities which propose to give for instruction to the poor only that which is wrung from their penury. The vision as pictured on our walls is divine. The American ideal is perfect. A weak or undeveloped race apparently might ask no better fate than the opportunity of maturing under the great wing of this nation and of becoming christianized under its spiritual ministrations.

It is no fault of the Negro that he stands in the United States of America today as the passive and silent rebuke to the Nation's Christianity, the great gulf between its professions and its practices, furnishing the chief ethical element in its politics, constantly pointing with dumb but inexorable fingers to those ideals of our civilization which embody the Nation's highest, truest, and best thot, its noblest and grandest purposes and aspirations.

Amid all the deafening and maddening clamor of expediency and availability among politicians and parties, from tariffs and trusts to free coinage and 16 to 1, from microscopic questions of local sovereignty to the telescopic ones of expansion and imperialism, the Negro question furnishes the one issue that says *ought*. Not what will the party gain by this measure or that, not will this or that experiment bring in larger percentages and cash balances; but who, where, what is my neighbor? Am I my brother's keeper? Are there any limitations or special adaptations of the Golden Rule? If Jesus were among men today, is there a type of manhood veiled wherein, the Divinity whom our civilization calls Captain, would again, coming to His own, be again despised, rejected, because of narrow prejudices and blinding, pride of race?

Uprooted from the sunny land of his forefathers by the white man's cupidity and selfishness, ruthlessly torn from all the ties of clan and tribe, dragged against his will over thousands of miles of unknown waters to a strange land among strange peoples, the Negro was transplanted to this continent in order to produce chattels and beasts of burden for a nation "conceived in liberty and dedicated to the proposition that all men are created equal." A nation worshiping as God one who came not to be ministered unto, but to minister; a nation believing in a Savior meek and lowly of heart who, having not where to lay His head, was eyes to the blind, hearing to the deaf, a gospel of hope and joy to the poor and outcast, a friend to all who travail and are heavy laden.

The whites of America revolted against the mother country for a trifling tax on tea, because they were not represented in the body that laid the tax. They drew up their Declaration of Independence, a Magna Carta of human rights, embodying principles of universal justice and equality.

Professing a religion of sublime altruism, a political faith in the inalienable rights of man as man, these jugglers with reason and conscience were at the same moment stealing heathen from their far away homes, forcing them with lash and gun to unrequited toil, making it a penal offense to teach them to read the Word of God, nay, more, were even begetting and breeding mongrels of their own flesh among these helpless creatures and pocketing the guilty increase, the price of their own blood in unholy dollars and cents. Accursed hunger for gold!

To what dost thou not drive mortal breasts! But God did not ordain this nation to reenact the tragedy of Midas and transmute its very heart's core into yellow gold. America has a conscience as well as a pocket-book, and it comes like a pledge of perpetuity to the nation that she has never yet lost the seed of the prophets, men of inner light and unfaltering courage, who would cry aloud and spare not, against the sin of the nation. The best brain and heart of this country have always rung true and it is our hope today that the petrifying spirit of commercialism which grows so impatient at the Negro question or any other question calculated to weaken the money getting nerve by pulling at the heart and the conscience may still find a worthy protagonist in the reawakened ethical sense of the nation which can take no step backward and which must eventually settle, and settle right this and every question involving the nation's honor and integrity.

It gives me great pleasure to record the historians' testimony to the clear vision and courageous action of the Society of Friends[1] who persisted in keeping alive this ethical sense in some dark days of the past.

"The Quakers have the honor" says Von Holtz of having begun the agitation of the Slavery Question from the moral standpoint earliest and most radically. Thanks to the fiery zeal of some members of this Society, the religions and moral instruction of the slaves and the struggle against any further importation of the Negros were begun by the close of the 17th Century. By the middle of the 18th Century the emancipation of slaves had gradually become a matter of action by the whole Quaker body. By a resolution of 1774 all members concerned in importing, selling, purchasing, giving or transferring Negroes or other slaves were directed to be excluded from membership or disowned. Two years later this resolution was extended to cover cases of those who delayed to set their slaves free. In February 1790 the Quaker meeting in Philadelphia and the Quakers in New York sent addresses to Congress requesting it to abolish the African slave trade. Certain representatives from the North urged that the petitions of so respectable a body as that of the Quakers in relation to so great a moral evil, were deserving of special consideration. The representatives of the South replied with provoking irony and mercilessly castigated the Quakers. Year after year the Friends came indefatigably with new petitions each time, and each time had to undergo the same scornful treatment. In 1797 the yearly meeting at Philadelphia set forth some special wrongs in a petition, a prominent place in which was occupied by a complaint against the law of North Carolina condemning freed slaves to be sold again. Many Southern delegates in Congress expressed in a bullying fashion their scorn for the tenacity with which these men of earnest faith ever constantly came back again and again to their fruitless struggle. Not in America alone, England also witnessed the faith and works of this body of consistent Christians of unimpaired vision and unwavering determination. The first petition to the House of Commons for the abolition of the Slave Trade and Slavery went up from the Friends, and thro out the long agitation which ensued before that prayer was granted, the Society of Friends took an active and prominent part. Their own dear Whittier has sounded the keynote both of their struggle and its reward:

> "Whatever in love's name is truly done
>   To free the bound and lift the fallen one,
>     Is done to Christ."

And the Master Himself: Inasmuch as ye did it unto one of the least of these my brethren ye did it unto Me.

The colored people of America find themselves today in the most trying period of all their trying history in this land of their trial and bondage. As the trials and responsibilities of the man weigh more heavily than do those of the infant, so the Negro under free labor and cut throat competition today has to vindicate his fitness to survive in face of a colorphobia that heeds neither reason nor religion and a prejudice that shows no quarter and allows no mitigating circumstances.

In the darkest days of slavery, there were always at the North friends of the oppressed: and devoted champions of freedom who would go all lengths to wipe out the accursed stain of human slavery from their country's scutcheon; while in the South the slave's close contact with the master class, mothering them in infancy, caring for them in sickness, sorrow and death, resulted as pulsing touch of humanity must ever result, in many warm sympathies and a total destruction of that repulsion to mere color which betokens narrow and exclusive intercourse among provincials.

Today all this is changed. White and black meet as strangers with cold, distant or avowed hostility. The colored domestic who is no longer specially trained for her job or taught to look on it with dignity and appreciation, is barely tolerated in the home till she can do up the supper dishes and get away—when she can go—to the devil if he will have her. The mistress who bemoans her shiftlessness and untidiness does not think of offering her a comfortable room, providing for her social needs and teaching her in the long evenings at home the simple household arts and virtues which our grandmothers found time for. Her vices are set down to the debit account of her freedom, especially if she has attended a public school and learned enough to spell her way thro a street ballad. So generally is this the case that if a reform were attempted suddenly, the girl herself of the average type would misunderstand and probably resent it. The condition of the male laborer is even more hopeless. Receiving 50 cents a day or less for unskilled but laborious toil from which wage he boards himself and is expected to keep a family in something better than a "one room cabin," the Negro workman receives neither sympathy nor recognition from his white fellow laborers. Scandinavians, Poles and Hungarians can tie up the entire country by a strike paralysing not only industry but existence itself, when they are already getting a wage that sounds like affluence to the hungry black man. The union means war to the death against him and the worst of it is he can never be lost in the crowd and have his opprobrium forgotten. A foreigner can learn the language and out-American the American on his own soil. A white man can apply burnt cork and impute his meanness to the colored race as his appointed scape goat. But the Ethiopian cannot change his skin. On him is laid the iniquity of his whole race and his character is prejudged by formula. Even charity does not study his needs as an individual person but the good that love has planned for him must be labeled and basketed "special" for the Negro. Special kinds of education, special forms of industry, special churches and special places of amusement, special sections of our cities during life and special burying grounds in death. White America has created a *terra incognita* in its midst, a strange dark unexplored waste of human souls from which if one essay to speak out an intelligible utterance, so well known is the place of preferment accorded the mirroring of preconceived notions, that instead of being the revelation of a personality and the voice of a truth, the speaker becomes a phonograph and merely talks back what is talked into him.

It is no popular task today to voice the black man's woe. It is far easier and safer to say that the wrong is all in him. The American conscience would like a rest from the black man's ghost. It was always an unpalatable subject but preeminently now is the era of good feeling, and self complacency, of commercial omnipotence and military glorification. It seems an impertinence as did the boldness of Nathan when he caught the conscience of the great king at the pinacle of victorious prosperity with the inglorious seizure of the ewe lamb from a man of no importance. Has not the nation done and suffered enough for the Negro? Is he worth the blood and treasure that have been spilled on his account, the heart ache and bitterness that have racked the country in easing him off its shoulders and out of its conscience. Let us have no more of it. If he is a man let him stand up and prove it. Above all let us have peace. Northern capital is newly wed to Southern industry and the honeymoon must not be disturbed. If southern conventions are ingenious enough to invent a device for disfranchising these unwelcome children of the soil, if it will work, what of it?

On the floor of the most august body in the land, a South Carolina senator said: Yes; we bull dozed and terrorized niggers and we are not ashamed of it. If you had been in our place you would have done the same.

During the slavery agitation Garrison was mobbed in the streets of Boston for advocating abolition; but he kept right on and would be heard. In our day the simplest narrative in just recognition of the Negro meets with cold disfavor and the narrator is generally frozen into silence. A lecturer on the Spanish War attempted as an eye witness and with the aid of Stereopticon to tell a Richmond audience of the gallant charge up San Juan Hill and the brave part in it by the 10th Cavalry. His words were met by hisses, his lantern slides destroyed and he was obliged to close his entertainment in darkness and confusion.

A professor in a Southern school who in a magazine article condemned the saturnalia of blood and savagery known as lynching arguing that the Negro while inferior, was yet a man and should be accorded the fundamental rights of a man, lost his position for his frankness and fairness. The Negro is being ground to powder between the upper and the nether-millstones. The South, intolerant of interference from either outside or inside, the North too polite or too busy or too gleeful over the promised handshaking to manifest the most distant concern.

But God is not dead neither doth the ruler of the universe slumber and sleep. As a Nation sows so shall it reap. Men do not gather grapes from thorns or figs from thistles. To sow the wind is to reap the whirlwind.

A little over two years ago while the gentlest and kindest of presidents was making a tour of the South bent only on good will to men with a better understanding and the healing of all sectional rancor and ill felling, there occurred in almost a stone's throw of where he was for the time being domiciled an outburst of diabolism that would shame a tribe of naked savages. A black wretch was to be burned alive. Without court or jury his un-shrived soul was to be ushered into eternity and the prospect furnished a holiday festival for the country side.

Excursion trains with banners flying were run into the place and eager children were heard to exclaim: We have seen a hang-ing, we are now going to see a burning!

Human creatures with the behavior of hyenas contended with one another for choice bones of their victim as souvenirs of the occasion. So wanton was the cannibalistic thirst for blood that the Negro preacher who offered the last solace of the Christian to the doomed man was caught in the same mad frenzy and made to share his fate. A shiver ran thro the nation at such de-moniacal lawlessness. But a cool analysis of the situation elicited from the Attorney General of the United States the legal opinion that the case "probably had no Federal aspects!"

Just one year ago the same gentle people loving president was again acting out his instinct of mingling naturally and demo-cratically with his people. Again lawlessness, this time in the form of a single red handed unreasoning ruffian instead of many but the same mad spirit which puts its own will whether swayed by lurid passion or smoldering hate, on the throne of the majesty of law and of duty, made the nation shudder and bleed by strik-ing down unaccused and untried the great head of the nation. A fact may be mentioned here, which was unquestioned at the time by those around, but which was not often repeated afterwards, that it was the burly arm of a Negro that felled the assassin and dealt the first blows in defense of the stricken president.

I will not here undertake an apology for the short comings of the American Negro. It goes without saying that the black is cen-turies behind the white race in material, mental and moral devel-opment. The American Negro is today but 37 years removed from chattledom, not long enough surely to ripen the century plant of a civilization. After 250 years of a most debasing slavery, inured to toil but not, to thrift, without home, without family ties, without those habits of self reliant industry by which peoples maintain their struggle for existence, poor, naked, weak, ignorant, degraded even below his pristine state as a savage, the American Negro was at the close of the War of the Rebellion "cut loose" as the slang of the day expressed it, and left to fend for himself. The master class, full of resentment and rage at the humiliations and losses of a grinding war, suffered their old time interest to turn into bitterness or cold indifference and Klu Klux beatings with re-enslaving black codes became the sorry substitute for the overseer's lash and the auction block.

At this juncture the conscience of the Nation asserted itself and the federal constitution was so amended as to bring under the aegis of national protection these helpless babes whom the exigences of war had suddenly thrown into the maelstrom of remorseless life.

That they are learning to stem the current there is ground for hope; that they have already made encouraging headway even enemies cannot deny. The Negro's productivity as a free laborer is conceded to be greater than formerly as a slave, and the general productivity of the South where he constitutes the chief labor element, has since his emancipation more than doubled. Not having inherited the "business bump" his acquisitive principles have received some shocks and many times have been paralyzed and stunted by the insecurity of his property and the disregard of his rights shown by his powerful white neighbors. Such was the case in the collapse of the Freedman's Savings Bank[2] and the recent Wilmington massacre[3] when the accumulations of a lifetime were wantonly swept away and home loving, lawabiding citizens were forced into exile, their homes and little savings appropriated by others. In spite of this, however, some headway is making in material wealth and the tax lists in former slave states show a credit of several millions to the descendants of the enslaved.

But all his advancement in wealth and education counts for naught, and ought to count for naught, if it be true, as commonly reported in certain quarters, that the Negro is a moral leper and that sexually he is a dangerous animal in any community. It is said that those astounding exhibitions of fury and force which dizzy the head and sicken the heart of civilized people, are necessary to cower his brutish passions and guard the Holy Grail of Saxon civilization. That the sanctity of pure homes, the inviolability of helpless womanhood must be protected at any cost and that nothing short of devastation and war will suffice. That the beast must be kept under a reign of terror to make him know his place and keep his distance. The iteration and reiteration of sharp and swift retribution for the *usual* crime[4] is kept up altho the crime has been again and again proved to be unusual by more than 90 per cent and statistics of lynchings and their causes have been published from year to year showing every cause for a black man's being lynched from "Being impudent to a white man" to Preaching the Gospel of Jesus Christ to a doomed convict, and yet we are told that these things have "probably no *Federal aspects*." Dont you think we would find a way to give them Federal Aspects if it were poor old Spain lynching her obstreperous islanders?

Says Prof. Shaler of Harvard:

"When we recall the fact that there are now some five million Negro men in the South and that not one in ten thousand is guilty of crime against womanhood, we see how imperfect is the basis of this judgment. We have also to remember," he continues, "that this offense when committed by a Negro is thro action of the mob widely publicised while if the offender be a white man it is unlikely to be so well known. I therefore hold to the belief that violence to women is not proved to be a crime common among the blacks. I am inclined to believe that on the whole there is less danger to be apprehended from them in this regard than from an equal body of whites of like social grade."

Such is the calm testimony of an expert sociologist who speaks after scientific "investigation and careful analysis."

Is it credible that this race which has under freedom caught so eagerly on the rungs of progress in other respects has so shockingly deteriorated in this all important particular as to reverse all claims to humane consideration which they had won by patient service during long years of slavery?

Have a race of men to whom masters not over kind were not afraid to entrust their helpless women and children while faring forth to rivet the fetters more firmly on their dumb driven bodies and who without one single exception demonstrated remarkable fidelity, trustworthines, reverence for women and kindness toward children, suddenly become such monsters of lust and vindictiveness that a woman is not safe on the same highway with them?

A noble army of Christian workers and helpers have gone to the South ever since the War, have lived with these people on terms of Christian sympathy and perfect social equality. Have you ever heard of one of these pure minded missionaries who was insulted or outraged and her delicate sensibilities shocked by the unconquerable instincts and baser passions of the men they came to help?

You ask what is the need of today.

How can the Negro be best helped?

What can be done by the man who loves his fellowmen and needs not to be convinced of duties but only to be assured of methods? What is the best means of the Negro's uplift and amelioration?

In a word I answer: Christian Education. This is nothing new you say. That experiment has been tried and tried and there are even those whose faith in the efficacy of this expedient is beginning to wane and we are looking around to see if there be not some other, some quicker and surer way of doing the job. Is it not a mistake to suppose that the same old human laws apply to these people? Is there not after all something within that dark skin not yet dreamt of in our philosophy? Can we seriously take the Negro as a man "endowed by his Creator with certain unalienable rights such as Life, Liberty, Pursuit of Happiness" and the right to grow up, to develop, to reason and to live his life. In short can we hope to apply the key that unlocks all other hearts and by a little human sympathy and putting ourselves in his place learn to understand him and let him understand us? Assuredly, yes!

The black man is not a saint, neither can he be reduced to an algebraic formula. His thirty or forty checkered years of freedom have not transfigured *en masse* ten million slaves into experienced, thrifty, provident, law abiding members of society. There are some criminal, some shiftless, some provokingly intractable and seemingly uneducable classes and individuals among blacks as there are still unless I am misinformed, also among whites. But our philosophy does not balk at this nor do we lose our belief in the efficacy of Christian teaching and preaching. Turn on the light! Light, more light! There will always be some who do not live up to the light they have. But the Master has left us no alternative. Ye are the light of the world.

We cannot draw lines where He recognizes none. We cannot falter so long as there is a human soul in need of the light. We owe it, and owe it independently of the worthiness or unworthiness of that soul. Does any one question that Jesus' vision would have pierced to the heart and marrow of our national problem, and what would be His teaching in America today as to *who is my* neighbor?

For after all the Negro Question in America today is the white man's problem—Nay it is humanity's problem. The past, in which the Negro was mostly passive, the white man active, has ordained that they shall be neighbors, permanently and unavoidably. To colonize or repatriate the blacks on African soil or in any other continent is physically impossible even if it were generally desired, and no sane man talks of deportation now except as an exploded chimera. For weal or for woe the lots of these two thinking people are united, indissolubly, eternally on both sides are convinced that each race needs the other. The Negro is the most stable and reliable factor today in American industry. Patient and docile as a laborer, conservative, law abiding, totally ignorant of the anarchistic, socialistic radicalism and nihilism of other lands, the American Negro is capable of contributing not only of his brawn and sinew but also from brain and character a much needed element in American civilization, and here is his home. The only home he has ever known. His blood has mingled with the bluest and the truest on every battle field that checkers his country's history. His sweat and his toil have, more than any others, felled its forests, drained its swamps, plowed its fields and opened up its highways and waterways.

From the beginning was he here, a strong, staunch and not unwilling worker and helper. His traditions, his joys, his sorrows are all here. He has imbibed the genius and spirit of its institutions, growing with their growth, gathering hope and strength with their strength and depth. Alien neither in language, religion nor customs, the educated colored American is today the most characteristic growth of the American soil, its only genuinely indigenous development. He is the most American of Americans for he alone has no other civilization than what America has to offer. Its foibles are his foibles. Its youthful weaknesses and pompous self-confidence are all found here imitated or originating, as between sitter and portrait. Here in the warp and woof of his character are photographed and writ large even the grotesque caricatures, the superficial absurdities and social excrescencies of "Get-rich-quick" and "Pikes Peak-or-bust" America. Nor is it too much to hope that America's finer possibilities and promise also prefigure his ultimate struggle and achievement in evolving his civilization. As the character of Uncle Tom is rated the most unique in American literature, so the plantation melodies and corn songs form the most original contribution to its music. Homogeneous or not, the national web is incomplete without the African thread that glints and ripples thro it from the beginning.

In a description of the Rough Riders' charge on the Block House at El Caney a recent columnist has this to say: "Over against the scene of the Rough Riders set the picture of the 10th U. S. Cavalry the famous colored regiment side by side with Roosevelt's men they fought these black men. Scarce used to freedom themselves they are dying that Cuba may be free. Their marksmanship was magnificent, their courage was superb. They bore themselves like veterans and gave proof positive that from natures congenitally peaceful, carefree and playful, military discipline and an inspiring cause can make soldiers worthy to rank with Caesar's legions or Cromwell's Army.

Mr. Bryce in his study of the American Commonwealth says: "The South is confronted by a peculiar and menacing problem in the presence of a mass of Negroes larger than was the whole population of the union in 1800, persons who tho they are legally and industrially members of the nation are still virtually an alien element, unabsorbed and unabsorbable."

A similar judgment was passed by the gifted author of the Bonnie Briar Bush in his "Impressions of America" who thought that the Negroes were like the Chinese in constituting the sole exception to an otherwise homogeneous population. This misapprehension is common. The explanation obvious. Social cleavage in America is strictly along the lines of color only. Jim Crow cars[5] are not for the unwashed of all races, not for the drunken rowdy and the degraded, ignorant, vicious rabble, not even for the pauper classes who cannot pay for superior comforts in traveling. Quite simply the only question is "What is the tinge of pigment in your epidermal cells, or in the epidermis of your mother's grandmother? The colored man or woman of culture and refinement is shoved into the same box with the filthy and the degraded no matter what his ability to pay for and his desire to secure better accommodations. He cannot eat a sandwich in one of the "white" hotels nor set down his luggage in one of their waiting rooms at a railway station. The result is that students of American society like Bryce and Ian McClaren never see or suspect the existence of intelligent aspiring thinking men and women of color in the midst of this social system. Men and women who are pondering its adjustment chafing it may be under its rude and crude incongruities and gathering strength no doubt to snap asunder one of these days its tissue beltings and couplings.

The American traveler sees and can account for only the black porter and colored boot black, the waiter and barber and scullion.

And these only as automatons in a passing show. He cannot know them as human beings capable of human emotions, human aspirations, human suffering, defeats and triumphs. Our traveler is then introduced by design to the criminal records wherein the Negro, because the poorest, weakest, least shielded class in the community figures, of course, at his full strength. Taken for a drive thro what would in New York or Philadelphia constitute a slum appealing only to the Christ spirit in good men to send out their light and their love, to start a mission to provide wholesome living conditions for healthy living and clean thinking. But here both the Priest and the Levite pass by on the other side. The missions are to seek and to save the lost who are already fortunate enough to be born white.

Come unto me all ye *whites* who are heavy laden. The Poor (*whites*) have the Gospel preached unto them. Suffer the little *white* children to come unto Me! for of such is the kingdom of heaven. Love the Lord thy God with all thy heart, soul, and strength and thy *white* neighbor as thyself!"

But these Negro quarters, these submerged souls, this "darkest America"—Ah this is our terrible "Problem!" This mass that menaces Anglo Saxon civilization "unabsorbed and unabsorbable!"

But this time our traveler is wholly inoculated. "It is truly a *peculiar* problem to be sure." He does not quite see how question can be solved. He is disposed with Mr. Bryce to trust much to the *vismedicatrix* naturae and to hope that somehow, somewhere, and somewhen the Sphinx will answer its own riddle, and yet I am no pessimist regarding the future of my people in America. God reigns and the good will prevail. It must prevail. While these are times that try men's souls, while a weak and despised people are called upon to vindicate their right to exist in the face of a race of hard, jealous, intolerant, all-subduing instincts, while the iron of their wrath and bitter prejudice cuts into the very bones and marrow of my people, I have faith to believe that God has not made us for naught and He has not ordained to wipe us out from the face of the earth. I believe, moreover, that America is the land of destiny for the descendants of the enslaved race, that here in the house of their bondage are the seeds of promise for their ultimate enfranchisement and development. This I maintain in full knowledge of what at any time maybe wrought by a sudden paroxysm of rage caused by the meaningless war whoop of some obscure politicians such as the rally word of "Negro domination" which at times deafens and bemuddles all ears.

Negro domination! Think of it! The great American eagle, soaring majestically sunward, eyes ablaze with conscious power, suddenly screaming and shivering in fear of a little mouse colored starling, which he may crush with the smallest finger of his great claw. Yet this mad shriek is allowed to unbridle the worst passions of wicked men, to stifle and seal up the holiest instincts of good men. In dread of domination by a race whom they outnumber five to one, with every advantage in civilization, wealth, culture, with absolute control of every civil and military nerve center, Anglo Saxon America is in danger of forgetting how to deal justly, to love mercy, to walk humbly with its God.

In the old days, I am told that two or three Negroes gathered together in supplication and prayer, were not allowed to present their petition at the throne of Grace without having it looked over and revised by a white man for fear probably that white supremacy and its "peculiar" system might be endangered at the Court of the Almighty by these faltering lips and uncultured tongues! The same fear cowers the white man's heart today. He dare not face his God with a lie on his lips.

These "silent sullen peoples" (so called because sympathetically unknown and unloved) are the touchstone of his conscience. America with all her wealth and power, with her pride of inventions and mastery of the forces of nature, with all her breadth of principles and height of ideals, will never be at peace with herself till this question is settled and settled right. It is the conscience in her throat that is "unabsorbed and Unabsorbable!"

The despairing wail of Macbeth's blood stained queen in all her gilded misery at the moment of her sickening success, is profoundly and everlastingly true: "Better be that which we destroy!" It is in the power of this mighty nation to turn upon us in a St. Bartholomew's Massacre and in one bloody day reckon us among the extinct races of history. A governor of Georgia is reported to have declared that "a dead Negro in the back yard" was his suggestion for settling this question and another has recommended that a reward be offered for every one so disposed of.

But the Negro's blood on this great Nation becomes a heavier burden than the Negro's education and Christianization. His extermination will weigh more than all the weight of his uplift and regeneration. A nation's dishonor is a far more serious problem to settle than the extension of a brother's hand and a Christian's grip by a favored race bearing the torch, as a sacred trust from the Source of All light to lead, enlighten and lift. Ye who have the light *owe it* to the least of these my brethren.

> "Is your God a wooden fetish
>    To be hidden out of sight,
>    That his block eyes may not see you
>    Do the thing that is not right?
>    But the Destinies think not so;
>    To their judgment chamber lone
>    Comes no voice of popular clamor

There Fame's trumpet is not blown
But their silent way they keep.
Where empires towered that were not just,
Lo! the skulking wild fox scratches
in a little heap of dust."[6]

This it were well for great powers to ponder. The right to rule entails the obligation to rule right. Righteousness and Righteousness only exalteth a nation and the surest guarantee of the perpetuity of our institutions is alliance with God's eternal forces that make for rightness and justness in His world.

As for the Negro there can be no doubt that these trials are God's plan for refinement of the good gold to be found in him. The dross must be purged out. There is no other way than by fire. If the great Refiner sees that a stronger, truer, purer racial character can be evolved from His crucible by heating the furnace seven times, He can mean only good.

With hearty earnestness the million and half colored boys and girls in the public schools South repeat on June 14 the salute to their country's flag:

"I pledge allegiance to my flag and to the country for which it stands." I commend these boys and girls to you for as staunch and loyal a yeomanry as any country can boast. They are Americans, true and bona fide citizens not by adoption or naturalization but by birth and blood incontestable.

Whatever may be problematical about us, our citizenship is beyond question. We have owned no other allegiance, have bowed before no other sovereign. Never has hand of ours been raised either in open rebellion or secret treachery against the Fatherland.

Our proudest aspiration has been but to serve her, the crown of our glory to die for her. We were born here thro no choice of our own or of our ancestors; we cannot expatriate ourselves, even if we would. When the wild forces of hate and unholy passion are unleashed to run riot against us our hearts recoil not more in dread of such a catastrophe for ourselves than in grief and shame at the possibility of such a fall and such a failure for our country's high destiny. It is unconceivable that we should not feel the unnatural prejudice environing us and our children. It is like stones between our teeth and like iron in the marrow of our bones. If at such times we cannot sing America it is not because of any treason lurking in our hearts. Our harps are hung on the willows and in the Babylon of our sorrow we needs must sit down and weep. But no dynamite plots are hatching amongst us. No vengeful uprising brewing. We are a song loving people and that song of all songs we would love to sing, and we challenge the lustiest singer to sing it more lustily and more eloquently than we. But when the wound is festering and the heart is so sore we can only suffer and be silent, praying God to change the hearts of our misguided countrymen and help them to see the things that make for righteousness.

Then pray we shall that come it may for come it will for a' that.
That man to man the world o'er shall brothers be for a 'that.

# 5

# "Educational Programs"

## (ca. 1930)

Cooper argues for the development of strong educational programs for all members of society—from the most to the least fortunate. Her focus turns especially to the education and uplift of Black Americans. She argues against a "Jim Crow" educational philosophy and maintains that tried-and-true educational principles are no less suited to Black students than they are to white ones. She calls for the development of and support for Black schools of all levels and a broad approach to training people for dignified work for which they receive fair pay and respect.

SOURCE: Anna Julia Cooper Papers, box 23-4, folder 33, Moorland-Spingarn Research Center, Howard University.

## Foreword

No profounder duty confronts a state than the necessity of constructing sane and serviceable citizens out of the material of childhood. No higher privilege awaits the individual in this land of opportunity than the privilege of contributing to such an end. With all the wealth of all the ages at his disposal, with all the worlds that throng the universe and all the stars that hold their glittering galaxies in luminous orbits of mazy splendor, God's greatest, most precious gift to the world for all time is His Son.

The most valuable contribution that can delight a nation, the noblest gift that God or man can bestow, the proudest gem that monarch can covet, the crowning point of evolution's progress is the replica of that gift in the fullness of the measure of the stature of Christ Jesus, the perfect Man.

"There is nothing great in the universe but man," and "there is nothing great in man but mind."

Now education has been well defined as the building up of a man, the whole man: which, I take it, implies putting your crude material through whatever processes insure the highest return of the entire product at its best.

Manifestly nothing can more profitably engage the time and thought of statesmen and sages than the perfecting of these processes and the improvement of this product. The interest of the commonwealth in the result is transcendent. The smallest element is as vital to the state as heart's blood. No expenditure is extravagant that enhances the value of the output: no experiment but is suicidal if it results in the waste of any precious material. Indeed, so busy and so efficient are the forces of evil in working up the refuse into engines of deadly execution, it may with truth be said that from the standpoint of the state the most valuable part of all material, reckoned both in direction of what it may become and of what it may be saved from being, the item most momentous in potentiality is the refuse—the outcast. "And so our uncomely parts have put on more abundant comeliness," that there be no schism in the body politic. The high cannot say to the low, "I have no need of thee"; nor the well-conditioned to the lazzaroni:[1] "I have no need of thee." So long as the wretchedest hovel may culture germs of disease and misery against which the proudest palace is not immune, the submerged tenth take on a terrible significance in the building up of men, and the only salvation lies in leaving the ninety and nine in the wilderness and going after that which is lost.

The only sane education, therefore, is that which conserves the very lowest stratum, the best and most economical is that which gives to each individual, according to his capacity, that training of "head, hand, and heart," or, more literally, of mind, body and spirit which converts him into a beneficent force in the service of the world. This is the business of schools and this the true cause of the deep and vital interest of all the people in

## Educational Programs

As interested in the education of a neglected people, and as educators in a circumscribed field of work, we are confronted by a peculiar danger at the same time that we are buoyed up and helped by a peculiar inspiration and stimulus to devotion. Whether from force of circumstances or from choice and loving consecration, we are ministers of the Gospel of intelligence, of moral and material uplift to a people whose need is greater than the average need around us by reason of past neglect, a people who are habitually reasoned about en masse as separate, distinct, and peculiar; a people who must be fitted to make headway in the face of prejudice and proscription the most bitter, the most intense, the most unrelenting the world has ever seen. Every journeyman tinker thinks he can tell you what to do with the Negro; what sort of clothes he should wear, what sort of meat he should eat, what sort of books he should and should not study: in short, just what sort of education is sane, sensible and "practical" for one of his texture of hair and hide.

In the presence of this multitude of counsellors the danger is that we lose sight altogether of basic principles as such, and remember that we are educating Negroes before we have yet realized that we are educating men.

It cannot be denied that the wisest plan of education for any people should take cognizance of past and present environment, should not the forces against which they must contend, or in unison with which they must labor in the civilization of which they form a part. It should not be ignored, further, that the colored man in America, because of his marked appearance and his unique history, will for a long time need peculiar equipment for the intense, the unrelenting struggle for survival amid which he finds himself in the America of today. The weakest of the races here represented, at the same time the most conspicuous and undisguisable, the black race, has need truly of wise teachers and far-seeing leaders, to help them up the thorny road of life. When studying or planning a program of Negro education we shall need the clearest thot, the wisest counsels, the broadest charity. There is no place for jealousies or for hobbies.

We want light from whatever source it comes. We want to know the truth on all sides whatever the consequences to our particular line of activity or to our preconceived theories and prejudices.

But we must formulate our program according to bed rock principles of HUMAN development, and not by some shifting sentiment of ephemeral conditions and snapshot conclusions. We are ready for a frank and fearless discussion of our needs, and for suggestions, according to our lights, of plans and remedies.

Now there are certain fundamental verities and educational principles which have been formulated by practical educators for the human race. They are as universal as the law of gravitation, as unquestionable as the axioms of Geometry. Whatever the social conditions and circumstances, our foundations must be laid on the rock-bottom of these principles. What has been tested and established for mankind need not be questioned for the Negro. It may possibly require stronger doses and more frequent applications if your patient is hard to move, but the physic for the black man is the physic for man—no more, no less.

One of the great thinkers in the educational world lays down in a recent magazine article three principles for the aim of education as "supreme, comprehensive, and ultimate": education is to make the thinker, education is to make one appreciative, education is to make one righteous. "Let women and men," he continues, "be trained in those studies which train them to think, which will give them the power of appreciation and make them right doers, or adjust the individual to the highest relations of being. When they are thoroly trained to think, to appreciate, and to do right,—and when, having these qualities, they are called upon to go into the kitchen or the nursery, or on the farm, I am sure they will apply their power of thot to the solution of the problems of the kitchen or the farm or the nursery."

It is well known that the power to think, the power to appreciate, and the power to will the right and make it prevail, is the sum total of the faculties of the human soul. Education which is truly "educative" must strengthen, develop, "lead out" these faculties in preparation for those special activities which may be called "occupative," because they give the one line of training necessary for the occupation or trade of the individual. No one will deny that thot-power, will-power, and the power to discern and appreciate proportion and right relation are fundamental needs of the people for whom we toil, as of others. Indeed when we speak of their peculiar weaknesses and special lack to be overcome by education, I think if we analyse our criticism carefully, we shall find the fault resolve itself into one or all of these three faculties still latent or underdeveloped and in need of training. The Negro has had manual education throughout his experience as a slave. For 250 years he was practically the only laborer in the American market. His training was whatever his teachers decreed it should be. His skill represented the best teaching of the section in which he found himself. If he did not reckon a knowledge of machinery among his accomplishments it must be admitted that machinery was very tardily introduced into the Southland. But his methods as a farmer, as a mechanic, as nurse, as domestic, were the result of the best teaching the peculiar institution afforded. What was the lack? What is the need today? Is it not just the power to think, the power to will, the power to appreciate true relation, which have been enumerated as the universal aim of education? The old education made him a "hand," solely and simply. It deliberately sought to suppress or ignore the soul. We must, whatever else we do, insist on those studies which by the consensus of educators are calculated to train our people to think, which will give them the power of appreciation and make them righteous. In a word we are building men, not chemists or farmers, or cooks, or soldiers, but men ready to serve the body politic in whatever avocation their talent is needed. This is fundamental. No sort of superstructure can endure on any different foundation. This first for all men—whether for white men, red men, yellow men, or black men, whether for rich men or poor men, high or low, the aim of education for the human soul is to train aright, to give power and right direction to the intellect, the sensibilities, and the will. Certain studies, certain courses, certain exercises have been tested, tried, accepted by the experience of centuries in the steady progress of humanity.

Teachers from Aristotle to the present have sifted and analysed the various branches of learning to get at their relative worth as educative factors. The results of their experiments and analyses are not hidden in dark places. They are universally accepted by teachers and thinkers as a reasonable and proper basis for the education of mankind.

The only way to meet those skeptics who still ask with a half sneer "What is the use of this or that study for Negroes?" is with the query "is it good for *men*?" Has it been selected for curricula universally and has it stood the test for the discipline it gives in the direction of thought-power, power of appreciation, power of willing the right? These are the things we need. If these studies are means to those ends there can be nothing incongruous or unreasonable in trying them on our pupils in all faith as to the divine possibilities in all human development.

As to the second or "occupative" aim of our work, it cannot be denied that there has been some loss in the past through a certain lack of definiteness on our part. There has been a shifting or wavering of programs coupled with an acrimony in criticising the other man's program which promises little in the way of progress or of mutual esteem. This has been partly our fault, partly our misfortune. It has been a misfortune that too often our program has been handed down from above, along with the cash which was to constitute our sinews of war. The Negro, being an "interesting case," all the good old ladies in the country have had a hand in prescribing his medicine, and they mean to see that he takes it. No fumbling with the bedclothes and trying to spit behind the bed! Down it must go. As head nurses we have had little opportunity to interpose. Those who had the hardihood to object, did so at their peril. The time has come, however, when the educators of Negroes must see that one narrow pattern cannot meet the demands of this people whose life is as varied and whose need is as various as the life and needs of the American people. The time has come for a rational discussion of these needs on the part of those who are interested in the shaping of educational programs, for a frank admission of individual limitations (one man can't do it all—or know it all), and lastly for an intelligent and economic division of labor on the principle of each undertaking that which he does best and standing squarely for that specialty for which his plant, his general equipment and his endowment promise the best result.

There can be no doubt that the colored families are producing children enough to keep all the schools going, from the kindergarten to the universities; the high schools, trade schools, colleges, normal schools, professional schools,—all are needed to minister to the ever broadening demand of this people. Let Fiske, Atlanta, and similar schools have the support and encouragement they need as instututions of higher learning; let Hampton, Tuskegee and similar schools wear their well earned laurels as the correspondingly great trade universities; but let not Atlanta think she must extemporize a tin shop, nor Tuskegee make shift for a chair of oratory under the apprehension that each must aim at what the other is doing well.[2]

I feel that I can afford to speak for an occupation concerning which there has been much backwardness in schools for occupations because, perhaps, of certain suppressed odium that may attend the frank avowal of such purpose. I refer to the occupation of domestic servants. There seems a delicacy about deliberately and avowedly setting about the training for domestic service or the frank admission that the training adopted leads to such an end. On this point I can speak more freely than I would probably do if I represented a school of thought that looks towards the occupations but is hampered by this shy sensitiveness and the secret hope that somehow its young people will take a turn in this direction and do credit to their training without ever having planned a course with such a purpose in view.

We hear a great deal about Negroes leaving the rural districts and congregating in cities. Now the great cry of the cities is for *trained* domestic help. In the Northern cities especially the demand would give an almost fictitious valuation to a supply measuring up in every way to the requirement. Just here, it seems to me, some one good school—not all by any means—but some school fitted for that business might undertake to supply the training for this branch of industry—frankly, and with careful planning of program. You and I know what an agonizing wail there is throughout the country on the degeneration of the Negro servant. In fact I believe that most of the sentiment existing to-day adverse to the race is due to the bad record *left by our missionaries-----the servants!* Most people don't stop to think, and our average American public is just like "most people" in this respect. They tell you that the Negro is more degenerate under freedom than he was under slavery; they extol the virtues, the amiability and reliability of the old time servant class, whom they tell you they loved by reason of their excellencies of character as well as their faithfulness of service,—"but now,"—and then the howl of despair as the shiftlessness of the up-to-date "girl" is detailed, her untrained, unkempt disorderliness, her unmitigated emptiness of all the qualities that rendered her supposed ancestors loved and respected. And then the conclusion inevitable that the whole race is immeasurably worse conditioned than "before the war"; that some such system as slavery was needed to keep us all from going to the dogs.

Let us look at the facts. Under slavery there was the most vigilant, the most intelligent, the most successful natural selection known to civilized man to form this class of house servants who were to be in immediate and constant contact of the most intimate sort with the master class. There was absolutely nothing to mar this selection or thwart the most perfect adjustment of it to the needs of the system. The house servants were the cream by natural endowment first, and by most careful training and contact afterwards. Have these same people, and their children, degenerated since or have they *gone up higher?* I think the latter. Today they represent the thrift, the mechanical industry, the business intelligence, the professional skill, the well ordered homes, and the carefully nurtured families that are to be found in every town and hamlet where the colored man is known. The whole bed-rock has been lifted up by emancipation, stratum upon stratum, so that they who know the Negro only in their kitchens are too often brought in contact with a level which they never met under the old regime. And yet it is important for our cause, no less than for the employer class, that the quality of domestic service be improved through training and through intelligent comprehension of its circumstances and opportunities. In the first place, the association of the domestic in the home of her employer is by necessity most intimate and responsible. "The help" can by her silent, self-respecting dependableness preach unanswerable sermons before audiences that you and I can never reach.

She can refute pre-judgments, allay opposition, and mold favorable sentiment without ever opening her lips on the Negro problem; she can in her own person and by her own character offer a solution of that problem which will gainsay all cavil and all criticism. Is it not worth while for some school to undertake the work seriously, candidly, devotedly, of sending out a stream into these channels of usefulness so full of promise, so rich in opportunities for the race? The character of the service is important and the service itself when properly appreciated and performed has the same elements of dignity as other services. Browning has stated a universal truth in *Pippa Passes* when he says:

> "All service ranks the same with God-
> With God, whose puppets, best and worst,
> Are we; there is no last nor first."

Something must be done on both sides, I grant you. Our young girls must be protected from libertines and villains who lie in wait in gorgeous palaces to entrap the innocent. Not only must the girl be trained for the home but the home, too, must be selected and prepared for the new servant—a servant whose treatment shall be worthy her training, a servant whose dignity and whose serviceableness shall justify the expenditure for such a course in our educational program. We may not stem the tide rushing into our large cities. Certainly speech-making has very little to do with such things. But we may direct, guide, and help some in the cities, and, it seems to me, that the consideration of such a program is not unworthy the serious attention of thoughtful educators.

I have dwelt thus at length on the occupation of domestic service for two reasons: first, I hoped to make it clear that I have no word or thought adverse to this or any honest toil. Second, I expect to make it just as plain before I am through that neither domestic service nor any other service will ever be considered anything else than menial until it is put on a professional basis by having behind it a *thorough course of general education*. The conclusion is a corollary to this that the trained domestic, like the trained nurse, will demand the pay, and will deserve the treatment that are accorded intelligent and efficient services professionally rendered in whatever calling of life, and that it is not by persuasive essays on the dignity of labor, but by broadening and dignifying the laborer, that we can secure any respectable number of recruits for this most important field of occupation. Any act performed by an ignorant slattern is menial, while no amount of indignity can really degrade a soul truly in possession of itself through scientific development of its faculties.

And just here is the battleground. The fatal American faculty of cutting corners has taught us to call that program of education "practical" which makes the shortest out to the nearest dollar in sight. Before childhood has had time to grow, it is harassed with the feverish, mercantile question "what can you do"? Bears sometimes eat their cubs and humans not seldom fatten on child labor, but the crime becomes monstrous when whole communities systematize the stunting and warping of all normal child-development by premature specialization. The Germans understand this better than we. They realize as we do not that the total output of all industry is enhanced by the broader growth of the laborer. In her fierce competition with her foreign foes Germany set herself to building up the man,—a man useful to and to be used by the Fatherland in whatever capacity his services might be needed. To this end primary and secondary education are made the broad basis for technical or industrial training. In other words, technical schools are where colleges are with us and specialization (specializing) does not begin until the child has completed what answers to the high school course.

This places the educative before the occupative—the cultural before the special, the development before the industrial. This is the natural order of any educational program based upon scientific principles of human development.

Training of the eye to accuracy and the muscles of the hand and arm as in writing and drawing have an early place in any program of general education which, according to all enlightened planning, comprehends the culture of the physical as well as the mental and moral man. But it is well known that with the growing child a too early concentration of effort in the operation of special muscles is sure to result in partial or total atrophy of others. As a matter of course subsistence is the first problem with man as with every other animal and, if it is not at hand, the child must make shift as he can to get it or perish. But he does not grow in order to subsist; he subsists in order to grow, and if his growth be used up in the means of subsistence, the inevitable result is dwarfage. The natural father stores up this subsistence for the child during the growing or formative period in order that his development may proceed along normal and self-preservative lines. My plea is for the sacredness and inviolability of the growing period of the child. Guard it, nurture it, foster it. Give it the one thing needful,—time. If it costs sacrifice, it is richly worth it.

The state has provided in all advanced American communities free instruction for this period covering altogether about twelve years and roughly divisible into primary and secondary schools, or more accurately into kindergarten and primary, intermediate and secondary which constitute the common school course or what we are proud to call general public education. Superadded to this common course for all should come the special courses or training for avocation: a Normal course to train for teaching and a technical course to train for certain trades. The latter are the true "higher" schools and are equal in rank as fitting for earning a living. They ought to rank with professional schools, but American communities have not yet put all the professions on a public education basis, although without doubt the way should be provided somehow and somewhere to enable a poor boy of special aptitude to make his way to whatever equipment his talents can best employ in the service of the state. Such common school equipment is and of right ought to be the birthright of every American born child. The Japanese can claim it under treaty obligation.

"When the centurion heard that, he went and told the chief captain, saying, 'Take heed what thou doest: for this man is a Roman.'" Then the chief captain came, and said unto him: "Tell me art thou a Roman?" He said, "Yea."[3]

And the chief captain answered: "With a great sum obtained

I this freedom." And Paul said: "But I was *free* born." And so
our children bear the stamp of the original coin and they should
not be crippled by getting short allowance through either misconception or opportunism on our part. I care no more for a
doctor or a lawyer than I do for an engineer, but I expect each to
know something more than just the daily tools with which he
works.

"We learn by doing" is an educational axiom, but true as it is,
it does not mean as it is often attempted to prove that sense travels only from hand to brain. The normal direction of the current
would seem logically to go just the other way. Brain power insures hand power, and thought training produces industrial efficiency. We learn by doing when we dissect a crayfish or build a
Latin sentence in the secondary school, when we perform a
chemical reaction in the laboratory or express a thought in
French, German, or Spanish, as when we read, write, or draw
in the primary grades. Enlightened industrialism does not mean
that the boy who plows cotton must study nothing but cotton
and that he who would drive a mule successfully should have
contact only with mules. Indeed it has been well said "if I know
my son would drive a mule all his days, I should still give him the
groundwork of a general education in his youth that would place
the greatest possible distance between him and the mule." Prof.
Huxley who was one of the most distinguished and enthusiastic
exponents of the progressive tendencies of modern education
said as early as 1877 before the Working Men's Club and Institute Union in speaking on the subject of technical education, "In
my judgment, the preparatory education of the handicraftsman
ought to have nothing of what is ordinarily understood by 'technical' about it. The workshop is the only real school for a hand-
icraft. The education which precedes that of the workshop
should be entirely devoted to the strengthening of the body, the
elevation of the moral faculties, and the cultivation of intelligence; and, especially, to the imbuing the mind with a broad and
clear view of the laws of the natural world with the components
of which the handicraftsman will have to deal. And the earlier
the period of life at which the handicraftsman has to enter into
actual practice of his craft, the more important is it that he
should devote the precious hours of preliminary education to

things of the mind, which have no direct and immediate bearing on his branch of industry, though they lie at the foundation of all realities."

In many a hard-fought field the foe has been routed, not by a blunderbuss, but by an epithet. Advocates of the shortcut have made good use of this ruse. In the first place, the modern designation of secondary grades schools as "high schools" has favored the confusion with "higher education" which has already fallen under the disrepute of being "mere culture" or professional or "gentlemanly" training. In any exact thinking, *culture* is the term for those studies which disclose the child to himself and put him into possession of his dormant faculties. The physician puts the germ of diphtheria or tuberculosis into a "culture" of gelatine or some substance in which the hidden spark is nurtured into life and enabled to grow. The gardener calls the little pots of nursery plants "cultures." But the poor man is almost ashamed to harbor the thought of culturing his offspring and high schools are derided as giving impractical and useless accomplishments for the few who do not have to work and as making "scholars" and high-sounding wind-bags. "You can't make," says one conclusively, "beet-root sugar out of fine phrases." This is true. But neither can you make beet-root sugar out of foolish phrases. When you come to think of it the beet-root industry has never been known to be affected by any kind of phrases. But the industries and ideals of a nation cannot but be enriched by the sound of intelligence of all the people derived from thorough general education in its schools.

Any scheme of education should have regard to the whole man—not a special class or race of men, but man as the paragon of creation, possessing in childhood and in youth almost infinite possibilities for physical, moral and mental development. If a child seem poor in inheritance, poor in environment, poor in personal endowment, by so much the more must organized society bring to that child the good tidings of social salvation through the schools. "According to thy need so be it unto thee; arise into such attainment as the modicum of thy capacity may permit." And let us not be over bumptious about unlovely exteriors and unprepossessing personalities. Remember Cavanaugh and Helen Keller. There will be differences and degrees of aptitudes and faculties which, when awakened and discovered, will make demands upon all the various theories and methods of modern programs of education, so that no one scheme will suffer from neglect. Natural and normal development will in the end determine all differences without the need of man's premature and too conscious interference in favor of one Propaganda or another. Natural and normal development will produce symmetry. Man's Preconceptions, local or national prejudices, selfishness of special interests can produce only onesidedness.

Against these we must guard, and while with frankness and openmindedness we should weigh and consider whatever promises improvement in our educational system, we need constantly to remember that the one result aimed at above all others is a well trained manhood,—a useful citizenship. The Report of the Committee at the Nashville meeting of the National Council of Education set forth in the following words the truth which should always be borne in mind in the matter of educational programs:

"Society should see to it that the child who cannot choose the family into which he shall be born, shall have given him the best possible heritage fortune could bring him, namely, an education that awakens him to the consciousness of the higher self that exists dormant in him."

# 6

# "The Negro's Dialect"

*(ca. 1930)*

Cooper makes a linguistic argument in this essay, wherein she analyzes Paul Robeson's speech in *Othello*—especially claims that he uses the phrase "am dat"—and the voices of the characters in the *Amos 'n' Andy* radio show. She argues that white people, the press, and many of the mainstream, popular forms of entertainment, from *Porgy and Bess*, to *The Green Pastures*, to *Othello*, often misrepresent Black speech. She goes so far as to state that "there is no such thing as Negro dialect per se," and she explains how all languages naturally come to be and to change with time, place, and other contextual factors.

SOURCE: Anna Julia Cooper Papers, box 23-4, folder 35, Moorland-Spingarn Research Center, Howard University.

The story has gone the rounds of the press that Paul Robeson,[1] who himself tells us that he has toiled and spent to attain the accent not offensive to Mayfair, sometimes slips into the "soft slur of the Southern Negro" and even at the tragic moment of Othello's[2] sublime fury demands: "Where am dat handkerchief, Desdemona?"

Reporters and critics must sell their stuff and one should not grudge them their little joke. Nothing helps like a bit of local color to heighten tone effects. This story listens well for heart interest on this side the Atlantic, where a black man is not true black unless he says "am dat." Mr. Robeson in his impersonation of the noble blackamoor may on his own part deliberately allow himself the racial touch, not at all inconsistent to my mind with a highly artistic effect. If he did so, be sure it was not a slip; he had been instructed and believed that such a departure would give just the original flavor he was expected to create. But speaking *ex cathedra* I claim, as one who ought to know, that no artist who has intelligently analyzed the Negro folk-speech, whether he be poet, novelist, or impersonator, can ever accept "am dat" as a possibility in Negro or Southern vocalization.

It is universally conceded that racial groups attacking a foreign language with which they are forced to serve themselves, will invariably take the line of least resistance. Thus Franks, Burgundians, Goths and Visigoths uniformly clipped off the troublesome Roman terminations for declension and conjugation, points too fine to bother their matter-of-fact brains, and homo-hominis-homini-hominem lost everything but the essential tonic syllable or sound, which becomes for the Frenchman, *homme*, for the Spaniard *hombre*, the Portuguese *homem* and to the Italian *uomo*—a new tongue slowly evolved by characteristic differentiation thro adjacent families or groups as the real expression of racial distinctions and peculiarities of vocalization that go to make a language. Later on comes that change within the family itself that we call provincialisms or dialects, either a natural growth from age to age or resultants from movement, differences in locality and climatic conditions, differences in occupation, habits, way of living, contacts with nature, contacts with other men.

Says Bourciez, *Linguistique Romane*:

"The stability of a language is wholly a relative matter. If a given language is spoken almost identically by men of the same generation and belonging to the same social group, one must see a priori that his language will necessarily undergo certain modifications on being transmitted from one generation to another, and that *the sounds* of which the words are composed may be altered as well as the sense attributed to these words. This 'evolution' is not only possible, but in some sort inevitable. It is however more or less rapid according to historic conditions in the midst of which the people speaking a given language find themselves. If, it is slow at certain-epochs when a type of literary language taught in the schools predominates, there are other periods when change is accelerated, and when with the dissolution of the ancient social ties, there appears a corresponding disorganizat.on, even more prompt, of common idiomatic speech. One conceives equally that if a people, having formed at the beginning a vast empire, speaking a language almost identical, happen to separate and to live a distinct political life, these people, no longer communicating with one another, experience each in their language particular alterations. It will be found then that at the end of a certain number of generations languages primitively identical, will be so no longer at the different points where it continues to be spoken, and the differentiation may have been so considerable, that one finds himself in the presence of several distinct dialects."

This is precisely what happened to the language of Shakespeare and Milton on American soil, and what, before automobiles and airplanes achieved their amazing annihilation of time and space, differentiated the strong burr of the West, the soft slur of the South, and the choppy staccato of the Northern United States, all of which differ from Mayfair English, not only in vocabulary and use of words, but even more in the *placing* of vocables, the muscular and I may say mechanical formation of sounds. Into the melting pot in due course was poured a witch's mixture of races, Scotch, Irish, French, Italian, German, Swede, Negro, Pole, Slovak and what not, all bound to make their wants known in this language of Shakespeare and Milton the weaker less energetically than the strong, and some "with no language but a cry," but all murdering the King's English, each in his own way, modifications pivoting many times on slight differences in structure of vocal organs, or on environment, social contacts, etc.

Doctor Frissell, General Armstrong's friend and successor at Hampton, used to remark: "Our boys," as he affectionately called them, "are rather venturesome with their English." Now undoubtedly to this racial or temperamental "venturesomeness" Negro folk have added their own characteristic physical equipment and endowments of organic structure such as breadth of nostril, length of vocal chords and perhaps a certain peculiar resonance of chest tones that vary all the way from the rich *basso profundo* vibrations of "Andy" to the anaemic narrow chested head tones so well simulated by "Amos."[3] But the dialect, like all attempts of *beiwohners* to serve themselves with a speech acquired exclusively by ear, never having started with the ABC at mother's knee, develops naturally by a process nothing different from the experiments of European Barbarians, who centuries ago attacked the Latin.

"Andy's" *sitchation* runs true to phonetic form, preserving the tonic syllable and all of the sound that is essential to carrying the sense (as any winged word should); the u never having been seen or consciously stressed is of course entirely negligible. The same analysis applies to "regusted" which has nothing whatever in common with the Irish "rr" in its first syllable, being hardly more than the movable nu in Greek or the "eh-r-eh" so often heard in hesitating for a word—eh-r-eh *gusted*, that's the thing! the tonic syllable every time. "Propolition" is, if possible, even more characteristically fashioned according to racial instinct, since it directly seeks euphone in the exchange of the harsh sibilant "s" for the smooth liquid "l"; "propolition" is as accommodating and ready to please, or rather to avoid offense, as the head waiter at a summer hotel. By the same reasoning "*am dat*," ascribed to Paul Robeson by the press and vouched for by Mr. Hannen Swaffer, must go. It is as artistically impossible to Robeson as it is untrue to nature in the primitive Negro who has never seen a book or been near a school house (or a stage prompter)— the simple reason being that the combination of a labial mute followed by a dental (m d) requiring that the lips close on m then open again to send tip of tongue behind upper teeth for d, is too difficult for his easy going lips to negotiate. His genius leans to flowing sounds, easy liaisons, more French than German, a prevalence of vowels, semi vowels, and liquids. He might say: "wheat dat" or "wheah's dat," or even "whah dat hankycher"— but never, never, I pledge you my word, will you hear a Negro, not drilled into it for stage effect, utter of his own accord: "Where am dat handkerchief." It is simply impossible.

Much of the literary dialect such as "dis am," "he am," "him am," "ob dis" and "am dat" which our industrious press turns out by the scoop in its willingness to pander to popular taste for unsophisticated and "colorful" native speech, would fall flat if held up thus to Nature's mirror to be tried by the rules of organic growth. It is a principle of grammar, recognized in children as well as in adult beginners, that irregularities are accepted last and that in verbs the third singular is made to serve for irregular first and second. The child speaks of "both *foots*," says "I *drinked*," "he *hitted* me," "mine is *goodest*," learning rules before exceptions, and "*I is*" (when corrected often gets it "I are") never "*he am*." In fact I think you will find the form *am* rather late coming into play, having to be stressed and directed quite a bit before it stands without hitching, with its own proper subject. No child says "It is I," right off the bat. He seems to shy at "I am" with persisting disapproval meeting your well meant attempts with cunningly devised substitutes such as "Johnny is" and "me is" till sometimes his wrath gets the better of his pretty manners and he downs his tormentor with "AW—Me said Ahee!" "I's gwine," for instance is folk made and "dat's" for "dat is"; but "dat am" does not bear the hallmark.

The difficult *th* sound in *this* and *that*, the Negro, like the Frenchman, systematically reduces to *d*: "dis" and "dat" are his own peculiar contribution. But not all Southern deviations from standard English can be set down as Negro in origin. "Ole Virginny" for instance is heard just as frequently among untraveled whites of that locality as among uneducated blacks. The Negro simple speaks the language of his locale, gives back his version of what he hears.

I once had a domestic who was absolutely illiterate, could not write her own name or recognize it when she saw it, and yet her language was beautifully English—not Yankee but English. Aunt Charlotte came to us quite casually thro an employment agency, but I found her such an interesting character, so original, so genteel and withal so lovable, that I kept her long after she was too old to serve my household needs. She used to say: "*My* white folks wouldn't allow their servants (she never said slaves) to 'sociate wit de poorer clahses. Said hit would teach bad habits." Pronounced "gyerl" and "gyahd'n" with that peculiar soft purling sound that only those to the manor born can hope ever to approximate even after patient painstaking practice. An implacable aristocrat, Aunt Charlotte would let you know when she had finished berating some "low down human" as "the scum o' de yearth" that "fum de time she was six years ole clean twell she growed up" she slept on a cot in the room with her young mistress of the same age and was always taught "to carry myself 'cordin to who I am and who I be."

Much of the Negro talk that has burst into the picture since the apotheosis of the "Type" in post War literature is machine made and crassly overdone under the usual pressure of mass production. For the fact is there is no such thing as Negro dialect *per se* just as there was never such a thing as a unique Negro or African language, understood and spoken *ab origine* by all dwellers on the continent of Africa whose decendants were kidnapped for slavery. Says Du Bois: "The slave raiding drew upon every part of Africa—upon the West Coast, the Western and Egyptian Sudan, the valley of the Congo, Abyssinia, the Lake regions, the East Coast and Madagascar—Bantus, Mandingoes, Songhays, the Nubian and Nile Negroes, the Fula and even the Asiatic Malay were represented in the raids." A tribal group then, even if they could chance to preserve their identity thro the decimating welter of the Middle Passage had no possibility whatever of solidarity amid the winnowing vicissitudes of the auction block; hence one might even more properly seek for a "European" than for an African "dialect." The Gullah talk of those slaves segregated on the Sea Islands off the coast of South Carolina was as unintelligible to the aristocratic colored servants of French Huguenots in Charleston as to their equally aristocratic owners; while in comparing Virginia and Texas with reference to those who really have nothing in common but their color, the differences in tone idioms and fundamental root words are so radical and conspicuous as to suggest that they are not racial at all, but traceable possibly to climate, environment and general habitat. It is more correct to speak of an Ohio brogue, or a Georgia drawl than of a "Negro" dialect and yet it may be conceded that the lip laziness ascribed by phoneticians to Americans in general is naturally and temperamentally exaggerated perhaps among persons of heavier maxillae and weak orbicularis oris, until developed by the gymnastics of energetic exercise, such as the French give in "*tantot le rat tata le riz*" etc. Again, it may be that the circumstances and conditions that gave rise to the bon mot: "Keep a stiff upper lip" and "Don't let on" can be held accountable in part at least for a complex that has resulted in greater immobility of those muscles that control speech organs, so noticeable here in comparison with natives of France and England. For after all the English, or attempt at English, of the American Negro is purely an American product and may be traced in each elemental characteristic to its roots in American life. Many of its syncopes and elisions are as old as Chaucer or the King James Version of the Bible, e.g. "afeard" for afraid; "holpen" or "holp" for helped (pronounced without the l); "hit" for it, "til" for to:

> "Is lykned til a fish that is waterless," Chaucer.
> "Moot" for must or might: "Men moot yeve
> silver to the povre freres" Chaucer
> "Hit mought and den agin hit moughtn't" Negro.

The common demonstrative "dis here" has its prototype as far back as the classic Latin, hic-haec-hoc, formed of the blending of an older demonstrative with "ce," adverb of place, written as late as Cicero enclitic on certain case forms like *hosce, hisce, huiusce,* the ce meaning "here." The accusative humce and hamce of course could not be pronounced. Accordingly we have *hunc* and *hanc,* but the union is evidently "this / here" as "this here man." Again, "swich" or "sich" for such and "for to":

> "For to delen with no swich poraille." Chaucer.
> "What went ye out for to see?" Bible.
> "Comin' for to carry me home." Folk Hymn.

On the other hand the conscious eye-minded "improvements" made in folk speech to render it up to date and grammatical are as undeniably racial as any dialect so labeled. The change made by present day *culture* in the beautiful spiritual

> "Were you there when they crucified my Lord?"
> "Sometimes *it causes me* to tremble, tremble"

grammatical but not nearly so close to the heart of the people as the folk version:

> "Oh-h-h-Sometimes hit *makes eh me* tremble, tremble"
> "Were you there when they nailed Him to the Cross?"

I heard Paul Robeson sing Water Boy and I have not yet made up my mind whether it was the real Robeson I heard or the actor impersonating a shuffling, sprawling, crap shooting, chain gang Negro. True, the perfection of art is to conceal art and if Mr. Robeson, the impersonator, does perfectly the type he chooses to present, the only criticism that can attach to him is for choosing one type and not another. One feels differently about Roland Hayes; when he sings Negro words he seems to interpret, not a race, but music, and that speaks a universal language—a human language that all souls understand. *Green Pastures* in the opinion of the writer falls just short of being great for this very reason of over-specialization. As a portraiture of naive and elemental folk-reaction to a group of Bible stories reflected thro the prism of the untutored imaginations of a primitive and essentially religious people, it had the chance of being an immortal epic scintillating with all the hues of their rich and vivid temperament. But, not withstanding all the stage accessories and wealth procurable thro the modern theater this elaborate study would peter out as a cheap and rather bizarre melodrama were it not saved by the sincere artistry of Richard B. Harrison and the really good and true singing of their undying spirituals by a chorus that knows, feels and loves them. The author with his fish fry and bone in cherubic throats has labored to bring forth a pour rire for an audience already committed to the judgment that whatever is done by Negroes must be ludicrous, sincere self expression being out of the question. Such a judgment is the result of a myopic habit of studying behavior only, and concluding egocentrically that all behavior is "put on" for effect on the observer. I have no quarrel with the author's empyrean menu— fried fish or even pigs feet would suit me quite as well as milk and honey—but it is lugged in adventitiously, with malice prepense, and does not at all grow from the roots of this people, having no place whatever in the racial or human imagination.

Mr. Harrison presents artistically the kindly indulgent patriarch that adequately embodies the anthropomorphism of his people. All races gifted with any imagination at all represent their deities in terms of their own qualities actual or hoped for. Michael Angelo's "God the Father" done in pigments for the *Last Judgment* in the Sistine Chapel is no more ethereal or spiritually satisfying than Harrison's done in the personality and tones of a living man; and the heart weary cry with which he utters: "I'm *tired of this people's disobedience and crooked doings*" comes as close to shaming us wayward moderns into the conviction of a guilty conscience as the literal translation in Genesis of the Hebrew: "and the Lord God *repented* that he had made man."

The author achieves a touch of genuine Negro humor when he makes the bibulous Noah plead with the Almighty to grant "jes one mo Kag o' likker for the forty days cantonment in the ark; he is not so happy on the other when he puts undignified words in the mouth of "the Lord," however common such words may be in the supposed Negro lingo. "Doggone it" strikes home with ease in the character of "Amos," but no Negro would ever imagine the Lord using that expression. For the folk mind of the Negro is essentially reverent even when it seems grotesque to the un-understanding mind of a foreign or unsympathetic genius. He takes his religion seriously and never spontaneously creates a burlesque on things and thots that he holds sacred.

Turning to the "Amos 'n' Andy" creations, one is puzzled to find the secret of their tremendous vogue and irresistible appeal for all classes and all ages. Opinions differ. Some ascribe their popularity to the consummate skill with which the actors put over the Negro's dialect. Some claim it is their clever imitation of the tones, so characteristically racial. Some hurriedly turn off the radio and resent the skit *in toto* as injurious to the taxicab industry. Apprehension is expressed by others that for American youth the "well of English" is no longer undefiled and the sheer popularity of these consummate impersonators of Negro humor actually threatens the language of Shakespeare and Milton.

As a matter of course we appreciate an artist and esteem him great just so far as he succeeds in holding a glass to Nature to interpret for the less gifted thro the medium mastered by his own skill, her myriad moods, her cryptic meanings, her "various language." He becomes eyes to the blind, ears for the deaf, and sympathetic insight for those calloused with prejudice. Messrs. Gosden and Correll have the gift or have caught the trick of human insight, of seeing and painting rock bottom essentials, so that in spite of superficial differences, the picture remains human, acts, speaks and reacts with that touch of Nature that makes all kin. The worries and anxieties of little "Amos" (you image him both little and threadbare) over his "hundud an' twenty fi' dollahs" interest and amuse a nation of millionaires just as Gulliver's Lilliputians perennially interest and amuse men of normal stature because they see that the little fellows after all are human. It is like looking at your reflection in the concave side of the mirror—you see your own foibles and follies, but on a scale so unheard of, so unsuspected and withal so amusing that you get a thrill from the very freshness and novelty of your own face. In sympathetic good humor you laught at the good natured caricature. "This Amos is a likable guy after all—and what a conceited ass is Andy! Oh well-a-day. Shouldn't wonder if there's a bit of the same thing in all of us!" The miracle is that you have had revealed thro "the soft slur of the Southern Negro" and those resonant tones the Soul of a Folk you had never seen before at closer focus than the outer rim of some epidermic cells—the same miracle that the creative artist must unfailingly bring to pass, whatever his tools and whoever his public. Whether he works with pigments or chisel, with tone pictures or muscular action, he must reveal to you, whoever you are a human kinship, the great human fact, whatever his race and whatever his theme. DeBose Heywood can thus paint Porgy of Catfish Alley and Mamba's Daughters, not because of any personal photography from experience with "Types" in those environs, still less because of any sermon or theorem he has to promulgate, but because he has the genius to look into that ant hill down deep enough and sincerely enough to find that "Fate under the hood of environing conditions is the inexorable protagonist of Man in Life's Drama, whether the hero be Oedipus or Jean Val Jean, Porgy or Othello. In the last analysis: "The Play's the thing"— not the Dialect and not the race of the Players.

# 7

# "Loss of Speech Through Isolation"

## (ca. 1923)

In this essay, Cooper recalls her interactions with a local family that kept to itself and rarely—if ever—spoke.
She finds the children's rare speech to need tutoring,
and she takes it upon herself to help. Cooper later
learns that the family had been isolated from the surrounding community and cut off from the town because its people charged the father with a crime and
lynched him, only to learn of the true perpetrator later.
The story reveals the ongoing impact of both the lynching and its aftermath as the family struggles in isolation. In opening the sketch, Cooper makes reference to
her summer serving as a supervisor of War Camp play-
grounds during World War I. The essay appears under
the title heading *A Problem in American Education:
Sketches from a Teacher's Notebook*, suggesting it may
have been part of a larger project as well as a chapter in
what Cooper outlined for her writings in *On Education*.

SOURCE: Anna Julia Cooper Papers, box 23-4, folder 36,
Moorland-Spingarn Research Center, Howard University.

One summer during the World War as director of War Camp
Community Service I had charge of a playground in West Virginia.

Standing out conspicuously in my impressions of that summer's experiences is a family whom I shall call Berry—chiefly

because that is not their name. The two lads, about ten and twelve, who first presented themselves to my acquaintanceship were perfect little Ishmaelites—their hand against everybody and every man's hand against them. Teachers of the neighborhood said that their school record was simply an annual repetition of suspensions and expulsions. They would present themselves regularly in September all spic and span with clean shirts, clean, if patched trousers, and clean eager faces for the year's start; but something always happened before the first lap of the course was run, and everybody thought the Berry boys lucky if October found them still on "praying ground where e'en the vilest sinner may return."

They were rather shy of the playground, especially when other children were there having a good time. Decidedly anti-social, they would slip in after the gates were shut and the swings locked, pick or break the locks to enjoy criminally what they might have had freely by simply being in the current with other people. They were never openly and bravely bad—they were only bad as rats are bad—with a passion and a genius for getting around all constituted authority. They would delight in climbing a hill overlooking the playground whence they would roll down boulders and huge stones that came crashing to a full stop just outside the limits of my jurisdiction. I noticed that their bedevilment was peculiarly voiceless. Most urchins of that type would be ready to sing out in fiendish glee when they thought they had you wrought up to a charming pitch of impotent rage. Not so the Berry boys. In fact they resembled nothing more than the silent little old men of the mountains that Rip saw amusing themselves at ninepins; and if you uttered the word "police!" the whole panorama would disappear so quickly, vanishing so completely you would imagine it had all been a horrid nightmare, and there wasn't any such thing as Berry boys after all.—You had been dreaming!

One day when I was almost alone on the playground in consequence of a steady drizzle all forenoon, I noticed a forlorn little figure with a pair of big round mellow eyes, peeping at me through chinks in the palings. As I started down to speak to her, the frightened little creature, a child of five or six made a dash as tho she would run away. I coaxed her in and putting her in one of the little folks' swings, stood by giving her a gentle push now and then, an excitement that she enjoyed very much. Tho she said nothing, one could read her gratitude in those lustrous round eyes—her joy was too deep for utterance. Alas, short lived joy! A tall soldier lad in khaki, puttees and an over-seas cap, came stalking up the walk. Without recognizing me or uttering a word he took up a position at the rear where he caught the eye of the little mite in the swing. The effect was electrical. The child fell out of the swing as if she had been shot! and pit-a-pat, pit-a-pat, as fast as her little legs could carry her she flew, neither looking back nor waving goodbye. Startled out of my Olympian calm, I turned on the stranger and demanded to know what was the matter.

"Meh wants her home," he replied sententiously.

"Yes? but why didn't you say your mother sent for her? You haven't said a word!"

"She know what I mean."

"Perhaps! But it isn't right for you to deal in dumb signs in conveying what you mean. You owe that child the English language. You are grown and have travelled. You can express yourself and interest her in the wonderful world outside that you have had glimpses of. She will never be anything but a dumb, shut-in creature unless you make opportunities for her to cultivate human speech!" More of the same sort I poured forth out of a full heart from my accustomed store. What struck me all the time I was talking was the unbroken stolidity with which my bursts of eloquence were received. He showed neither resentment at the lambasting I gave him nor a gleam of appreciation that it was fairly well done for a woman. He was chewing a bit of wheat straw pulled in the field and regarded me with the patient, passionless eyes of a yoke of oxen at the end of a furrow when the day is done. Finally in sheer desperation at getting no response, I turned on my heel and left him. Reaching down he pulled another bit of straw which he caught in his teeth and stalked out as he had stalked in. My notebook records this day: "Encounter with the oldest and youngest of the Berry family."

Act II, Scene 1, discovers me in the midst of my basket weavers, reed and rafia all around and busy little fingers holding up mats and baskets in various stages of imperfection—all

clamoring to be set right and shown how at the same instant.[1]
Walter Berry, the younger of the two tormentors I had known
from the first on the playground, now becoming less shy and
perhaps, too, a little less savage, was hovering near in the background, evidently struggling with something he wanted to say
but having a hard time getting it out. At last he sidled up, and
speaking over my shoulder from behind he managed to blurt out
desperately:

"Mith Coo' show—*I* make bick *too!*"

"Why certainly, Walter," I said with ready comprehension.
"I'll be glad to show you how to make a bas-ket," speaking very
distinctly and letting him observe the motion of my lips in pro-
nouncing "bas-ket." "You must try to come every day and you
have to take lots of pains, you know. But it will be real nice to
make a basket for your mother.—Don't you think so?"

Well, from that day till the end of my stay I was taming Walter
and incidentally getting a basket ready to present to his mother.
Not infrequently I had to take out at night what Walter had put
in by day so as to have him start right the next day, but on the
whole the basket, between us, got on amazingly well and I determined to use it as a card of introduction to Mrs. Berry the
"Meh" of whom I had heard much but never seen. Accordingly,
armed with my playground products I fared forth to break the
ice and force a passage into some homes I had never succeeded
in luring out to any of our many tempting "occasions" at the
playground. Mrs. Berry's was my first coup de main. The house
was at the top of a high hill with more steps to climb to reach the
porch which spanned a plain but scrupulously neat living room.
The floor was freshly scrubbed with white sand, there was a deal
table also scrubbed to snowy whiteness and a few splint bot-
tomed chairs scrubbed likewise. All this I noted standing on the
threshold of the front door which stood wide open from habit,
one could see, rather than with any notion of inviting wayfarers
to enter. I knocked on the floor with the point of my umbrella
and after some minutes a comely little black woman appeared in
the doorway just opposite and stood with hands crossed in front
of her waiting to learn the cause of the intrusion. "Oh," I said
with an ingratiating smile; "This is Mrs. Berry, is it not? I am
Mrs. Cooper, Walter's teacher on the playground. I came to

bring you a little basket that Walter made for you—I taught him how," I added truthfully. "Rather pretty don't you think?" Appealingly now—for I was becoming a wee bit phased at whipping my own top. For the lady held her pose of dignified aloofness in queenly silence. She might have been an artist's conception of Juno just after that goatherd Paris had pinned the blue ribbon on his amorous little charmer. She did not frown, neither did she beam a smile. She did not ask me in nor say that she was glad I brought the basket. She did not make a pretence of thanking me for any interest I had taken in Walter nor did she try to act out the lie that she was glad to meet me, and yet with it all her manner was singularly free from active repulsion. Byron's line comes to mind: "*I seek to shun, not hate mankind,*" and yet Byron's misanthropy was a pose put on to write about it, and the curl of his patrician lip, the négligé of his open collar and the somber lilt of his dreamy eyes were sedulously cultivated before the mirror by all the dudes and dandies in New York and London. But here in this solitary little woman was something that was no pose, something commanding respect, almost akin to awe and reverence, something, I felt instinctively, too sacred for prying eyes and inquisitive "investigators." She stood and appraised me with that same unfrowning eye I had noticed in her first born that made you think of uncomplaining oxen, too strong to weep, too weighted down to smile. After a while she parted her lips—and this is what she said: "I keep to myself; I don' want nothin' to do wit nobody." Her tone was even and clear without the slightest suspicion of hysteria or overwrought emotion. The words might have been borne in from a disembodied spirit, so passionless were they, so sublimated, so purified of the tenseness and dross of the physical and earthy.

"But Mrs. Berry," I persisted, "You can't *live* that way! You can't be in the world without having something to do with other people!"

"I been livin that way longer'n you been livin' yo' way," she rejoined, "I'm older'n you." (She wasn't at all; but a comparatively young woman.) I accepted the compliment without debate, however, and tried by the most beguiling arts I knew to entice her out of her solitude. After using all the illustrations and arguments I could think of to suggest the interdependence of man on man I was rewarded by seeing the merest ghost of a smile flit across her countenance, more like the quivering gleam of far-away lightning than the steady radiance of sunlight and dawn. We were still standing where I could look out from the threshold of the porch on the muddy water of the Ohio River. "There's nothing you could get to eat," I continued, "without calling in someone to help you out. You can go to the river and fish—"

"And then I'd have to have lard to cook 'em wit," she put in brightly.

Good! I knew I had struck fire and we were friends at last.

As I came down the steps she called out almost shamefastly, "When you come to W.—— again, come to see me!"

"Oh, no," I bantered—"you don't want to see anybody!"

"Well, if all was like you," she answered dismally.

It was not till I had left W.—— that I understood the tragedy of Mrs. Berry's grim struggle with life. Her husband, an innocent man, had been torn from her arms by an infuriated mob and brutally murdered—lynched. The town realized its mistake afterwards when the true culprit confessed but it was too late to bind up that broken family, and the humble drama of that obscure black woman like a wounded animal with her cubs literally digging herself in and then at bay dumbly turning to face—*America*—her "head bloody but unbowed"[2]—I swear the pathos and inexorable fatefulness of that titanic struggle—an inescapable one in the clash of American forces, is worthy an Epic for its heroic grandeur and unconquerable grit!

And I wondered what our brand of education, what our smug injunction that the home "is expected" to cooperate with the school will find or create for the help and guidance of such a home, a type as truly evolved from American environmental conditions as are the blind fish in the Mammoth Cave or the bronchos of the western plains.

A Problem—Will isolation solve it?

# 8

# "College Extension for
Working People"

*(no date)*

This essay reiterates Cooper's calls for support to make higher education accessible for people from all backgrounds and in all fields so that they may demand fair pay and respect for their work and participate in US societies as educated and engaged citizens. Cooper argues that it is Black college-educated leaders' responsibility to make higher education available to wage earners. She details America's dutiful work to educate its underprivileged white population, but she finds that African Americans' access to higher education has nearly disappeared despite an earlier period when schools were beginning to admit Black students. In the outline for her writings *On Education*, the seventh essay is listed as "The Higher Calling for the Teacher of Underprivileged Adults." While an essay bearing this title does not appear in the archives, "College Extension for Working People" explicitly addresses how serving as a teacher for "underprivileged adults" constitutes a higher calling for African Americans who have secured higher education. It is likely, therefore, but not certain, that this is the essay Cooper was referencing in the outline.

SOURCE: *The Journal of the College Alumnae Club*, nd, in Anna Julia Cooper Papers, box 23-5, folder 61, Moorland-Spingarn Research Center, Howard University.

The criticism is often brought against our "culture" (and with what justice the conscience of the individual must decide) that we are not "good radiators." That education, well-being, personal refinement, instead of making torch bearers and missionaries of the Gospel of a better day and a brighter hope for the less privileged, has the effect of encasing us in a sheath of self-centered dilettantism supersensitive to the rough elbows of the vulgar herd, and ego-centrically devoted to the betterment solely of our own immediate environment; and that, even more narrowly, for the sake and satisfaction solely of our own soul's growth and well-being. Nay, there are some, even, who go a step farther and assert that the selfishness or exclusiveness, to some degree inherent in the intensive cultivation of personality everywhere, takes on with us a tinge of rancor and resentment far more withering than the selfishness of other groups. That there is here a positive repulsion and an insurmountable antagonism against the "untouchables" whose existence is thought to cause and explain and to some extent excuse all their social handicaps and, however innocent, to be responsible for the origin and spread of the contagion of race prejudice; so that, as the human sediment is stratified lower and deeper in the social scale, the poignant prejudices of race and color become more and more galling, and the sufferers from it themselves inflict the same clannish bitterness with intensified fury on each caste a little below themselves.

In so far as this is mere emotion there is no use arguing with or about it. The writer will undertake in the present essay merely to bring forward a few facts and comparisons that reveal a broad and inviting field for earnest, thoughtful college women of today to address themselves to the really exhilarating task of College Extension for *Working People*, or, in other words, to furnishing opportunity for steady intellectual growth and a satisfying pursuit of the higher Education for those whose economic status places them in the category of wage-earners. In doing so I shall not appeal to my readers' sympathies for the downtrodden or try to enlist charity for the under dog or emphasize unduly the racial handicap. A broad interest in his community is not only a duty and responsibility of the college bred man and woman, it is a characteristic and essential function, an answer and a justification in return for the privileges with which they have been favored and the advantages they have enjoyed.

To study with trained intelligence this social ferment of his time, to cast into the unguided and misguided, the hysterical and often riotous turbulence of the seething, writhing, raging mass the calm sanity of a well-disciplined leadership, a purposeful initiative and wisely systematized restraint—such is the high task and the sacred obligation of the elect few who, from contacts within college walls with the noblest, the truest, the best, are prepared as heirs of all the ages to take their rightful place as guides, as torch bearers to lead order out of chaos and to direct the trend of the social movement and social aspirations along the upward passes. Leadership is the college man's duty to society— a duty which automatically lifts him above the sordid selfishness which threatens the economic world of today. Service is his slogan, and brotherhood in his vocabulary is limited only by the world's need and his own enlightened resourcefulness. He feels that he owes all and is glad to give all for universal betterment.

Not long ago prospectors and engineers were looking for an ideal spot to locate a summer camp for our Chief Executive. They found one on the banks of the Rapidan, in historic Virginia, a spot to drive away dull care and to forget the jangling and the wrangling of human affairs. But one day a human affair obtruded itself into that peaceful retreat. It was not pleasant. In fact it was found that those mountains were "infested" so to speak, "with tribes of undiscovered Americans," ignorant, unkempt, unclean. They were benighted white Americans in almost a state of savagery within a stone's throw of the heart of the nation, in fact literally sitting on the doorstep of the Chief Executive.

What concerns us here is the instant and spontaneous reaction of progressive America to this embarrassing problem. Something must be done and at once. The Associated Press hastened to assure an amazed and wondering public that living conditions disclosed in the neighborhood of the Rapidan were not to be regarded as a mark of inferiority either in mentality or in social advancement. Isolation here in the mountain fastnesses had left these human waifs without that contact which is needed for any progress. Immediately the latest and finest products of invention and science were put on foot, on wings, to hurry civilization overnight to the mountaineers. Trucks, planes, telephones, radios, wireless, were pressed into service as if to make amends for the neglect. Most significant and in the forefront for emphasis went the modern school-house and the sympathetic teacher with her carefully selected "methods" and her wise adaptation of means to ends.

A certain Metropolitan daily gravely suggested that in order to transplant an "atmosphere" of culture some of the retired teachers and Government employees whose pensions enabled them to disregard salaries be invited to make there a college settlement and colonize the ideas and ideals of our advanced civilization. Admittedly education was the indispensable doctor and the unfailing remedy for regaining the lost step and the impaired touch with humanity and the moving world of thought and wide-awake activity.

By education we fall in line and hold our own with the vanguard of civilization, and the incident here mentioned shows the readiness and liberality with which enlightened men and women of our day take up responsibilities for backward groups and unprivileged classes, and the unhesitating spontaneity with which the best thought, the best discoveries, the best inventions are poured forth for the rehabilitation and the spurring on of their lagging forces. It is as if to pay a debt long overdue—as if the rich and powerful were ashamed to enjoy wealth and prominence under pressure of the consciousness that there are living in outer darkness and neglect their brothers after the flesh, rightful heirs of the common inheritance and entitled by inalienable birthright to a blood brother's share in all the rights, privileges, and advantages derived from the toil and production of their forebears. There is this tradition inherent in culture. It yearns with a mighty yearning to propagate itself—to send the idea "missionarying," to strike its roots and send its seedlings further and further, and to see to it that in the next generation and the next and the next a glorious immortality shall be its reward.

Good tidings of salvation by enlightenment, by right living, by harmony, sane adjustment, and good will to men is not an idea that can be preempted and monopolized within a narrow group or egocentric race. It cannot be stifled, it must come out; and like the divine spark that it is, it gives its possessor no peace till it has been passed on and on kindling a new light and inflaming a new want in the souls of men—the Saviors of the world.

That there should be artificial barriers and man-made handicaps in this cosmic advance seems incredible, contradictory, stultifying. Above all, in America, the Open Door of Opportunity to learn, to get in step, to appreciate the good things of life surely ought to be the rule, the norm, the unvarying law of this land "conceived in liberty and dedicated to the proposition that all men are created equal."

Germany is responsible for teaching the world many things by her high-powered efficiency in the World War, an efficiency built up admittedly and deliberately by her Educational System. Not the least of these lessons, good for peace time though learned and tested by the bitter experience of war, is the incalculable value, the indispensable first necessity to a Nation of its Man-Power. When our country went up against Germany in the World War, America realized for the first time in all her history, perhaps, that Roosevelt's slogan *"All Men* Up!" was at such a crisis immeasurably safer and saner than the exploiter's maxim "Some Men Down." Since our dearly bought experience in that trying ordeal, the States and the Federal Government have courageously addressed themselves to the general problems of illiteracy and Adult Education.

There has been formed the National Organization for Adult Education headed by the former Secretary of War, Newton D. Baker; also an important department has sprung up in the Office of Education (formerly known as the Bureau of Education) under Commissioner Wm. John Cooper, stimulating and abetting College and University Extension—the actual enlargement of college campus boundaries by correspondence, by radio talks, by traveling professors, traveling libraries, laboratories, moving pictures—every possible and imaginable help in the promotion of the education of adults. L. R. Alderman, specialist in adult education in the Office of Education, is authority for much detailed information of interest to the large number of people who for any reason cannot go to college, and may profit by having the college come to them. Four hundred forty-three institutions are listed as offering some type of extension work for the years 1928 and 1929 for the benefit of persons anxious to further their education by study during leisure hours. Again, there is the National Illiteracy Crusade, Inc., in the Washington Building under Mrs. Cora Wilson Stewart, Director, John H. Finley, President, Jane Addams and Glenn Frank, Vice Presidents. The whole movement is a titanic push to lift, as it were, the opprobrium felt as a national disgrace in the presence of our World War Allies, that we were sending men to save the world for Democracy who had not themselves been saved from the ignominy and shame of ignorance and degradation.

It is a comfort to be able to state that this rebirth of a great national interest in education has shown already gratifying results, especially among classes hitherto overlooked or neglected.

A comparison of the latest census with that of 1920, taking the District of Columbia alone as symptomatic of the general trend throughout the entire country, will disclose some very significant figures and facts embodying a real awakening in the United States to the deep and crucially important element which the education of all the people has to contribute to the national efficiency. The number of persons from 5 to 20 years of age attending school in the District in 1930 is 83,701 as compared with 64,475 in 1920; the number of persons 10 years of age and over unable to read and write in 1930 was only 6,611 as against 10,509 in 1920, the percentage of illiteracy having been reduced from 2.8 to 1.6. But what concerns the present argument most directly is the telling reduction of illiteracy among Negroes by more than 50 per cent in the same decade. In 1920 there were, in a population of 93,782 Negroes, 8,053 who could not read or write; in 1930, out of a population of 111,224, there are only 4,591 reported illiterate; that is, a reduction from 8.6 in 1920 to 4.1 at present accounting. As was well said by G. F. T. Cook, the first and last man of this race to be superintendent of schools in Washington without a hyphen attached: "No colored school has ever failed for want of scholars; the parents sent their children even when too poor to be decently fed or clothed."

A brief survey of universities and colleges of Washington shows but one colored in a list of seven recognized as full time universities, while in a list of part time colleges and special schools compiled by Harry O. Hine for the District of Columbia, out of 88 listed there is not one that will admit a Negro whatever his qualifications.[1]

In "Washington Past and Present," a four volume history by Proctor and Williams, the late Dr. Carusi has contributed a thirty-six page article on Higher Education in the District of Columbia. In this article he points out that there are many white institutions of learning that look back on the uncertainties of poverty and general financial instability. We know of several colored lawyers who hold degrees from those schools. But not one of these institutions today will admit a colored man or woman whatever his qualifications.

As then, the lines have been drawn tighter and tighter, the man who is both colored and poor finds himself left out of the educational reckoning and surely in need of those agencies for college extension and higher education which may be initiated by the resourceful sympathies of his own leaders.

# 9

# *The Social Settlement:*
# *What It Is, and What It Does*

*(1913)*

In this 1913 pamphlet, printed by Murray Brothers Press, Cooper explains the history, purpose, and work of the social settlement. She addresses the need for a social settlement to serve Black communities, especially the poor, and recognizes the first colored social settlement in Washington, DC. Social settlements sought to address the ill conditions of the city by offering classes, social and academic clubs, access to libraries, affordable food, health care, recreational programs, safe water, and more. Cooper describes the settlement's purpose "to stimulate ambition, raise moral standards, strengthen character and develop capacity for self-help."

SOURCE: Printed by Murray Brothers Press, Washington, DC, 1913, in Anna Julia Cooper Alumni File, Oberlin College Archives.

The Social Settlement idea is as old as the fact that "The Word was made flesh and dwelt among us." It is an attempt to carry into the city slums the incarnate Word, the idea of better living, the ideal of higher thinking, embodied or energized in earnest and resourceful men and women who LIVE THERE. It is the heart of sympathy, the hand of brotherly grip, the brain of understanding insight, of efficient and masterful good will indwelling in the midst of down-and-out humanity. It is the gospel of the good neighbor, the evangel of helpful sociability. It is a democracy that "levels up" by throwing into the breach its best and its holiest, it is a creed that believes in the Christianity that can save society, a religion that interprets its commission "into all the world and to every creature" to include also our own back alleys and the drunkard whom our laws and customs have helped to undo. It is set on fire with the conviction that all men are created with the divine right to a chance, and sets about hammering down some of those hideous handicaps which hamper whole sections of a community through the inequalities of environment, or the greed of the great. It sees in a little child the most precious possibilities and at the same time the most awful peril of the universe; and it endeavors to promote, for his sake, a home, as seedling soil that cultures the best, with guiding lines and props and God's own sunlight and the God-ordained chance to grow up right.

In point of time the Social Settlement movement in England antedates the attempt to form such centers in America by twenty-five or thirty years. In the early [18]60's the universities of Cambridge and Oxford were manifesting a social conscience under the influence of such men as Ruskin, Toynbee, Chas. Kingsley, Prof. Seeley and Green, the historian. The Workingmen's College in London was founded by F. D. Maurice in 1860. In 1867 Edward Denison, an Oxford man of means, went to Stepney, London, making his home among the people, seeking to understand their needs and to help them.

Toynbee Hall, in the White Chapel district, East London, is possibly the earliest full embodiment of the modern social settlement. Arnold Toynbee, a brilliant young Oxonian, gave his life in devotion to this cause, and after his premature death friends who had caught the fire of his enthusiasm took up the work as a memorial. The oldest Social Settlement in the United States is "Neighborhood Guild," now known as University Settlement in New York City. It was founded by Dr. Coit, in 1887, and has had remarkable influence in municipal reform, sanitary housing, extension of parks into crowded neighborhoods, and improvement of conditions among working girls.

Hull House, in Chicago, probably the most widely known

Settlement in America, was established in 1889 by Miss Jane Addams and Miss Ellen Starr. A characteristic remark of Miss Addams maybe quoted as almost a warning in general how not to succeed: "SETTLEMENTS SUCCEED THRU THE CHARACTER, FORCE AND INSIGHT OF SANE AND INFORMED RESIDENTS. WORKING PEOPLE ARE QUICK TO DETECT SHAMS; AND MERELY LODGING IN A TENEMENT DISTRICT WILL NOT MAKE ONE USEFUL."

The educational work is carried on at Hull House by college men and women and by lectures under the extension work of the University of Chicago. All service, even of resident workers, is gratuitous, and it is counted an honor to have a share in the admirable work.

A few typical examples taken from activities in the Settlements in Philadelphia, New York or Chicago will illustrate what many do and what all aim to do. A library and reading room, generally a branch of the public library, is maintained for the benefit of the neighborhood, where recreation clubs and study classes enjoy social advantages under ideal circumstances. The kitchen or coffee house wages a bloodless warfare against the groggery by furnishing at low cost wholesome drinks and nutritious foods with clean, cheerful and comfortable surroundings. There are art exhibitions to cultivate the esthetic sense, and often a circulating picture library sends out mounted photographs of great pictures into the homes of the people, a printed slip giving a sketch of the artist and a description of the subject being pasted on the back.

Sometimes a co-operative coal club is formed, saving to its members several dollars per ton on coal which was formerly purchased by the bucket. This sort of lesson in economy and thrift is among the most useful means of promoting social efficiency. It is notorious that the poor pay the highest prices for necessities, and they are gilt-edge customers for the "on-time" salesman. And so the stamp system of collecting savings by the friendly visitor from the settlement inculcates the habit of saving the pennies with the result of larger returns from provident expenditures.

Lectures on economic, social and hygienic subjects attended by workers in various charitable and philanthropic institutions furnish a means of training specialists for other fields. The college settlement in a certain city found in their neighborhood a space covered by old tenements unfit for human habitation. The workers went before mayor and aldermen with a request to have the property purchased by the city and made open space for fresh air, health giving sunshine, room for play and chance for beauty. Persistent effort was crowned with success.

In a Jewish quarter in New York City flourishes the "Gospel" settlement established by a Christian woman of whom the *Outlook* says: Mrs. Bird has not endeavored to induce Jews to accept a Christian creed nor has she desired to do so. Her object is not to teach theology, but to impart life. Her home is open from early morning to late at night; and in it are classes and clubs to which boys and girls, men and women of every faith, or none at all, receive equal welcome.

Paradoxically enough, the very period of the world that witnesses the most widespread activity in uplift movements and intensest devotion to social service finds in America the hard wall of race prejudice against Negroes most emphatically bolted and barred. This is perhaps because the transfer in narrow minds from individual selfishness to group selfishness covers with the glamor of religious consecration the sordid meanness of one race toward another. Let a man convince himself that natural selection and survival of the fittest in some way involve responsibility for the uplift of his entire group, and if he is mean anyhow, it will not be hard for him to conclude that he is doing God's service by excluding hated groups or races from all enjoyments and advantages sought for his own. A white woman said to me: "I cannot hold mothers' meetings in connection with my school, or in any way touch the social life of its people." This woman is, and has been for years, principal of a colored school in the south. Yet she confesses that she has not at all touched the social life of the people who need that touch far more than they need either books or trades.

In 1901 there came to Washington a white man, Chas. F. Weller, as executive officer of the Associated Charities of the District of Columbia. His method was to learn how best to minister to the needs of the poor by being a "good neighbor" in neglected neighborhoods; his religion, that every message to man must come expressed in the life of brother-man. He was not conscious of a color line, or, if he was, he did not believe it should fetter the soul of Service. In fact, he seemed to deepen his sense of responsibility with the knowledge of the deeper need and long neglect of colored Americans; and to feel that the social body could not be two-thirds well and one-third sick, two-thirds clean and one-third unwashed, or two-thirds virtuous and one-third impure. He rented a room in an alley given over to colored people of the poorest class, and with the aid of his trusty camera began to study conditions. In his book, *Neglected Neighbors in the National Capital*, he pays tribute to a colored family with whom he thus sojourned: "Out of such a hole as this, Charley, Mrs. Malcolm's older son, has come—clean, honest and ambitious." For this is the hope, beneath all social horrors, that even

> "In the mud and scum of things
> There alway, alway, something sings."

But Mr. Weller was not allowed to work out this hope in his own way. The compulsion of public opinion, that psychic force which controls society, willed that no white man shall play the part of the Good Samaritan if he answers the question, "Who is my neighbor?" broadly enough to include the neediest class of the social body.

> "Prone in the road he lay,
>   Wounded and sore bested;
> Priests, Levites passed that way
>   And turned aside the head.
> They were not hardened men
>   In human service slack;
> His need was great; but then,
>   His face, you see, WAS BLACK."

And the pity of it all is its obviousness to the American mind— its finality and undebatable inexorable fatefulness. It is as if you said: "Why, of course the Christ could not have meant YOU. No conception of universal brotherhood could ever be made to include YOUR race variety! That were preposterous to imagine!"

And so Mr. Weller had to modify his plan of personal work in a colored settlement, but he formed a conference class of willing workers among the colored people themselves, who met in the office of the Charities building and organized the first colored social settlement in Washington, and perhaps the first distinctive settlement of its kind in the world. A sympathetic young white woman—a woman not rich in this world's goods, only a salaried clerk in government employ—donated rent-free a small six-room house on M street southwest, in a section that had borne the ill-omened name of Bloodfield. Here clubs and classes were conducted and after a residence was secured, day nursery, a kindergarten, penny saving through the stamp system and friendly visiting were added. The influence of the settlement on the neighborhood has been marvelous, and its workers have proven helpful agencies in promoting civic improvement and supporting law and order. The growth of the work has called for a larger building, which was erected three years ago, on L street southwest, about a block away from its first home and in the neighborhood of the same general need.

A milk station supplied by a philanthropic citizen has furnished wholesome nourishment to about sixty babies each day; a nurse and doctor, under the same generous provision, have given instruction in "What to Do and How to Do It" to numbers of little mothers whose slender shoulders have burdens beyond their years. Thrift and provident saving are inculcated through the friendly visitor and the penny stamps. A good library is maintained as a branch of the public library, and useful arts and crafts are taught by competent teachers. The response of the neighborhood in support of the work has been admirable. The colored people have realized that without their loyal support the work must fail, and never have people shown greater willingness. The Settlement music department contains interesting possibilities and already numbers many anxious applicants. A swimming pool is one of our dearest ideals, not yet in sight, and it is hoped that some Abou Ben Adhem,[1] who has realized the saving grace of plentiful water, may make public baths as accessible to all the people as Andrew Carnegie has made libraries and learning. A wealthy citizen of Baltimore has established public laundries among the work people of that city where a poor washer-woman may, at reasonable cost for soap and starch, wash and iron under perfectly sanitary conditions and with the best approved appliances—a philanthropy, it seems to me, more directly blessing the class who give than these who receive, if we reflect on the terrible consequences that may result from ignorant laundering under squalid conditions. It is one of the stultifying humiliations of American manners that the group pariahed as the great Unwashed are not only not encouraged to be clean, but are actually barred out from water. Personally, I would struggle to get water if I had to purchase it by the pint. If I went to hunt big game in the jungle I would wash—I think. But after living through some hours of American railway service (not the best to be had for the money I paid, but the best I could get at any price), on going for refreshment and accommodation to a waiting room provided for the purpose, my preference generally is to endure the dirt and stains I have rather than fly to that so palpably pestiferous.

If only a millionaire would care for my advice. Baths! Baths! Baths! for the plain people, for poor people, for colored people! Endow swimming pools, establish showers, finance laundries! Give us water, oh land of mighty rivers, give water of thy gushing fountains and mighty cataracts! Give water, oh, fatherland, to thy children of sweat and toil; water to wash in, water to play in, water to love and trust and know on terms of intimate familiarity!

In my walk to the Settlement Home I pass a saloon at every corner. The door is of easy swing, the display of obtrusive sociability and alluring hospitality. There are some churches in the neighborhood, too, but closed and dark nine-tenths of the time. At one recently, even on a Sunday, I had to stand outside a bolted door fifteen minutes because I had chanced to come one minute late. The one man, the one door that gives a comforting welcome to a colored man at all hours of the day and night, the one entertainment where his money is as good as any other is that of the saloon and its unctuous keeper. Not a lecture hall, theater or cafe, not a musical or pictorial exhibition, not a place to catch an ideal or inspire a purpose but deliberately, relentlessly, RELIGIOUSLY, slams the door in the black man's face. One of my neighborhood friends works eight hours a day underground in the sewers of this great city. I find him sometimes in the evening fixing up a tiny flower bed in front of his little home, while his wife sings in preparation of the family meal inside. It is easy to believe that if I had to breathe the gases of the city's sewerage for my eight-hour working day, year in and year out, the good temperance people would have to offer something better than a "don't" to keep me from taking the beaten track to the dazzling hospitality that promises a forgetting.

Washington has the largest colored population of any city in the world. Whatever obtains here will stand as a model of the best or a symptom of the worst in American life. It is to the interest of this entire nation that no plague spots of hidden or segregated depravity be overlooked and ignored as outside the nation's current of life. It is to the interest of every man, woman and child in Washington that each child here, the least important in our reckoning as well as the most important, shall have the chance to develop into serviceable citizenship.

The Social Settlement with its home life, its neighborhood visiting, its clubs, classes and personal service, is endeavoring to bring higher ideals of life and character to many who are largely cut off from good influences and opportunities; to stimulate ambition, raise moral standards, strengthen character and develop capacity for self-help.

We hear a great deal these days about a fitting memorial to the immortal Lincoln, whose name will stand through all the ages as the great Emancipator of a much-exploited people. In what truer way can we endorse and perpetuate the elemental human good for which the martyr President died and to which the great founder of Hampton devoted his life than to build and maintain at our nation's Capital a working bureau of ideals and opportunities—a "level bridge" reaching sheer to the shores of complete emancipation, the land of honest toil and self-respect, of self-control and social efficiency.

# 10

# "The Tie That Used to Bind"

## *(no date)*

This story is told in the first person and recounts the narrator's attempts to care for an older Black woman whose husband served in the Spanish-American War and has recently died, while also narrating an attempt to secure a war pension for the widow. After her husband's funeral, the woman becomes confused and looks for her husband, thinking he is still alive. The narrator attempts to care for her, but the woman is ultimately sent to a "hospital for the colored insane." This story also demonstrates how an elderly Black woman's health and well-being are affected directly and indirectly by violence, war, and loss.

SOURCE: Anna Julia Cooper Papers, box 23-4, folder 38, Moorland-Spingarn Research Center, Howard University.

## A Mid-Victorian Negro Marriage

She did not cry. Her eyes were dry and her lips trembled and twisted just a little as she tried to smile.

With native courtesy she bent at the waist to greet me. How you do, Sis Annie. Whe'eh's Ander? I told her as gently as I could that the body could not have come thro on the same train with me, altho I had thot that every arrangement was complete and the station master at Old Point assured me when I bought the tickets for myself and—*the box* that it would be put in the baggage car of my train to Raleigh. She asked only one question:

"Does he look po?"

"Oh no; I answered with brave cheerfulness.

"He looks all right."

At the same time visions of the shrunken figure in army blue trousers, long rows of metal file cases like compartments of a huge oven, drawer upon drawer, drawer upon drawer, all ticketed and provided with knobs so that the efficient attendant could conveniently pull out one or shove in another as easily as the baker man looks into the compartments of his huge stacks of browning bread. And when the right one ticketed Andrew J. Anderson; disease pneumonia; department— and so on and so on I said quietly: His wife wants me to bring him home for burial.

"You will have to see an undertaker over in town for that. We provide just the plainest interment here at the Home."

I choked back my visions and dwelt only on how natural and peaceful he looked. She turned to the kitchen to prepare a meal for me in spite of my repeated insistence that I wanted nothing. I heard her mutter to herself: "Dat po' soul out dere in all dis rain by hisself."

She went thro the funeral with the same more than natural calm. Chose the hymns herself from the Hymnal: No. 660. "Oh for a closer walk with God" and "How firm a foundation" cause, she said, "Ander always liked dat one."

I had slipped to the undertakers and ordered suitable clothes and a handsome casket so that he would not "*look po.*" Friends sent flowers not stiff set pieces from florists, but familiar loving blooms from home gardens and friendly yards; and the little front room of that humble cottage where her Ander lay in state was as dignified and solemnly beautiful as a millionaire's castle could have been made. The impressive burial service of the Prayer Book, the same alike for Prince or peasant, the rich harmony of full throated voices unspoiled by instrumental accompaniment, the simple dignity of that silent form lying there seemed to await and claim as its just and fitting due the final homage and ultimate tribute of reverential adoration from all the living.

I had to get back to my work almost immediately and in Washington busied myself at once to secure a pension for her as a Spanish American War Widow.[1] As the cottage in which she lived free of rent was mine and she seemed physically fit to look after herself, I felt the pension tho small was sufficient for her simple wants the rest of her natural life. To prove her marriage I had the frayed and yellow leaves of the family Bible:

*Andrew J. Anderson married to Caroline McPherson Jan. 1, 1867.*

No need, for every citizen of Raleigh, white or black knew her and could testify that from the time that memory runneth not to the contrary she had always been a faithful and devoted wife, a loyal and even ostentatiously proud supporter and defender of her liege lord as any medieval vassal. For 50 years they had lived together in an ideal union and not even the vilest ever dared a breath of suspicion against her fidelity to her marriage vows. Tho wise gossips would shake slanderous heads with "Calline's plum crazy 'bout her Ander as she calls him, and he aint no better'n he ought to be. She'd sell her soul to de debble jes to please him. Jes' look a' dat bastard o' his 'n she took to raise." "Aint he de very spit o' Ander? She would say proudly. "Jes' look a' de way he walks and de way he th'ows his hands, and dem eyes jes' Ander right over again." Then she would chuckle to herself and hang her head self consciously: "Well I reckon de Laud took dat chile to punish me. Hit dont do to set your heart too much on nothin nor nobody in dis worl."

In an altercation once with a very important personage she was told "You must remember, Caroline I am Mrs. So and So." "Yes sum," she replied bending at the waist as always in her courtly fashion "An; an' you mus 'member, Ma'am, dat I am Mrs. Ander Anderson," which was no joke for this Mrs. So and So could have consigned both Mr. and "Mrs." Ander Anderson to the poor house by the flick of a pen. In the way the love begins as often happens she had pitied and mothered Andrew who was several years younger than she, thro a spell of sickness in a hospital for contagious diseases in a lonely deserted spot outside the city limits. She was not a nurse and of course not allowed to enter. But love finds a way and Calline would take her knickknacks to the woods and give the signal by firing a pistol. If by any chance she was caught, she was shooting at a big black snake that "Jes run right under dem bushes there."

Absorbed in my own affairs I dismissed this case from my mind, easily assuming that with the house and garden (she was fond of gardening) and her regular pension money for food and simple necessities her life would resume its even tenor neither poverty nor riches, the happiest ideal. But one day a letter from a social worker at Raleigh brought a shock to my smug satisfaction. "Aunt Calline was surely not herself. Found wandering in the woods looking for 'Ander.' Obviously demented." I wrote Dr—— and tried every expedient to avoid a trip to Raleigh for myself. When finally I had to go I found her to all appearances so docile and simply childlike, I concluded the symptoms of insanity that had alarmed the neighbors must have been due solely to lack of normal social contacts and that what she needed was the renewal of her accustomed associations in an ordinary comfortable home wherein her presence would be taken as a matter of course and where she would encounter only kind looks and loving words. I was not unaware of a District Law which forbids the bringing of insane persons from the States into Washington. I did not at all believe her to be insane but knew that she could be quickly rendered so by being put into an asylum with crazy people and less quickly, perhaps but just as surely if left to the solitary life she had been leading since her husband's death. Again I suppose with the conceit which I hope is pardonable in an inveterate School Marm, I may have overestimated the efficacy of my own powers of suggestion and mental control. I thot that kind treatment in an ideal environment and constant companionship of a potential psychiatrist would keep her as well as most minds commonly considered simply morbid. I brought her into the bosom of my own family, ministering personally and directly to her wants physical and mental. I bathed her, dieted her, coiffured her hair becomingly, took her out for walks and sight seeing, to church every Sunday—and at night when she had had a nice warm dip in the big tub, her face shiny with the clean smell of good wholesome toilet soap and she was cosily tucked in bed, together we would repeat the good old 23rd Psalm; her voice trembling naturally and pathetically with the emphasis; The Lord's my Shepherd *I shall not want*; He resto 'eth my soul—and after my cheery Good night, Sleep tight" she would sink peacefully and happily into a restful natural, child-like sleep.

Indeed as I remember her in those early days in our home, she seemed perfectly normal, tractable as a sweet and trustful child, responsive, ready to obey, kindly and open minded to guidance. Those were to me the happy days of fulfillment of a teacher's task with a mind under apparently perfect control, a mind less distracting than a group of youngsters, however intelligent, more challenging to originality of method, more inspiring to the urge for experimenting on a *tabula rasa* with a new untried method, more satisfying from the unexpected thrill of having met a real human need and at the same moment receiving adequate and grateful appreciation. True I recognized at times a confusion of places and persons between Raleigh and Washington—a blending of present and past associations that did not always yield to treatment. One day for instance when Griffith Stadium was mentioned as the Base Ball Park, she startled me by saying knowingly "Oh yes; That's where Ander, my husband works." I said you mean he used to work at the Park in Raleigh. This you know is Washington. "Yessum, I know but Ander is at the Park right up the street here. I been there many a time. Oh yes ma'am I understan. But Ander aint dead. He works up here at the Base Ball Park. I been intendin' to go up dere and see him but I been sort er sick and kept puttin' it off." Then without arguing the point I tried to call to mind the day of the funeral. "Dont you remember the hymns you chose for the service that day and the beautiful long stem chrysanthemums Miss Phoebe sent and how we laid him to rest beside grandma and Big Brother. I'm sure you remember how sweetly your Miss A—— sang "Oh *rest in the Lord Wait patiently for him*! You said it was the sweetest thing you had ever heard."

"Yes'm. I know there's some says Ander's dead, but—" and

after that she would watch her chances with the utmost cunning and steal out of the house to find the Base Ball Park. That one expression seemed to stick. The chance change on a word had upset the entire fabric I thot I was building. I seemed to have lost all power to start her over again. I plead with her to stay in the house, telling her that the City Fathers would not leave her to stay with me if she kept running away and had to be brought home by the police. Thinking to convince her that this was not Raleigh and that the Ball Park in Washington was not the place where "Ander" had worked I let her follow her bent one day and meekly walked beside her without trying to direct or in any way hinder her route. She stopped a strange man to ask if "this wasn't the right way to the Base Ball Park and added didactically: "de place where de teams comes to play Ball." He pointed to the Park which wasn't far and she kept on triumphantly. Our roles had changed completely. She was the teacher and naturally enough mistook my silence for docility. "You see Sis Annie" and she would go on into details of Ander's history and why she hadn't been up to see him etc, etc. Finally we reached the Park and went inside. "They've changed it," she said and pitifully "They've sent Ander somewhere else to work." I took the whip hand again and made her promise to give up these excursions to the Base Ball Park. I told her honestly that they would say she was crazy and send her to the Asylum and I would be powerless to keep her any longer. She seemed to understand for the time being and promised sweetly as ever that she would stay in the house till I came from work every day and then we would take our walk together. This promise however, she was wholly incapable of keeping. The police were very considerate and brought her home several times but finally she was taken to Gallinger adjudged insane by the Court and sent to St. Elizabeth's and after that to the hospital for the colored insane in North Carolina her native State.

The nurse who brought her in on my first visit to her there whispered: "She is such a nice patient. Such a perfect *lady*." So clean and comfy she looked—and there was the same unforgettable bending at the waist curtsy. "How you do, Sis Annie. I never can fergit you." We sat holding hands for a while and repeated together our old familiar Psalm while the hospital attendant stood at a respectful distance with moist sympathetic eyes. "*I shall not want. He leadeth me beside—Yea tho I walk— He resto'ith my soul—*" then breaking off she pinned me with a piercing look "Sis Annie there's jes one thing I want to ask you." It was the look a judge might give a culprit with the command to tell the truth the whole truth and nothing but the truth: "I wants to know is Ander dead or is he not?"

# Christmas Bells:
# A One-Act Play for Children

### (c. 1940?)

In this musical pageant, set on a Christmas Eve during World War I, three children ponder the meaning of democracy and Christianity while their mother works and their father is away serving in the military. A local group brings the family a tree and gifts, which they could not themselves afford. A second scene depicts the Nativity and includes much singing of hymns. A third shows soldiers and Red Cross nurses singing and praying for peace. And a final scene returns to the family, who awaken from dreams of the above scenes, as the mother returns home to her children. Cooper wrote this one-act play, likely in the 1940s, to raise funds for Frelinghuysen University. It was performed with Cooper's great-grandniece Madeline Beckwith starring in it (Hutchinson 1981).

SOURCE: Anna Julia Cooper Papers, box 23-4, folder 39, Moorland-Spingarn Research Center, Howard University.

## DRAMATIS PERSONAE

HANNAH, aged eleven, "the little Mother," who has the care of her two sisters, while the Mother works by the day, away from home. The Father is a soldier, across the sea.

NANNETTE, aged eight

ANNIKINS, aged four

THE THREE KINGS,—

    Gaspard, a European,

    Melchior, an Asiatic,

    Balthazar, an African.

Chorus of Angels

Chorus of Shepherds

Sunshine Club of the Community Service. Soldiers. Red Cross
    Nurses.

# SCENE I

*Before the curtain rises, Christmas chimes are heard, playing
distinctly,—"Christians, awake! Salute the happy morn, Whereon
the Savior of mankind was born." At the close of the chimes a
pause of 30 seconds absolute silence; after which there sounds
shrill and clear a single stroke of a bell. The curtain rises, disclos-
ing a room of a humble family of three children. "The little
Mother" is busy about the evening meal; Nannette is setting the
table; Annikins, on the floor, cuts pictures for paper dolls.*

### NANNETTE

What are the bells ringing for?

### HANNAH

Why, don't you know dear? They're ringing for the Christmas
Child—for His birthday. This is Christmas Eve!

### ANNIKINS

Is Christ Child coming here?

### HANNAH

*(Thoughtfully)* Why yes, Annikins. He will come to us if we try
to be kind and good.

### NANNETTE

Sister, can't we possibly have a Christmas tree this year?

### HANNAH

I'm afraid not, deary. But we'll try to be happy just the same. We'll play "make believe" and make each other wonderful presents. It's lots of fun! And write letters to Daddy, and we'll ask the Christ Child to bring Daddy safe home to us, and then mother will not have to work so hard down town. And we'll ask the Christ Child to bring us sweet Peace and Good Will. Because He is the Prince of Peace, and that's what He is coming for. And then I s'pose we ought to pray for Democracy, 'cause that's what Daddy is fighting for.

### NANNETTE

What is Democracy?

### HANNAH

I'm not sure I know, little sister. It's kind of hard to understand. But it must be what the Christ Child wants every where in the world— for it means every body will be good and kind to every body and there'll not be any poor people who can't get enough to eat, nor any unkind people who scorn and hate. Just all the world will love each other like you and I and Annikins love one another. Every body will be helping to make the world good and pleasant for every body else and so the Christ Child will come back to us again and He will be our Big Brother and all the people will be brothers 'cause you see they will all be His brothers. Come now Annikins, put away your paper dollies. Supper is ready.

*(She smoothes the child's hair, examines hands and face to see that they are clean, and lifts her into a high-chair at the table. The others take their places and, with bowed heads and folded hands, sing the grace)—*

> God is great and God is good,
> And we thank thee for this food;
> By thy hand must we be fed,
> Give us, Lord, our daily bread. Amen.

### ANNIKINS

Pass the sugar! *(correcting herself)* Excuse me sister, *please pass the sugar!*

### HANNAH

Oo-h Annikins! *Don't* take quite so *much*, love! Uncle Sam says we can't have any more sugar till next month!

### ANNIKINS

*(Confidentially to her big sister)* you tell the Christmas Child *I want some sugar,*—hear? *(Carol singers are heard outside)*

### HANNAH

Hush, child, listen. It's the carol singers!

### CAROL SINGERS.

Christmas where children are hopeful and gay,
Christmas where old men are patient and gray,
Christmas with peace, like a dove in its flight,
Over brave men in the thick of the fight.
Everywhere, everywhere, Christmas tonight!

*Immediately after the carols the Sunshine Club come bursting in, covered with snow. The boys wear mufflers. Some have ice-skates hung over their shoulders. Two of the boys lug in a tree all ready to set up. The girls have their arms full of trinkets for the tree and presents for the children. They are bubbling over with spirits and gayly shouting,—"Merry Christmas Hannah! Merry Christmas Nannette! Hello, Annikins! Merry Christmas!" Their leader gives the child a bear-hug, and presents her with a wonderful doll, almost as big as the four-year-old herself. Nannette gets a beautiful red dress and a string of beads. The children clap their hands in glee. While dressing the tree they sing.*

There's a wonderful tree a wonderful tree
The happy children rejoice to see.

Spreading its branches year by year
It comes from the forest to flourish here.
Oh this beautiful tree with its branches wide
Is always blooming at Christmas Tide;
And a voice is telling its boughs among
Of the Shepherds' watch and the Angels' songs;
Of a holy Babe in the manger low—
The beautiful story of long ago—
When a radiant star threw its beams so wide
To herald the earliest Christmas Tide.

*(Joining hands, and singing, they dance around the tree)*

#### HANNAH

*(A little shyly at first) Oh thank you!* Thank you so much girls. What a beautiful tree! Oh, we are so happy—I had no idea we would have a *tree!*

#### 1ST SUNSHINE GIRL

*(Hanging a small doll on the tree)* Here is a baby-doll for Annikins; skates for Nannette. And here, little Mother, is a gay peasant-kerchief and a picture storybook for *you.* I know you'll read the stories to the rest. Hannah never keeps anything all for herself!

#### HANNAH

*(Somewhat embarrassed)* Oh girls, I—I can't tell you how much—Oh, I mean you are *so* good and kind—I just don't know how to thank you.

#### 1ST SUNSHINE GIRL

Oh don't thank us at all, just thank the Christ Child!

#### 2ND SUNSHINE GIRL

All who love the Christ Child are trying to make little children happy tonight, don't you know? We don't want a single child to be forgotten. His love will warm and cheer the loneliest child on earth.

### HANNAH

*(Thoughtfully)* Yes. All for the Christ Child who was born tonight. To love Him is to love all little children.

### SUNSHINE GIRLS

*(Putting on their wraps, waving Merry Christmas to all; shaking hands affectionately with Hannah).* Good night everybody! Be good children! Good night,—good night!

### THE CHILDREN

Good night! Merry Christmas!

### ANNIKINS

*(Piping up)* Au revoir-au revoir! *(Exit S.S. Club laughing and throwing kisses. A pause)*

### NANNETTE

What a wonderful tree! *(They examine the presents)*

### HANNAH

*(Bustling to hide her emotion)* Come now *(takes Annikins by the hand)*. The Christ Child has sent us perfectly lovely friends and I am so glad you have your Christmas tree after all! Kneel down children. Annikins, put your hands together. *(They all kneel and repeat a prayer)*

> Oh holy Child of Bethlehem!
> Descend to us we pray;
> Cast out our sin and enter in,
> Be born in us today.
> We hear the Christmas angels
> The great glad tidings tell;
> Oh, come to us—Abide with us,
> Our Lord, Emanuel.

*(During the prayer the stage is gradually darkened, so that the children are no longer visible)*

# SCENE II

*The Children's Dream City.*

CHRISTMAS ANNO DOMINI.[1] *Two strokes of a bell. On the screen a still life night scene of the City of Bethlehem. Shepherds with flocks in the middle distance chorus by radio transcription:*

### HYMN.

*(Chorus or transcription)*

> O little town of Bethlehem,
> How still we see thee lie!
> Above thy deep and dreamless sleep
> The silent stars go by;
> Yet in thy dark streets shineth
> The everlasting Light;
> The hopes and fears of all the years
> Are met in thee tonight.
>
> For Christ is born of Mary,
> And gathered all above
> While mortals sleep, the angels keep
> Their watch of wondering love.
> O morning stars together
> Proclaim the holy birth,
> And praises sing to God the King
> And peace to men on earth!
>
> How silently, how silently
> The wondrous gift is given!
> So God imparts to human hearts
> The blessings of His heaven.
> No ear may hear his coming,
> But, in this world of sin,
> Where meek souls will receive Him, still
> The dear Christ enters in.

## HYMN.

*(Chorus or transcription)*

> While shepherds watched their
> flock by night,
> All seated on the ground,
> The angel of the Lord came down,
> And glory shone around.
>
> "Fear not," he said, for mighty dread
> Had seized their troubled mind;
> "Glad tidings of great joy I bring
> To you and all mankind."

*(A strong white light is thrown on the stage. A shining Angel descends and sings)*

### ANGEL.

> From Heaven above to earth I come
> To bring glad news to every home;
> Glad tidings of great joy I bring
> Whereof I now do tell and sing.
> To you tonight is born a child
> Of Mary chosen Mother mild;
> This little child of lowly birth
> Shall be the Joy of all the Earth.

*(There appears suddenly from all sides a throng of angels who sing in chorus)*

### ANGELS.

> All glory be to God on high,
> And to the earth be peace.
> Good will henceforth from heaven to men
> Begin and never cease.

*For chorus of angels, "Glory to God:" from Handel's Messiah may be used if preferred. Angels disappear suddenly (effected by manipulation of lights). Enter, left back, Shepherds wearing loose tunics, carrying crooks, and singing:*

### SHEPHERDS.

Hark! the herald angels sing
Glory to the new-born King;
Peace on earth and mercy mild,
God and sinners reconciled!

Joyful, all ye nations, rise,
Join the triumph of the skies;
With the angelic host proclaim,
Christ is born in Bethlehem!

*(Exeunt Shepherds right. The stage is dark. There appears, dimly at first, a star just visible in the darkness. As the star grows brighter the three Kings, L, back, pass to the front, R, singing):*

### THE KINGS.

We three Kings of Orient are,
Bearing gifts we traverse afar,
Field and fountain,
Moor and mountain,
Following yonder Star.

*(Refrain)*
O Star of wonder—star of night—
Star with royal beauty bright,
Westward leading, still proceeding,
Guide us to thy perfect light.

### GASPARD.

Born a King on Bethlehem's plain,
Gold I bring to crown Him again,

King forever, ceasing never
Over us all to reign.

### MELCHIOR.

Frankincense to offer have I—
Incense owns a Deity nigh.
Prayer and praising, all men raising,
Worship Him—God on high.

### BALTHAZAR.

Myrrh is mine; its bitter perfume
Breathes a life of gathering gloom;
Sorrowing, sighing, bleeding, dying,
Sealed in the stone-cold tomb.

*(Refrain)*

### THE THREE KINGS.

Glorious now behold Him arise,
King and God and Sacrifice.
Alleluia, alleluia!
Earth to heaven replies.

*(Refrain)*

*(As the Kings leave, the stage is again dark. The star alone is seen, in the middle distance. Gradually one spot begins to glow till, in the full radiance, is seen the group around the manger cradle [based on Correggio's Holy Night]. While the Chorus sings softly, the Shepherds enter and adore; later the Kings)*

### ANGELS.

Holy night, Silent Night!
All is calm all is bright
Round yon Virgin Mother and Child.
Holy infant, so tender and mild,
Sleep in heavenly peace!

Silent Night, Holy Night,
Shepherds quake at the sight,
Glories stream from Heaven afar,
Heavenly hosts sing Alleluia,
Christ the Savior is born.

Silent Night, Holy Night,
Son of God, love's pure light
Radiant beams from thy holy face,
With the dawn of redeeming grace,
Jesus, Lord, at thy birth.

### SECOND CHORUS.

Sleep, Holy Babe, upon thy Mother's breast;
Great Lord of earth and sea and sky!
How sweet it is to see thee lie
In such a place of rest!
Sleep holy Babe, thine angels watch around,
All bending low with folded wings,
Before th'incarnate King of Kings.

*(The scene fades in darkness. A long silence. Three strokes of a bell)*

# SCENE III

## 1942. CHRISTMAS ON THE BATTLEFIELDS

*(Where now are "Peace on Earth, Good Will to Men"? In a ghastly gleam of red, soldiers in helmets, gas masks, marching, marching, marching, falling, dying. Red Cross Nurses minister to the wounded)*

SONG OF THE SOLDIERS. *(THE ROSE OF NO MAN'S LAND)*

There's a rose that grows on No Man's Land,
And it's wonderful to see;
Tho' dimmed with tears

It will live for years
In my garden of memory.
It's the one red rose the soldier knows,
It's the work of the Master's hand;
Mid War's great curse
Stands the Red Cross Nurse:
She's the Rose of No Man's Land.

THE NURSES. (HOLDING THEIR ARMS ALOFT)

Lord God of Love, let us have peace!
From War's vain sacrifice
Give us release.
Grant Peace the victories
War cannot know.
God of the Ages!
Hast Thou not seen
Thy fields and meadows green
Red with the blood of men where War hath been?
Dost Thou not know War's fearful endless roll—
The countless graves of those who paid the toll?
Teach us to build, Oh gentle Lord, not to destroy.
Forge these bleeding swords into plowshares,
thy fields to increase.
Lord of the lives to be—Let us have peace!

(They kneel)

God of the fatherless, we pray to Thee,
Father of all of us, hear Thou our plea;
Peace and Good Will to men are willed by Thee—
Lord God of Love, Let us have Peace!

QUARTETTE. (SOFTLY)

Peace, perfect peace, in this dark world of sin?
The blood of Jesus whispers Peace within.

Peace, perfect peace, with sorrows surging round?
On Jesus' bosom naught but calm is found.

Peace, perfect peace, with loved ones far away?
In Jesus' keeping we are safe, and they.

Peace, perfect peace, our future all unknown?
Jesus we know and He is on the throne.

Peace, perfect peace, death shadowing
us and ours?
Jesus has vanquished death and all its powers.

*Once more on the darkened stage there appears the shining way of the Angel, who spreads protecting wings over the sisters (sleeping center). Nurses still kneeling L, Soldiers R. Angel, elevated center, over children. Angel sings with deep significance and tenderness:*

He shall feed His flock like a shepherd:
He shall gather the lambs with his arm,
and carry them in His bosom,
and shall gently lead those that are with young.

*After the Angel's song of promise, Nurses and Soldiers, inspired with hope and courage, burst forth in a triumphal strain.*

### CHORUS.

Ring out, wild bells, to the wild sky,
The flying cloud, the frosty light;
The year is dying in the night;
Ring out, wild bells, and let him die.

Ring out the old, ring in the new,
Ring happy bells, across the snow;
The year is going, let him go;
Ring out the false, ring in the true.

Ring out the grief that saps the
mind,
For those that here we see no more;

Ring out the feud of rich and poor,
Ring in redress to all mankind.

Ring out the want, the care, the sin,
The faithless coldness of the times;
Ring out, ring out my mournful
rhymes,
But ring the fuller minstrel in.

Ring out the shapes of foul disease,
Ring out the narrowing lust of
gold:
Ring out the thousand wars of old:
Ring in the thousand years of
peace!

Ring in the valiant man and free,
The larger heart, the kindlier
hand;
Ring out the darkness of the land,
Ring in the Christ that is to be!

*The Christmas Chimes, which have been playing through-
out the hymn, as if in the distance, now peal forth in a loud
and joyful clamor. After which darkness, and again a silence.*

## SCENE IV
## (AS IN SCENE I)

*The children are discovered asleep at their prayer.*

#### HANNAH

*(Arousing herself)*: Twelve o'clock! Dear me! Almost time
for Mother to come home, and Annikins hasn't been put to

bed! What will Mother say! *(Staring in front of her as if dazed)* But I have had a most wonderful dream! I thought I saw—*(rubs her eyes as if trying to make sure she's awake. Turns to waken the other children)* Annikins! Nannette! wake up! Wake up, Dear. We ought to have been in bed long ago!

### ANNIKINS

*(rubbing her eyes and looking around—points center)*: Christ Child! He was wight dere—'cause I *seen* Him!

### NANNETTE

I dreamed I saw Daddy marching and the Angel was bringing him home to us.

*Hannah gives her a startled, half incredulous look.*

### NANNETTE

*(Arguing the point)*: Well, didn't *you say* that the Christ Child would come to us if we tried to be kind and good? And didn't *He say* He loved little children and wanted them to come to Him? And didn't *we ask* Him to come to us just a little while ago?

### HANNAH

*(slowly and dreamily)*. Yes, Dear—and may be—

*(Mother enters)* Oh Mama! *(Conscience stricken as she remembers her charges)*.

### NANNETTE

Oh Momsie! We've got a Christmas tree!

*(The Mother soothes her excited children and takes Annikins in her arms.)*

ANNIKINS

An'—An' Muvver! Christ Child Come! He brought me
some sugar!

*The tree is mysteriously alight. It glows marvelously as the
curtain slowly descends.*

## TABLEAU

# Two Scenes from the *Aeneid:*
# A Translation from Vergil, Arranged
# and Directed by Anna J. Cooper

*(ca. 1928)*

Cooper translates these scenes from Vergil's *Aeneid* in
which Aeneas and his fellow Trojans are welcomed to
Carthage (modern-day Tunisia, in North Africa) by its
queen and founder, Dido, a strong and heroic leader
who is presented as Aeneas's equal and fellow exile.
Dido hosts a celebration during which she and Aeneas
exchange gifts and Aeneas recounts the battle of Troy at
Dido's request. Cooper directed and arranged the play,
and it was performed in February 1928 by the Latin
Club of Dunbar High School. The students' performance of the play and Cooper's request that W. E. B.
Du Bois report on it in *The Crisis* magazine is the subject of several correspondences between Cooper and Du
Bois (see part 4, Cooper—Du Bois Correspondences).
The play and its production represent Cooper's extensive training and years of teaching Latin, as well as her
commitment to showcasing an Afrocentric approach to
the classics of Western tradition. Friend and colleague
Felix Klein noted Cooper's excellence in teaching Latin,
and specifically in explicating the *Aeneid*, in his 1905
book, *In the Land of the Strenuous Life.*

SOURCE: Anna Julia Cooper Papers, box 23-4, folder 42,
Moorland-Spingarn Research Center, Howard University.

# SCENE I THE ATRIUM OF PRIAM'S PALACE.

R. An altar with the Lares and Penates, nearby and shading the altar a very old laurel tree. Enter Hecuba L. followed by daughters singing a hymn to Diana. All bear palms and register prayer and supplication. They kneel or crouch around the altar clinging to the household gods while attendants execute a sacred dance in slow rhythmic reverence beseeching and adoring the gods.

(PUELLAE) HYMN TO DIANA:

1. Dianae sumus infide
   Puellae et pueri integri
   Dianam pueri integri
   Puellaeque canamus.

(PUELLAE)

2. O Latonia, O Latonia
   O Latonia, maximi
   Magna progenies Iovis,
   Quam mater prope Deliam
   Deposivit olivam

(PUERI)

3. Montium domina ut fores
   Silvarumque virentium
   Saltuumque reconditorum
   Amniumque sonantum
   Amniumque sonantum

4. (Puellae)
   Omit

5. (PUERI)
   Omit

6. (PUERI ET PUELLAE)
   Sis quocumque tibi placet
   Sancta nomine, Romulique
   Antique ut solita es, bona
   Sospites obe gentem.

*Shouts and clashing of swords heard without. Enter Priam from rear stage, tottering with age and breathlessly girding on a long unused sword.*

HECUBA: *(Rises to meet him)*

What madness wretched spouse
Has placed that Helmet on thy brows?
Come, whither fare you Times so dire
Bent knees, not lifted arms require:
Could Hector now before us stand
No help were in my Hector's hand.
Take refuge here and learn at length
The secret of an old man's strength;
One altar shall protect us all;
Here bide with us, or with us fall.

*(She leads him to a seat at altar)*

*Enter Polites running, Pyrrhus in hot pursuit with spear levelled at his head. They circle court and corridor and when just before the altar where sit the horror stricken parents Polites falls and expires.*

PRIAM: *(Sternly)*

May Heaven if Heaven be just to heed
Such horrors render worthy meed
For this atrocious bloody deed
Which makes me see my dear son die
And stains with blood a father's eye.
But he to whom you feign you owe
Your birth, Achilles—'twas not so.
He dealt with Priam, though his foe:
He feared the laws of light and truth;
He heard the suppliants prayer with ruth;
Gave Hector's body to the tomb,
And sent me back in safety home.

*(He feebly hurls his dart which Pyrrhus scornfully catches on the boss of his shield)*

PYRRHUS:

Take the news below
And to my sire, Achilles, go
Tell him of his degenerate seed
And that (striking) and this my bloody deed.
Now die:

*(Drags the father sliddering in his son's gore to the altar*
*stone and glares ferociously at his Blasphemous deed.)*

Curtain.

Carmen!!! (Horace)

*Sung softly behind the curtain.*

Aequam memento rebus in arduis
Servare mentem non secus in bonis
Ab insolenti temperatam
Laetitiā, Moriture Delli.
Omnes eodum cogimur omnium
Versatur urna serius ocius
Sors exitura et nos in aeternum
Exsilium impositura cymbae.

– – – – – – – – – – –

*Strains of Carmen ad Dianam as echo of opening prayer &*
*supplication.*

# SCENE II THE BANQUET AT DIDA'S COURT

## DRAMATIS PERSONAE:

Dido. . . . . . . . . . . . . . . . . . .     Queen of Carthage

Bibias. . . . . . . . . . . . . . . . . .     Prime Minister

Iopas (the long haired). . . . . . .     Poet Laureate

Balzar. . . . . . . . . . . . . . . . . .     a Moor

Herald, Maids of Honor,
    Guards, Page, full retinue
    of attendants on the
    Queen. . . . . . . . . . . . . . . .

Aeneas. . . . . . . . . . . . . . . . . .     Trojan hero
       shipwrecked near
       Carthage

Ascanius. . . . . . . . . . . . . . . .     His son afterwards
       changed to Cupid

Achates (Fidus). . . . . . . . . . . .     His faithful friend and
       Follower

### GRAND ENTRY—MARCH—PROCESSION
### ORDER OF MARCH

Two Heralds (trumpet music)
4 Soldiers
2 Flower girls. Strew roses
*The Queen* & Prime Minister
Train bearer
Color bearer
Ladies in waiting
Iopas, with lyre
Tyrian maids
Balzar
Page.

## SCENE II THE THRONE ROOM
## IN DIDO'S PALACE, CARTHAGE

PAGE: *(Approaches the Throne and*
*Kneels Forehead to Floor)*

Most gracious Queen, a stranger waits without. He
desires audience before your Royal Highness.

DIDO:

Bid him enter.

*(Enter Aeneas attended by Achates)*

AENEAS:

Of Troy am I, Aeneas is my name
Who, Driven by war forth from my native land,
Put sails to sea to seek out Italy
And my divine descent from sceptend[?] Jove;
With twice ten Phrygian ships I plowed the deep
And made that way my mother Venus led;
But of them all scarce seven do anchor safe,
And they so wrecked and weltered by the waves,
That ev'ry tide tilts twixt their oaken sides;
And all of them unburdened of their load,
Are ballassed with billows watery weight.
But hapless I, God Wot, poor and unknown
Do trace these Lybiam deserts all despised,
Exiled from Europe and wide Asia both
And have not any coverture but Heaven.

## DIDO:

Alas what trials, Goddes born, pursue you thro'
such perils!
What storms, what violence drives you to these
wild shores!
But drive fear from your heart now, O Trojans,
Banish care.
Who does not know the race of Aeneas.
Who is ignorant of the story of Troy, that splendid
city—
Its valiant men and noble women and—its unhappy
fate.
Who has not heard and thrilled with scenes of
the stupendous
Conflagration that ended that great war!
We Carthaginians do not wear such blunted sensibilities
Nor does Sol yoke his steeds so far from our
Tyrian City
As to leave us unmoved with sympathy
For sufferings such as yours,
Whether you choose the great Hesperia and the
Saturnian fields
Or prefer the country of Eryx and King Acestes,
I will send you safe with aid.
The resources of my kingdom are at your disposal.
If you wish to settle with me in this realm,
This city which I am building is yours
Haul your ships upon the beach.
Trojan and Tyrian shall be treated by me
With no discrimination.


## AENEAS:

Thou alone of all the world, O Queen,
Dost pity the unutterable woes of Troy.

Thy generosity alone offers to share
City and home with needy Trojans bereft of all things
Exhausted now by all the buffetings of sea or calamities
    of land.
To pay thee worthy honors, most noble Dido
Is not in our power,
Nor is there anywhere in the Dardanian Race
Any adequate return that we can offer—
The race now scattered thro' out the great circle of the
    world.
May the Gods requite you, if Gods there be
That regard human devotion;
If Justice counts for anything anywhere
A pious heart conscious in itself of rectitude
Deserving well of the celestials.
            Most Gracious Queen
                Happy the age that gave you birth
                Ever blest the parents unveiling such worth!
                So long as rivers run to the deep,
                So long as shadows o'er hillsides creep
                So long as stars in heaven's fair Pastures graze
                So long thine honor, thy name and praise
                Shall unfading live—where'er my destined
                    home shall be.


                        DIDO:


And art thou really that Aeneas
Whom nurturing Venus bore
To Trojan Anchises on the waves
Of Phrygian Simois?
In fact now I do remember
Teucer came to Sidon, from his native land expelled
Seeking new realms by the aid of Belus.
Just then Father Belus was laying waste rich Cyprus
And victorious held it under his sway.
Ever since that time the story of the Trojan city

To me has been familiar. Your name and the
Grecian Kings have been like household words.
Belus too, tho publicly your enemy used to extol
The teucri with signal praise, and would have it
that he was sprung from the same ancient stock.
Wherefore, come now; O Friends rest and refresh
yourselves under our roof. *(reflectively)*
A like misfortune
Has pursued me thro many trials and I am trying
In this land at length after many hardships
To build the foundations of my battered fortunes.
Not ignorant of troubles myself, I know how to
sympathize with misfortune and love to succor the
wretched.

*(To Balzar)*

Go Balzar, Proclaim a thanksgiving in all the
temples of the Gods:
To the shores send down for the associates of
our guest my royal salutation: twenty bullocks,
One hundred head of big bristling boars,
One hundred fat lambs with their dams
Present our royal gifts and congratulations.

*(Exit Balzar)*

AENEAS: *(To Achates)*

Go Achates, Bring to the city
The boy Ascanius. Fetch too a few princely gifts
for the Queen.
Precious relics, Madam, snatched from the ruins of
Troy. The cloak heavily embroidered with designs
of gold, and the ornaments of Grecian Helen—
Wonderful gifts of her mother Leda.
Fetch too, the sceptre which I lone bore

And the necklace of pearls and the coronet with
double band of jewels and of gold.

*(Exit Achates. Reenter Balzar)*

DIDO:

Sit down Aeneas, sit in Dido's place.

AENEAS:

Your pardon, noble lady,
Not in this garb, drenched by the waves
Of Lybian seas.
For tho my garb be great, My fortune's mean,
Too mean to be companion to a queen.

DIDO:

One's fortune may be greater than his birth,
But rich adornment never substitutes true worth.
Aeneas is Aeneas, tho' he were clad
In weeds as foul as ever true had.
*(To Balzar)* For those our honored guests
Let the cup be brought.
With messy gold and jewels wrought
Whence ancient Belus quaffed his wine
And all the kings of Belus' line.

*Balzar bows, backs out, brings in cup & places it on altar.
Flower girls weave garlands around altar crowning the
cup. Appropriate music.*

*(Takes cup and pours libation on table. Music for ceremo-
nial crowning of the wine by cup bearers.) (Prayer as she
pours the libation.)*

Omnipotent Jupiter, thou who know'st
The mutual rights of guest and host;
O make this day a day of joy
Alike to Tyre and wandering Troy.
And may our children's children feel
The blessing of the bond we seal!
    Bacchus, Giver of glad cheer,
    And Bounteous Juno, be present here!
    And Tyrians you with frank good will
    Our courteous purposes fulfil.

*(Touches lips to goblet's edge and passes it to [unclear] who drains it)*
*(Enter Achates leading Iulus)*


DIDO:

If this be thy son as I suppose, Here let him sit.
Be merry, lovely child.


IULUS:

Madam, you shall be my mother.


DIDO:

And so I will sweet child. Come sit here.
*(fondles him)*

Iopas shall sing for us and play the golden lyre
Mighty Atlas taught.
*(soft music as Iopas touches the lyre)*
He sings the wanderings of the moon
The sun eclipsed in deadly swoon,
Whence human kind and cattle came,

And whence the rain spout and the flame
Arcturus and the two bright bears
And Hyads weeping showery tears;
Why winter must so softly go
And why the weary nights move slow

*(Tyrians and Trojans wandering applaud
Iopas' music)*


DIDO: *(Aeneas)*


Now Guest, wilt thou vouchsafe a space
The tale of Grecian fraud to trace.
How Troy was overcome.
Tell me of Prism—Tell me of the great Hector and
Oh do tell me all about the Ethiopian Prince Memnon:
How did he look? What sort of armor was it that
Vulcan forged for this Son of Aurora? And
How did his Ethiopian forces behave in the battle?
Tell me all about those brave black soldiers—
And, too, the great Achilles. Tell me of him!
And those horses of Diomedes—Nay Friend,
Recount from the beginning the dire misfortunes of
your race and let us prolong the night in interesting
discourse.

*(Music interlude. Introducing Aeneas' story.
Music short but suggestive.)*


AENEAS: *(sighing deeply)*


A woeful tale bids Dido to Unfold.
Oh the enchanting words of base Sinon
Made us to think Epeus' pine-tree
horse
A sacrifice t'appease Minerva's wrath!
The rather since that one Laocoon,

Breaking a spear upon its hollow breast
Was with two winged serpents stung to death.
Where at aghast, we were commanded straight
With reverence to draw it into Troy.
In which unhappy work was I employed;
These hands did help to hale it to the gates.
O had it never entered, Troy had stood!—
But so came in this fatal instrument
At whose accursed feet, as overjoyed
We banqueted; till overcome with wine
Some surfeited and others soundly slept.
Which Sinon viewing caused the Greekish spies
To haste to Tenedos and tell the camp:
Then he unlocked the horse; and suddenly
From out his entrails, Neoptolemus
Setting his spear upon the ground, leapt forth,
And after him a thousand Grecians more.
I then ran to the Palace of the king,
And at Jove's altar finding Priamus,
About whose withered neck hung Hecuba,
Folding his hand in hers; and joinly both
Beating their breasts and falling on the ground.
Pyrrhus, his falchion's point raised up at once,
And with Megaera's eyes stared in their face,
Threatening a thousand deaths at every glance;
To whom the aged king thus trembling spoke:
"Achilles Son! remember what I was:—
Father of fifty sons, but they are slain;
Lord of my fortune, but my fortune's turned.

AENEAS:

King of the city, but my Troy is burned.
And now am neither father, lord nor king.
Not moved at all, but smiling at his tears,
This—butcher, whilest his hands were yet
up held,
Treading upon his breast, *Struck off his head!*

DIDO:

O end, Aeneas! I can hear no more.


AENEAS:

By this I got my Father on my back,
This young boy in my arms, and by the hand
Led fair Crensa, my beloved wife;
And we were round environed with the Greeks.
Others—I lost my wife! and had not we
Fought manfully, I had not lived to tell this tale.

*A short interlude*


DIDO:

Trojan thy ruthful tale hath made me sad;
Come let us think upon some pleasing sport,
To rid me from these melancholy thots.

*(To Blazar)*

Go now, and if the Tyrian Band
Of royal maids is here at hand,
Bid them on this our festal day
Their native drill in arms display.
And let the company here retire
And leave the circus free.

*(All groups to back stage)*
*(Enter Tyrian Drill)*

*Finale.* Curtain.

BY MISS WILLIAMSON

# PART III

# SCRAPBOOK, 1931–1940: NEWSPAPER ARTICLES AND OTHER WRITINGS

This section contains newspaper articles and other writings that Cooper collected and archived in a scrapbook identified as "Scrapbook no 2, 1931–1940" in the Anna Julia Cooper papers held at the Moorland-Spingarn Research Center at Howard University. It appears most of the articles were published in the *Washington Tribune*, a semiweekly Black newspaper from Washington, DC, where her numerous articles and bylines suggest Cooper may have had a regular column during the 1930s and into the early 1940s. The articles were clipped, pasted, and preserved in *The First Fifty, 1889–1939*, a book by F. Lawrence Babcock published in 1939 relating the triumphant rise of the Standard Oil Company in Indiana. While it is unknown how Cooper came to possess the book or why she chose to archive her newspaper writings in this particular book, the content of her articles often conflicts directly with narrative related in *The First Fifty*. Images of drilling rigs, oil wells, service crews, and refineries, and short blurbs about improvements in the refinery process and the role of gasoline in propelling the automobile industry are truncated and overtaken by Cooper's writings and words. Over and above the celebratory narrative of industrial capitalism *The First Fifty* constructs, Cooper pastes her articles critiquing the "mass production" ethos of the "machine age." (See a digital image of the scrapbook at https://bwoaproject.org/cooper.) The documents archived in the scrapbook constitute an important addition to our recognized archive of Cooper's writings and demonstrate that Cooper continued to engage and shape local and national conversations about issues affecting African American communities well into her seventies and eighties. That Cooper archived and preserved her works in the scrapbook also suggests that she saw the value in her writings and sought to preserve them for future generations.

# 13

# "A Revolting Portrait"

Published in *New Journal and Guide* on February 16, 1935, Cooper discusses the role of newspapers not only in printing the news, but also in publishing articles that promote "social betterment" rather than material that "panders to morbid curiosity of human depravity."

SOURCE: Anna Julia Cooper Papers, box 23-7, folder 89, Moorland-Spingarn Research Center, Howard University.

Editor, Journal and Guide: I like your paper and I am sure the Negro press today has a unique opportunity as well as a grave responsibility. The danger is, as too often is the case, that power is valued as a hammer to knock somebody rather than as a fulcrum to lift and guide. Representatives of the weak and incoherent are apt to take their leadership as grounds for self aggrandisement and not as an opportunity for wide and unselfish service along with the unceasing struggles for social justice.

I admit that a newspaper must print the news—the bad as well as the good. But a high and worthy purpose involves an intelligently constructive policy and this at all times requires selection and rejection—selection of what is promotive of its fundamental principles, constituting and justifying its reason for existence; rejection, systematic and unrelenting of all that is subversive of those well-determined essential objectives that one puts before subscription lists and paid up ads.

Good taste, too, must come in to dictate the suppression of what merely panders to morbid curiosity, human depravity. Such would be revolting portraits of pitiful degenerates like the one allowed on the front page of your February 2 edition. But there is always the high and holy mission to publicise those movements that aim at social betterment and to welcome those individuals who lend weight to juster views, finer harmony and wise cooperation in world affairs, and particularly in American problems and social adjustments.

An example may be cited from a recent Literary Digest release which sets forth far reaching advantages vital to our people, which well deserve the follow-up emphasis of our newspaper and if the facts are found as stated, should stimulate enthusiastic support and coloration of every one who loves his kind. I refer to the Shriners Hospital for Crippled Children, said to be 100 per cent charity regardless.

WASHINGTON, D.C.
ANNA J. COOPER

# 14

# "No Flowers Please"

This handwritten poem in Cooper's scrapbook relates how she would prefer to be remembered for promoting greater learning and understanding rather than to receive large bouquets of flowers in her memory.

SOURCE: Anna Julia Cooper Papers, box 23-7, folder 89, Moorland-Spingarn Research Center, Howard University.

Oh, just a rose perhaps, a few violets
Or even a handful of wild honeysuckle
Or Star of Bethlehem and sweet alyssum
Which says you remember kindly.

For this I shall thank you, Wherever I am.
And more for the courage and strength
You gave in the Struggle we call Life.
By the touch of your shoulder to shoulder
And the understanding glance of your eye
And the hearty Pull together of a sympathetic heart.
Priceless and undying these as God's gracious bounty.
    And I shall thank you, Wherever I am.

But *please, please,* don't pass the hat for big florist's
    offerings
Or take up a collection to crowd the room and cover my
    poor bier
With mute withering symbols of God's eternal love and
    Christ's unspeakable Prayer

Agonizing that we all should be one and love one
   another
Even as He and the Father are One in Love.

   No flowers please, just the smell of sweet understanding
   The knowing look that sees Beyond and says gently
   and kindly
   "Somebody's Teacher on Vacation now.
   Resting for the Fall Opening."

ANNA J. COOPER
AUGUST 10, 1940

# 15

# "Dr. Cooper Doesn't Like the Hughes Poem"[1]

"To Midnight Nan at Leroy's" was a poem by Langston Hughes first published in *Vanity Fair* in September 1925 and reprinted in the *Washington Tribune*. Cooper expresses disappointment in the *Tribune*'s decision to republish the poem, which Cooper argues revolves around the caricature of a Black female sex worker. Cooper notes that caricatures of Black male sexuality would not have been deemed acceptable to print in the Black press. While she does not challenge the quality of Hughes's body of work, she does suggest that a different poem would have been more appropriate to print.

SOURCE: Anna Julia Cooper Papers, box 23-7, folder 89, Moorland-Spingarn Research Center, Howard University.

Editor, Tribune:

I think it a pity that the high note of your editorial page should be vitiated by a selection that presents the very opposite ideal from the one you so ably advocate.

That so serious minded a paper as the Tribune, which condemns Amos 'n' Andy as pernicious propaganda and a vicious caricature of the race, should allow "Midnight Nan" to "strutt and wiggle" through the same page where-on we find earnest advice for "Children's Reading" must surely have been an oversight. A full survey of Langston Hughes' poetry ought to furnish, I am sure, some samples of his genius more in keeping with the high standard announced by the Tribune than this nauseating

portrait of a colored prostitute. My criticism is not against
Hughes for writing about whatever he sees and happens to know;
but I do object to pictures of the gutter and sewer being culled
and paraded by preference from all the ennobling and inspiring
examples of art that present themselves—examples that are just
as true to life, just as humanly appealing, and just as artistically
acceptable.

Walt Whitman did much that was coarse and vulgar in his poetic creations, but one has to wade through his unexpurgated
works to find it. You will not be confronted with the filth of
"Leaves of Grass" on the editorial pages of a cosmopolitan
newspaper, and this is not from race squeamishness either, but a
mere matter of literary taste and fine selection according to the
eternal fitness of things.

# 16

# "Educational Aims"

In this article, Cooper summarizes and discusses Julian S. Huxley's recent *Atlantic Monthly* piece on African education, which puts forth a proposal as to how Africans can and should be educated.

SOURCE: Anna Julia Cooper Papers, box 23-7, folder 89, Moorland-Spingarn Research Center, Howard University.

The current **Atlantic Monthly** carries an illuminating article by Julian S. Huxley on African Education which would suggest useful ideals for educators of any people anywhere and particularly in countries or districts whose economics must be based on agriculture rather than manufacture.

As his main thesis he says: "Education in Africa means native development. Black men are not white men, but they are men, and as such essentially educable,—the natives want education, and in spite of everything natives are being educated to do—and often to do well—things which only one generation back were not even dreamed of by the African. I have seen dressers in charge of dispensaries, clerks keeping the records of native courts, girls running maternity and infant welfare stations with white inspection only once a month, men in charge of a power station on a big estate, school-masters who taught well and had their heart in their job, foremen in sole control of building operations—all blacks. I have seen black nuns, black school prefects, black drill sergeants, black students who were dissecting a cadaver with commendable thoroness, a black choir singing Bach Motets and singing them well, black health workers who, unsupervised produce admirable malaria surveys and maps." He proceeds to give the main heads of his plan as follows: "To insist on hygiene, drill, and practical agriculture, to encourage respect for tribal history and customs and the practice of native handicrafts; to begin with general education in which, after a grounding in the three R's emphasis is laid on the native's own environment—African geography, African history, local nature ture study, hygiene, agriculture; to build on this foundation by special vocational training for the great majority of boys and girls, reserving the higher academic education for the exceptional few who can profit by it, and so quite apart from its direct effect upon production, education will pay for itself over and over again by raising the native's demands upon life, reducing the wastage of life and health, cutting down the expenditure on military and police and replacing many alien cogs in the administrative machine by indigenous ones." Further he adds: "There must be a supply of white teachers, government and missionary alike, who do not think of the natives as 'niggers' to be taught useful trades, or as heathen to be converted, but as human beings who have a culture of their own, making native education to the fullest extent the instrument of native development."

Is not this the elemental principle and foundation of all education everywhere? namely the fullest development of the individual in and by and for the best possible environing society. The writer cogently concludes: "Hundreds of black boys and girls are being today let loose over the country charged every year with new knowledge, new practical arts, new thots and ideas. There is no stemming the tide. We are certain. . . . the remedy for education is more education."

"We of the U.S.A. have also our problems in education of primitive or backward groups—and they are not all black! The public press has thrilled recently and we have all been touched and inspired by the spirit of sympathetic kindness with which the best brain and heart of the country responds to the need of a group of arrieres lately discovered in the vicinity of the Rapidan. Wealth has rushed to the rescue—radios, automobiles, desks, books, and abundance, to be sure, of much needed soap and water, assuring the world that to have been by any trick of fate marooned for a time off the high ways of civilization is by no means to be imputed as a mark of inferiority, or any inherited tendency, but should be promptly and dutifully atoned for by all the forces of the onrushing tide."

# 17

# "Another Apostle of Race Integrity"

Cooper summarizes and critiques the argument made in Alexander Harvey Shannon's 1930 book, *The Negro in Washington: A Study in Race Amalgamation*, in which Shannon advocates for his African repatriation program and asserts racial causes behind the unemployment of unskilled white workers.

SOURCE: Anna Julia Cooper Papers, box 23-7, folder 89, Moorland-Spingarn Research Center, Howard University.

The crop of literary solutions of the race problem by gratuitous assumptions and statistical charts and graphs is gradually taking on a slightly less abusive and contemptuous tone while losing none of its nervy determination to find or make a place for the American Negro, put him in it and keep him there.

Even the author of the "Rising Tide of Color" in his discussion in the Forum with Dr. Locke[1] disclaims the purpose to marshal his forces on the old "Inferiority argument." Negro music, Negro art, and Negro poetry, drama, and cinema have won an interest amounting to a fad in the ever restless, ever changing taste of the American public. Nevertheless it is worthy of note that the old propaganda cult has the same passwords and secret countersign, however neatly padded superficially with sympathetic and even laudatory phrasing to catch the eye and tickle the fancy of the Negro public who have been but lately discovered as able to read, analyse and talk back.

The Reverend A. H. Shannon,[2] former chaplain of Mississippi State Penitentiary has brought forth a book on The Negro in Washington, A Study in Race Amalgamation;[3] using Washington merely as a peg on which to hang his general preachment for what he calls "re-patriation" i. e. a national arrangement for unscrambling the mess by removing to the Upper Congo (and to Abyssinia for mulattoes) all normal and healthy Negroes reaching the age of 21 or younger who marry and produce children. He argues from the enthusiasm created by Garvey that the Negroes themselves would be 10 to 1 glad of the chance to escape persecution from race prejudice here if assured of the opportunity to found a Negro state under most favorable circumstances. All this is worked out in the pure desire of "philanthropy" to preserve the Negro's race integrity and save him from vicious whites as well as to keep "the stream of Caucasian protoplasm" pure from pollution by his presence.

"The courts fail utterly," he wails, "in reference to race protection. Religion has failed to control the situation. Race prejudice has failed as a complete control and will continue so to fail. Only complete separation of the races can prove a complete protection for either race."

I shall not attempt here to review the book since it contains little that has not been answered over and over beyond the very serious clash he attempts to foment among shades of colored people themselves.

The one bit of really significant propaganda which I consider of vital and pressing importance is what he has to say regarding unemployment of the unskilled white man. "The matter of the poor white is one of the most serious problems of the present day. America can learn much from South Africa." Quoting Sir Walter Hutchins who speaks of the poor white class of Natal: "Kaffirs' work they will not do, skilled work they cannot do. They sink and sink, live in misery and wretchedness, objects of compassion and contempt even to the natives, relying, not a few of them on the natives to preserve them from starvation." Here in America, Shannon continues, a similar situation is the direct result of colored environment. There has been no effort, he charges, to protect the poor white from the competition of the Negro. "Those who must work in order to live, find on seeking employment they must meet conditions created by the Negro, accept his wage; show his docility, do his work, or there is no place for them in a Negro dominated industrial order."

Not long since the daily news noted a white man who went to a factory seeking work. The employer told him to come in the next morning. On his way out he saw a solitary Negro at work and asked how long he had had the job. He was told, and he peremptorily ordered the Negro to clear out. The man thus ordered left at once and was shot in the back dead in his tracks as he was making his way from the place of his employment.

The economic situation looms even more grave than either the social or political, if they can be isolated and viewed in contrast. It is a situation that cannot be conquered by force nor negotiated by logic. Only the counter tactics of mutual help and racial patronage dictated by enlightened group interest and concerted economic enterprise can hope to furnish even partial and gradual relief. But it will help some.

# 18

# "Shannon's Book Continued"

Continuing the discussion that appears in "Another Apostle of Race Integrity," Cooper makes further comment about, and argues against, Reverend Shannon's contention that African Americans are depriving unskilled white laborers of work.

SOURCE: Anna Julia Cooper Papers, box 23-7, folder 89, Moorland-Spingarn Research Center, Howard University.

My readers will possibly remember that last week's column noted a recent publication considered by the writer more than usually significant. In fact "The Negro in Washington" with its pious platitudes and sympathetic yearning to "save the Negro from loss of precious Race Integrity thru contact with vicious whites," is put in such a way as to stir more bitterness and work a deeper, a more enduring economic hardship than the most brutal insults and diatribes anent "missing links" and malodorous inferiority could ever have done. Insulting lies can be passed over with silent contempt; and even in Mr. Shannon's book his chimerical scheme of getting all not-whites happily herded into Africa may well be ignored. But economic facts, so marshaled as to lead inevitably to group conflicts and irreconcilable racial bitterness bring us face to face with a situation which I deem of sufficient moment to call for more than a cursory review. I have singled out this week two specific quotations which I will ask the thotful reader to consider,—not for the purpose of academic discussion or sulphuric denunciation, but by way of offering perhaps an opportunity on both sides for clear constructive thinking and some inter-racial understanding.

When one sees clearly the subtler forces that are so astutely and so insidiously at work, there should be, in place of the usual hysteria and soap box declamation, a calm, intelligent and quiet thinking the thing thru, arriving here and there eventually at individual purposive judgments. This seems to me the only safe and sane way of approaching hoped for results and building up something in the way of a sound policy and a useful, if not organic, line of action.

Organization doubtless is an approved method, but it is conceivable that a handicap can be utterly paralyzed by over-organization. "The strength of the wolf is in the pack" says Kelly Miller.[1] "Except when they are drowning!" say I. A solidarity of suffering and of opposing forces is only too evident and undeniable. But there are circumstances that would be rendered increasingly awkward and painful by too great solidarity of machinery. The big thing is that we get to know and trust,—a community of interest, a community of simple sympathy. At any rate we ought to understand one another better, and when we realize that the hurt is after all a part of the great human hurt, we shall not go futilely, striking friend and foe blindly as an irritated infant uses arms, legs, and diaphragm to kick the air. As already said the unemployment problem is the one biggest "hurt" in the economic world of today. The man of color is by no means the only sufferer. His color simply accentuates it in his neighborhoods and punctuates the bitterness in the struggle for bread. It may be that our western civilization has not mastered the technique of distribution and may be that man's greed is wholly to blame for the sickening chasms between wealth and poverty, where the rich grow automatically richer and the poor poorer. Surely the earth is productive enough to afford sustenance for all its children, and a man with brains and energy in the wide stretches of the United States ought not inertly to rot like a cabbage in one spot because he happened to be born there. It may be, that the onward stride of scientific invention and the craze for mass production, like the car of Juggernaut, is trampling in the dust and grinding to powder the helpless victims of a machine age. Sure I admit that something is wrong when wages are being paid for tree-sitting and Niagara barrelling instead of for wheat harvesting and cotton picking; and when Alabama takes more pride in Bobby Jones for playing golf than in Booker Washington for inaugurating a system of education in practical farming for the larger half of its population. There is something wrong I admit, and am equally sure that weeping and wailing and gnashing of teeth will not right it.

But here are the quotations from Shannon's book. Read them silently, think them over calmly, then judge what is best or simply what can be done about it. It may be you will decide, as I do, to do your work that comes to hand tomorrow as you have done today, to plan your household, train your children, support your institutions, give a fair wage to the few you are able to hire and go whistling on your way. Certainly not to hire a hall to "discuss" the problem, nor yet to conclude that none of these things touch you; but understandingly and fellow-feeling to help where, when, and if you can.

"For every Negro trained as a skilled artizan a white skilled artizan, actual or potential is displaced. For every such Negro who builds a home and rears a family, somewhere a white man is either deprived of the chance to build a home and rear a family or is driven to contend with highly unfavorable conditions in his efforts to do so. The Negro schools in Washington are training carpenters, bricklayers, cement workers etc. Also these schools are fitting men for professional life. Every one of these Negroes will, in so far as he works at his trade here, displace a white worker actual or potential.

"Construction of a large apartment house at G and 18, Washington. Very little of the skilled labor done by Negroes except laying of brick. Hardly a white man was employed at unskilled labor. It was usually the cast that for 25 to 75 white men would be on hand at beginning of work each day in hope of being given a job, some remaining till after work was well under way. It was frequently the case that some of these men would be present at the Union Gospel Mission where a light meal and a free bed could be had by those unable to pay for food and lodging. It is at such missions and at Salvation Army stations—and in Jails that one sees the real significance of the meaning of conditions existing in Washington."[*]

---

[*]Shannon: *The Negro in Washington*, p. 175.

# 19

# "Anna J. Cooper Makes Comment on the Lindbergh Kidnapping Affair"

Writing for the *Washington Tribune*, Cooper comments on the unfortunate Lindbergh baby kidnapping and uses it as an opportunity to discuss mothers' universal sorrow over lost children as well as Americans' tendency to focus on, and celebrate, sensational rather than genuine accomplishments.

SOURCE: Anna Julia Cooper Papers, box 23-7, folder 89, Moorland-Spingarn Research Center, Howard University.

Editor Washington Tribune:

Allow me to commend the timely and very forceful editorial in last week's Tribune on the Lindbergh case.[1]

The restraint and breadth of human sympathy in this particularly well-written article make it stand out in sharp contrast against the too often hypersensitive, crassly denunciatory and rabid effusions of those who think black, and only black all the time. For after all the agony of that silent Mother-Heart at Sourland Castle, the cynosure at present of the richest and most powerful nation on earth, is no different from the sorrow that wrung the Mother-Heart of Mary weeping over the Crucified One, or of the least "blessed among women," the unrecorded Mother of the sinful Judas, or yet again of the lowly and despised Mother of Some black victim of mob fury and rape, whose bitter anguish, unheard and unsung can only spend itself in inarticulate groans as she sits rocking with empty arms folded over the aching void, hugging helplessly her hungry aloneness: "Jes tell 'em I'm hungry for ma chile! You hear? I want's ma chile!"

The same ruthlessness of power and selfish greed has driven the bloody knife into the quivering breast of each bereaved mother, and none can better understand the suffering human heart than they who themselves have suffered.

That our country is passing through a baptism of fire under a ruthless reign of gangdom, class suspicion and bitter hatred, no one in his senses will attempt to deny. That the colored people are the only or chief sufferers, or that they can be separated and set over against the suffering as a symbol of retributive justice of an avenging God only an unspeakable egoism and exaggerated self-importance could imagine. Still less that an overruling Providence could design such a cataclysm to teach a monstrous object lesson to a chosen people. And yet the weakest and least articulate element in a self-asserting democracy may well be the test and gage by which to measure the depth and sincerity of its principles and professions. "Inasmuch as ye have done it unto the least." There is no rubbing out the injustice to the Negro—the offense is rank and smells to Heaven. But the American race problem is only a phase of the American ideal and master passion, which is quite frankly and unblushingly the worship of "the Beast."

Power, the big noise, the top notch, the unbeatable record! The under dog in any walk of life is weak, and we don't like weakness. The lowly Nazarene who had no where to lay his head would have a hard time gaining recognition in a land where the king of law breakers could be sent up only for evading his income tax. Lindbergh himself, who was never a particularly glib talker, and could not pass 1A English at Eastern High School, would not have been hailed across the corner at the avenue unless he had put over a stunt that set the whole world agape, while we prostrate ourselves five times a day before the brilliancy of such minds as Loeb's and Leopold's.

Dazzling achievement, not useful service, is the spur, and the goal to set imaginations tingling and give fresh impetus to hope. The wife of an honest poor man sees success writ larger in any idiotic stunt that she can afford, so she gets out of washing dishes and making beds for the rest of her life by having some one to pilot her a short distance over the Atlantic on the first convenient sailing vessel that comes along, and yet we wonder that young people are frivolous, that high schools and colleges are turning out vain and purposeless puppets, and that we have greater demand for houses of detention, reformatories and jails than for lecture halls, boys' clubs and evening classes. Can organized lay society do anything about it? I believe it can, and I am sure it is as much my duty and privilege as it is that of the richest and most powerful in the community to join vigorous hands with men and women of good will, be they white or black to help "ring in the Christ that is to be."

It may be, as one has said, that it is the hunger for brotherhood that is at the bottom of the unrest of the world, and perhaps after all it is not over production of wheat, but a certain underproduction of the milk of human kindness, somewhere, somehow, that makes one-half of the world seem ready to take the other half by the throat. Is there no cure? None better than that enunciated twenty centuries ago—"My neighbor as myself." We have sinned and fallen short, as a nation, as individuals, none excepted. In the pride of our prosperity we have sown the wind and may expect to reap the whirlwind. We have had respect to the high lofty, the lowly we have allowed to be trampled under foot. Well might the prophetic pen of Jefferson write: "I tremble for my country when I remember that God is just."

# 20

# "The 14th Amendment: A Confession of Faith"

Published the week after "'A Pitiful Mouth,'" Cooper explains why she does not fall into the category of "New Negro." She states it is primarily because she is not young, she thinks "the New Negro racket has been a bit overdone," does not want her children to marry across the color line, and is not distressed by the fact that she lives in an African American neighborhood, suggesting that her critiques of the New Negro also relate to what she sees as capitulation to popular white cultural norms. Cooper goes on to argue that as a Black woman, she is a "true blue American" in the sense that her ancestors are a mix of Native Americans, those who came over on the *Mayflower*, and the first Africans to arrive on North American soil.

SOURCE: Anna Julia Cooper Papers, box 23-7, folder 89, Moorland-Spingarn Research Center, Howard University.

I am not a "New Negro."

This is not merely because my hair is gray and unbobbed; but, to say the truth, I think the New Negro racket has been a bit overdone. I confess I am a trifle weary of it.

Second: I do not want my son or my daughter to marry a white person on the other side of an imaginary line that belts this planet known as the "Color Line." This is not because of any prejudice against race or color on my part. I know that there are individuals on the other side of that amazing line just as good as

I am, just as true-hearted, just as noble, just as generous, just as fine. Some of these I have met,—really met, not as one rubs elbows with the hoi polloi at a drawing room crush or a yamping, gwaping carrousel; but where soul actually reaches out and touches soul in the solitude "a deux," confident that there is no beguiling camouflage, no treacherous quicksands to tempt and destroy the unwary. Yes; friends true and tried I have known and know; but I do not want to marry them nor that any my kith and kin should do so.

Neither on the other hand do I feel it incumbent on me to sheath myself and all my kin with porcupine quills of cruelty and hatred in order to prevent what I do not want and what no one can possibly force me to accept. When, therefore, I see the Army, Navy and Air forces of my grand and glorious country all mobilized and concentrated, getting bolts and bars in place to make a few hoboes keep off the grass, I fall to wondering what it's all about. There seems to be a panic of anticipated bombardment or of an overwhelming invasion and I want to say "There, there— don't take on so. Nobody's going to marry you! Nobody's axed you Sir, have they? Why this unaccountable distress?"

Third—and I expect in saying this to have to dodge all the God save the mark!—but Third: While guiltless of an inferiority complex, I am not greatly distressed over the fact that I live in a "colored" neighborhood, so long as adequate police protection and those material comforts and services for which I pay taxes are fairly and justly provided. To be quite candid again, "I do not choose" to live among savages, whatever their complexion, and I answer the question "Who is my neighbor?" in language quite different from throwing stones to smash his windows and raising a small riot merely because another's accident of color scheme does not happen to coincide with my own.

Thus much by way of preface.

Not that I imagine for a moment that my personal attitude has any interest for the general public or that it will command a following even from the man across the street. But there are around 12 millions of me, born into American citizenship, loving our country with an overflowing, sentimental, nay even, if you will, a pathetic affection, wishing and, according to our lights, working for the best things for this, our native land, just as truly and as sincerely as the elect of God, who blush self-consciously whenever We, the People are mentioned and who say (not always in undertones) WE are IT!

The first Lady of the Land has no better right to sacrifice and die for our fatherland (hers and mine) than have I. The part of my ancestors that did not come over in the Mayflower in 1620, arrived, I am sure, a year earlier in that fateful Dutch Trader that put in at Jamestown in 1619. If there be any higher percentage among the "Hundred Percenters" it must be for the aborigines, and I believe that the third source of my individual stream comes clean even from the vanishing Red Man, which ought, according to my arithmetic, reckon my points up to one hundred thirty three and one-third per cent to the manor born and "inheritor of the glebe": genuine F.F.A.'s (First Families of America,) incontestable, undeniable, and unalienable. True blue American, if there be any honor in that, I claim it.

While however, some may be interested in checking up, testing, measuring and comparing these three strains in the curl of my hair, or the breadth of my nostrils, or the color of my epidermis, myself, as a thinking, feeling, willing entity, am not the least bit conscious of thinking, feeling or willing through and by the pigment cells in that epidermis. If different, I don't know it. I am absolutely sure that I am not an alien and could not, even if I wanted to, expatriate myself. With clear-eyed vision of its human imperfection and short comings I sing "America" and mean every word of it because I know it is my duty and my privilege to strive as mightily as the mightiest to help truth to overcome error, justice to prevail over corruption, and that Righteousness, which alone exalteth a nation shall triumph over all the hosts of evil.


## A CORRECTION

A printer's point made me say last week that we paid Mr. Darrow two dollars for his advice that "the Negro should learn to give tips." What I wrote and meant to print was two hundred dollars—a rather respectable tip, all things considered.

# 21

# "'A Pitiful Mouth'"

Cooper examines the irony that involves Americans
boasting about being well to do, yet reluctant to tip
servers, and compares the practice in the US to the one
in Europe, where tipping is not an option, but rather
built into the system.

SOURCE: Anna Julia Cooper Papers, box 23-7, folder 89,
Moorland-Spingarn Research Center, Howard University.

Clarence Darrow advised the Negro race to give tips instead of
taking them. We paid Mr. Darrow $2.00 to tell us that and I
could have told it for 2 cents. But that was Darrow and it was
worth the price of admission. Now I want to add, for nothing a
line, that "Tips" given or taken is a state of mind, an attitude, an
inherited tendency, an atavistic formula of the Mendelian Law,
so to speak. It is not a matter of race, color or creed. There are
some people who never get over the habit of being poor. They
think poor, feel poor and, when it comes to paying a just debt,
they talk poor, even tho they dress in silk and drive expensive
automobiles. They will boast of the high cost of their bridge favors and yet refuse a Christmas gratuity to the tshmtn.[1] "The
poor in spirit" see God. The mean in spirit cannot see a fellow
man. There's a difference.

I have heard the owner of three or four rented houses higgling
with a colored plasterer whose price was already less than three-
fourths of what she would have had to pay a white contractor for
the job. Still the colored workman had his family to support all
through his long extended slack times with no Union help or unemployment insurance to tide him over.

The American public resent the giving of tips to Pullman porters and yet the son of the great Emancipator himself said in a
well known investigation before Congress: "All will admit it is
not desirable that Negroes shall be paid high salaries." A nation
as an individual is just before it is generous, and, if we are bent
on getting the laborer's service with as little return as possible in
the form of his "worthy hire," then we are all tip takers and not
givers.

In Europe an understood 10 percent of every charge is gratuitously added for service, a pour boire or "for a drink" which
translated into plain Americanese signifies "a tip." The usher
who shows you to your seat at the theater, expects it. The check
man who takes your umbrella, the attendant who politely helps
you on with your wraps, the janitor the bootblack, the femme de
chambre, all expect a substantial "tip," and they write you down
as awfully "cheap" if they don't get it. Quite inconsistently
Americans are the only people that make a fuss about it, while
proudly boasting that they are the richest and most prosperous
nation on earth.

Just before leaving France from my last sojourn there, I had an
autobus sight-seeing trip through the regions devastated by the
War. It was a regular itinerary arranged by the American Express and the "atmosphere" of the All-Americas was there.
Needless to say my unaccustomed ears were regaled for a full
day with the nasal twang and the Georgia drawl of my native
heath. At one of the stops where we went in for refreshment, one
of my-eh-fellow-passengers who had not given evidence that she
had been aware of my existence at any time during the journey,
in the lavatory sidled up and observed: "I heard you talking
French to that—girl who seems to be in charge. Do you have to
pay them?"

"Oh certainly, give them something," I said. "You don't have
to, of course. Our trip is prepaid, but the service is worth a little
extra."

"Well," she faltered, "I left my money with my husband—will
you pay her for me?"

I promptly handed her my purse of small change telling her to
give Mademoiselle whatever she wanted to. At that time French
girls were really pitiful to look at and a whole franc, which

would have seemed munificent to this one, was worth less than five cents, an amount which would have made an American servant spit at you for merely suggesting so insignificant a tip.

We read some time ago of a pitiable imbecile who had amassed his millions. His architects had built him a palace with broad lawns and beautiful terraces. Interior decorators had furnished it with paintings, statues, books—every physical comfort that heart could wish or modern invention supply. The poor wretch literally had gained the whole world and lost his own soul in the process. His nerve centers could never get over the hardened activity of grasping and getting. He would leave the downiest couch to sleep on the cellar floor; refuse the daintiest viands to feed on husks. His sons in their distress appealed to psychoanalysis and nerve specialists in vain. Every trick of scientific suggestion and environmental allurements were tried without avail. The fixed idea of abject destitution and unsatisfiable want and misery was like the Rock of Gibraltar against which the efforts of science and art pounded futilely. Worse than the thirst of Tantalus, his restless yearning gave him no peace and all his wealth could not batter down the sordid fastnesses of an imprisoned soul nor wash away the parsimonious accretions of a lifelong habit of meanness. We are as rich as we think ourselves and the measure of our opulence is the skyline and horizon of our brotherhood. The dear old couple saying grace over a breakfast of corn bread and molasses were undeniably rich in their contented summing up of their happiness balance sheet: "All this and Jesus too." One is more than apt to find the truest, the most genuine and untarnished philanthropies in just such lowly hearts, who without herald or brass band are actually sharing their truly primitive wealth simply and contentedly with their brethren in distress.

Verily penury hath its compensations, not the least of which may be exemption from penuriousness.

# 22

# "Say 'Thank You'"

In this article, Cooper defends and advocates for the practice of saying *thank you*, asserting it should be done even if other formal social niceties have grown cumbersome.

SOURCE: Anna Julia Cooper Papers, box 23-7, folder 89, Moorland-Spingarn Research Center, Howard University.

There are many hackneyed expressions of pure formalism, hypocritical civilities which had better be packed away in moth balls and forgotten. They are intolerable and meaningless when they have no original flavor and represent no sincerity of feeling or genuine warmth on the part of the speaker. In this category would fall, surely, the smirking "Pleased-to-meet-you" on receiving an introduction that you did not desire and which you have already shown the palpable hypocrisy by withholding your greeting under the well-nigh belligerent demand: "Name please!" thus signaling in action anything but pleasure at the courtesy thrust upon you. This last seems to me particularly offensive, if not gratuitously insulting. Here comes, let us suppose, a mutual friend, smilingly expectant, leading party of the second part to begin a lifelong friendship with the party of the first part. Presumably, Mr. Mutual Friend has already rehearsed the antecedents in the case. Where she's from, how much her grandfather owned, her own special accomplishments at bridge, jazz, ice cream etc., while party of the first part stands a not unwilling victim ready for the sacrifice, having made it plain to all possible comers that she is on the tapis for the express purpose of being introduced and stands with the glad hand barely concealed in the shimmer of chiffon and rhinestones. Now comes the anti-flop, so to speak: "Miss Smith, allow me to present Mr. New-comer who is just dying to have a number on your card." When Mr. New-comer stiffens with what he considers becoming dignity and hesitantly demands before proceeding another step: "Name please." Whereupon Miss Smith should spell with a flash "S-m-y-t-h vamoose! Now git!"

But "I thank you," fortunately, is not one of those inanities that we can afford to taboo.

Even the million and one "phthankew-s" from a million and one telephone girls have all a cherry ring that heartens the listener even though he has been given the wrong number. Who does not enjoy the hearty "Thank you, Family" in the Good Night of Major Bowes for his Capitol Theater Family in New York. How homelike and friendly it is! How full of real appreciation and gratitude! He might say: "I don't see why I should thank these people. They are not singing and playing for me personally. It's their livelihood. They're paid to do it.—Then why thank them?" But on the other hand, what an atmosphere of good fellowship and camaraderie emanates from that simple Thank you. Who would not sing better, play better, work better if the boss somehow gave out the feeling that he appreciated every little effort,—not as a cog on a wheel of a cast iron machine—but as a human palpitating sentiency, vitally promoting the big Cause actually at stake, and directly and personally boosting his interests and undeniably heartening and strengthening him. For after all, in the last analysis it is our enthusiasms that lift us above the brutes and only because we feel, admire and appreciate that we deserve to lift our head, look the sun in the face and assert our divine kinship. As one has well said:

"No orator ever made a great speech to a cold and clammy audience.

"No actor ever gave a great performance to a house that sat on the back of its neck and dared him to make it laugh or cry. No man lies awake at night thinking how he can do better work for a boss who never notices what he does except to find fault.

All our labor, all our effort, all our enthusiasm falls flat if we fail of the recognition we know we have earned."

A simple "Thank you" is easily said, costs nothing, and goes far. Let us not grudge the praise and thanks due honest effort—and don't wait to say it with flowers.

# 23

# "Courtesy"

Recounting an experience in which she walked into a barbershop seeking to buy moss and was treated rudely, Cooper uses the example to highlight the need for courtesy in society.

SOURCE: Anna Julia Cooper Papers, box 23-7, folder 89, Moorland-Spingarn Research Center, Howard University.

I was attracted recently by some fine Irish moss, growing rather widely and unkept in a show window out Seventh street way. As my own pots of moss had unaccountably lived all winter to die wildly and unkept in a show window seemed badly in need of expert thinning out, I determined to stop and barter for a few sprigs here to start a fresh pot. As I entered, I saw the place was a barber shop, with nothing doing for the time being. Two lads of about high school age lounged in the front, one chewing gum, the other "jes looking on." I am sure that they were not conversing. Neither rose as I paused at the door and inquired pleasantly if I could buy a bit of the moss in the window. The boy with the gum, who on the whole seemed less wooden of the two (at least his jaws were alive) jerked his head toward the west without releasing his gum, by which gesture I discovered a third occupant of the room, whom I judged to be the proprietor, enjoying his ease with becoming dignity near a barber chair in the rear of the room.

Now I submit that by all odds, I would have been rated as a prospective customer to be met with the ingratiating bow and smile of the trade.

"Madam, would you like your hair bobbed or your face lifted, or eyebrows plucked, or third chin reduced? We have all styles—satisfaction guaranteed. . . ."

But no; he does not even straighten his backbone from on the highest round of a chair, but waits as woodenly as the two boys had done until I repeat my offer to buy a bit of moss, and then emits, without so much as moving his eyes, the grunted monosyllable, "Naw," with a finality that closes the incident.

I had to indulge in an ironical "How delightfully accommodating!" as I tried to smile away my chagrin and disappointment on leaving the non-social trio-disappointment, not on failing to get a sprig of moss, but a sense of failure in our whole scheme of education which, while aiming to adjust the individual to life and its environing requirements, could project such an object life before our young people in practice.

It is either merely a groundless suspicion on my part, or there is more and more a noticeable disregard for the conventions of good manners—those little courtesies in our contacts which ought to pave the way to a happy adjustment in all the little affairs of life and which are most assuredly for the man in business, the foundation stone for all progress and success.

And again, am I wrong in wondering whether the deliberate rudeness I sometimes encounter in our city gives evidence of a widening gulf, a growing separation in sympathy and understanding between our self-styled intelligensia, and which I may call the "ignorantsia," or between the privileged (if ever so imperfectly) and the underprivileged classes.

Deplorable, if true, such a chasm would be at any time and under any circumstances. The first move to heal the breach should come from those whose opportunities and superior advantages enable them to appreciate the dangers of a house divided against itself, and whose cultivated powers impose the responsibility of sane leadership and sympathetic guidance and instruction.

For after all, our cause is one; our interests one. Together we rise and fall.

Mutual distrust and suspicion will never get us anywhere. Scorn and repulsion beget nothing but hate, jealousy, and vindictiveness. If the masses do not believe in our brand of brotherhood, it may be after all that there is a baser metal mixed in the alloy. Genuine kindliness needs no interpreter. It speaks a universal language. The discourtesy of plain people is too often but a reflection of something spurious found in the article that has been offered them.

But whatever the cause, our duty as teachers and leaders is to impress on our youth, along with the subjects and courses offered in the schools, the absolute value and essential bedrock importance of good manners in business and courtesy in every human contact.

# 24

# "The Community Chest"

In this article, published in an unidentified paper on January 23, 1931, Cooper speaks in favor of the Community Chest, a community-based charity organization, and suggests individualism is a potential enemy to the common good the Chest espouses.

SOURCE: Anna Julia Cooper Papers, box 23-7, folder 89, Moorland-Spingarn Research Center, Howard University.

To my mind Unity is the last word in the Chest idea. I can't say whether it is the egg or the hen that laid the egg, but sure I am that the Chest was spoken of and wished for years ago by forward thinking people at the Nation's Capital; but the knowing ones felt the time was not ripe because of the stubborn lines of demarcation in feeling even more than in fact that existed at the time among the people themselves.

I don't know if the fundamentals of my loyalty may be called in question when I say that this growing sense of unity so essential in the drive for the Chest, is a matter of slower attainment in our city, perhaps, than in others which, presumably can boast no higher ideals or purer purposes, by and large, and this backwardness, it seems to me, is due to those very isolating and disintegrating forces that keep alive the individualistic interests and strive to build up group by group from within instead of by a common circulatory system directed and nourished by one heart and one head.

Nor are color lines and race lines, complicated and all-pervasive as they are, from whatever angle you view them, the only barriers walling in petty prejudice and provincialism, and walling out a

finer community interest. The "Home Towner" feels the importance of looking after the Oldest Inhabitants, the "Transients"
feel snubbed when confronted with a stand-off look that says as
plainly as words: "Who are you to tell us what to do?" And so
the Alabamans have their stimulating "get-toe-gethers," the Bos-
tonians enjoy their little fling at the brand of "cultua" they behold, New Yorkers broadcast that the narrow gauge way of
running things "down heah" is horribly antiquated, and westerners are sure (with a tremendous roll of the "R") that the capital
should be more centrally located, and there you are. A sort of
God bless me and my wife, my son John and his wife, which is as
disastrous for unity of sentiment or purpose,—not to speak of a
common money box—as an early frost on sweet peas.

For my poor part I like to feel that my little dollar, which I
give of my own volition, quite as surely as the taxes I am forced
to give, will possibly reach in its travels even as far as those who
may ignore or dislike me and, as drop by drop water wears
stone, so these voluntary and cherry littles will eventually batter
down mighty strongholds.

I say then that the Community Chest, here and now,—having
passed safely both the Scylla and Charybdis of its teething year
with its manifold critical dangers of infancy, has triumphantly
proved its vitality and is here to stay. That it is at once the efficient cause and the hoped-for effect of a wholesome development
of unity in the Community and is the very best school master
our divided, stratified and segregated National City could have
to bring our group-mindedness into harmonious articulation
with cosmopolitan philanthropy. Having weathered the storms
of hyper-critical prejudices of all sorts and from all sources, and
having battered down the obstructions of selfish narrowness and
hide bound preferences, it is worthy—eminently worthy, to receive the whole-hearted support and unqualified cooperation of
every public spirited citizen of our Washington, because it means
not giving, but sharing, not cold charity but warm brotherliness,
and because it stands for and believes in that oneness of Fatherhood and brotherhood without which all our efforts at lifting or
climbing will be but spasms and spurts of a galvanized corpse,
not the effective power and wholesome vitality of a living, growing, and healthy organism.

# 25

# "Educational Chit-Chat"

In this article Cooper laments the focus on speeding up educational efforts and pushing children through school as quickly as possible. She suggests that, instead, children be allowed to mature and exercise physically as well as mentally.

SOURCE: Anna Julia Cooper Papers, box 23-7, folder 89, Moorland-Spingarn Research Center, Howard University.

## SPEEDING

A machine age with its top-notch goal on mass production necessarily overrides the individual, sacrificing spiritual values as it throws open the throttle to "let her go" for all she's worth! Smash the record! Never mind about the scenery—just get there! a few hundredths of a second quicker, a few millimeters faster, a few feet higher and a few rounds of refueling longer than the latest and most startling topnotcher.

It is most unfortunate that this craze for speeding and topnotching should strike our educational programs. Youth is the time for growth—and growth, to be healthy, should be normal and without artificial forcing.

"Only God can make a tree," and He has never yet made one overnight. Mushrooms come that way, but trees never. "Skipping grades" and making four years in three may flatter teachers and stimulate the superiority complex of some students, but I always feel that there is something lost—something of solidarity and strength, something that will be sorely missed when one comes to stand up before the inexorable demands of a cold and calculating world. Educational speeding is like glimpsing Niagara from an express train. It takes time for observation, reflection, appreciation—the basis and essential condition of that genuine mental growth which we call education and which is power.

Particularly disastrous are those fads for speeding up education which inject the insidious stimulant of "something to prove." Propaganda, whether for or against, is artificial and baneful when applied to human cultures. It is high time that those who are holding the whip hand thought out their own program to meet the needs and direct the development of their charges, and parents and guardians must insist that children, shut out from so many cultural contacts calculated to make growth largely a matter of natural absorption from a congenial atmosphere, shall not be forced under the strain of "stunt" performances into exceeding the speed limit, just to show that we can. The sequel to young Sidis and Katherine Stover, the two top-notchers in speeding through college, does not inspire emulation for our children. Above all we must conserve their health. See that the "medicine ball" is mixed in with the day's responsibilities. Old and young need it, regularly, systematically, purposefully. The studious child more than all others needs it. Envious about marks and the honor roll, he is under a strain that few parents realize and not many teachers appreciate, because both are keyed up to the same pitch, and most are ready to fight to the last ditch for the paltry difference between a V.[ery Good] G.[ood] and E.[xcellent].

Relax, relax, I say. Take a deep breath and smile. If the youngster is doing his best (and many, I grant, are not), let him have the reward of your satisfaction. Give him time, and a real romping, rollicking vacation for swimming, tennis, camping in the woods with only Mother Nature's big reference books to study over.

# 26

# "For Barbers:
# Boards of Examiners"

Cooper calls attention to the licensing laws and tests being implemented in a variety of states supposedly to protect public health, but which, in reality, are designed to prevent Black barbers from practicing their trade.

SOURCE: Anna Julia Cooper Papers, box 23-7, folder 89, Moorland-Spingarn Research Center, Howard University.

There are more ways to kill a dog than by choking him to death with butter. One way, approved and much in demand is to have him go before a duly appointed board of examiners and "pass" the examinations. At least this seems a satisfactory solution of both Negro unemployment problems as settled in the minds of leading tonsorial artists in U.S.A.

According to The Nation the organized white barbers of the country are gradually securing the adoption of bills in the various states, (always in the interest of the health of the public, of course) setting up boards of barber examiners to pass on the qualifications of applicants and issue or revoke licenses. Twenty-six states including Maryland have already passed such laws. The Virginia legislature was the last to make a try out, with the State Federation of Labor, the four railway brotherhoods and the National Women's Trade Union League backing the measure, and the Virginia Commission on Interracial Relations opposing. The bill failed at this session. A few sample questions quoted by The Nation will show how eager these "protectors of the public health are to secure competent, clean and intelligent hands to wash and trim the public hair:

> "1. How many hairs are there to the square inch on the average scalp?
> "2. Where is the arrector pili muscle located and what is its function?
> "3. Describe the function and location of the sebaceous glands, etc., etc., etc."

While it is loudly proclaiming that the object of these examinations is "to protect the public against diseased and incompetent barbers," it is freely admitted among those pushing these bills that they desire their enactment in order to run the Negroes out of business and raise the tariffs in their own shops. Similar legislation is being offered at almost every session of every state legislature in the Union. In Virginia the plumbers, realtors, and embalmers have come forward with schemes setting up stiff requirements for would-be practitioners, with boards of examiners to say who shall be licensed. In this way all professions and trades will be able to set up monopolies against competition by legalizing their various boards of examiners.

We learn that a bill to make the Virginia Bar Association an agency of the state was defeated at this year's session. Members of the Senate having shown that lawyers who supported it aimed to prevent many deserving persons from practicing in Virginia. Undoubtedly, those who offered it claimed that it was "solely for the protection of the public."

Thirty years ago those who foolishly opposed Booker T. Washington's plan of Industrial Education, thought they were fighting for the rights to higher culture through avenues of advanced studies; today the struggle is on for man's chance to earn an honest living by the sweat of his brow. The competition is absolutely sagacious, terribly relentless, horribly ruthless.

# 27

# "'O Thou That Killest the Prophets and Stonest Them Which Are Sent Unto Thee'"

Cooper discusses the American tendency to dismiss, demean, or commit violence upon those who stand and fight for equality as a result of prejudice.

SOURCE: Anna Julia Cooper Papers, box 23-7, folder 89, Moorland-Spingarn Research Center, Howard University.

If one were inclined to believe in a foredoomed curse upon a long suffering race, no more convincing evidence of the most pessimistic fatalism could be adduced than the merciless, unmitigated, unrelenting fanaticism with which our leaders and special advocates are systematically and unceasingly beaten down and trampled underfoot or else ruthlessly thrown to the blood-thirsty beasts.

—"Crucify him" is the jawp that is snarled up as soon as any self-sacrificing service has come sufficiently into prominence to earn the Hosannas and win the palms of an appreciative multitude. It matters not how meek, how honest, how devoted to the general good that Service has been, it matters not how brilliant, how phenomenally successful, how unprecedentedly efficient— nay, even it would seem because of this very efficiency and indispensable usefulness the cry is all the more insistent: "Not this man, but Barabbas!" yes; with the parenthetical absurdity; "Now, Barabbas is a robber."

It might add somewhat to the sympathy of our perspective if

we reflect that, however proud of our race we are or claim to be, there is actually nothing within the range of our gifts to lure the self-seeking and foresighted geniuses either of our own or of other races in America today to cast in their lot preferentially with us or in any way undertake voluntarily and disinterestedly to help us. The plums are all in one side of the pudding, and it is seldom indeed that any little black Jack Horner has the luck to pull out one. We are not the guys who furnish distinguished service medals and offer honor, preferment and emoluments for conspicuous devotion to our cause; and yet, such is our forthright and downright "100 per cent Americanism," that more genuine enthusiasm can be detected today in our sympathetic mourning for the Norwegian football coach, Knute Rockne than for the comparatively unheralded passing of Moorfield Storey, that greatest exponent of the noblest and best in American ideals, who unflinching and without condescension laid on the altar of Service for this race the finest talent and the most convincing logical inheritance the soil has yet produced.

Whenever a citizen of the U.S.A., black or white, stands before the great white throne of the dominant sentiment of his country to plead for a square deal, equal opportunities and a man's chance for all regardless of race, color or previous condition, he does so because he has a passion for justice and loves his fellow man. Such a man is more than likely to face persecution, ostracism, misunderstanding and misrepresentation and the loudest and bitterest of these will come from the very people most in need of his intercession and support.

> "I do not like you, Mr. Pell;
> The reason why I cannot tell
> I do not like you, Mr. Pell."

Now shall we never learn to sink these petty differences, our little jealousies and dislikes, our pitiable scrambling for a place on the band wagon when someone else has set it in motion? Can we not put shoulder to wheel and give a solid big push all together for the common good and the upbuilding of the great big interests, instead of eternally nursing some narrow grouch and incessantly chewing upon some imaginary slight, as if our ego-centric little selves were the only important pivot in the whole universe.

"The fault, dear Brutus, is not in our stars, but in ourselves
That we are underlings."

No amount of prejudice, oppression, or segregation could stifle and hold down forever a free people in a free country who understood their opportunities and appreciated the advantages of consecrated leadership. The man at the helm has a hard enough task without the carping criticism and the treacherous machinations of a disloyal, self-seeking few, rash and reckless followers of the ship for sake of the loot, whose unvarying motto is Rule or Ruin, and who would rather wreck the entire cargo than go safely into port with a pilot untrammeled by their own pettifogging leading strings.

# 28

# "The Problem of the City Child"

Cooper highlights the tendency of specific communities, Black, white, or otherwise, to focus on others' faults and not on their own. This has, according to Cooper, produced children who behave poorly. She advocates for self-awareness and modeling politeness in front of all children to disprove the stereotype that America is "the worst mannered nation in the world."

SOURCE: Anna Julia Cooper Papers, box 23-7, folder 89, Moorland-Spingarn Research Center, Howard University.

A new note for the Crisis and a very much needed note, is struck in the October Postscripts where Dr. Du Bois calls attention to the swaggering insolence in manners of certain of our young people. As a leader of thot and teacher of good manners and correct social intercourse, as well as a fighter for rights and recognition, our newspapers and magazines are likely to be so absorbed in the latter as to crowd out entirely all criticism of morals and manners among ourselves; and, from persistent examples and illustrations with due condemnation and bitter denunciation of wrongs inflicted on members of the colored race, too often the cue is taken to wear the perpetual chip on the shoulder and imagine that common politeness and decent behavior will be construed as some sort of inferiority complex.

There is nothing in my judgment more deplorable in all the disadvantages and drawbacks from American race prejudice than the ingrowing race consciousness that narrows every thot and every act into relativity with "The Question" and prevents young and old from seeing, feeling, acting as human first and black, brown, yellow or white accidentally and secondarily.

Life has its own problem for all of us, and when you get down to the core the Souls of Black Folks[1] are just like the souls of set and the individual, whatever other folks. For each the task is his handicap, must set to with what power he has to make the most of it or else to smash the slate.

To suppose our wrongs and our suffering the only wrong and the only suffering in the universe is to become self-centered and an intolerable bore; while to think and talk perpetually from this center eventually shuts out all harmony of action, all beauty in human contacts, all appreciation of artistic achievement. A certain detachment is necessary in order to judge even ourselves and a certain open-mindedness, a sweeping the cobwebs of prejudice and narrowness from our own brains and hearts and souls before we can see life in the round and enjoy the fullness of human sympathy and human striving. We may yet learn to pity prejudice as a disease, a sort of myopia or near-sightedness which calls for light—more light and better light, rather than for heated declamation and fisti-cuffs. At any rate it is a good practice to see whether there may not be the same fault, or one at least just as unreasonable, in our own camp. First pull out the beam that is in thine own eye then shalt thou see clearly to pull out the mote from thy brother's eye.

Young people, however, are not philosophers, they take their cue and set their pace generally from what they hear their elders say. It becomes us therefore to remember "a chiel's amang ye takin notes," and in their presence refrain from discussions that engender bitterness and hard feeling. If on both sides the Great Divide, the good rule: Speak no evil were strictly followed especially in the presence of children and other irresponsibles, there would be fewer senseless clashes and insulting behavior which so easily run into riot and bloodshed, and Americans of all shades might hope to live down the reputation they now seem to have as the worst mannered nation in the world.

# 29

# "The Return of a Favorite"

In this 1931 piece, Cooper celebrates the return of the actor Nathaniel Guy to Frelinghuysen University by way of his appearance in *The Servant in the House*.

SOURCE: Anna Julia Cooper Papers, box 23-7, folder 89, Moorland-Spingarn Research Center, Howard University.

Editor, Tribune:

The Washington public will rejoice to welcome again to the dramatic stage that veteran artist and finished actor, Nathaniel Guy; and the patrons of Frelinghuysen University are indeed fortunate if they can win him back from his long seclusion at Landover to take the leading role in their forthcoming play "The Servant in the House." Mr. Guy's histrionic ability, his interpretative genius is so well established and so thoroughly appreciated in Washington that it has seemed a real deprivation to have missed so long his vibrant voice and thrilling personality in the legitimate theatre. We hope he "comes home again" and to stay, and that the Community Players will have for a long time to come his brilliant leadership and inspiring association. Frelinghuysen University is trying very hard to secure his permanent service as teacher of dramatics and public speaking.

The remark is trite and often made flippantly that there is latent much high grade talent among our group that wants only the opportunity to prove itself. But dramatics' latent demands is public and the public must insist on unceasing service,—and that service must be devoted and single-minded. Art does not tolerate a divided allegiance. She is a jealous mistress. And this, I take it, has been the real handicap—not lack of opportunity to express, but lack of grit to endure hardness and to throw business, trade, money, every other consideration to the winds and cling to the one love. And so while we have many with the talent to do, if "only they had the time," "if only they didn't have to slave for their bread" "if only—" but we really have few, very few professionals whose art is the same thing as the breath of their life. Mr. Guy is almost unique in this respect. He is normal and happy only in his art. Any other life is to him unnatural and irksome, however rich it may be in material things and creature comforts.

The public has waited too long, his race needs him and would be the poorer without his contribution. He owes it to himself as well as to his many friends and admirers to get into his stride once more and as the war horse that scents the battle, to know what it is to feel the giver of muscle and the tingling of nerve that is Life!

# 30

# "The Unprivileged"

Class divides are highlighted in this piece as Cooper argues that neither the poor nor the privileged are inherently good or evil and that improving society is a matter of respecting each class's interests and working toward "mutual regard."

SOURCE: Anna Julia Cooper Papers, box 23-7, folder 89, Moorland-Spingarn Research Center, Howard University.

A noted writer a while ago likened society to a stage coach on which the "Privileged Classes" had all seats reserved for themselves, their baggage, their dogs and their golf sticks. The common people drew the coach on its toilsome way, thro mire and mud, over ruts and stones. Gaily riding on top, amusing, chattering, pampering, petting, grumbling at every jolt, but care-free and indifferent so long as the roadway was smooth, the Privileged knew little and cared less about the common herd that dragged the car.

Interesting food for thot as regards group psychology or individual attitudes, the analogy does not hold as a generalization. It is not to be derived that too often we wrap ourselves in smug satisfaction as long as our own head is above water and pharisaically thank God we are not as other men, while our brother is left to lift his load unheeded and alone; or we throw a beggar a bone to have it advertised as charity or as philanthropy according to the size and succulence of the bone, and yet sordid selfishness is not characteristic of the social order of our generation; and the self centered passengers, laughing and chaffing luxuriously in the human drawn stage coach would be a libel on modern thot and conduct if taken as a generalization.

# GENERALIZING

Nothing so beclouds our thought and so disastrously warps our understanding and our judgments as the devastating habit of generalizing. It has been well said that the Israelites managed to come thru the wilderness only because there were no statisticians along to prove that it couldn't be done. Human nature is ever variable, ever changing and no specimens have yet been found that squared algebraically with the most perfect formula. The typical man, woman, group, race simply does not exist; and therefore, the most dangerous leaders of thought and painters of society are the dogmatists who undertake to lay down rules and deduce general principles from social statistics.

The fact is that among the hardest working members of society today are the very rich men, and those bearing the heaviest, most nerve-racking strain of pulling the coach are people who are thot to be riding on top and cracking the whip. True servants and benefactors of humanity are those who regard the great accumulations from their own thrift and foresight as a sacred trust to benefit mankind and who devote that same power of intelligence and efficiency of organization, which in the first place rendered them captains of industry and directors of men, to the foundation and extension of those big philanthropies which permanently bless and enrich the race of men, and which never could have been devised in a purely communal organization. It is a mistake to suppose that the "man farthest down" if put on top will be uniformly wise and good; or that all wealth is predatory and therefore a redistribution of it count by count would eliminate forever all selfishness from the world. Wealth with philanthropy has actually done more for the world,— stamping out diseases, spreading intelligence and giving the human race a better and brighter chance in the struggle for existence and pursuit of happiness than the rosiest dreams of the communists can picture as resulting from their wild schemes of unseating the efficient and handing over the reins to a yelping multitude.

# PLEAD FOR JUSTICE

The poor man's plea and every man's plea should be unceasing and unvarying for Justice—indeed this is not only his right but his sacred duty. Justice for all—not merely his class, clique, or color, but an equal and impartial administration of law; a free chance in the pursuit of happiness. The unprivileged need not be inarticulate—Self-expression becomes a duty—but let him not imagine that the blessing he seeks is secured or enhanced by hatreds and antagonisms, or by abrogating all social restraint and disregarding established rights. Anarchy has absolutely nothing to offer the poor man or the social weaklings. While it proposes to cut the earth from under the classes, it has only the law of the jungle to substitute for the self interested orderliness of Big Business,—unorganized guerrilla selfishness for selfishness disciplined and broadened by experience and training. As well stand unshielded before the car of Moloch as to dare the vicissitudes of force in the hegemony set up by anarchists.

Interests there always will be—clamoring, even clashing interests. It would be Utopia to find these interests at once reasonable and altruistic. Self-seeking they naturally are and will be. Adjustment and mutual regard for the other fellow's interest is the acme of the aim and purpose of good administration. Despotism cannot endure. It may have its day, but inexorably it carries within itself the seeds of its own destruction. All history proves this, common sense supports and bears it out. No individual, no class, no color can ultimately and finally hog it all. The irreconcilables must give way at last and be content to take what they can get, and the "peace makers" who are "blessed" will be those who preach sanity in judging another's view-point and a sweet reasonableness in persistently maintaining one's own.

# 31

# "Thy Neighbor as Thyself"

In this article, Cooper argues that exploitation and asking for the world's pity "is the quintessence, the sum total of the most monstrous, the most heinous, the most ungodly" crime.

SOURCE: Anna Julia Cooper Papers, box 23-7, folder 89, Moorland-Spingarn Research Center, Howard University.

Of all the crimes of the universe, exploitation is the quintessence, the sum total of the most monstrous, the most heinous, the most ungodly. Exploitation means using your neighbor for yourself—shoving his body between your body and the bullets, manipulating his fingers to claw chestnuts from the embers, the savage expression at the Nth degree of human selfishness, the hoggish principle among men which makes self the center of the universe and stands ready to trample ruthlessly underfoot or greedily devour the entire not-self regardless of right, rhyme or reason. Exploitation is at the bottom of all the wickedness that ever plotted human woe, it has staged and enacted all the world suffering and sorrow from the tragedy of Cain to the latest crooked maneuver in watered stocks. It has more shapes than Proteus, more colors than the chameleon. Its Big Business is not merely enslaving the proletariat by the privileged as in Russia before the Revolution, nor blacks by whites as in this country before emancipation; it crunches its monstrous jaws upon the helpless victims of peonage today, wherever criminals are expertly manufactured in the mass production of cheap laborers, wherever the embers of racial passions are fanned to flames in order to run out of town friendless weaklings who are getting "too damn prosperous," wherever pogroms, or lynchings, or "rides" are suggested and conducted by disturbed debtors who have "insufficient funds."

The weak, too, have their come backs and right adroitly and efficiently learn to exploit "their betters"—for the trick works both ways and under many guises, and altho less bloody in the manipulation of the worm (till he turns!) than when worked by the "Lords of the jungle," the tiger, the panther, the bear, nevertheless the humble disguise is just as contemptible, just as selfishly mean.

Exploitation of rich by poor, of white by black, of philanthropist by charity promoters, tho its features are less harsh and it wears with insinuating humility the velvet glove over the iron claw, yet this colossus of crimes exploitation, the real thing is there and must plead guilty at the bar of humanity nothwithstanding all its pious posing. The sniveling beggar with a comfortable bank roll of his own, who holds up traffic to get a dime in his tin cup, is guilty and guilty too is the rummage sale that masquerades as church work but re-enacts the comedy of Annias and Sapphira and smilingly "holds back part of the price." Most insidiously does this protean monster work his way into the philanthropies of a people, teaching subtle ways of appealing for sympathy and money thru the beaten paths of pity and human kindness.

I was in a hotel once when an entertainer appeared with a pitiful group of Negro children to "sing for the guests." Of course the children sang Spirituals—"Nobody knows the trouble I See"—"Aint got no friend but Jesus"—"Way down yonder by mahself, couldn't hear nobody pray," and then the inevitable collection was "lifted" and the wheedling beggar who posed as leader and "head of a school" trying to be facetious in what he meant to be a tremendous climax to his address: "Ladies and gentlemen. I just thot I'd bring mah face along."

Now this column's excuse for all the foregoing high powered indignation, or rather long drawn out and somewhat lurid introduction to our "Educational Aims," is the writer's firm conviction that appealing to the world's pity is pretty surely inviting its contempt. While poverty is no disgrace (as we are fond of reciting rather unconvincingly) it is, we must admit, quite systematically charged up to social inefficiency: and if any group expects to dictate either policies or personnel it ought to square its shoulders, set its jaw, and heave to under its load. To come down to person-alities: we cannot blame the white employer when he has a job to give out and white men with families to support are standing in the bread line asking for work, if he does not leave it impartially to the flip of a penny or a purely psychological test as to whether he will choose a colored man for the place. We have been hearing much of late of "colored management for colored institutions, and not a few of the out-spoken news agencies came back with the cynical but unanswerable retort: "Yes; with white money." We are not independent. Let's admit it, and if it's any comfort to know it, neither is anybody else. Independence is all a big bluff. You've either got to serve, or wheedle, or bulldoze. For my part, I prefer service. Earn your way, and, if you desire that high chested feeling that we call honor;—give more than the specifica-tions call for. Let humanity have the lagniappe. You feel better, it boosts your trade, and is in the long run sounder business promo-tion than exploitation. Honest work for an honest dollar, the quid pro quo with due regard for the other fellow's Self—Thy neighbor as Thyself.

# 32

# "'Let the Scottsboro Boys Forget,' Woman Tells Bill Robinson"

In this letter to famed entertainer Bill Robinson published in *The Pittsburgh Courier* on September 11, 1937, Cooper asks why he offers to fund the education of only one Scottsboro boy, and suggests that the education of all six should be funded. However, Cooper also clarifies that the Scottsboro Boys should not be exploited and should be permitted to forget their ordeal and start over in life if they wish.

SOURCE: Anna Julia Cooper Papers, box 23-7, folder 89, Moorland-Spingarn Research Center, Howard University.

An Open Letter to:

"Bogangles" Robinson, Tap Dancer,[1] Care Pittsburgh Courier:

Dear Mr. Robinson: I read with great interest in The Pittsburgh Courier your admirable offer to pay three years' tuition for one of the liberated Scottsboro boys. That is certainly fine! But why not get together on a plan to educate all of these boys and thus turn their terrible experience into a message of hope with the satisfactions of normal growth as useful American citizens. How splendid a demonstration! What an over-whelming vindication of Mr. Leibowitz's loyalty and devotion.[2] And it must not be left to one individual. A syndicate of Negro athletes and entertainers could put it over splendidly with the Negro Press to help unselfishly and unitedly.

We must fight shy of any exploiting of the boys. They have suffered enough and are entitled to the balm of a forgetting. Let them start life all over again with the simplest, pleasantest associations. Let them get away as far as possible from the agitation and the bitterness and the horror of those six years. Let them learn that life has a friendly side, a welcome beckoning side of opportunity for growth and service and helpfulness to others.

I thank you for that gesture and I thank The Courier for publishing it. That move may gather strength and the inspiration for a team and just so surely will do more good for all of us than all the speeches and arguments and all the indignation meetings and caustic resolutions for the so-called Advancement of Colored People, I am

Very sincerely yours for advancement through education and training.

ANNA J. COOPER
WASHINGTON, D.C.

# 33

# "Mistaken Identity"

Urging tolerance between whites and African Americans, Cooper argues that humans are too complex to be boiled down to race formulas. She also suggests that Christian and democratic doctrines are not currently being followed and that the first step to getting on the path to Christianity and democracy is tolerance for one another.

SOURCE: Anna Julia Cooper Papers, box 23-7, folder 89, Moorland-Spingarn Research Center, Howard University.

An Irishman once spied a Jew sunning himself in the streets of Cork and at once fell to belaboring him with his shillalah.

"But why?" cried the Jew. "What have I done?"

"You dog of an unbeliever," shouted the son of Erin between blows, "you crucified my Lord!"

"But leave off," pleaded the Jew, "I never saw your Lord."

"Ah, that's the accursed infidel! the heretic blasphemer! The spalpeen denies the Saviour of the World!"

Much of the race prejudice around us today is as senseless if not as ludicrous, as the misplaced zeal and religious fervor of this inquisitor of the Emerald Isle, and it is by no means confined to one side of the color line.

"Do you expect me to treat as equals these people whom my grandfather held as slaves?"

"Do you expect me to treat with politeness and respect these people who lynch and burn my people and who use the most contemptuous language they can find to insult and degrade us?"

"It is just because of the unreasonableness behind our

emotions and the tragic consequences of all bitter emotion, that pulpit and press, teachers and leaders should combine to guide aright and allay by every honorable and sane expedient the hysteria and blatant bitterness of the race question in America today.

Such news as the item mentioned in last week's Tribune, the authenticated fact that an honorable and respected white in one of the high record lynching states of the South quietly and unobtrusively submitted to a transfusion of his blood to save the life of a colored woman, is news, quite as truly as that when a man bites a dog, is news. It is news, too, that ought to open all eyes to the big fact that human association is a matter of individual and group adjustment, and that life is far too complex and variable to be reducible yet, even by a Freud or a Niebschi, to an algebraic formula.

Not all white people are lynchers at heart; not all colored people are servile tip-seekers. Human behavior cannot be graphed and diagrammed just by the shape of a skull, not can a column of figures settle what ought to be done with twelve millions rooted in the soil. Race prejudice feeds on cheap talk. It grows and multiplies, it fattens and battens in the hot-beds of agitators and statisticians. We've got to learn to tolerate our neighbor before we can love him. Christianity hasn't failed—we just haven't got to it. It has never yet been given a chance by any Christian nation. No Christian statesman today dares advocate the principles of Jesus Christ as a guide for a League of Nations.

Democracy, too, is meat admittedly too strong for this generation. Our ideals have jumped way ahead of the procession and are demanding the impossible. Christianity and democracy, as abstractions, are too sublimated for modern thinking to get a grip on them. While they are being interpreted by the theologians and reasoned out by the philosophers, the barbarians of today will have brained the teacher and burned down the schoolhouse. If Christian brotherhood is too hard a doctrine we shall have to drop the gauge a peg or two, as the Church of Rome did in dealing with the Barbarians of the Middle Ages. She instituted what was known as the Truce of God, and actual compromise with lawlessness which agreed to leave off atrocities for three days of every week. And so now, if you really cannot love one who does not look like you, the solidarity of your race and the perpetuity of your traditions can hardly require that you slay him. Christ says, love our enemies. You don't and you won't. Well then, tolerate them. The primitive savage at the cannibal stage eats his enemies; a little higher up he enslaves them; not much higher he exploits them and eats their labor; it is quite a step up to be willing to live and let live.

Tolerance, then, I suggest as a first lesson in the lowest form or group D for the "retarded" pupils. Let that be the first round of your ladder. Tolerance of differences, tolerance, too, of similarities—for there is often as much bitter hatred for those who approximate uncomfortably near our own condition and standard of life as of those whose abject want of all that we hold dear, appeals to our pity and tempers our repulsion. It is not an easy lesson to learn—this of allowing the other fellow to be himself, to live his life, to think the thing through for himself and above all to look the part kind nature created him for and predestined him to represent in her setting up of the great drama— in a word—respect, his personality.

We are told a new Gospel of Tolerance is being preached this week in the great gathering in New York of more than 1,000 Jews, Christians, Moslems, Hindus, Sikhs, a tolerance of religious beliefs as well as of races and colors. Rabbi Israel Goldstein characterizes it as a signal event in the direction of comity and good-will. "Mutual appreciation," says he, "is the culminating virtue of civilized society. The ideal humanity will never be a 'melting-pot,' but a harmonious orchestration."

# 34

# "Belle Sadgwar"

An obituary for Belle Sadgwar, one of Cooper's former students whom she considered a friend.

SOURCE: Anna Julia Cooper Papers, box 23-7, folder 89, Moorland-Spingarn Research Center, Howard University.

Among the unforgettable experiences in an old teacher's memory chest are those rare glimpses deep down straight into the heart of things, beyond the rub and fret of marks, the routine of percentages and averages, the statistics of ratings, and gradings of promotions and retardations, and the weary rest of it. It not unfrequently happens thus in the contacts of our profession that soul actually touches soul, not officially, as teacher meets pupils, but in the one supreme and essentially "extra-curricula activity" as friend meets friend in naked truth and genuine simplicity.

Such a precious remembrance have I of dear Belle Sadgwar,[1] whom it is impossible for me to picture to myself as having so soon "finished her course." Life's school already completed and now really and truly "promoted" to a higher grade beyond our ken. I shall always remember her as the same charming young creature, deliberately choosing in class the front seat nearest my right with that intimate understanding smile of hers, characteristic of an innocent child nestling up to its mother.

Strangely enough we have not met since she graduated—another proof that while the earth has grown smaller our circles of contacts are immeasurably larger, so that although individuals for a while meet daily in the regular routine of life, their several orbits may later swing apart never to cross again till one day the shock comes that a being we had come to regard almost as a part of our own has passed out of reach, perhaps, forever.

Indeed the last conscious meeting I recall with Belle Sadgwar was at a surprise party which she had engineered at my house bringing together her classmates in Cicero, June 22, 1927. They left on my mantel a beautiful framed sentiment beginning, "You are my friend," and I gave each member a card of the Dunbar Alma Mater Song, having inscribed on the back the well-remembered passage from Marcellus which begins, "This ought not to be considered your life which is limited by body and breath; that, that I say, is your life which eternity itself will keep and care for." Many choice spirits were in that party that 22nd day of June, and I can only dare to hope that the souvenir passed on to them has been held as precious in their memories as this which they left for me will always be. Here it is:

> "You are my friend, you warm my heart,
>   In all my thoughts you have a part,
>   In all I say, in all I do
>   There is a comforting bit of you;
>   I see your smile, I feel your hand,
>   I hear your voice and understand.
>   No word will mar, no deed will end
>   This comradership of yours, my Friend."

Priceless, wonderful, is it not?

# 35

# "Obituary"

Cooper laments the loss of three former students: Zenobia Bundy, Elaine Williams, and Audrey Wright. She writes that their deaths are a loss to the race as well as to her personally.

SOURCE: Anna Julia Cooper Papers, box 23-7, folder 89, Moorland-Spingarn Research Center, Howard University.

When one contemplates the untimely passing from us of three such rare spirits and promising intellects as Zenobia Bundy, Elaine Williams, and Audrey Wright, there is for their teachers a poignant sense not only of personal sorrow such as inevitably attends the loss of friends of peculiar charm and congenial personality, but an inconsolable feeling of shattered and blasted hope, second only to that of parents and immediate blood kin in the intimate closeness of its grief and sense of affliction. For are they not the offspring of our life work, brought forth in the travail of our brain and the agony of unseen hopes and fears, anticipations and longings?

But the crowning tragedy is for the race which can so ill afford the loss of its choicest and best just at the threshold of what would have been undoubtedly brilliant and universally valuable careers. Excellent students in high school, of honor standing in "scholarship, leadership, character, and service," these young ladies were all ambitious to go the limit in college and postgraduate courses. Miss Williams had shown such aptitudes in her chosen line at Howard that she was already employed as assistant pupil-teacher prior to her graduation, and, immediately after she won her degree, she qualified by examination and was immediately appointed to the science department of the senior high schools.

Miss Wright, with singular cheerfulness and energy in face of an early handicap had taken, after graduating from Oberlin, two successive years at Bryn Mawr in special post-graduate work, and just in the act of receiving her master's degree at Chicago when stricken.

The pity of it all is that our great loss in these conspicuous cases of eminent abilities is chargeable to overwork and unmitigated application to the pursuit of knowledge. Admirable as their industry is, one could wish that these three scholars had been less closely confined to study, and could have had with it more of the breezy ozone of pure fun and frolic.

Is there not a real danger that we take our degrees and our marks too seriously? It is not the work, but the worry, which eats into the vitality of the student. Deep down beneath all the tasks and achievements, eating its silent way by day and by night, is the terrible strain of lifting a race, and of treading the winepress alone.

# 36

# "An Appreciation of the Late Rev. William L. Washington"

An obituary for Cooper's colleague at Frelinghuysen University, the Reverend William L. Washington.

SOURCE: Anna Julia Cooper Papers, box 23-7, folder 89, Moorland-Spingarn Research Center, Howard University.

To the Editor:

The entire community will feel its loss in the passing of the Rev. Wm. L. Washington, and no organization or group more poignantly and more deeply than Frelinghuysen University in the irreparable loss of its trustee, instructor, friend and sympathetic helper who, even in the face of his failing health, came faithfully, and always cheerfully and loyally in proof of his unswerving support of the work and his unwavering faith in its value as an indispensable service to the race.

The present writer first knew the Rev. Mr. Washington in social service as resident worker and executive secretary for the first social settlement in Southwest Washington some twenty years ago.

He was always the same upright Christian gentleman, the same unassuming quiet worker, the same devoted loyal friend and genuinely sincere collaborator.

Where there are so many tributes from the host of interests faithfully served by Mr. Washington later in his eminently useful career in Washington, it seems but fitting the public should know the very significant remark made on his last official call at

Frelinghuysen just a few days before his final illness. He said to the writer:

"I feel the happiest culmination of my service in this community is the very satisfactory adjustment recently accomplished by which the $2,500 devoted by the settlement workers and friends to social betterment of colored people was finally accepted by the Chest as a sacred trust to that end. And I am gratified to have wound up thus, satisfactorily the first business in which I had a hand on coming to Washington twenty years ago.

ANNA J. COOPER

# 37

# "Lauds Robeson for Not Taking Part in Anti-Draft Rally"

Published in the issue of the *Washington Tribune* from September 21, 1940, Cooper expresses approval for Paul Robeson's refusal to take part in an anti-draft rally, arguing that wars come whether they are desired or not. Cooper also indicates Black Americans should not flinch from serving if called upon to do so.

SOURCE: Anna Julia Cooper Papers, box 23-7, folder 89, Moorland-Spingarn Research Center, Howard University.

It is significant that the TRIBUNE should give front page headlines in a recent issue to the refusal of Paul Robeson to take part in the anti-conscription demonstration at Washington. If that refusal was due, as I trust it was, to Mr. Robeson's determination not to shirk his country's service in her hour of need his loyalty and patriotic devotion to duty is worthy of highest honor and admiration from all true-hearted Americans.

Our Democracy like other noble ideals has its dangerous pitfalls and often needs protection from its friends against their excesses, their hysteria and panicky demagoguery.

Apostles of free speech, free press and the freedom of assembly can and often do overstep the bounds of sanity and safety in their misguided zeal for self expression or their hectic denunciation and not seldom persecution of the fellow with a different point of view.

In critical times like these many are they who have cause to exclaim with the ill fated, Madame Roland: "Oh, Liberty! What crimes are perpetrated in thy name!" Especially important, it seems to me while racialism is rampant in the one nation that threatens to subjugate the globe, that Americans of differing racial extraction should stand four-square on their Americanism.

Isolationist and anti-conscriptionists with their embittered name-calling and frantic insistence on academic theories, like sophomores in a college debate, must not cause us to ignore those vital issues that concern our very life stream in the body politic.

## BOMBS KNOW NO DISTINCTION

Presidential Third Terms and the disposal of over age destroyers are abstractions for constitutional lawyers to worry about; But the menace of bombs carrying tons and tons of deadly explosives to be ruthlessly dropped on our hospitals, our schools, churches, homes, little ones, look at no distinction of race, color, creed or condition.

No president has ever been willing or able to lead this country into a war. No man with sober judgment can read those solemn and sorrowfull inaugural words of Abraham Lincoln and again at Gettysburg and imagine even for a moment that the burdened soul purposed the Civil War.

McKinley certainly did not "lead into" the Spanish American; and as for Woodrow Wilson, those very volatile voters actually put him into his war term with the wild slogan "he kept us out of the War!"

## WARS CAME ANYWAY

The Wars came and the three men, martyrs all, conscientiously faced their responsibility. They did their duty as best they could and served their country in doing so.

Not without a running fire of carping criticism by the exponents of free, and too often intemperate, speech.

Colored Americans enjoy today a right that has been there

since the Fifteenth Amendment was enacted into law to vote with the party of their individual choosing.

But let us be done with "Rounding up the Negro Vote" and every soap box demagogue boasting that he'll "swing the election" this way or that for "a consideration."

Above all let the youth of this generation, knowing their rights, have regard also to their obligations. Let them prove themselves as ready to fight for justice and the preservation of the American Way as others are to whine over injustices that are manifestly a perversion of that Way.

Let them not flinch at their country's call for service in her hour of need nor stage an opposition parade when measures are under contemplation to train them to render such service effectively and efficiently in and for a land where, as in no other on God's earth, they are assured of life, liberty and the pursuit of happiness by the fundamental law of the land which is thank God inviolable by potentate or power, by dictator or despot. "Americans having nothing to fear but fear."

# 38

# "Writer Flays 'Native Son'; Would Like Story on Victor Hugo Theme"[1]

In this article, published in the *Washington Tribune* on August 17, 1940, Cooper admits to having not read Richard Wright's *Native Son* (1940) or having any desire to see it dramatized. Instead of a book that deals in tropes and has a particular purpose and message, Cooper expresses a preference for a book that details life in the vein of the wretch in Victor Hugo's *Les Misérables* (1862).

SOURCE: Anna Julia Cooper Papers, box 23-7, folder 89, Moorland-Spingarn Research Center, Howard University.

To the Tribune Editor:

When the nation is facing a crisis that threatens to undermine and disrupt the most sacred principles of its historic structure and traditions, it is well for racial minorities to pipe down on specialized counter irritants, however important they may seem to be locally and specifically, if they do not serve to promote the general welfare and thus tend toward harmony in adjusting internal differences in the body politic.

Like a burr under the saddle of a turbulent steed or sand in the spinach for an exasperated dispeptic, racial differences with minority rights and privileges clamored for at such a time can only result in snapping over wrought tempers and upsetting the entire applecart.

Conservative thinkers will view with some misgiving the announcement that Paul Green, who holds the Pulitzer Prize for his production, "In Abraham's Bosom," has offered his expert service as playwright in collaboration with Richard Wright to dramatize "Native Son," the sensational problem study of the year.

By way of accentuating the agony and crowding out the mourners they intend, I believe, to have Orson Welles and John Houseman parade their product in New York next season.

## WOULD BE "TORTURE"

I have not read and shall not read Mr. Wright's novel. Even to live through a dramatized hour of it before footlights would equal the torture of ten nightmares. No overflow of presumption, however, could tempt me to criticize it.

By the yard stick of "success" it is undeniably tops. As a money getter and as towntalk it displays a startling preview of what the public wants, and every pencil pusher is hot on the trail of another Bigger Thomas.

The type is etched in lurid lines and no delineator of Negro character has a Chinaman's chance who essays to depart from it. Added to a morbid taste for dirt in the realism of today which sends camera men snooping around moral cesspools and social garbage cans for available "copy," there is the more subtle, more persistent urge of the propagandist who knows how to inject the virus of social unrest and hide-bound antipathies into what seems a bold reproduction of reality.

The clash between law of organized society and human frailties and individual appetites is an unfailing source book for creative genius; and the tragedy of it has been portrayed in immortal pictures of classic literature.

I have often wished that another Victor Hugo might conceive "The Brute" of Negro life, comparable to the "Wretch" in Jean Val Jean. It will be a masterpiece for all time if ever we get it. It will not be a novel with a purpose, nor a "Problem of Today."

It will be Life As Is—Life in the raw, struggling, failing, falling, battling the hardships, buffeting the onslaughts, accepting the handicaps, but toiling on and up, irrepressibly up and always human—always understanding by every other human, not a monster of race, color or creed.

Nor will this novel, if truly great, undertake to establish a thesis, prove a point and fix the norm of human relations contrary to nature and subversive of the Gospel rule.

Peace among men of goodwill is both sane and safe. Society does not need the fiery Cross of a lynching to further terrorize victims of long injustice, nor hooded night riders to prevent an orgy of interracial tolerance and American fair play.

ANNA J. COOPER

# 39

# "The Willkie Smear"

In this article, published in the *Washington Tribune* edition of October 26, 1940, Cooper discusses the controversy surrounding President Franklin D. Roosevelt seeking a third presidential term and the accusations about dictatorship that Roosevelt's Republican opponent, Wendell Lewis Willkie, had been making.

SOURCE: Anna Julia Cooper Papers, box 23-7, folder 89, Moorland-Spingarn Research Center, Howard University.

To the Tribune Editor:

It is indeed most unfortunate that if and when politicians must indulge in the gentle pastime of mudslinging they have to pick on a racial group that can least afford that bad eminence and send them over the top.

One is filled with the dismay of the out witted spirit in Booker T. Washington's story, who, in his eagerness to get to heaven, obligingly served as pack horse for his white brother only to hear the sainted gatekeeper say at journey's end: "Just hitch your horse outside and come right in."

Surely the friends of Mr. Roosevelt have no need of such questionable and highly dangerous tactics, which can only result in a boomerang for any one so foolish as to make the attempt.

In the President's case both the facts and the law are an open book for any one with enough intelligence to heed the Constitution, to understand and apply.

There is no law against a Third Term and those who charge it leads to dictatorship must know without being reminded that the Constitution provides for impeachment and removal from office by the people's representatives of any President found guilty of malfeasance in office whether it be third or first term. Mr. Willkie[1] promises Utopia. Mr. Roosevelt has in hand accomplished facts every one of which is endorsed by Mr. Willkie in his promises to keep going without a hitch if the other man is put out he, Mr. Willkie, is put in.

At a time like the present unprecedented world crisis, when the forces of hate and racial intolerance seem bent on destruction of all that mankind holds dear, when civilization itself and its precious achievements through toiling sweat and thought and inspired dreaming of centuries seems doomed to annihilation in the universal holocaust under the ruthless bombs of powerful despots, we Americans, especially we colored Americans, have a sublime opportunity to keep our heads, to stand firmly by our convictions and to fight loyally with all the consecration and devotion of souls that have known oppression.

ANNA J. COOPER

# 40

# "Freedom of
the Press and Negro
Public Opinion"

Arguing that literature cannot be honest if the author is striving for fame and wealth, Cooper is critical of a system that privileges white approval in recognizing and validating Black literature. She is particularly critical of the way in which Richard Wright and Langston Hughes have been elevated as the faces of African American literature. A flyer announcing Hughes's reading in Pasadena, California and including a reprint of his poem, "Goodbye Christ," is pasted alongside this article in Cooper's scrapbook.

SOURCE: Anna Julia Cooper Papers, box 23-7, folder 89, Moorland-Spingarn Research Center, Howard University.

Fear makes cowards of us all. Cowards are, by implication, self-conscious, and a self-conscious personality is never forceful. It is the curse of minorities in this power-worshipping world that either from fear or from an uncertain policy of expediency they distrust their own standards and hesitate to give voice to their deeper convictions, submitting supinely to estimates and characterizations of themselves as handed down by a not unprejudiced dominant majority.

In no phase of modern culture is this inarticulate weakness more apparent and more directly hurtful than in literature and art and in that which holds the mirror up to both, the public and press.

Above all things the outpouring of the soul of a people, its poetry, its music, its art should be downright and forthright, simple, sincere, untrammeled. It cannot be honest with itself while straining for effect and panting for the gleam of purse strings like bad actors whose next meal hangs on the applause from the gallery gods.

It is important to know values and to discriminate between values fundamentally human and those that may be narrowly racial, temporary or individual. Economically it may vitally concern some that Tom Jones lands a good job; politically it seems as vital to others that Bill Smith is or is not made superintendent of Crab Tree Alley.

Loyalty and race solidarity may even dictate that persons not immediately affected resolve themselves into cheering squads or crape hangers or a committee on "keeping mum" according to the considered policy of the moment.

But when it comes to those deeper issues that penetrate to the very heart and character of a people,—its art, its literature, the elemental outcry and up-spring of its untutored soul, then, surely it becomes a sacred duty to throw policy to the winds. Tom Jones and Bill Smith may have to be sacrificed.

The cry of the children must not be stifled nor must the standards of a race be vitiated or its mouthpiece be allowed to utter falsely the message entrusted to it from on High.


## BE TRUE TO SELF

Here as always the maxim applies:

"To thine own self be true and it must follow as night the day thou canst not then be false to any man." Thus Public Opinion will feel the force of the collective sensitivity and the group or racial reaction becomes dependably sound and effectively representative, being rooted and grounded in truth and honest conviction.

A self sufficient columnist declares, "I can say what I please in this newspaper; I don't mind what Negroes think of what I write." (Sic!!!).

Paul Laurence Dunbar[1] had to await commendation from William Dean Howells before our parlor socials would admit him in "select readings."

Antonin Dvorak came all the way from Mulhausen, Bohemia, to disclose to us the native poetry and simple beauty of our sorrow songs. Today we make bargains to exploit them.

## PENDULUM SWINGS THE OTHER WAY

Occasionally the pendulum swings the other way. We are afraid to criticize "Native Son," richly upholstered as it is by cash and comment, and silence counts for acquiescence in face of the indecent blasphemies of Langston Hughes, since Vachel Lindsay has given him the accolade of the immortals. His "Goodbye Christ," recently paraded by Saturday Evening Post as the nauseating effusion of a "Young Negro Poet" is so tawdry in workmanship and above all so impious in tone, one cannot help feeling a certain exhilaration in disclaiming any kinship with its misguided author.

## HIS RACE IS HONORED

In fact his race is honored rather than snubbed by his peremptory exclusion from the banquet in Pasadena, Calif., where he was to have appeared before the Book and Authors Club in November. There is no good will intent on the part of the Post which adds information that the "distinguished Negro Poet is Member of the American section of Moscow's International Union of Revolutionary Writers."

These be parlous times and many there are who are on their toes to "view with alarm" or point with conviction at the first pimple that may indicate a symptom of the "black peril," "the yellow peril" or the "folks-I-don't-like-peril."

A weak minority such as ours can ill afford the stigma of untried leadership. The Negro people are neither un-godly nor un-American. As a race the Negro is mentally and temperamentally incapable of scoffing at sacred things.

Mr. Hughes speaks for none but himself, and while we do not wish to curtail his freedom to speak and to write, we do most earnestly insist that on his devoted head alone rest both the honor and the responsibility due his peculiar genius.

# Letter to Frederic J. Haskin, Director Star Information Bureau

In this handwritten letter to Frederic J. Haskin, Cooper responds to a printed translation of the United States Army Air Corps motto "Ut viri volent," which Haskin wrote meant "As they wish to be alive" or "As the living desire." Using her knowledge of Latin, Cooper suggested two alternative translations: "Fly as heroes!" or "Let men fly."

SOURCE: Anna Julia Cooper Papers, box 23-7, folder 89, Moorland-Spingarn Research Center, Howard University.

> *Frederic J. Haskin*
> *Director Star Information Bureau*
> *Washington, D.C.*

Dear Sir: Not having a Latin lexicon at hand at the moment, it is with some diffidence I venture another translation of the insignia of the Air Corps: "Ut viri volent" as given in your column of tonight's Star.

I noted that the translation given regards volent as derived from volo to be willing of which it may be future Indic. 3d pl. May it not be as well pres. subjunct. of volare to fly. If so viri may be it seems to this writer nom. plural of vir, (man, in highest sense hero). Fly as heroes! how would that do? or "Let men fly."

Q. What is the motto of the United States Air Corps?—K. H.

A. The words on the insignia of the caps worn by members of the Air Corps are "Ut viri volent" and are translated "As they wish to be alive" or "As the living desire."

# PART IV

# CORRESPONDENCES

Part 4 is divided into two sections. The first section reprints together, for the first time, the Cooper–Du Bois correspondences from 1923 to 1932, held in the W. E. B. Du Bois Papers at UMass Amherst Libraries. These correspondences document the long and evolving relationship between two intellectual giants, Anna Julia Cooper and W. E. B. Du Bois. They provide context for understanding the emergence of some of the most significant events and publications of the twentieth century, with exchanges related to the accessibility of the Pan-African Congresses for Black women and working people and the need for an extended reply to a racist history of the Reconstruction era, which would give rise to Du Bois's seminal tome, *Black Reconstruction in America: 1860–1880*. They also document the development of several of Cooper's intellectual projects and provide important insights into the processes that shaped, and often curtailed, Cooper's efforts to participate fully in Black public intellectual life. They provide a new perspective on the commitments that shaped Cooper's intellectual work, teaching, and pedagogy, and they also reveal Cooper as a tenacious editor and intellectual who worked to ensure her community was given voice and representation in national publishing outlets.

The second section publishes additional correspondences that represent Cooper's personal relationships and professional challenges as well as her national and international networks and spheres of influence. The personal correspondences represent the relationships Cooper nurtured over long periods of time and that fanned out across the US and abroad. They reveal Cooper as central to her community—deeply respected by those who knew her and a cherished member of a broad network of care and support. Her friends were fellow travelers—suffragists, educators, community activists, and public intellectuals—and Cooper's personal correspondences constitute an important resource for understanding the multidimensional aspects of her life and work. The professional correspondences relate challenges Cooper faced, as well as social critiques she mounted, throughout her career as an educator and public intellectual. Several letters relate to the sexist and retaliatory actions she faced as an administrator and later teacher at M Street/Dunbar High School, while others document the racism, sexism, and ageism she ran up against as she sought to preserve, publish, and distribute her own writings, as well as those of educator and author Charlotte Forten Grimké. Beyond these professional roadblocks and challenges, this section also demonstrates the reach of Cooper's influence and her circle of correspondents that extended to include French scholar Felix Klein; journalist and adviser to former French president Charles de Gaulle, Jean de Roussy de Sales; suffragist and poet Alice Dunbar Nelson; as well as the first African American elected to US Congress, Oscar De Priest (whose election was won in part through the efforts of Black women suffragists like Ida B. Wells, Mary Church Terrell, Cooper, and others). These correspondences, collated from five different archives, suggest the ways in which the private, professional, personal, and political were intertwined. They expose the racial and gendered dynamics, and sometimes outright duplicity and hostility, Cooper confronted, and they affirm the support and care offered by Cooper's friends, family, and colleagues as she met these challenges.

## 42

# Anna J. Cooper to
# W. E. B. Du Bois

*(September 4, 1923)*

Cooper asks for Du Bois's advice regarding travel arrangements to the third Pan-African Congress being held in London and Lisbon in 1923. Cooper and Du Bois had served alongside each other as two of the six US delegates to the first Pan-African Conference at Westminster Town Hall in London, July 23–25, 1900. The delegates would not realize their plans for a 1902 Pan-African Conference in Boston, as they had hoped, and it would be almost two decades before the conference would reconvene (referred to in the later iterations as congresses rather than conferences) in 1919, under Du Bois's leadership.

The first Pan-African Conference in London was an outgrowth of the African Association, founded by Henry Sylvester Williams in 1897, and convened to address "the treatment of native races under European and American rule . . . in South Africa, West Africa, West Indies [and the] United States of America" and to advocate for Black self-rule in the colonies in Africa and the West Indies.[1] At the conference, Cooper delivered her paper "The Negro in America," which held the US accountable for its failings as a "Christian nation," and Du Bois presented his talk "To the Nations of the World," in which he called for the rights of self-government for Blacks at home and abroad as "soon as practicable."[2] The inaugural meeting in London was significant in asserting the right of Black people in Africa and throughout the diaspora to speak collectively in claiming authority for representing their own needs and concerns.[3]

SOURCE: W. E. B. Du Bois Papers (MS312), Special Collections and University Archives, University of Massachusetts Amherst Libraries.

*201 T. St. N.W.*
*Washington, D.C.*

*September 4, 1923*

*Dr. W. E. Burghardt Du Bois,*
*The Crisis—New York City.*

My dear Mr. Editor:
Most assuredly you can help in a very "specific way" if only you will + I shall be under great + lasting obligation for your advice + suggestions.

I did not know the date of the "3[d] Pan African Congress" but shall be glad to make it if I can arrange it.

When do you sail + by what line? I have not yet booked my passage but want to leave Washington Oct. 31 P.M. I had thot to look out for a French steamer + go direct to Cherbourg or Boulogne but am open for advice if I can take in the London meeting.

TRULY
A. J. COOPER.

(OVER)

Could you have some one in the Office telephone the Steamship Companies to forward me their time table + rates? I shall greatly appreciate your advice as you gave it once when I was making up a globe-trotting itinerary far more taxing in time + thot. —"Times have changed + we have changed in them"—but perhaps you can spare this much in helping me get started.

A.J.C.

# 43

# W. E. B. Du Bois to
# Anna J. Cooper

*(September 20, 1923)*

Du Bois gives Cooper advice regarding travel arrangements to the third Pan-African Congress.

SOURCE: W. E. B. Du Bois Papers (MS312), Special Collections and University Archives, University of Massachusetts Amherst Libraries.

*September 20, 1923*

*Mrs. A. J. Cooper.*
*201 T. Street N.W.*
*Washington, D.C.*

My dear Mrs. Cooper:—

I would advise you concerning steamship travel to write to the Bennet's Travel Bureau, No. 500—5ᵗʰ Avenue, New York City, who could make arrangements for you. They served us very nicely at the time of the Second Pan-African Congress.

You can reach London by either French or English steamers. Practically all of the French steamers stop at an English port on their way to France. I will send you further information about the Pan-African Congress as our plans develop.

VERY SINCERELY YOURS,
WEBD/W

# 44

# Anna J. Cooper to
# W. E. B. Du Bois

*(September 10, 1924)*

Cooper asks Du Bois if, based on current interests in the topic, the NAACP would consider undertaking a translation of Jean-Philippe Garran de Coulon's four-volume history of Haiti, the *Rapport sur les troubles de Saint-Domingue* (1797). She also requests that he send her a copy of Jessie Fauset's 1924 book, *There Is Confusion*, and Du Bois's history of the Negro race.

SOURCE: W. E. B. Du Bois Papers (MS312), Special Collections and University Archives, University of Massachusetts Amherst Libraries.

*September 10, 1924*

Dear Doctor Du Bois:

As a by-product of my thesis for the Sorbonne I have come across a very interesting history of Haiti in the *Rapport sur les Troubles de Saint-Domingue* par Garran-Coulon.[1] It seems to me splendid propaganda material for our cause, and I am thinking of attempting an English edition. Do you know if it has been translated? Do you think the present interest in Haiti would make such a work worth while? Would the N.A.A.C.P. care to promote such an undertaking?

I wish a copy of Miss Fauset's book "There is Confusion" also one of your History of the Negro Race. Will remit one receipt of bill.

VERY TRULY YOURS,
ANNA J. COOPER.


*Address:*
*201 Tea St. N.W.*
*Washington D.C.*

# 45

# W. E. B. Du Bois to
# Anna J. Cooper

*(September 12, 1924)*

Du Bois responds to Cooper's query about the NAACP's interest in a translated history of Haiti by stating that the NAACP is not in the business of publishing books due to the expense. The NAACP was founded in 1909 as an interracial civil rights organization. Founding members included Du Bois, Mary Church Terrell, Ida B. Wells, and others. Cooper's attention to Garran de Coulon's text, however, proved discerning as the study has served as an important source for subsequent histories on Haiti and is cited extensively in Laurent Dubois's authoritative work of the Haitian Revolution, *Avengers of the New World: The Story of the Haitian Revolution.*

SOURCE: W. E. B. Du Bois Papers (MS312), Special Collections and University Archives, University of Massachusetts Amherst Libraries.

*September 12, 1924*

*Mrs. Anna J. Cooper*
*201 Tea Street, N.W.*
*Washington, D.C.*

My dear Mrs. Cooper:

I do not know of the history by Garran-Coulon to which you refer and I doubt very much if it has been done into English. You will, of course, find some difficulty in getting it published but I should think it would be worth trying. Possibly you could get some Haitian support.

The N. A. A. C. P.[1] has never undertaken to promote any publishing because of the high cost of book-making. I do not think they would do it in this case.

I am sending you a copy of Miss Fauset's book and my "Negro." Mr. Dill will send you the bill.

VERY SINCERELY YOURS,
WEBD/KF

# 46

# Anna J. Cooper to W. E. B. Du Bois

*(May 18, 1925)*

Cooper notes that she sent Du Bois some of her "Educational Sketches" for *The Crisis* to aid teachers of colored youth and has received neither a response nor a return of her postage. Cooper is likely referring to her essay, "Loss of Speech Through Isolation" reprinted in part 2 of this edition.

SOURCE: W. E. B. Du Bois Papers (MS312), Special Collections and University Archives, University of Massachusetts Amherst Libraries.

*201 T. St. N.W.*
*Washington, D.C.*

*May 18, 1925*

*Doctor Dubois*
*New York City.*

Dear Doctor Dubois:

I sent you some months ago an instalment of Educational Sketches which I thot would not only interest but help the thousands of teachers of colored youth who read the Crisis. I also enclosed postage for return of my sheets in case you did not like them. As I have heard nothing of the communication + did not get my stamps back I am wondering if the package ever reached you.

VERY SINCERELY,
ANNA J. COOPER.

# 47

# Unknown to
# Anna J. Cooper

*(May 26, 1925)*

Cooper receives a reply that Du Bois is out of town and cannot respond to her previous letter in which she requested Du Bois respond to her previous submission of her essay "Educational Sketches." There is a handwritten comment across the bottom of the typed letter stating "manuscript returned," with initials that appear to be D. W.

SOURCE: W. E. B. Du Bois Papers (MS312), Special Collections and University Archives, University of Massachusetts Amherst Libraries.

*May 26, 1925*

*Mrs. Anna J. Cooper*
*201 Tea Street, N.W.*
*Washington, D.C.*

My dear Madam:

We have received your letter and the information which you kindly sent. Dr. DuBois is out of the city and will not return until July. At that time I shall be glad to call these matters to his attention.

VERY SINCERELY YOURS,
WEBD/PF

# 48

# Anna J. Cooper to
# W. E. B. Du Bois

*(December 4, 1925)*

Cooper demands the return of "Educational Sketches,"
which she sent to Du Bois and the return postage if the
essay is not "acceptable" to "ye editor."

SOURCE: W. E. B. Du Bois Papers (MS312), Special Collections and University Archives, University of Massachusetts Amherst Libraries.

*201 T. St. N.W.*
*Washington, D.C.*

*December 4, 1925*

Doctor W. E. B. Du Bois
Editor The Crisis.
New York City.

Dear Doctor DuBois:
   Something over a year ago I sent you one of a series of "Educational Sketches" which I thot would interest readers of the Crisis, enclosing at the same time return postage in case the sketch submitted should not prove acceptable to "ye editor."
   I shall thank you very much to let me have the manuscript now if you are thro with it + notice of charges, if any, for excess postage.

VERY TRULY YOURS,
ANNA J. COOPER.

# 49

# W. E. B. Du Bois to Anna J. Cooper

*(December 9, 1925)*

Du Bois responds to Cooper's request regarding her "Educational Sketches" and agrees to look into the matter.

SOURCE: W. E. B. Du Bois Papers (MS312), Special Collections and University Archives, University of Massachusetts Amherst Libraries.

*December 9, 1925*

*Mrs. Anna J. Cooper*
*201 T Street, N.W.*
*Washington, D.C.*

My dear Mrs. Cooper:

I will look up the matter which you sent us and write you about it in a few days. I am sorry to have kept it so long.

VERY SINCERELY YOURS,
WEBD/KF

# 50

# Anna J. Cooper to
# W. E. B. Du Bois

*(December 21, 1927)*

Cooper submits a notice to Du Bois that she would like to see included in *The Crisis* and states her intention to send photographs as well. This letter is in reference to Cooper's students' production of Two Scenes from the *Aeneid* included in part 2 of this edition.

SOURCE: W. E. B. Du Bois Papers (MS312), Special Collections and University Archives, University of Massachusetts Amherst Libraries.

*December 21, 1927*

My dear Doctor DuBois

Mr. Smith would like the enclosed notice to get in the February Crisis which we believe comes to us the last week in January.

We shall send you from Scurlock[1] in a few days photos of "Dido" + "Hecuba" which we hope will be in time to get in the same issue.

CORDIALLY YOURS + WITH XMAS GREETINGS,
A. J. COOPER.

# 51

# W. E. B. Du Bois to
# Anna J. Cooper

*(December 27, 1927)*

Du Bois agrees to include some of Cooper's submissions in *The Crisis*.

SOURCE: W. E. B. Du Bois Papers (MS312), Special Collections and University Archives, University of Massachusetts Amherst Libraries.

*December 27, 1927*

*Dr. A. J. Cooper*
*201 "T" Street, N.W.*
*Washington, D.C.*

My dear Dr. Cooper:

I shall be very glad to use some of the matter which you sent me and especially the photographs. I am afraid, however, that they are going to be too late for the February CRISIS which appears January 15th. At any rate, send them along.

VERY SINCERELY YOURS,
WEBD/PF

# 52

# Anna J. Cooper to
# W. E. B. Du Bois

*(January 13, 1928)*

In this telegraph, Cooper corrects the misprinting of a student's name in the school production of a play submitted to *The Crisis*.

SOURCE: W. E. B. Du Bois Papers (MS312), Special Collections and University Archives, University of Massachusetts Amherst Libraries.

DOCTOR DUBOIS=
THE CRISIS 69 FIFTH AVE NEWYORK NY=
AENEAS IN THE PLAY IS AUBREY GORDON NOT
AUBREY MORTON=

ANNA J COOPER.

# 53

## Anna J. Cooper to
## W. E. B. Du Bois

*(January 22, 1928)*

Cooper expresses her disappointment to Du Bois that the production of the Dunbar High School's play was not mentioned in the most recent issue of *The Crisis*. She also questions some of the facts within that issue about the policies of the national Girl Scouts, noting that Dunbar High School had been denied the authority to organize a "colored" troupe.

SOURCE: W. E. B. Du Bois Papers (MS312), Special Collections and University Archives, University of Massachusetts Amherst Libraries.

*January 22, 1928*

Dear Doctor Du Bois:

We are disappointed not to find notice of our play for Dunbar High School in your February issue just received. Perhaps you plan to put it in the March no. [number]

I would like to know if you are assured of the facts mentioned p. 55 regarding policy of national office Girl Scouts on organizations of colored girls. I know that Jenny Taylor Wilder applied at headquarters for authority to organize in Dunbar H.S. and was told they were not ready for that yet. Have they changed?

VERY TRULY YOURS,
ANNA J. COOPER

# 54

# W. E. B. Du Bois to
# Anna J. Cooper

*(January 24, 1928)*

Du Bois explains why the production of the Dunbar High School's play was not included in *The Crisis* and agrees to contact the Girl Scouts to ascertain the veracity of the error printed in *The Crisis*.

SOURCE: W. E. B. Du Bois Papers (MS312), Special Collections and University Archives, University of Massachusetts Amherst Libraries.

*January 24, 1928*

*Dr. A. J. Cooper*
*201 T. St. N.W.*
*Washington, D.C.*

My dear Dr. Cooper:

We so often have the same difficulty with our friends. You wrote us December 21st saying that you were going to send information and pictures concerning your play. I waited until December 27th and wrote you saying that we should be glad to have the matter and especially the photographs, but that if you did not rush them they would be too late for the February CRISIS, which goes to press January 4th and appears January 15th. One picture came in January after THE CRISIS had gone to press marked Suzanne Payne as Hecuba. It was not a particularly interesting picture. Nevertheless, if it had come on time we should have used it. A telegram came about Aubrey Gordon's picture, but no picture has appeared.

Under these circumstances you were, of course, disappointed in seeing nothing in the FEBRUARY CRISIS, and even in the MARCH CRISIS we have nothing of real interest, except, of course, a short note that you gave the play. The general public is not much interested in that, but if you had had a real dramatic picture of a group, we could have given you good publicity.

I am writing the Girl Scouts concerning the point which you are bringing out. I will let you know their answer.

VERY SINCERELY YOURS,
WEBD/DW

# 55

# Anna J. Cooper to
# W. E. B. Du Bois

*(January 26, 1928)*

Cooper critiques Du Bois's editorship and discussion of the "New Negro" in *The Crisis* and asks that he publish information about the Dunbar High School's play production, allowing readers of *The Crisis* to decide what interests them.

SOURCE: W. E. B. Du Bois Papers (MS312), Special Collections and University Archives, University of Massachusetts Amherst Libraries.

*January 26, 1928*

Dear Doctor DuBois:

Of course "every crow"—+c. but "according to me" a thing of beauty cut from the classic contacts of a people is as "interesting" (it surely is more stimulating educationally) as the picture of two morbidly dull + "greasy" individuals, each boring the other because they have nowhere to go but the movies. All of which means to say quite frankly that I think much of the New Negro stuff you are feeding us is flat, stale, + unprofitable.

The two scenes from Vergil we are going to put on in February will employ nearly a hundred students of our Latin Department + illustrates some of the best work accomplished in the Dunbar High School.

The communication sent you before Xmas mentions facts worth featuring. Our staging alone will cost several hundred dollars which is a good deal for poor folks + amateurs. Our costumes are not rented but in the main made by the students themselves. They will, nevertheless, conform to classic models + present for the student correct notions of time + place. The photograph that I rushed thro to the Crisis as advance notice was what we could put before the camera so far ahead. We shall have two group pictures as soon as scenery is completed + I trust you will give readers of the Crisis an opportunity to judge for themselves whether the effort is "interesting."

CORDIALLY,
ANNA J. COOPER

# 56

# W. E. B. Du Bois to
# Anna J. Cooper

*(January 28, 1928)*

Du Bois requests photographs of the Dunbar High School students participating in the play, believing that it will give the play more publicity.

SOURCE: W. E. B. Du Bois Papers (MS312), Special Collections and University Archives, University of Massachusetts Amherst Libraries.

*January 28, 1928*

*Dr. Anna Cooper*
*201 "T" Street, N.W.*
*Washington, D.C.*

My dear Dr. Cooper:

Please have two or three good, clear photographs, at least 8x10 taken of your group in costume, either before or right after the performance. It would be better to have a daylight picture. All this will be trouble, but only in this way can you get the right sort of publicity, which I should be very glad to give if I ever receive photograph.

VERY SINCERELY YOURS,
DW

# 57

# Anna J. Cooper to
# W. E. B. Du Bois

## (February 10, 1929)

Cooper regrets that she will not be able to attend the Pan-African Congress due to the expense.

SOURCE: W. E. B. Du Bois Papers (MS312), Special Collections and University Archives, University of Massachusetts Amherst Libraries.

February 10, 1929

My dear Doctor Du Bois:

Your notice of the 5th PanAfrican interests me. I should love to go. But cant see it yet. However shall tell all my wealthy friends—maybe I can help swell the 200 that way.

YOURS TRULY,
ANNA J. COOPER

# 58

# Anna J. Cooper to
# W. E. B. Du Bois

*(October 27, 1929)*

Cooper regrets that she will not be able to attend the Pan-African Congress and questions why Du Bois chose not to schedule it during the summer when teachers and working people might be more likely to be able to attend.

SOURCE: W. E. B. Du Bois Papers (MS312), Special Collections and University Archives, University of Massachusetts Amherst Libraries.

*October 27, 1929*

Dear Doctor DuBois

Sorry I cant make the trip to Pan African.

But why, oh why dont you have your Congresses in summer time when working people might go without having their heads thrown to the crows?

REGRETFULLY,
ANNA J. COOPER

# 59

# Anna J. Cooper to
# W. E. B. Du Bois

*(December 31, 1929)*

Cooper urges Du Bois to address *The Tragic Era* in *The Crisis*. *The Tragic Era: The Revolution after Lincoln* (1929) was written by Claude Bowers and depicted a racist history of Reconstruction that was later used by white segregationists to oppose civil rights legislation.

SOURCE: W. E. B. Du Bois Papers (MS312), Special Collections and University Archives, University of Massachusetts Amherst Libraries.

*December 31, 1929*

My dear Doctor Du Bois

It seems to me that the Tragic Era[1] should be answered,—adequately, fully ably, finally. + again it seems to me Thou art the Man! Take it up seriously thro the Crisis + let us buy up 10 000 copies to be distributed broadcast thro the land.

Will you do it?

Answer.

FAITHFULLY
ANNA J. COOPER

# 60

# W. E. B. Du Bois to
# Anna J. Cooper

## (January 9, 1930)

Du Bois expresses a willingness to address *The Tragic Era* in *The Crisis*, but states that he does not have the funds to do it unless Cooper can facilitate a financial contribution.

SOURCE: W. E. B. Du Bois Papers (MS312), Special Collections and University Archives, University of Massachusetts Amherst Libraries.

January 9, 1930

*Dr. Anna J. Cooper*
*201 "T" Street, N.W.*
*Washington, D.C.*

My dear Dr. Cooper:

I should like very much to devote an issue of THE CRISIS to answering the Tragic Era, but it would cost some extra money. If you can think of any plans by which this can be raised, either by selling ten thousand extra copies, or advertising in THE CRISIS, or in any other way, I should be very glad to undertake the project. I could contribute something myself and there are several experts who would be glad to write. Think the matter over and consult friends and let me hear from you again.

VERY SINCERELY YOURS,
WEB/DW

# 61

# Anna J. Cooper to
# W. E. B. Du Bois

*(January 18, 1930)*

Cooper pledges support for an extended response to the *The Tragic Era*. She also requests information so that her students can send proceeds of their performance in support of Elizabeth Prophet. Prophet, of Native American and African American ancestry, was an accomplished sculptor who struggled to show her work or make a living due to the racism and sexism of the art world.

SOURCE: W. E. B. Du Bois Papers (MS312), Special Collections and University Archives, University of Massachusetts Amherst Libraries.

*January 18, 1930*

My dear Doctor Du Bois:

I think the extended distribution of an effective answer to Tragic Era can be arranged. At least I can pledge to do my part in helping. Get it out and make it snappy. Carter Woodson has a review in this month's Journal which I have not yet seen but that need not interfere with yours.

There is another matter that calls for the present letter. The Crisis, month before last, spoke of the struggles of Miss Prophet, the young sculptress in Paris—and we want to help.

I have a club of girls at Dunbar H.S. whom I have interested in the project. We are already at work on a play which we hope to put on this spring. Will you let us know how to reach Miss Prophet with the proceeds and what is her present address.

Thank you.

VERY TRULY YOURS,
ANNA J. COOPER

# W. E. B. Du Bois to
# Anna J. Cooper

*(January 28, 1930)*

Du Bois agrees to try to release an issue of *The Crisis* on *The Tragic Era* and also connects Cooper with Elizabeth Prophet.

SOURCE: W. E. B. Du Bois Papers (MS312), Special Collections and University Archives, University of Massachusetts Amherst Libraries.

*January 28, 1930*

*Dr. Anna J. Cooper*
*201 T. St. N.W.*
*Washington, D.C.*

My dear Dr. Cooper:

I shall see if I can get out a copy of The Crisis on "The Tragic Era." I will let you know my plans later. Mrs. Elisabeth Prophet, the sculptor, is at present the guest of Mrs. Du Bois at 226 West 150th Street. She has some busts on exhibition in New York and is hoping to sell some. I am sure she would appreciate hearing from you and your club.

VERY SINCERELY YOURS,
WEBD/DW

# 63

# Anna J. Cooper to
# W. E. B. Du Bois

*(February 2, 1930)*

Cooper thanks Du Bois for connecting her with Mrs. Prophet and recommends Dr. Carter G. Woodson's review of *The Tragic Era* as a start to creating an issue on the subject. Woodson was a renowned historian of African American history and the African diaspora. He is credited with founding Black History Month and spent most of his career as a professor and later dean at Howard University.

SOURCE: W. E. B. Du Bois Papers (MS312), Special Collections and University Archives, University of Massachusetts Amherst Libraries.

*February 2, 1930*

Dear Doctor DuBois
Thank you for Mrs. Prophet's address.

I admire her greatly + shall write her.

Doctor Woodson has reviewed "Tragic Era" in the "Journal of Negro History, but I think some thing more detailed as to facts + figures is demanded to meet the situation adequately.

VERY TRULY
ANNA J. COOPER

# 64

# Anna J. Cooper to
# W. E. B. Du Bois

*(September 19, 1930)*

Cooper submits a copy of one of her articles to *The Crisis* that she believes will benefit teachers. Cooper is referring to her essay "The Humor of Teaching," published in *Crisis* (*November* 1930): 387 (available in Lemert and Bhan).

SOURCE: W. E. B. Du Bois Papers (MS312), Special Collections and University Archives, University of Massachusetts Amherst Libraries.

*September 19, 1930*

My dear Doctor Dubois:
I thot this suggestion might be of some use to teachers who read Crisis.

VERY TRULY
ANNA J. COOPER

# W. E. B. Du Bois to
# Anna J. Cooper

*(September 23, 1930)*

Du Bois agrees to include her article in an issue of *The Crisis*.

SOURCE: W. E. B. Du Bois Papers (MS312), Special Collections and University Archives, University of Massachusetts Amherst Libraries.

*September 23, 1930*

*Dr. Anna J. Cooper*
*201 "T" Street, N.W.*
*Washington, D.C.*

My dear Dr. Cooper:

I am going to use your article in an early number of The Crisis. Thank you for letting me see it.

VERY SINCERELY YOURS.
WEB/DW

# 66

# Anna J. Cooper to
# W. E. B. Du Bois

*(October 30, 1930)*

Cooper proposes that Du Bois create a series on her friend, educator and author Charlotte Forten Grimké, and Grimké's grandfather James Forten in *The Crisis* that she would write. She states that she has been given some of their materials and requests any advice he has about researching their lives further. Several of the correspondences in part 4, Additional Correspondences, refer to Cooper's role as steward of Charlotte Grimké's writings.

SOURCE: W. E. B. Du Bois Papers (MS312), Special Collections and University Archives, University of Massachusetts Amherst Libraries.

*October 30, 1930*

Dear Doctor Dubois:

Doctor Grimke has placed in my hands much material + I am now engaged in searching for more for a "Life of Charlotte Forten Grimke."[1]

There are many features of this Life which I think would not only inspire + hearten your colored readers but I am sure would enlighten + helpfully influence the general American public.

I would like to know your views about the reception of such a work for the Crisis + shall appreciate your suggestions + advice. I am on the hunt just now for further facts regarding her grandfather,

[AJC insertion: James Forten[2]] who was a sail maker in Philadelphia + was captured by the British in the Revolutionary War + was exchanged in the give + take of prisoners. Perhaps you can tell me where to search in the archives of Phila. for contemporary account of this fact.

I hope it is not too much of a gamble to say beforehand whether you trust my ability to make a readable Crisis series of articles on this subject.

Please answer.

VERY TRULY
ANNA J. COOPER

# 67

# W. E. B. Du Bois to
# Anna J. Cooper

*(November 10, 1930)*

Du Bois agrees to include "something" on Charlotte Forten Grimké in *The Crisis*, but cites the constraints of the magazine as a reason for not making it a series. He also offers resources for Cooper's research on James Forten.

SOURCE: W. E. B. Du Bois Papers (MS312), Special Collections and University Archives, University of Massachusetts Amherst Libraries.

*November 10, 1930*

*Dr. Anna J. Cooper*
*201 "T" Street, N.W.*
*Washington, D.C.*

My dear Dr. Cooper:

We should like very much to publish something about the late Mrs. Grimke but we can hardly make it a series of articles. A succession of articles on the same subject do not go well in a small magazine like The Crisis. One, or the most, two articles would be enough. You will find a great deal about James Forten in Philadelphia. There were two or three collections of books on the Negro which were variously disposed of but I am sure could be found in the city. I have mentioned Forten on pages 23-24 of my Philadelphia Negro.

VERY SINCERELY YOURS,
WEB/DW

# 68

# Anna J. Cooper to
# W. E. B. Du Bois

*(February 8, 1931)*

Cooper requests a copy of an issue of *The Crisis* that included an article on "Negro Dialect."

SOURCE: W. E. B. Du Bois Papers (MS312), Special Collections and University Archives, University of Massachusetts Amherst Libraries.

*February 8, 1931*

My dear Doctor Du Bois:

There appeared sometime ago an article in The Crisis on Negro Dialect—just when or by whom I am unable to recall. I have ransacked all my back numbers and interrogated all my friends with no success. Finally Mrs. Clifford suggests the "Home Office" which I might have that of long ago—and here I come! Help by return mail if possible—if not, as soon as you can. Send copy and bill me. Thank you.

VERY TRULY YOURS,
A. J. COOPER

# 69

# Anna J. Cooper to
# W. E. B. Du Bois

*(February 24, 1931)*

Cooper regrets that Du Bois did not include her response to Benjamin Stolberg's essay "Classic Music and Virtuous Ladies: A Note on Colored Folks' Prejudices," which ran in the January 1931 issue of *The Crisis*. Cooper felt Stolberg's essay preached "an insidious doctrine" dismissing African American achievements in classical music and art in favor of popular performances of jazz and spirituals, and she stresses the importance of countering his argument.

SOURCE: W. E. B. Du Bois Papers (MS312), Special Collections and University Archives, University of Massachusetts Amherst Libraries.

*February 24, 1931*

Dear Doctor DuBois:

I think Stolberg's note on "Colored Folks' Prejudices" ought to be answered + I am frankly sorry you do not think my answer, sent in January, good enough to place before readers of the Crisis.

There is a very insidious doctrine being preached + practiced in literary circles, viz., + to colored youth especially: "Assume a vice if you have it not,—it will lessen the distance between you + white people + give you truly a part in the gay abandon of this free + frank generation."

I for one should like Mr. Stolberg to know that there are some thotful colored persons who are not ashamed to differ.

VERY TRULY
ANNA J. COOPER

# 70

# Anna J. Cooper to
# W. E. B. Du Bois

*(January 20, 1932)*

Cooper requests that Du Bois print information about the creation of a new "Societe" meant to encourage engagement with the French language and culture.

SOURCE: W. E. B. Du Bois Papers (MS312), Special Collections and University Archives, University of Massachusetts Amherst Libraries.

*January 20, 1932*

My dear Doctor Dubois: Here is "News" for your "Color Line" + I hope a hand out for colored America. This "Societe" was inspired + organized by Dantés Bellegarde +, but for diplomatic considerations, he should be its president.

Of course we had a French "Cercle" since the days of Arthur Gray, Hillyer + Albert, but nothing to compare in seriousness of outlook + loftiness of aspirations with the Constitution drawn up by Bellegarde.

The news note enclosed herein is typed by his secretary + is a part translation into English of his "Statuts." He says you have his cut already + we should like his photograph to appear as Honorary life member of the "Société des Amis de la Langue Française.

We are looking to a nation wide organization + affiliation with l'Alliance Française of the world.

I am sure the Crisis can help. Will <u>you</u>?
Thank you.

ANNA J. COOPER.

There was organized in October at Washington LE CERCLE FRANCAIS, société des Amis de la Langue et de la Culture françaises, whose object as set forth in their Statutes is:

1. to spread among its members the knowledge and appreciation of the French language and culture;
2. to enter into relations with friends of French culture whatever may be their race, their nationality, or their religion, in order to establish among them and its members bonds of moral and literary sympathy.
   Among the special activities enumerated are:

a/ Periodic meetings for exchange of views among the members and practice of the French language;
b/ Conferences in French or conferences in English on subjects bearing upon French-speaking countries, particularly France and Haiti;
c/ The organization of courses in the French language and literature;
d/ The distribution of suitable awards for the encouragement of the teaching of French in the schools;
e/ Foundation of a French Library and Reading Room;
f/ Publication of a Review;
g/ Circulation of books among students of French.

The Society, under direction of delegates named by it, may organize local Committees in all centers that offer the necessary conditions. These local organizations will be autonomous.

The membership is classified as active members, members for life, benefactors and honorary members. The Officers—President, Vice-President, Recording and Corresponding Secretaries, Treasurer and Librarian-Archivist—together with an Executive Committee of ten, form the Board of Directors who will administer the affairs of the Society in conformity with the

Constitution. This Board is elected for two years by the General Assembly composed of active and life members and meeting each year on December 26.

The Headquarters of the Society will be at Washington D.C. in the rooms of the Frelinghuysen University, 201 T Street, N.W.

# 71

# Anna J. Cooper to
# W. E. B. Du Bois

*(January 22, 1932)*

Cooper expresses her dismay that Du Bois mistakenly printed the death of Judge William Clarence Hueston (1880–1961), a lawyer and civic leader who had recently accepted a position as dean of the Law Department at Frelinghuysen University. She also notes that she had submitted information about him to *The Crisis* prior to the printing of the issue.

SOURCE: W. E. B. Du Bois Papers (MS312), Special Collections and University Archives, University of Massachusetts Amherst Libraries.

*January 22, 1932*

Ohhh DuBois!

How on earth could you make such a blunder? Dont you read your notices at all?

Judge Hueston is not dead! He has accepted the Deanship of the Law Department of Frelinghuysen University + is very much alive! Hence my notice for the February Crisis which comes today to horrify + humiliate me.

What can be done about it?

Please acquaint yourself with facts sent you.

YOURS DISTRESSED,
ANNA J. COOPER

# 72

# Anna J. Cooper to Hannah Stanley Haywood

*(July 29, 1898)*

Letter from Anna "Annie" Julia Cooper to her mother, Hannah Stanley Haywood, in which Cooper gives updates concerning friends, family, and acquaintances. In her autobiographical reflections (see part 5), Cooper identifies her mother as the "finest woman I have ever known" and states that her most important accomplishment was the founding of the Hannah Stanley Opportunity School, "named for [her] slave mother," and serving African Americans with cognitive disabilities. This letter reflects the sense of community Cooper cultivated as she provides updates on family and friends, including suffragist Anna Jones, with whom she continues corresponding into the 1920s, John Love, and Francis and Charlotte Grimké, along with an update on the Hampton Institute and its conference.

SOURCE: Anna Julia Cooper Papers, box 23-1, folder 5, Moorland-Spingarn Research Center, Howard University.

*HAMPTON, VA*

*July 29, 1898*

Dear Mother: I wrote Littlebud Sunday & thought that would do for you too as I was so busy & had so little time. Miss Anna Jones was here and we spent the day at Shellbanks together. You remember the lady I spoke of having you come down to Hampton with. She is gone now & Johnny Love is here learning the carpenters trade in the Hampton shops. He works like a Trojan and has already sawed two of his own fingers. Mr. Grimke is here too but Mrs. Grimke did not come. The people here like his preaching very much. When I went down to Old Point to see Miss Jones off I saw Dr. Smedes of St. Augustine on the boat and ran on board to speak to him. He seemed very glad to see me and inquired particularly about you. I told him I would bring you out to hear him preach when we get back to Washington. He has a church in one of the suburbs of Washington called Woodside. He is looking older & bent but seems in good health. He spoke of all the old people of St. Augustine's and told me of some of them whom I had lost track. Jane Thomas or Mrs. Caspar came over from Norfolk during the Conference here at Hampton. She is going to Raleigh about the 2nd or 3rd of August & I thought it would be a good time for you to start back to Washington if you have seen enough of the soldiers. You were having such a gay time when you wrote, dining with the officers + all that, I fear you will not want to settle down as a plain citizen again. I thought it would be nice to go home & have all the house cleaning done before you get back so as to have you avoid all the confusion. I shall have the parlors painted + papered + a new mantel put in the front parlor. I enclose a letter from Maggie which will tell you about the baby. Prof. Atkins attended the conference here after which he stopped at our house in Washington. Now when you are ready to leave let me know. You may want to stop a few days in Raleigh to see your old friends & then come on to Norfolk. Miss Jane will see you safely on the Washington boat & you will have no trouble. Enjoy yourself + have a good time. I am glad you are with Mrs. Gibble. Give my love to their family.

AS EVER,
ANNIE

# 73

# Anna H. Jones to
# Anna J. Cooper

*(August 16, 1925)*

Letter from Anna H. Jones to Anna Julia Cooper in which Jones reaches out to Cooper because she is nearby due to a class reunion. She thanks Cooper for her account of her travels to Europe. Jones is likely referring to Cooper's travels to France to complete and defend her dissertation, *L'Attitude de la France à l'égard de l'esclavage pendant la Révolution (France's Attitudes toward Slavery during the Revolution)*,[1] at the University of Paris, Sorbonne. Anna Jones (1855–1932) was a prominent Canadian-born suffragist, clubwoman, and educator who lived and worked in Kansas City, Missouri, later in life and sought to improve the conditions of African Americans through education.

SOURCE: Anna Julia Cooper Papers, box 23-1, folder 5, Moorland-Spingarn Research Center, Howard University.

*505 Shelton Ave.*

*August 16, 1925*

Dear Anna

I am as much nearer to you than I have been for years that I must scribble a line to you. I was called out from my Calif. home by a class reunion that I could not say "no" to, our 50th, so while I was comparatively near, I came down close to see my niece who is married and living here. I don't feel able to get any farther east so I am renting a few days before beginning my westward [unclear]

I have enjoyed so much your account of your European experiences that I must thank you for them. You don't know how proud I feel of you and enjoyed seeing your picture in the "Crisis."

Send me a line. I shall be here about 2 weeks.

YOURS ANNA H. JONES

# 74

# John L. Love to
# Anna J. Cooper

*(no date)*

Letter from fellow teacher and member of the American Negro Academy John "Johnnie" Love (1868–1933) to Anna Julia Cooper, marked "Easter Morning" (likely April 12, 1925, as the reference to his ambivalence about attending the upcoming NAACP meeting convening in Denver from June 24 to 30, 1925, suggests). In the letter, Love congratulates Cooper for her achievement of becoming a doctor and expresses the profound joy and pleasure he takes in Cooper's accomplishment. This letter conveys the close and personal nature of their relationship, as well as Love's admiration for Cooper and deep respect for her achievements.

SOURCE: Anna Julia Cooper Papers, box 23-1, folder 7, Moorland-Spingarn Research Center, Howard University.

*Easter Morning*

My dear Annie:

Congratulations on your splendid achievement—the winning of the goal for which you have so long looked forward to and have so deservedly earned. Yet how weak these words are as an expression of the very great joy and satisfaction I feel for what you have so signally accomplished. How much I would rather be near you, and let you see the joy I experience & have waited anxiously and towards the end somewhat impatiently, I must confess, for the news.

Friday a card came from Sis saying you had arrived with the promise of your letter the next day. It came yesterday morning while I was planting in the garden which forthwith I left and was so overcome with joy, I hardly cared to go back to rustic occupation. Then in the afternoon the paper which you sent came, just as I was about to make a trip in the city with Robert W. Bagnall of the New York Office. We both read the article—he with pleasure and I with a joy I could hardly suppress.

So glad to have you back and a Doctor! A great victory. I suppose it will take time for me to learn to change my former way of greeting you. Maybe I won't be able to learn entirely. You will be Doctor and also—.

I am so glad you had the ocean trip just after the supreme effort you had made and that you were able to reach home refreshed and reinvigorated thereby. It was so fine that Gittie was on hand, which confirms a dream I had to that effect something over two weeks ago. I have not yet had the opportunity to read over your letter as deliberately and intimately as I shall have, I hope, today. The newspaper article I shall turn over to-morrow to our local paper for it to reprint. No doubt the Washington representative of the Negro Press association has already taken up with you the matter of a special article. About this I would like to know.

I am anxious to learn more definitely about your status upon your return to the work then. Doubtless you suspect my anxiety about this and will soon let me know.

Now the next job for you is a larger one and may I hope, prove pleasurable and profitable—that is the preparation for a lecture or speaking tour, dealing with such subjects as may seem to you fundamental and appropriate.

Now is the season I should like to come on, especially when the ceremony with the District Commissioners takes place. But, sad indeed for me, this may be one summer which does not promise the great privilege. In the first place the NAACP Conference will be in Denver this year and even to this I am not looking forward to attending, first because I cannot afford the personal expense these trips have always entitled in spite the allowance made and secondly I feel that I ought to let others have the privilege of going, though of course there will be the disposition to send me. This has been a very hard year with me financially, due largely to the slipping back occasioned by the frequent trips the past three or four years and the extraordinary expenses this way. In consequence my nose has been a little more than next to the grindstone. Then too I shall probably have some connection with the summer work at Lincoln University. (Lincoln Institute). Young and I are just taking the matter up through correspondence. Young has very frequently asked about you. When I write him, I tell of your achievements after becoming settled again and resting from your strenuous efforts, think about the speaking trip and let me know your views.

This Easter morning is glorious indeed for its brightness and warmth and splendor, a fitting foil for the joy I feel over your success.

VERY DEVOTEDLY AS EVER,
JOHNNIE

# 75

# Lula Love to
# Anna J. Cooper

*(August 11 [no year])*

Letter from Lula E. Love Lawson (1871–1951) to Anna
Julia Cooper (addressed here as "Cookie") marked
"Thursday the 11th" (presumably August 11, since the
tenth is Cooper's birthday). In it, she wishes Cooper
well after her birthday and, among other things, tells
Cooper how much she means to their friends and the
people of Washington, DC. After the death of a friend,
Cooper assumed responsibility for foster siblings Lula
and John Love.

SOURCE: Anna Julia Cooper Papers, box 23-1, folder 7,
Moorland-Spingarn Research Center, Howard University.

*Thursday the 11th*

My Dear Cookie:

Well, how do you feel after a birthday!! I was with you all day
yesterday. If there's any truth in the old saying your ears must have
burnt all day, for I was telling every body "This is Cookie's birthday." All my friends here know you and constantly ask "how's
Cookie?" The Western Union telegraph girl phoned your message
and then mailed it to me. I am so glad you wore the dress and liked
it. I thought of you when I first saw it hanging on the rack in Lane-
Bryant's store. The only fear was that it would not fit. I went out
to call on Jaunita Howard at Ruth's home, and we talked a lot
about you and what you meant to the Washington people, plus

others. Juanita + her husband drove out here, making stops all along the way out. They left today for D.C. and will make stops on way back. She will see you when she returns for she was sorry not to be there on the 10th. I suppose Dillon got back ok. I just know you had a fine day, and we all are happy. I guess for this you have manila envelope with the other forgotten trinkets. Be sure to use the in soles in your slippers—let the rubber side be down and the leather side up next to your feet. I realize now I should have sent some foot powder. I once kept you well supplied with Scholl's foot powder. Remember? That will keep your feet from sticking to the pad, unless you have stockings on. Now don't strain your eyes to write me—this is a good time to get Regia's pen in hand to write me. Or Father John: Ha! Ha!

MORE NEXT TIME. BEST LOVE, LULA

76

# Francis J. Grimké to
# Anna Julia Cooper

*(November 19, 1910)*

The Reverend Francis Grimké (1850–1937) updates
Cooper on the activities of the Board [of Education]
(likely in reference to Cooper's reinstatement at M
Street High School), as well as meetings and correspondences he has had with Roscoe Conkling Bruce (1879–
1950), the assistant superintendent of public schools in
DC in the early 1900s. Grimké also updates Cooper on
the status of his wife, and Cooper's dear friend, "Lottie" (Charlotte Grimké)—who is unwell.

SOURCE: Anna Julia Cooper Papers, box 23-1, folder 5,
Moorland-Spingarn Research Center, Howard University.

*1415 Corcoran Street, N.W.*
*Washington, D.C.*

*Nov. 19, 1910*

Dear Mrs. Cooper:

You have, doubtless, been wondering why you have heard nothing from this side of the line; we have also been surprised at the slow pace at which matters have been moving. No action was taken at the last meeting of the Board. The matter did not come up at all. The alleged ground was that the examining committee had not, up to the time of the meeting of the Board, rendered a report. I have just had another interview with Mr. Bruce, and he assures me that matters will turn out all right, in the end and, he wished me to say that to you. The real cause of the delay, he now assures me, is due to the fact that Supt. Stewart wanted first to talk the matter over with each member of the Board, before making the recommendation, in order to make sure that his recommendation would be sustained. It seems that the only member of the Board who has raised any objection, is Mr. Horner. Miss Barrier called me up a few days ago, and told me that she had also understood that such was the case. I went out immediately to Howard University and saw Tunnell, with whom I had talked before about the subject, and he told me to give myself no uneasiness about the matter, that he would see Horner and set him straight on the matter. So don't give yourself any uneasiness. Be a little patient, and soon everything will be all right. What Mr. Bruce said to me, of course, is confidential. Lottie is still quite poorly, and sends a great deal of love to you. We all wish to be kindly remembered, and with best wishes, I am,

YOURS TRULY,
FRANCIS J. GRIMKE

# 77

# Anna J. Cooper to
# Garnet C. Wilkinson

*(May 24, 1926)*

Cooper requests that Wilkinson take a stand for justice
with respect to her ousting and being bypassed for promotion by the Board of Education of Washington, DC,
when she was rehired. Notably, she states that those
who were preferred for promotion over her were of
lesser qualifications. Dr. Garnet C. Wilkinson (1879–
1969) was an educator known for his work in the DC
school district, where he was appointed as principal of
Dunbar High School (formerly M Street) before he became assistant superintendent. In addition to being
Cooper's colleague through M Street and the school
district, Wilkinson was a graduate of the M Street High
School (1898) as well as a fellow alumnus of Oberlin
College (1902).

SOURCE: Anna Julia Cooper Papers, box 23-1, folder 6,
Moorland-Spingarn Research Center, Howard University.

*201 T. St. N.W.*
*Washington, D.C.*

*May 24, 1926*

Dear Mr. Wilkinson:

Once again I shall try (without offense I hope) to write you as a man rather than as an official.

The year 1927–1928 will mark my fortieth year as a teacher in the High School of the District of Columbia, barring an interim of four years as a college professor at Lincoln University. One year later (1928–9) I shall be retired automatically from the system by the age limit rule. I have therefore only about three years more of public school service before me, even if I am not excluded before that time by some unforeseen disability. My ratings by officials immediately concerned have been uniformly "excellent" and "excellent superior." There has never been, to my knowledge, any question of my efficiency as a teacher or of my spirit of willing co-operation in all the deepest concerns of our school population. Much of my aims, ideals and principles of action is personally well known to you and many of my achievements have been consciously aided, inspired and abetted by you. I believe that I have had many evidences of the sincere esteem and appreciation with which my service is regarded by the humble laity whom I serve, and yet it must be admitted that official recognition still seems tardily and grudgingly accorded and pecuniary emoluments, so eagerly sought by most persons, is stubbornly withheld while every opportunity is seized in some quarters to excuse this material injury by detraction and misrepresentation.

Now I should utter no word of complaint for all this were it not my firm conviction that nothing vitiates the morale of any educational system more completely than a sense of unfairness in the distribution of rewards. Once let the conviction take root that merit does not count, that service, however long and fruitful and efficient can be outstripped any day by sheer pull or flimflam, and no administration would be secure. The strength of the head rests on those loyal hearts that respond to a sense of justice and fair play and on that support that goes out spontaneously always to unselfish devotion.

It may be that you can without jeopardizing your own interests prevent the perpetuation of those studied attempts at persecution and humiliation which have been so patent in my case. I do not ask you to say or do one thing to embarrass yourself. But as it seems to me now and as it has seemed all along to a few very thoughtful friends of mine, it could only strengthen your hold on the community and give real significance to your position in the eyes of the country, if you would take a firm stand for justice and fair play in the bestowal of those favors that involve the taxpayers' burdens. You, if any one, can say that neither N. E. Weatherless nor Marion P. Shadd can convince one who has ever been a student under Anna J. Cooper that she does not know her subject. Surely the testimony of Oberlin and Columbia and La Sorbonne should not be allowed to be discredited by any factitious "board of Examiners" in the Washington Public Schools.

A report from Mr. Hine dated May 11, 1926 in re my appeal before the Committee on Complaints contains this paragraph: The Committee is impressed with Mrs. Cooper's attainments as a scholar and student and takes pride in the recognition which her work has lately received. But a "passing mark" on the written examination is required for promotion and as Mrs. Cooper at the hearing held before the Complaints and Appeals Committee did not claim that she should have been given a passing mark on the written examination it is therefore impossible for her appeal to be granted.

The whole ground of my complaint and appeal to the Board was from the first that several candidates were given the promotion over my head whose educational claims were admittedly below mine, altho their written examination papers by the first set of judges had been marked below the required passing mark, as had my own presumably. I have never raised a question of those markings. I think I could show if I were allowed to see my papers that I gave a fairly good account of myself. I have never in my life failed in a written test and I have taken on an average I am sure one at least for every year of my teaching experience. The quantity of work required in these Washington examinations is purely arbitrary and the questions themselves designed rather to "stump" the candidate than to test his ability to teach the subject. In this case the questions had been carelessly mimeographed or typed and

were full of errors that had to be unraveled in order to give any
sort of intelligent answer. The translation was wholly sight work
and as I recall it the first question had five or six subheads for comments, mythological, historical, or interpretive, on certain lines of
a poem that must first be scanned to mark the rhythm, show the
caesura and classify the meter. There may have been ten or could
have been fifty questions after this—I never knew. I think I answered something like two or three after the first which had consumed most of the forenoon. Then since as you know there is no
hostelry near the Franklin where a colored person can procure a
glass of milk, I had to walk all the way to the "Y" 9th and R. I.
Ave. for lunch. Caught a cab coming back but was not so fortunate
going. When I returned the others were already under way, but I
put in the time remaining as best as I could, on the afternoon work
consisting of principles and methods, conduct of department, etc.
etc. I mention these trifling details to show why I employed a lawyer to plead for the "merging" of the written and "oral" marks in
giving the final standing. The law of Congress provides that
"Teachers shall be promoted for superior work from Group A of
Class 6 only after oral and written examinations by the Boards of
Examiners upon recommendation of their respective principals
thro and with the approval of the Superintendent of Schools and
with the additional recommendation of the Colored Assistant Superintendent for the Colored Schools, and provided further that
"No teacher shall be eligible to Group B who has not attained the
maximum of Group A." Fixing the entire weight of eligibility exclusively on the written test papers is in the opinion of my lawyer
wholly extra-legal. Indeed the law nowhere says that the written
examination shall even be passed or any defined standard shall be
met therein. The teacher is promoted for "superior work" only after oral and written examinations." Now the word oral as interpreted in practice by the Superintendent of Schools sums up the
whole arc of personal efficiency in the work of the schools and
should if anything be made the sine qua non of a "superior" teacher's claims for promotion. Yet strangely enough I was excluded
from consideration under this head until the Board of Education
at the instance of my lawyer ordered first that the Oral be given me
and later that the ratings be affixed to the several items. It was on
this so-called oral test that my complaint rested and still rests. The

law was clearly violated in promoting to group B a teacher who had not reached her maximum in Group A; it was violated only by implication in promoting those whose test papers in a written examination were rated below 210. Again all the more was it violated in my case in altogether disallowing the "oral examination," just as legally necessary as the other, and insisting, on an arbitrary standard of 210 on the written examination before any other claims could be considered. Now altho the board at the instance of my attorney granted my plea for a rating on the oral involving the most important items of personal fitness, educational qualifications and general efficiency as a teacher these items largely demonstrable by documentary evidence that would be incontestable in any educational center of the civilized world were systematically discredited and given a mark below passing in each particular. My complaint then is solely against these ratings a copy of which is enclosed herewith. It will be noted that the items discredited are questions of fact open to mathematical proof. One item only (B under III) is given full credit and here personal judgment is fairly permissible and a "zero" could not have been gainsaid. One successful candidate had been in the system less than five years, had no degree whatever when taking the examination, took it then as a kindergartner and failed according to the first ratings received from competent judges of her test papers. The attainment of [unclear] to disrupt the proceedings and to curtail his very [unclear] before the Board was literally true. It is well known that several were promoted in spite of the fact that they did not receive a passing mark on their written examination from the first judges who rated them the longevity law which is very explicit was not always enforced. In "Educational Preparation" and Educational Courses taken, in both of which I am rated below passing by the Chief Examiner, I think I can say without self-conceit or egotism that there is no one in the system producing a more extensive record by actual count and measurement. If Miss Shadd can say that my scholarship is not up to standard I have a right to inquire what is the standard and who the judge. This is just why I appeal from Miss Shadd to you, not only the First Assistant Superintendent in charge of colored schools but is one better qualified, in every way to pass judgment on the academic question involved. I expressed to the committee my dissatisfaction at your absence from the hearing as likewise my opposition to the presence there of the already discredited N. E. Weatherless who presumed to criticise the revisions action of the Board of Education in allowing any consideration whatever of the "Oral Examination" and had the hardihood to employ the expression "Speaking as a lawyer" when the committee knew the circumstances under which my own lawyer had been unjustly disbarred from appearing there.

The Superintendent's circular had estimated 300 points for written, 300 for oral and 400 Personal characteristics and Teaching Ability. My 700 superior points as elements of actual teaching service were discredited for the first 300, a purely arbitrary element of written examination.

I wish distinctly and unequivocally to disclaim responsibility for any disrespectful remarks concerning either the Superintendent of Schools or any member of the Board of Education made by David A. Pine who was employed to present my appeal to the Board. He may not have been tactful; he certainly was not successful in representing my own attitude of mind regarding the question at issue. But the Administration cannot be willing to play the role of persecuting a faithful servant who has from the beginning been innocent of any intention to offend.

And may I not at least hope, Mr. Wilkinson, that you with your usual judicial mind will see this somewhat from my point of view and that your natural love of justice and fairness will not rest till due consideration is given where it deserves.

VERY RESPECTFULLY YOURS,

# 78

# Anna J. Cooper to
# George Hamilton

*(ca. 1916–1917)*

Cooper, writing to the president of the DC Board of
Education, expresses her discontent with the fact that
her children and their school were used as a subject of
ethnological study. This letter references Dr. John Van
Schaick Jr., then president of the Board of Education,
granting Herman Marie Bernolet Moens, a Dutch ethnologist, permission to photograph children in the DC
public schools. Cooper states her protestation against
the exploitation of her children and others for the sake
of the ethnologist's study.

SOURCE: Anna Julia Cooper Papers, box 23-1, folder 5,
Moorland-Spingarn Research Center, Howard University.

*To Mr. George Hamilton*
*President of the Board of Education*
*Franklin Building*

Dear Sir:

    While sharing fully in the indignation felt by the colored com-
munity at the outrages perpetrated by the fake "scientist" and pretended ethnologist, Moens, I crave the privilege as a guardian of
five children in the schools of entering here and now a solemn protest against the whole theory of exploitation which in the first
place gave admission to our schools to a "scientist," were he as
pure as an angel of light, with the expressed purpose of using the

material in this group as a laboratory. I claim the right to know and be assured that I send my children to school to be taught, developed, trained and so far is possible to be inspired to their highest possibilities as human beings—not to be analyzed, labeled and catalogued as zoological specimens.

# 79

# Anna J. Cooper to
# A. G. Comings

*(October 1, 1928)*

Cooper communicates to Albert Gallatin Comings, treasurer of the Oberlin Committee Campaign Fund of 1928 of the Anti-Saloon League of America that, although she is supportive of the Eighteenth Amendment (banning the production, transport, and sale of intoxicating liquors), she is unwilling to support their campaign against Alfred E. Smith, then governor of New York and Democratic Party presidential candidate, in his 1928 bid for the US presidency. She doesn't believe the Oberlin group has taken the protections of Black rights as seriously as their fight against the Eighteenth Amendment, or stood sufficiently against Black disenfranchisement and lynching.

SOURCE: Anna Julia Cooper Papers, box 23-1, folder 5, Moorland-Spingarn Research Center, Howard University.

*201 T. St. N.W.*
*Washington, D.C.*

*October 1, 1928*

Mr. A. G. Comings, Treasurer
Authorized Oberlin Committee
Campaign Fund of 1928
of the
Anti Saloon League of America.

Dear Mr. Comings:

I am sorry I cannot enter wholeheartedly into the campaign for downing Gov. Alfred E. Smith. My own vote, it is true, if I had one, should go to Hoover as, of the two, the man coming nearer to representing the best in American ideals. But personally the 14th & 15th amendments to the Constitution are just as precious in my sight as the 18th. & I am unable to warm up very enthusiastically with religious fervor for Bible "fundamentalists" who have nothing to say about lynching Negroes or reducing whole sections of them to a state of peonage worse than slavery. I do not at all question the sincerity of the little band of Oberlin workers for those ideals that Oberlin, as I know it, has always championed & which I most heartily endorse. But Al Smith has the same right to his opinions that I have to mine & even if elected could not carry the country any further than our representatives in Congress would allow.

VERY SINCERELY YOURS,
ANNA J. COOPER

# 80

# Anna J. Cooper to
# *The Afro American*

## (September 2, 1958)

Cooper requests that the money contributed in honor of her hundredth birthday be deposited at interest to later be used in publication of her work on the "Ethics of Negro Problem and Dialect."

SOURCE: Anna Julia Cooper Papers, box 23-1, folder 5, Moorland-Spingarn Research Center, Howard University.

Frelinghuysen University
A Group of Schools
For Employed Colored Persons

*201 T. St. N.W.*
*Washington, D.C.*
*Telephone North 7-6206*

Personal to the Afro

It is my wish that two hundred seventy nine dollars 65 cents contributed in honor of my hundredth birthday be deposited at interest in Savings Dept. of National Savings and Trust Company to be used later in publication of my work on Ethics of Negro Problem and Dialect.

With thanks & appreciation to all concerned I appoint my niece Madeline Beckwith & my friend West A. Hamilton joint Trustees & administrators of this fund.

SIGNED ANNA J. COOPER
201 T ST. N.W.
WASHINGTON, D.C.


*September 2, 1958*

# 81

# Cooper, Note from
# Scrapbook 1881–1926

When Cooper was preparing to retire from Dunbar High School, Frank Ballou, superintendent of DC schools, attempted to withhold from Cooper status that would have guaranteed her the full retirement benefits and annuity. As part of the supporting documents for her case, Cooper's lawyer turned over letters of support that had been written over the years testifying to Cooper's scholarly merits and qualifications. Cooper expresses her regret at having entrusted a set of her original materials to someone so hostile to her case and requests that they be demanded back again. These letters can be found pasted in Cooper's 1881–1926 scrapbook housed at the Moorland-Spingarn Research Center (MSRC).

SOURCE: Anna Julia Cooper Papers, box 23-7, folder 88, Moorland-Spingarn Research Center, Howard University.

I do not know what discount may be made of these poor relics of the good opinions of others not directly "earned" perhaps, certainly not consciously sought, & precious therefore to none but myself. It is not my wish to have the superintendent see these for I do not care to have anyone with sinister purpose start a commercial apprising in percentages & probable promotions growing out of what no man can measure & it [is] sacrilege to weigh with money. It was very foolish of me to leave my original papers in such hostile hands, but I am so accustomed to laying all my cards on the table I played right into the enemy's hands. Please demand them again. I have indicated a few paragraphs that may interest you. The class letters were on our 25$^{th}$ anniversary when I was chosen class historian—the pages marked are my own contributions. You asked about my book and I enclosed some of the clippings from the press. Dr. Ballou need not be at such pains to try to stamp out recognition of my life's work, he can withhold a paltry increase in salary but he can never take from me the realities that are beyond his comprehension.

# 82

# Adelia A. Field Johnston to
# Anna J. Cooper

*(May 4, 1892)*

Adelia A. Field Johnston, the first female faculty member of Oberlin College and later dean and professor of medieval history, certifies that Cooper graduated from Oberlin College in 1884 and attests to her ability as a scholar and educator.

SOURCE: Anna Julia Cooper Papers, box 23-7, folder 88, Moorland-Spingarn Research Center, Howard University.

*Oberlin College*
*Ladies' Department*
*Oberlin, OH*

*May 4, 1892*

This is to certify that Miss A. J. Cooper graduated from this College in 84.

Miss Cooper was among the very best scholars in the class. My present memory is that she stood first in Greek. In English Literature and Rhetoric she was especially good.

Miss Cooper is in every way qualified to fill a Professor's Chair. She is a successful teacher, a Christian lady and has an executive ability not often equaled.

A. [ADELIA] F. [FIELD] JOHNSTON

# 83

# A. A. Allen to
# Anna J. Cooper

*(July 8, 1926)*

Allen responds to a previous letter from Cooper on a matter regarding Cooper's grandnieces and nephews. Allen suggests Cooper seek the assistance of Mr. Edward de Veaux Morrell's wife, Louise Bouvier Drexel Morrell, in relation to the matter. Edward de Veaux Morrell formerly served in the US Congress from 1900 to 1905, during Cooper's tenure as principal at M Street, and as chairman of the School Subcommittee of the District Committee.

SOURCE: Anna Julia Cooper Papers, box 23-7, folder 88, Moorland-Spingarn Research Center, Howard University.

*July 8, 1926*

*Mrs. A. J. Cooper*
*201 "T" Street*
*Washington, D.C.*

My dear old friend, Mrs. Cooper:

I am in receipt of your very wonderful letter of July 5th. I would do anything in the world that I could to help you in your splendid thought of building into good citizens the orphan nieces and nephews for whom you have already done so much.

I know practically no one in Philadelphia although my dear father was born there.

Mr. Morrell, while Congressman, was the most understanding man on the Floor of the House, and as Chairman of the School Sub-Committee of the District Committee, he forced seventeen of our twenty proposed school reforms down the throats of his colleagues, many of whom were unwilling. He did this even against the opposition both of the District Commissioners and of the Members of the Board of Education.

As a consequence (unknown to him of course) of his just and intrepid advocacy of these reforms and his success in pushing them through, what happened? Among other things, you lost out and from being a successful, inspiring and admired High School principal, you were demoted to a plain teachership and have had trouble in keeping even that ever since.

So, in a sense, one might say that if any one over deserved the good will of the Morrell family and had a claim upon their consideration and good offices, it is Anna J. Cooper, Ph. D., late principal and now teacher in the "M" Street High School, Washington, D.C.

If this letter can in any wise aid you, I hope that you will not hesitate to use it in whole or in part with Mrs. Morrell.

Assuring you of my great and continued regard, I remain

VERY SINCERELY YOURS,
(MRS. A. A. ALLEN)
40 WEST 59TH ST.
NEW YORK CITY

# 84

# W. G. Ballantine to
# O. O. Howard

*(May 17, 1892)*

William Gay Ballantine (1848–1937), fourth president
of Oberlin College, writing to Oliver Otis Howard, the
founder and namesake of Howard University, recommends Cooper for a position at Howard University citing that she is a lady of "thorough culture and of the
highest moral character."

SOURCE: Anna Julia Cooper Papers, box 23-7, folder 88,
Moorland-Spingarn Research Center, Howard University.

*Oberlin College*
*Oberlin, Ohio*

*May 17, 1892*

My dear Sir:

I am informed that Mrs. Annie J. Cooper is a candidate for the
position in the Faculty of Howard University and am asked to say
a word in her behalf to you.

Mrs. Cooper is a graduate of Oberlin College of the class of '84.
She is a lady of very thorough culture and of the highest moral
character.

In scholarship in all departments she Ranked among the best
educated whom the College has graduated.

I have no hesitation in recommending her for any position which she will consent to accept. With high esteem [unclear] me.

VERY SINCERELY YOURS,
W. [WILLIAM] G. [GAY] BALLANTINE

PRESIDENT
O. O. HOWARD
NEW YORK CITY

# 85

# Anna J. Cooper to
# George M. Jones

*(August 21, 1926)*

Cooper writes to the secretary of Oberlin College seeking a US publishing house to publish, advertise, and
help distribute her translation of *Le Pèlerinage de
Charlemagne*. She is notably willing to cover the full
cost without reservations about price or profit she
could make from it.

SOURCE: Anna Julia Cooper Alumni File, Oberlin College
Archives.

*August 21, 1926*

*Mr. George M. Jones*
*Secretary of Oberlin College*

Dear Sir:

I can only thank your considerate generosity that makes you refrain from reminding me that it is time for my "285" promise to
materialize, altho there has been hardly a minute that I have not
been conscious of the fact, nor a day that I have not hoped that the
realization of my dream was approaching. I have not been just idly
hoping as the enclosed notices from French periodicals will show.
My edition of the "Pelerinage de Charlemagne" was first prepared
as an M.A. dissertation at Columbia University + afterwards
printed in France with the express desire to make it a material contribution to Oberlin, my beloved Alma Mater.

Beyond the giving away of several copies I have done no advertising in this country, but have the 500 copies (minus those few complimentary ones) all expenses fully met—ready for the middle man (an American publishing house) who will take over the stock at 50/50 sending the whole of my share to Oberlin. I am not figuring on one cent of profit for myself or any refund of expense of printing, shipping etc. all of which I have met already. I ask only that the publisher be found who will relieve me of the advertising + pushing to get it introduced into colleges where French is taught + into prominent libraries.

Frankly I think my color will be a barrier in this country, + that is why I would have the work taken solely on its merits without reference to the personality of its editor; + it may be that your intervention at this juncture can save the day without embarrassment to Oberlin.

I trust you have time to at least consider the matter + advise me.

VERY SINCERELY YOURS,
ANNA J. COOPER

# 86

# George M. Jones to
# Hermann H. Thornton

*(October 9, 1926)*

Jones writes to Thornton requesting his "frank opinion" on Cooper's translation of *Le Pèlerinage de Charlemagne* and whether it would be suitable for publication. He also mentions a friend, "R. P. J.," in Paris, who might be able to assist.

SOURCE: Anna Julia Cooper Alumni File, Oberlin College Archives.

*October 9, 1926*

*Mr. Hermann H. Thornton*
*83 Elmwood Place*
*Oberlin, Ohio*

My dear Thornton:

Will you kindly do me the favor to read the enclosed letter and the comments on Mrs. Cooper's book, and give me your frank opinion whether or not it would be even remotely possible for us to undertake to do anything about the publication of her work. Mrs. Cooper is a rather distinguished colored graduate. She seems to have a realizing sense of the difficulties her color adds to the situation, but I would like to write her if I may, frankly in regard to the question she asks. Perhaps I can wish it on our friend, R. P. J., in Paris if you have no suggestions, but I would value your own personal opinion.

CORDIALLY YOURS,

# 87

# George M. Jones to Hermann H. Thornton

*(October 12, 1926)*

George M. Jones asks Hermann H. Thornton to send the materials he had sent him to Professor T. A. Jenkins (of the University of Chicago and president of the Modern Language Association—according to chapter 88, "W. F. Bohn to Anna J. Cooper, October 14, 1926"). Katherine Shilton chronicles Cooper's efforts to donate copies of her translation of *Le Pèlerinage de Charlemagne* (from medieval to modern French), an old French epic poem dealing with the fictional pilgrimage of the protagonist and his knights, and the way her efforts were thwarted by those whose assistance she sought with disseminating her work.[1]

SOURCE: Anna Julia Cooper Alumni File, Oberlin College Archives.

*Oct. 12, 1926*

*Professor Hermann H. Thornton*
*83 Elmwood Place*
*Oberlin, Ohio*

My dear Thornton:

I shall be very grateful to you if you will forward the material I sent you the other day to Professor Jenkins, and any help you may lend in this connection will be appreciated.

VERY SINCERELY YOURS,

# 88

# W. F. Bohn to
# Anna J. Cooper

*(October 14, 1926)*

William Frederick Bohn (1878–1947), secretary of the
Oberlin Shansi Memorial Association, tells Cooper that
he received a copy of her translation from Secretary
George Jones and that he had referred that matter to
Professor Thornton. Professor Thornton told Bohn that
he would refer the matter to Professor Jenkins at the
University of Chicago and requests that she send her
materials to him.

SOURCE: Anna Julia Cooper Alumni File, Oberlin College
Archives.

*October 14, 1926*

*Mrs. Anna J. Cooper*
*201 T St., N.W.*
*Washington, D.C.*

Dear Mrs. Cooper:
  Secretary Jones has put in my hands your letter of August 21st,
concerning your publication "Pelerinage de Charlemagne," and
I am of course very naturally interested not only in securing proper
recognition of the work itself but also in your very generous offer
to share any profit there may be in the sale of the book with Oberlin. In the absence of Professor Jameson, the head of our Department of Romance Languages, I referred the matter to Professor
H. H. Thornton, who is the acting head of the department.

Professor Thornton tells me that he would be glad to take the matter up with Professor T. A. Jenkins, of the University of Chicago, who is at present President of the Modern Language Association, and who will be interested. Will you, therefore, be good enough to send at once to Professor Jenkins, University of Chicago, Chicago, Illinois, a copy of this dissertation? In the meantime, Mr. Thornton will write Professor Jenkins telling him that a copy is coming and asking for his cooperation. It is quite possible that Professor Jenkins may know of a suitable way to secure its distribution.

WITH ALL GOOD WISHES,
SINCERELY YOURS,

# 89

# Anna J. Cooper to
# W. F. Bohn

*(October 17, 1926)*

Letter from Cooper to Mr. W. F. Bohn at Oberlin College, dated October 17, 1926, in which she thanks him for his letter and communicates that she will send a copy of her translation of *Le Pèlerinage de Charlemagne* to Professor Jenkins of the University of Chicago, per Mr. Bohn's instructions. She also requests that, if the work meets his approval, he aid her in the printing and republication of the work for personal distribution, again stating her willingness to cover the full cost of printing, publishing, and distributing the work, without reservations about price or profit she could make from it.

SOURCE: Anna Julia Cooper Alumni File, Oberlin College Archives.

*October 17, 1926*

*Mr. W. F. Bohn*
*Oberlin College*
*Oberlin, OH*

Dear Mr. Bohn:

I thank you for your letter. I am sending by this post as per your instructions a copy of the Pelerinage de Charlemagne to Professor Jenkins of the University of Chicago. I shall also take the liberty to send your Professor Thornton a copy together with my thesis on

Slavery for his personal perusal. And will you allow me to offer a suggestion that really seems like shirking responsibility. That is if you decide that the work is acceptable you will allow me to ship the whole consignment to Oberlin to be handled from there with such machinery as you have for distributing + accounting. Just let me disappear from the picture if you can take the 400 or 450 copies as squaring off my promissory note for $285. I ask no further consideration in the profits + have no concern in fixing prices. All expenses so far have been fully met by me + I will pay freight from Washington to Oberlin if you please to accept such a settlement.

I await your reply.

VERY SINCERELY YOURS,
ANNA J. COOPER

# 90

# Hermann H. Thornton to
# W. F. Bohn

*(October 30, 1926)*

Thornton tells Bohn that Jenkins thinks Cooper's translation is "pretty bad" and explains that he will try to find publication for it "as opportunity presents itself." Notably, despite the negative assessment the work received, Thornton expresses that it will likely be useful for classroom use in various respects, highlighting the way racial and gender politics limited Cooper's opportunities for publishing and disseminating her work.

SOURCE: Anna Julia Cooper Alumni File, Oberlin College Archives.

*Hermann H. Thornton*
*Department of French and Italian*
*Oberlin College*
*Oberlin, Ohio*

*October 30, 1926*

My dear Mr. Bohn:

I am returning herewith Mrs. Cooper's papers, which I have recently had back from Prof. Jenkins. I regret to say that Jenkins thinks the work is pretty bad and does not feel that he can commend it for use in American schools. He has, however, bought a copy for his own library and written to Mrs. Cooper a letter discussing certain points in connection with the edition.

Prof. Bourland of Western Reserve to whom I mentioned the work was inclined to think that, on account of the inclusion of the Koschwitz text, it might be of use in Old French classes. I asked Mrs. Cooper to send him a copy, and should not be surprised if he would use it in his classes. While we must, I think, accept Jenkins' opinion as apt to prevail in this country, I shall continue to speak a discreet word for the edition as opportunity presents itself. Needless to say, I have mentioned it and shown it to my class in Old French Literature, as well as to the little Faculty French Circle.

Assuring you of my desire to be of service whenever I may in connection with the work of the President's office, believe me,

SINCERELY,
HERMANN H. THORNTON

# 91

# Unknown to
# Anna J. Cooper

*(January 11, 1927)*

The sender tells Cooper that they have discovered some profitable way of distributing her book (likely her translation). He explains that Professor Thornton has been in contact with Professor Jenkins as well as Professor Benjamin Parsons Bourland of Western Reserve and that, although Bourland is interested, the men had expressed their doubts about the likelihood of putting her books into immediate circulation. He suggests that she send the copies she has on hand to Professor Azariah S. Root to see if he could "make good disposition of them."

SOURCE: Anna Julia Cooper Alumni File, Oberlin College Archives.

*January 11, 1927*

*Mrs. Anna J. Cooper*
*201 T St., N.W.*
*Washington, D.C.*

Dear Mrs. Cooper:

I have hoped that I might before this write you that we had discovered some profitable way of distributing your book so that it would have the reading it doubtless deserves and also might produce a certain amount of profit which could be applied on your

2-3-5. Professor Thornton of our department of Romance Languages has been in correspondence with Professor Jenkins of Chicago and also with Professor Bourland of Western Reserve. Professor Bourland particularly seemed interested but none of these men seemed to think that there is any likelihood that a considerable number of these books could be put into immediate circulation. I suspect that if you have no better disposition to make of them, it might be a good plan to send the copies you have on hand to our Professor A. S. Root, and let him see if he could from time to time make good disposition of them. He seems to have a veritable genius for exchanges and might use the books that way.

VERY CORDIALLY YOURS,

# 92

# Anna J. Cooper to
# Howard President and Trustees

*(May 5, 1944)*

Cooper explains the duty and responsibility left to her by Dr. Francis Grimké in the preservation and dissemination of Charlotte Forten Grimké's writings and diary materials. She explains that two of the five diaries went to Howard's collection by oversight, that she is having Ray Billington type and edit the journals she has, and requests that Howard allow the two diaries in their possession to be deposited with the three that she owns. Cooper regarded the preservation, publication, and stewardship of Charlotte Grimké's papers, given to her by Francis Grimké, as her "sacred trust."

SOURCE: Anna Julia Cooper Papers, David M. Rubenstein Rare Book & Manuscript Library, Duke University.

*May 5, 1944*

*To the President & Trustees of Howard University*

Gentlemen:

It is commonly known that the Rev. Dr. Francis J. Grimke entrusted to me for editing & publication the writings of his wife, my life long friend Charlotte Forten Grimke. In pursuance of the implied trust and confidence, also in line with my own view of a valuable service possible for the colored race in a worthwhile contribution to its history, I have prepared with numerous cuts and photographs "Personal Recollections of the Grimke Family" in one volume, and in another the Life and Writings of Charlotte Forten Grimke.

Now in separating the material of his wife's letters articles, diaries, & c. meant for me, from the great mass of books, papers, & c. of his own which he sent to Howard University, two of her five diaries went to Howard by an oversight. I have no doubt, tho quite understandable with such a collection—all priceless, to sort and pack. I think you will agree that from the standpoint of future historians it will mean much to the honor of our race, as well as to the place in literature of our Charlotte Forten Grimke to have the diaries all together and in a place accessible to the entire American public—foes as well as friends. I enclose a letter of Dr. Ray Billington who will edit the diaries and has typed copies of all five.

He will deposit the originals of the three in my possession and would appreciate your permission to add the two now—held by you in order to make a complete unit. Believing as I do that such a move will distinctly enrich the racial contribution to American historic literature and bring deserved honor to the life and character of Charlotte Forten Grimke, I earnestly hope you will acquiesce in this disinterested ambition of mine by allowing the diary collection to be housed together in one place known and read by all.

SINCERELY YOURS,
ANNA J. COOPER

# 93

# Dorothy B. Porter to
# Ray Billington

*(June 21, 1944)*

Letter from Dorothy B. Porter (1905–1995), supervisor of the Negro Collection at Howard University, to Professor Ray A. Billington at Smith College in Northampton, Massachusetts, dated June 21, 1944, in which she expresses her interest (and requests Professor Billington's help) in persuading Cooper to deposit the manuscript materials that she was using for her book on the life of Charlotte Forten Grimké to Howard University for preservation in the library's special section for the Negro Collection.

SOURCE: Anna Julia Cooper Papers, David M. Rubenstein Rare Book & Manuscript Library, Duke University.

*June 21, 1944*

*Professor Ray A. Billington*
*Smith College*
*Northampton, Massachusetts*

Dear Professor Billington,

Some time ago I discussed with Dr. Anna Cooper the question of what shall be done with certain manuscript materials which she is using for a book on the life of Charlotte Forten. I understand from her that you are helping with the editing of the diaries. I have a great interest in this subject and it happens that I became acquainted with Dr. Cooper when I went to her home to interview her concerning the material she had in her possession on Charlotte Forten. I had become interested in Charlotte Forten and had begun myself an article of her life. When I found that Dr. Cooper was going to work on the book I immediately put at her disposal the diaries which had been deposited at Howard University Library. These diaries I considered of great great value and as treasures of our library.

Recently, I discussed with Dr. Cooper the possibility of having the Grimke material deposited at Howard University when the manuscript is completed. The question in the mind of Dr. Cooper is the need of making this material available for scholarly use and the need for preserving it for the future. She was not aware that in our new million dollar building we have a special section set aside for the Negro collection which we have been emphasizing and building for the last fifteen years. At the present time we have about 18,000 cataloged items on the Negro about 17,000 of these are books and pamphlets. We have in the collection over 5,000 manuscripts. The Library of Congress regularly sends scholars to our library who come to Washington to do research. Many authors of books on the Negro have spent many days working here. I can truthfully say from years of experience that research workers on the Negro can find in our special collection information on the Negro much more easily than they can at the Library of Congress, as it is more easily available. There is here a card catalog of approximately 60,000 cards and in addition special supplementary indexes. With this in mind it seems that any research materials on the Negro should be first deposited in the Negro collection at Howard whose major aim is the collection and preservation of books and documents on the Negro.

I should like to suggest that you think this matter over and write to Dr. Cooper concerning it. I am sending her a copy of this letter and I shall do what I can to persuade her to feel as I do about this matter.

I spent a most pleasant week in the Graduate house at Smith College, when I was in Northampton two years ago doing a piece of research on a Negro abolitionist, who founded a watercure establishment in Northampton. I shall send you a reprint of the article which I believe will be of interest to you as a history professor and a resident of Northampton. I expect to write up my notes into a full biography, as I have much material on hand, some of which I collected in Northampton and other New England Towns.

I hope that you will visit our library when you are in Washington.

VERY TRULY YOURS,
(MRS.) DOROTHY B. PORTER

SUPERVISOR OF NEGRO COLLECTION

# 94

# Ray Billington to
# Dorothy B. Porter

*(July 2, 1944)*

Billington sends a copy of the letter he has sent to Cooper to Porter. He explains that he has pressured her to deposit the volumes that belong to her (that he currently has) to the Howard Negro Collection.

SOURCE: Anna Julia Cooper Papers, David M. Rubenstein Rare Book & Manuscript Library, Duke University.

*Smith College*
*Northampton, Massachusetts*
*Department of History*

*July 2, 1944*

Dear Mrs. Porter:

Enclosed is a copy of the letter that I am sending to Dr. Cooper. I have, from the beginning of our correspondence, urged her to deposit the materials at Howard University—particularly after I learned that some of the diaries were already your property. I have been especially insistent that the diaries be kept together—either you turn over your volumes to the Library of Congress, or she allow the volumes that I now have in my possession to go to you. I think the latter course vastly preferable, and have so said many times. My hope is that your pressure, and perhaps my letter, can persuade her to take this step.

I will look forward to receiving the reprint that you mention—especially because by the time I receive it it will also awaken memories of Northampton in me. For I am moving to the department of history at Northwestern University this fall. If there is anything more that I can do to persuade Miss Cooper, please let me know at that address.

SINCERELY YOURS,
RAY A. BILLINGTON

# 95

# Ray Billington to Anna J. Cooper

*(July 2, 1944)*

Billington tries to convince Cooper that Howard is the best place to deposit the diaries of Grimké, despite the fact that she has communicated that she wishes to deposit them at the Library of Congress. He states that he will send them to either library she decides (in chapter 96, "Ray Billington to Rayford Logan," seven years later, he admits that this was never his intention and tells Howard professor Rayford Logan about planning to wait until she passed away to deposit them at Howard).

SOURCE: Anna Julia Cooper Papers, David M. Rubenstein Rare Book & Manuscript Library, Duke University.

*Department of History*
*Smith College*
*Northampton, Mass.*

*July 2, 1944*

*Dr. Anna Cooper*
*201 T. St. N.W.*
*Washington, D.C.*

Dear Dr. Cooper:

Mrs. Dorothy Porter of the Howard University Library has written me concerning the disposition of the historical materials concerning Dr. and Mrs. Grimke, and has sent a copy of her letter to you. She has, as you know, asked me to send you my opinion on the matter, and that is the purpose of this letter.

You may remember that when we first discussed the fate of the diaries and other materials I suggested that they be given to Howard University or some other library specializing in Negro history. At that time I know that Howard was actively collecting these materials but had no idea of the size or usefulness of their collection. Mrs. Porter's letter has convinced me that the materials certainly should be sent there if you can bring yourself to do so.

I appreciate your feelings on the matter. You wish to erect a monument to two good friends, and believe that that can best be done by depositing their diaries and papers in a national institution. There is something to be said for your wish, but on the other hand I sincerely feel that their memories could be better perpetuated at Howard University than in the Library of Congress. You, as a scholar, know that manuscripts will be used most widely when they are with other manuscripts that bear on the same subject. In the Library of Congress the diaries would be buried amidst thousands of other documents on many subjects; at Howard University they would be in a position to attract the attention of every student interested in Negro history.

Please know that I have no other interest in this matter other than the cause of scholarship. I will, of course, send the copies that I have to either library as you direct, when I have finished with them. But I honestly feel that both learning and the memory of the Grimkes will benefit if you decide on Howard University.

We are, as you can see, still in Northampton and will be here for about three more weeks, I'm afraid. Mabel has been laid up with a week in the hospital and we have been forced to put off the move correspondingly. Glad that the books reached you safely and that they will be of some use.

SINCERELY YOURS,
RAY A. BILLINGTON

# 96

# Ray Billington to
# Rayford Logan

*(August 20, 1951)*

Billington notifies Howard University professor Rayford Logan that Cooper has decided to deposit the diaries he has to Howard University and brags about having stolen the materials from Cooper and how he planned to wait until she passed away to go against her previously stated wishes and deposit them at Howard. Likewise, he requests that there be a "thank you" celebration or gesture for Cooper, saying that she would be "tickled pink" and that it would make "an old woman very happy." This letter documents the ageism, sexism, and duplicity with which Cooper contended as she sought to process and preserve the writings of Charlotte Grimké.

SOURCE: Anna Julia Cooper Papers, David M. Rubenstein Rare Book & Manuscript Library, Duke University.

*Department of History*

*August 20, 1951*

*Professor Rayford Logan*
*Department of History*
*Howard University*
*Washington, D.C.*

Dear Logan:

This is returning to a subject of which we have spoken before, and where I need your help right now.

You may remember that the diaries of Charlotte Forten Grimke were entrusted to Dr. Anna Cooper by Mr. Grimke after his wife's death—with the exception of two of the notebooks that by chance or design, ended up in the Howard Library. You may remember, too, that Dr. Cooper turned over her notebooks to me for publication, and that I have been working for some time preparing those Journals of Charlotte Forten for the printer. They will be published this winter by Dryden Press.

Against this background, let me say that I have been working on Dr. Cooper for some years to give the manuscript journals to Howard. She has held out for the Library of Congress, and because she has, I am afraid, I have held onto the journals. Just between us, I was planning to wait until she passed away, and then turn them over to Howard. Now I have received a letter from her, stating that she has decided to present them to Howard, and asking me to send them to her attorney: Mr. Louis Rothschild, 1006 Munsey Building, Washington. Needless to say, I am most pleased, and will send the diaries to Rothschild at once. Your library should receive them in due time.

I tell you all this, partly because I feel that someone at Howard should know they are on the way, and should see to it that they get to your library. I tell you also, however, because obviously old Dr. Cooper would be just tickled pink if something in the way of an elaborate "thank you" could be sounded. She wants Howard to acknowledge as her gift not only the books she is giving you, but the two you already have. If you could see to it that this is done, with as much fanfare as possible, you would make an old woman very happy.

Hope your summer has been a good one; we have been so consistently cool in these parts that I have been in Lake Michigan only once—an unpleasant record.

With best personal regards,

CORDIALLY YOURS,
RAY A. BILLINGTON

# 97

# Dorothy B. Porter to
# Anna J. Cooper

*(October 8, 1951)*

Porter thanks Cooper for choosing to deposit Grimké's diaries at Howard University. This letter documents that Cooper and Porter corresponded outside of Billington. Porter expressed tremendous respect for Cooper and had included *A Voice from the South* among the list of books she recommended for reprint by the Negro Universities Press.

SOURCE: Anna Julia Cooper Papers, David M. Rubenstein Rare Book & Manuscript Library, Duke University.

*October 8, 1951*

*Mrs. Anna J. Cooper*
*201 T Street, N.W.*
*Washington 1, D.C.*

Dear Dr. Cooper:

It is with a feeling of deep gratitude that I write to thank you for presenting to Howard University this morning, the unique diaries written by Charlotte Forten Grimke. It is needless to say that Howard University is greatly honored in the selection of it as the depository for these valuable diaries. I can assure you that they will be well preserved and treated as rare documents with the future generations of race scholars in mind.

I wish also to congratulate you on the final completion and publication of the *Life and Writings of the Grimke Family*. It must give you great satisfaction that it is completed.

With best wishes, I remain,

YOURS SINCERELY,
(MRS.) DOROTHY B. PORTER

SUPERVISOR, NEGRO COLLECTION

# 98

# Ray Billington to
# Dorothy B. Porter

*(October 17, 1951)*

Billington expresses his pleasure at having heard that the Grimké diaries were deposited at Howard University. He tells Porter that Cooper was determined to give them to the Library of Congress, but that he held on to them until Cooper decided to deposit them at Howard. He likewise expresses how he found Porter's comments on Cooper's *Life and Works* to be humorous and that he believes they never should have been published as they were.

SOURCE: Anna Julia Cooper Papers, David M. Rubenstein Rare Book & Manuscript Library, Duke University.

*Department of History*

*October 17, 1951*

*Mrs. Dorothy B. Porter*
*University Library*
*Howard University*
*Washington, D.C.*

Dear Mrs. Porter:

I was most pleased to receive your letter and to learn that the Forten materials have been safely deposited at the Howard University Library. What caused Dr. Cooper to reverse herself I will never know; until recently she had been determined to give them to the Library of Congress. I am afraid that I did not make myself too popular with her as a result, for I was frankly sitting on them until she decided to place them where they belonged—which was with you. Hence my pleasure that the deed has been done, and that I could be relieved of responsibility for them.

Your remarks on Mrs. Cooper's *Life and Works* were good for a chuckle on my part. I have struggled with the problem of those for many years, for her one great ambition in life was to have them published. Of course they never should have been, and I shudder to think how much some printer charged that nice old lady for the job. I suppose that her satisfaction is worth any sum, however.

Thanks for your kind words on the fragment of the diaries that I have published. I certainly hoped that the entire volume would be out before now. It has been accepted for publication by the Dryden Press, in New York. Shortly after they agreed to do the job they began to show signs of fright at declining college enrollments, which meant fewer textbook sales for them, and hence fewer profits to spend on such an enterprise as Miss Forten's diary. I have prodded them regularly, and they promise to act as soon as possible, but I have had no definite word. If anyone around Howard could help convince Dryden that the book would sell a thousand copies within a year or so (as I am convinced it would) I will be eternally grateful.

Thanks again for your good letter.

CORDIALLY YOURS,
RAY A. BILLINGTON

# Anna J. Cooper,
# Original Letter for Grimké Books

*(ca. 1951)*

Cooper conveys her original request for Grimké's diaries to be made available to future generations of students and scholars. She also states that Dr. Francis Grimké had left her in charge of all of Mrs. Forten Grimké's writings, including the ones accidentally deposited at Howard along with his materials.

SOURCE: Anna Julia Cooper Papers, box 23-6, folder 71, Moorland-Spingarn Research Center, Howard University.

It is deeply gratifying to have the privilege thro courtesy of the president of Howard University to make available for future historians, scholars & pathfinders the unique contribution of Charlotte Forten Grimke in her simple, direct, sincerely truthful diaries, covering a most fateful period in our country's development.

This is a consummation devoutly desired by her beloved husband, Dr. Francis J. Grimke who entrusted to me *all* her writings—poems, letters, diaries, magazine articles & news clippings; & I wish here to add my appreciation of the honor by requesting my publishers to send two copies of my *Personal Recollections of the Grimke Family* one for the general library, the other to be honored by a place along with Dr. Ray A. Billington's commentary on the Charlotte Forten diaries.

With profound appreciation of the courtesy,

SINCERELY,
ANNA J. COOPER

## 100

# Anna J. Cooper to Mrs. Paul Laurence Dunbar [Alice Dunbar-Nelson]

*(December 31, 1901)*

Cooper expresses her gratitude for poet and suffragist Alice Dunbar-Nelson's previous letter and her commitment to women's causes.

SOURCE: Alice Dunbar-Nelson Papers (MSS 0113), Special Collections, University of Delaware Library, Museums and Press, Newark, Delaware.

*Dec. 31*

My Dear Mrs. Dunbar,

I appreciate deeply your good wishes so kindly & so heartily expressed & I truly hope that the cause of woman may never receive a setback through any lack of efficiency or of worthiness on my part. Wishing you & Mr. Dunbar a happy New Year.

I AM SINCERELY YOURS,
ANNA J. COOPER

# Anna J. Cooper to
# Mrs. Paul Laurence Dunbar
# [Alice Dunbar-Nelson]

*(June 23, 1904)*

Cooper writes to Alice Dunbar-Nelson to ask if she would entertain an offer for a post at M Street High School.

SOURCE: Alice Dunbar-Nelson Papers (MSS 0113), Special Collections, University of Delaware Library, Museums and Press, Newark, Delaware.

*June 23, 1904*

My dear Mrs. Dunbar:

Please inform me whether you are at liberty to entertain an offer of a post in the M. St. High School salary the first year 750 or 800 dollars.

VERY TRULY YOURS,
A. J. COOPER

# Felix Klein to
# Anna J. Cooper

*(October 5, 1923)*

Abbé Felix Klein, the French priest and scholar whom Cooper befriended when he was first touring the United States and who remarked about the impression Cooper's lessons on Vergil left on him, informs Cooper that he has commenced the administrative process of transferring her student records from Columbia University to the University of Paris, Sorbonne, so that she can complete her PhD. Throughout Cooper's doctoral studies, Klein remained a dear friend and an ardent supporter of her work.

SOURCE: Anna Julia Cooper Papers, box 23-1, folder 4, Moorland-Spingarn Research Center, Howard University.

*Meudon, Seine et Oise*

*October 5, 1923*

My dear Mrs Cooper,

As soon as I came back to Paris I started the administrative process, as promised, and I hope you soon find out the results. The important question is whether diplomas from Arlington are recognized as equivalent—that is not the case for all Universities.

I gave your entire file (including your original diplomas which I received not long after your letter) to the organization most apt to obtain grade equivalencies and to facilitate your stay in Paris in every way: the Collège des Etrangers, 24 rue Caumartin, Paris. The director promised me that he will do all in his power to help you, and that he will write you directly and keep me informed as well. Moreover, if I do not receive news promptly, I will go back and stimulate their zeal.

The Collège was founded and is supported specifically by Americans. I'm attaching their prospectus. I ardently wish that you come among us, and I will be very pleased to see you again.

May God protect you and bless your courageous plans,

In Him, believe me, dear Miss,

YOUR MOST DEDICATED
FELIX KLEIN

# 103

# Anna J. Cooper to Felix Klein

*(January 15, 1924)*

Cooper requests the assistance of Klein in helping her access materials for her dissertation, "The attitude of France towards the equality of the races," from the French National Archives and expresses her appreciation for a course he taught that she attended ten years before at La Guilde Internationale.

SOURCE: Anna Julia Cooper Papers, box 23-1, folder 4, Moorland-Spingarn Research Center, Howard University.

*4 rue Rollin, Vème*

*January 15, 1924*

Sir,

I would like to request the assistance of a collaborator with the access to the national archives necessary for me to prepare my dissertation: "The attitude of France towards the equality of the races," which I wish to present to the Faculté des Lettres at the Sorbonne. I am looking for

1)  The History of the Société des Amis des Noirs, founded in 1788 with the goal of abolishing slavery. Speeches made at the Assemblée Constituante on this topic. The works of Abbé Grégoire.

2) Current law regarding the citizenship rights of colonials
3) Current law regarding immigrants from Japan, Africa, India, etc.

Allow me to tell you, Sir, that I have the most pleasant memories of your precious course at the International Guild ten years ago, and I hold the certificate signed in your hand among my dearest treasures.

I know that you already have the materials I want and will not need to search them, and that you could direct me to the books and manuscripts I need without too much bother.

I hope you will grant me the privilege of once more benefitting from your clever mentorship.

RESPECTFULLY YOURS,
ANNA J. COOPER

# Felix Klein to
# Anna J. Cooper

*(December 19, 1925)*

Klein conveys his appreciation for Cooper's December
4 letter (not included here) and concern for her health.
He expresses his hope for her recovery in time for an
upcoming celebration.

SOURCE: Anna Julia Cooper Papers, box 23-1, folder 4,
Moorland-Spingarn Research Center, Howard University.

*Meudon*

*December 19, 1925*

Dear Friend and Madam,
   You would not believe how happy I was to finally receive news
of you in your December 4th letter. As you will have read in the
letter I recently sent you, I was beginning to worry about your
health. The little flu you mention notwithstanding, I am now reas-
sured and I hope you will be fully recovered for the beautiful university celebration of December 29th. Give my best wishes to your
colleagues and friends and tell them that I wish I could be with
them in the chapel at Howard University. Allow me to give my
warmest Christmas wishes to you and your nephews.

WARMLY,
FELIX KLEIN

# Felix Klein to
# Anna J. Cooper

## (December 14, 1934)

Klein thanks Cooper for her postcard and Christmas greetings. He also sends prayers and greetings to her and her friends. He also updates her on the status of his governess and requests Cooper's prayers for her.

SOURCE: Anna Julia Cooper Papers, box 23-1, folder 4, Moorland-Spingarn Research Center, Howard University.

*Meudon*

*December 14, 1934*

Dear Mrs Cooper,

I thank you very warmly for your faithful remembrance, your lovely postcard and Christmas wishes. Please receive my best wishes and the assurance that my prayers are with you and your friends.

It is with great pain that I must tell you that my excellent governess passed away on December 3$^{rd}$ after surgery. You know she liked you very much. Pray for her, for her children and for your faithful friend,

FELIX KLEIN

# Felix Klein to
# Anna J. Cooper

*(December 1, 1936)*

Klein sends Cooper early Christmas wishes along with two images of "Black Madonnas," which he says French Catholics do not find "at all surprising." Cooper collected images of, as well as composed poetry dedicated to, the Black Madonna (see "Black Madonna" in part 5).

SOURCE: Anna Julia Cooper Papers, box 23-1, folder 4, Moorland-Spingarn Research Center, Howard University.

*Meudon*

*December 1, 1936*

My Dear Friend,

This time, I would like to be the first to give my best Christmas wishes, and you can see I am starting rather early.

You will appreciate, I believe, the two images I am sending you: "Black Madonnas," which French Catholics do not find at all surprising.

YOUR FAITHFUL FRIEND
FELIX KLEIN

# Felix Klein to
# Anna J. Cooper

*(December 27, 1944)*

Klein expresses his joy at having received Cooper's previous letter and his remembrance of her and of the causes they share.

SOURCE: Anna Julia Cooper Papers, box 23-1, folder 4, Moorland-Spingarn Research Center, Howard University.

*Meudon*

*December 27, 1944*

Dear Mrs Cooper,

Yours is the first letter I receive from America since 1939. It gave me great joy for this reason, but even more so because it proved to me the faithfulness of your memory. Do believe that I have not forgotten you either. I pray with all my heart the Divine baby Jesus may bless and protect us, those you love, and the great causes we have in common.

YOURS, AND WITH YOU,
FELIX KLEIN

# Oscar De Priest to
# Anna J. Cooper

*(November 16, 1932)*

In this letter, Oscar De Priest (1871–1951), the first African American elected to US Congress after Reconstruction, expresses his gratitude for well-wishes sent him by Cooper from Frelinghuysen University. De Priest served as US representative from Illinois from 1929 to 1935 and credited Black women suffragists like Cooper, Ida B. Wells, and others with his election.

SOURCE: Anna Julia Cooper Papers, box 23-1, folder 5, Moorland-Spingarn Research Center, Howard University.

*Nov. 16, 1932*

*Dr. Anna J. Cooper*
*President*
*Frelinghuysen University*
*201 T Street, N.W.*
*Washington, D.C.*

My dear Dr. Cooper:

I beg to acknowledge receipt of your letter of the 9th on behalf of yourself and Frelinghuysen University and to thank you for your kind words of congratulation and confidence.

SINCERELY YOURS,
OSCAR DE PRIEST, M.C.

# Jean de Roussy de Sales to Anna J. Cooper

*(October 11, 1941)*

Count Raoul Jean De Roussy de Sales, a French jour-nalist and historian who was viewed as spokesperson for French president Charles de Gaulle during World War II, informs Cooper that he has arrived from Paris. He also relays news and information about Paris and Felix Klein per Klein's instructions. He says that "the spirit of Paris is very dignified and the mass of the peo-ple, though suffering morally and physically, are in strong opposition to all ideas of 'collaboration,'" likely with the invading German army, and that they look to the British and Roosevelt with confidence. He states, however, that they know how those in the US "are se-vere in their opinion of them."

SOURCE: Anna Julia Cooper Papers, box 23-1, folder 6, Moorland-Spingarn Research Center, Howard University.

*12 East 82nd Street*
*New York City*

*October 11, 1941*

Dear Mrs Cooper:

I have just arrived from Paris and am happy to give you very good news of our dear mutual friend, the Abbé Klein. I left Paris on July 22nd—he was then in very good health, having wonderfully stood the ordeal of the Leoire[1] cold winter—also as interested in these terrible worldly events as if he was a young man of twenty, having a combative and the right spirit and morale— This most likely will not astonish you— The spirit of Paris is very dignified and the mass of the people, though suffering morally and physically, are in strong opposition to all ideas of "collaboration" thus hopes are with the British and they look to them and Roosevelt with confidence— They know how the U.S.A. are severe in their opinion of them; it pains them terribly because they feel they are unjustly associated with the Vichy government. They can only murmur and protest inwardly. I beg of you and am also speaking for the Abbé Klein, please enforce this and try to appease this malentendu.[2] If you only knew how they look towards Roosevelt— the Tradesmen, the shopkeepers I have spoken to many of them—"d'etre-celle que nous l'attendons"[3]—

Of course there may be, and there is a minority, thinking differently, these are among the financial and big industrial world; a few also in society, very few. I am speaking of Paris,—in occupied territory, I can vouch the same for Brittany and Alsace–Lorraine. I have lived in Paris for fifty years. So I feel I can say I well know the people being in touch with them and having many friends, dear friends in different "milieux."

The Abbe wanted me to tell you all this. If by chance you came to N.Y. I would be most pleased to meet you.

MOST SINCERELY,
JEAN DE ROUSSY DE SALES

# 110

# Anna J. Cooper to
# Alfred Churchill

*(January 21, 1941)*

Cooper recalls to Alfred Churchill, the son of Professor Charles H. Churchill, how the faculty decided in her senior year at Oberlin whether they would have a commencement speaker or a long list of essays from every member of the class. She recalls that she delivered her address "mannishly" and is thankful to report that she is in good health and teaching at Frelinghuysen.

SOURCE: Anna Julia Cooper Alumni File, Oberlin College Archives.

*January 21, 1941*

My dear Alfred: (Churchill)

It is more than kind of you to speak so pleasantly of me in your book of Oberlin Reminiscences + I am grateful for it.

Your letter brot up precious memoires, as hearing from you + Mrs. Anderegg always does—memories the dearest + most precious of my entire life, of Oberlin on its most generous side, its noblest + truest + best. There were giants in those days, big hearted, high towered giants of spiritual elevation + self forgetful devotion. Of course, you know: I was "on my own" + glad of every opportunity to eke out my slender savings by earning what I could in spare hours. Hence it was like an unexpected legacy from Heaven when Anna Waddell called on me to supplement her failing eyesight by reading Guizot's History of Civilization aloud for her so that she was enabled to pass her term's examination in it without using her own eyes. Then coaching students sent me by "Lady" Johnston + best of all the 3d term Algebra class in French Hall in my senior year.

I recall it was debated by the Faculty whether to break precedent for commencement in '84 in order to have a commencement speaker instead of the long + rather wearisome list of "essays" from every member of our unprecedentedly numerous class. "Proff." Ellis our rhetorical professor for the year said somewhat sarcastically I thot, "But your paws & maws will be disappointed if they have to leave without hearing every one of you." I stopped after class to let him know he might save one five-minutes by leaving me off & no "paws & maws" would feel the worse. My offer was not accepted. I came on with "Strongholds of Reason" & to Mrs. Morris' infinite disgust delivered it mannishly, not pretending to read an "essay" as a lady properly should.

I am thankful to say my health is good & tho I retired from public schools ten years ago I am still teaching & carrying on the work in Adult Education at Frelinghuysen. At 81 I read without glasses & write occasionally for publication. At the moment I am engaged on "The Life & Writings of Charlotte Forten Grimke," a dear friend of mine whose diaries & other writings cover the interesting period from 1854 to the late 80s. She corresponded intermittently with Whittier, Phillips, Garrison, Col. Higginson & the gallant Col. Shaw. Articles by her on the Sea Isles off S.C. appeared in the Atlantic Monthly, the Congregationalist, elsewhere. Enclose one or two samples of present activities.

AS EVER,
ANNIE

# Anna J. Cooper to
# Alfred Churchill

*(February 9, 1941)*

Cooper answers Churchill's query about Fanny Jackson Coppin's school in Philadelphia, stating that her school is "distinguished by the high standard of 'liberal' and classical subjects taught there." She also goes on to recount information about the other Oberlin alumni whom she knows personally. Fanny Jackson Coppin (1837–1913), educator and missionary, was famous for teaching and serving as principal at the Institute for Colored Youth, a Quaker school in Philadelphia.

SOURCE: Anna Julia Cooper Alumni File, Oberlin College Archives.

*February 9, 1941*

My dear Alfred Churchill,

To answer your last question first, Fannie Jackson Coppin's school in Philadelphia was distinguished by the high standard of "liberal" & classical subjects taught there. Many in her day berated her as a "Blue-Stocking" & thot the work she was doing quite useless & inappropriate for the people whom she served. However she added industrial features from time to time & her school was both popular & practical. It was supported I think by the Society of "Friends" (Quakers) & has since been removed to Cheyney & made strictly Normal i. e., to train colored teachers from Pennsylvania & the South.

The half-dozen or so of Oberlin graduates whom I mention below may or may not be outstanding as the world goes but I happen
to know them.

1. Mary Church Terrell, '84 O.C. socialite & club woman.
   Taught only a short while. Married Robt. H. Terrell one
   time Principal M St High School later municipal Judge.
   Mrs. Terrell has recently written "A colored Woman in a
   white world," widely commented on.
2. Ida Gibbs Hunt '84 O.C. Taught several years. Her husband
   served a notable number of Administrations as U.S.
   Consul in France & elsewhere.
3. Judith Carter Horton, Teacher & Social worker in
   Oklahoma.
4. John L. Love (deceased) noted historian & teacher
5. Anna H. Jones, (deceased) Teacher, Kansas City Mo.

Some fine work has come from O Conservatory graduates notably Nathaniel Dett Composer & musician, Roy W. Tibbs Professor at Howard University.

BEST WISHES,
"ANNIE" COOPER.

P.S. so far as I have learned Fannie Jackson & I are the only ones
who have been employed as teachers in Oberlin.

# PART V

# ADDITIONAL WRITINGS

The selections in this section provide a fuller picture of Cooper as a poet, while also offering Cooper's reflections on her own history and what she identified as her most significant contributions. Some of the writings included in part 5 were drafted on scraps of paper or the backs of envelopes and had been previously unpublished. Others were privately printed in program booklets or written and rewritten in numerous drafts. Some were published in the Hampton Institute's monthly journal, the *Southern Workman,* and document the founding and operations of important cultural and civic groups and organizations, including the Hampton Folklore Society and the American Negro Academy. The writings in this section also showcase Cooper as a poet whose verse was often composed with religious themes and in conventional forms and constituted poetic acts of commemoration, memory, and resistance.

# 112

# Autobiographical Note

## (no date)

In this short note, Cooper provides context about the circumstances of her birth and upbringing. Born during the Civil War, Cooper notes that she was the child of Hannah Stanley Haywood and most likely her mother's white enslaver, Fabius J. Haywood. Cooper rebukes owing her father anything, and instead focuses on the commitment to education and self-sacrificing service she inherited from her mother. She also relates the hope the enslaved had for a Union victory and the faith they put in her childhood visions to foretell the future.

SOURCE: Anna Julia Cooper Papers, box 23-1, folder 1, Moorland-Spingarn Research Center, Howard University.

I was born in Raleigh North Carolina. My mother was a slave & the finest woman I have ever known. Tho untutored she could read her Bible & write a little. It is one of my happiest childhood memories explaining for her the subtle differences between q's and g's or between b's & l's. Presumably my father[1] was her master, if so I owe him not a sou & she was always too modest & shamefaced ever to mention him. I was born during the civil war & served many an anxious slaves' superstition to wake the baby up & ask directly "Which side is going to win de war? Will de Yankees beat de Rebs & will Linkum free de Niggers." I want to say that while it may be true in infancy we are nearer Heaven, if I had any visions or second sight[2] in those days that made my answers significant to the troubled souls that hung breathless on my cryptic answers, such powers promptly took their flight with the dawn of intelligent consciousness. In the later struggle for existence I could not have told you how the simplest encounter with fate would end.

# 113

# Note About "Courageous Revolt"

*(no date)*

Cooper asserts the role she played in opposing a lesser education for Black students at M Street High School and her achievement in getting several of her students into prestigious universities, notably Harvard, Yale, and Oberlin. While the so-called M Street controversy, in which the DC Board of Education failed to reappoint Cooper as principal of M Street, has often framed Cooper as the victim of debates over industrial versus classical education that were dominated by Booker T. Washington and W. E. B. Du Bois at the turn of the century, in this note, Cooper suggests that the actions of the school board were retaliation for her protests against the segregated "colored" curriculum in Washington, DC, schools and her success in preparing Black students to excel at M Street and to gain admittance into top universities.

SOURCE: Anna Julia Cooper Papers, box 23-4, folder 28, Moorland-Spingarn Research Center, Howard University.

The most significant fact, perhaps, in Mrs. Cooper's contribution to education in Washington certainly the most directly promotive of the cause of Higher Education in her own segregated Group is the courageous revolt she waged against a lower "colored" curriculum for the M Street High School.[1] The proposal was already in Congress to "give the pupils of this school a course of study equal to their abilities." The proposal looked innocent & benevolent, but Mrs. Cooper at the risk of Insubordination insisted that her pupils should have equal opportunity to choose whatever subjects might be chosen if they were in one of the other High Schools. While the discussion was at white heat, she actually prepared pupils who entered Harvard, Yale, Brown, & Oberlin & won for the first time a place in the list of accredited High Schools for the Washington High School for colored children known then as the M St. High School.

# 114

# "Discussion of the Same Subject by Mrs. A. J. Cooper of Washington, D.C."

## *(1893)*

This speech is Cooper's response to Fannie Barrier Williams's[1] speech at the 1893 Congress of Representative Women at the Chicago World's Fair. African Americans were previously excluded from the world's fair, but women received space for this congress after protesting their exclusion. Cooper was one of only three Black women (Fannie Barrier Williams and Fanny Jackson Coppin) allowed to address the congress, and Black women were not involved in planning the "Woman's Building" organized by the congress. Cooper focuses here on the unique positionality of Black women—whom she describes as "doubly enslaved" because of their race and gender—as heroic exemplars of womanhood, morality, and intellect despite the oppression they face in the US. Cooper offers a brief history of schools, universities, and women's organizations that evidence Black women's work toward true universal equality.

SOURCE: *The World's Congress of Representative Women*, edited by May Wright Sewall, Chicago: Rand McNally, 1894, pp. 711–15.

The higher fruits of civilization can not be extemporized, neither can they be developed normally, in the brief space of thirty years. It requires the long and painful growth of generations. Yet all through the darkest period of the colored women's oppression[2] in this country her yet unwritten history is full of heroic struggle, a struggle against fearful and overwhelming odds, that often ended in a horrible death, to maintain and protect that which woman holds dearer than life. The painful, patient, and silent toil of mothers to gain a fee simple title[3] to the bodies of their daughters, the despairing fight, as of an entrapped tigress, to keep hallowed their own persons, would furnish material for epics. That more went down under the flood than stemmed the current is not extraordinary. The majority of our women are not heroines—but I do not know that a majority of any race of women are heroines. It is enough for me to know that while in the eyes of the highest tribunal in America she was deemed no more than a chattel, an irresponsible thing, a dull block, to be drawn hither or thither at the volition of an owner, the Afro-American woman maintained ideals of womanhood unshamed by any ever conceived. Resting or fermenting in untutored minds, such ideals could not claim a hearing at the bar of the nation. The white woman could at least plead for her own emancipation; the black woman, doubly enslaved, could but suffer and struggle and be silent. I speak for the colored women of the South, because it is there that the millions of blacks in this country have watered the soil with blood and tears, and it is there too that the colored woman of America has made her characteristic history, and there her destiny is evolving. Since emancipation the movement has been at times confused and stormy, so that we could not always tell whether we were going forward or groping in a circle. We hardly knew what we ought to emphasize, whether education or wealth, or civil freedom and recognition. We were utterly destitute. Possessing no homes nor the knowledge of how to make them, no money nor the habit of acquiring it, no education, no political status, no influence, what could we do? But as Frederick Douglass had said in darker days than those, "One with God is a majority," and our ignorance had hedged us in from the fine-spun theories of agnostics. We had remaining at least a simple faith that a just God is on the throne of the universe, and that somehow—we could not see, nor did we bother our heads to try to tell how—he would in his own good time make all right that seemed most wrong.

Schools were established, not merely public day-schools, but home training and industrial schools, at Hampton, at Fisk, Atlanta, Raleigh, and other central stations, and later, through the energy of the colored people themselves, such schools as the Wilberforce, the Livingstone, the Allen, and the Paul Quinn were opened. These schools were almost without exception co-educational. Funds were too limited to be divided on sex lines, even had it been ideally desirable: but our girls as well as our boys flocked in and battled for an education. Not even then was that patient, untrumpeted heroine, the slave-mother, released from self-sacrifice, and many an unbuttered crust was eaten in silent content that she might eke out enough from her poverty to send her young folks off to school. She "never had the chance," she would tell you, with tears on her withered cheek, so she wanted them to get all they could. The work in these schools, and in such as these, has been like the little leaven hid in the measure of meal, permeating life throughout the length and breadth of the Southland, lifting up ideals of home and of womanhood; diffusing a contagious longing for higher living and purer thinking, inspiring woman herself with a new sense of her dignity in the eternal purposes of nature. To-day there are twenty-five thousand five hundred and thirty colored schools in the United States with one million three hundred and fifty-three thousand three hundred and fifty-two pupils of both sexes. This is not quite the thirtieth year since their emancipation, and the colored people hold in landed property for churches and schools twenty-five million dollars. Two and one-half million colored children have learned to read and write, and twenty-two thousand nine hundred and fifty-six colored men and women (mostly women) are teaching in these schools. According to Doctor Rankin, President of Howard University, there are two hundred and forty-seven colored students (a large percentage of whom are women) now preparing themselves in the universities of Europe. Of other colleges which give the B. A. course to women, and are broad enough not to erect barriers against colored

applicants, Oberlin, the first to open its doors to both woman
and the negro, has given classical degrees to six colored women,
one of whom, the first and most eminent, Fannie Jackson Coppin,[4] we shall listen to to-night. Ann Arbor and Wellesley have
each graduated three of our women; Cornell University one,
who is now professor of sciences in a Washington high school. A
former pupil of my own from the Washington High School, who
was snubbed by Vassar, has since carried off honors in a com-
petitive examination in Chicago University. The medical and
law colleges of the country are likewise bombarded by colored
women, and every year some sister of the darker race claims
their professional award of "well done." Eminent in their profession are Doctor Dillon and Doctor Jones, and there sailed to Africa last month a demure little brown woman who had just
outstripped a whole class of men in a medical college in Ten-
nessee.

In organized efforts for self-help and benevolence also our
women have been active. The Colored Women's League,[5] of
which I am at present corresponding secretary, has active, energetic branches in the South and West. The branch in Kansas
City, with a membership of upward of one hundred and fifty,
already has begun under their vigorous president, Mrs. Yates,[6]
the erection of a building for friendless girls. Mrs. Coppin will,
I hope, herself tell you something of her own magnificent creation of an industrial society in Philadelphia. The women of the
Washington branch of the league have subscribed to a fund of
about five thousand dollars to erect a woman's building for educational and industrial work, which is also to serve as headquarters for gathering and disseminating general information relating
to the efforts of our women. This is just a glimpse of what we are
doing.

Now, I think if I could crystallize the sentiment of my constituency, and deliver it as a message to this congress of women,
it would be something like this: Let woman's claim be as broad
in the concrete as in the abstract. We take our stand on the solidarity of humanity, the oneness of life, and the unnaturalness
and injustice of all special favoritisms, whether of sex, race,
country, or condition. If one link of the chain be broken, the
chain is broken. A bridge is no stronger than its weakest part,

and a cause is not worthier than its weakest element. Least of all can woman's cause afford to decry the weak. We want, then, as toilers for the universal triumph of justice and human rights, to go to our homes from this Congress, demanding an entrance not through a gateway for ourselves, our race, our sex, or our sect, but a grand highway for humanity. The colored woman feels that woman's cause is one and universal; and that not till the image of God, whether in parian or ebony, is sacred and inviolable; not till race, color, sex, and condition are seen as the accidents, and not the substance of life; not till the universal title of humanity to life, liberty, and the pursuit of happiness is conceded to be inalienable to all: not till then is woman's lesson taught and woman's cause won—not the white woman's, nor the black woman's, nor the red woman's, but the cause of every man and of every woman who has writhed silently under a mighty wrong. Woman's wrongs are thus indissolubly linked with all undefended woe, and the acquirement of her "rights" will mean the final triumph of all right over might, the supremacy of the moral forces of reason, and justice, and love in the government of the nations of earth.

# 115

# "More Letters Concerning the Folklore Movement at Hampton"

## *(1894)*

In response to plans for a society in Hampton involving the study of Black folklore, literature, and ethnology, Cooper sends a letter of support at the behest of society organizer Alice Bacon,[1] who had made a call for support in a previous issue of *Southern Workman*. Cooper feels that this movement can foster a greater pride in Black cultural production and establish Black folklore as worthy of study.

SOURCE: *Southern Workman* 23, no. 1 (January 1894): 5.

From Mrs. A. J. Cooper of Washington, author of that able little collection of essays entitled "A Voice from the South," comes this tribute to Gen. Armstrong's work combined with her approval of our new plan.

"Your letter expresses a want that has been in my mind for a long time. In the first place the "Hampton idea" is one for which I have long entertained an enthusiastic regard and I have been sorry that my fate has not yet given me an opportunity of coming in contact with its work. I do not at all discourage the higher courses for those who are capable among my people, but I am heartily in favor of that broad work begun with so much thoroughness at Hampton. You have large views of things at Hampton and it must have been a large heart that inspired the movement and a wise, well-balanced head that conceived and developed the plan. General Armstrong is one of our national heroes, and his work is no whit inferior because it supplements and rounds off that begun by Lincoln and Grant.

As for your plan for collecting facts that disclose and interpret the inner life and customs of the American Negro, I believe such a work is calculated to give a stimulus to our national literature as characteristic as did the publication of Percy's Reliques to the English in the days of Scott and Wordsworth. It is what I have wanted long to take part in in some way and nothing would give me greater pleasure than to become a part of your plan. What you say is true. The black man is readily assimilated to his surroundings and the original simple and distinct type is in danger of being lost or outgrown. To my mind, the worst possibility yet is that the so-called educated Negro, under the shadow of this over powering Anglo-Saxon civilization, may become ashamed of his own distinctive features and aspire only to be an imitator of that which can not but impress him as the climax of human greatness, and so all originality, all sincerity, all self-assertion would be lost to him. What he needs is the inspiration of knowing that his racial inheritance is of interest to others and that when they come to seek his homely songs and sayings and doings, it is not to scoff and sneer, but to study reverently, as an original type of the Creator's handiwork."

# 116

# Paper
# [to the Hampton Folklorists]
# by Mrs. Anna Julia Cooper

*(1894)*

Cooper, representing the Washington Negro Folklore Society, presented this paper, following William
Wells Newell (a white folklorist and founder of the
American Folklore Society), at the meeting of
the Hampton Folklore Society,[1] which was held at the
Hampton Normal School, in Virginia, on May 25,
1894. In her paper, Cooper calls for Black folklore,
customs, art, and history to be given serious attention
and respect. She implores folklorists to move beyond
narrow conceptions of Black production as merely imitative, and instead posits that Black Americans are,
like all great artists, original creators worthy of critical
study. In the paper, Cooper makes one of the earliest
statements about the need for Black folklore to serve as
a basis for a distinctive African American literary tradition.

SOURCE: *Southern Workman* 22, no. 7 (July 1894): 132–33.

Mrs. Cooper of Washington was next presented to the audience
and read the following paper.

## PAPER BY MRS. ANNA J. COOPER

In the direction of original productiveness, the American Negro is confronted by a peculiar danger. In the first place he is essentially imitative. This in itself is not a defect. The imitative instinct is the main spring of civilization and in this aptitude the Negro is linked with the most progressive nations of the world's history. The Phœnecians imitated the Egyptians, the Greeks borrowed from the Phœnecians, the Romans unblushingly appropriated from the Greeks whatever they could beg or steal. The Norman who became the brain and nerve of the Anglo Saxon race, who contributed the most vigorous and energetic elements in modern civilization, was above all men an imitator. "Whenever," says one, "his neighbor invented or possessed anything worthy of admiration, the sharp, inquisitive Norman poked his long aquiline nose," and the same writer adds, "wherever what we now call the march of intellect advanced, there was the sharp eager face of the Norman in the van." It is not then where or how a man or race gets his ideas but what use does he make of them that settles his claim to originality. "He has seen some of my work," said the great Michael Angelo of the young Raphael when he noticed an adroit appropriation of some of his own touches. But Raphel was no copyist. Shakespeare was a veritable freebooter in the realm of literature, but Shakespeare was no plagiarist.

I heard recently of a certain great painter, who before taking his brush always knelt down and prayed to be delivered from his model, and just here as it seems to me is the real need of deliverance for the American black man. His "model" is a civilization which to his childlike admiration[2] must seem overpowering. Its steam servants thread the globe. It has put the harness on God's lightning which is now made to pull, push, pump, lift, write, talk, sing, light, kill, cure. It seems once more to have realized the possession of Aladdin's wonderful lamp for securing with magic speed and dexterity fabulous wealth, honor, ease, luxury, beauty, art, power. What more can be done? What more can be desired? And as the Queen of Sheba sunk under the stupendousness of

Solomon's greatness, the children of Africa in America are in danger of paralysis before the splendor of Anglo Saxon achievements. Anglo Saxon ideas. Anglo Saxon standards, Anglo Saxon art. Anglo Saxon literature, Anglo Saxon music—surely this must be to him the measure of perfection. The whispered little longings of his own soul for utterance must be all a mistake. The simple little croonings that rocked his own cradle must be forgotten and outgrown and only the lullabies after the approved style affected. Nothing else is grammatical, nothing else is orthodox. To write as a white man, to sing as a white man, to swagger as a white man, to bully as a white man—this is achievement, this is success.

And, as in all imitations that means mere copying, the ridiculous mannerisms and ugly defects of the model are appropriated more successfully than the life and inner spirit which alone gave beauty or meaning to the original. Emancipation from the model is what is needed. Servile copying foredooms mediocrity: it cuts the nerve of soul expression. The American Negro cannot produce an original utterance until he realizes the sanctity of his homely inheritance. It is the simple, common, everyday things of man that God has cleansed. And it is the untaught, spontaneous lispings of the child heart that are fullest of poetry and mystery.

Correggio[3] once wandered from his little provincial home and found his way to Rome where all the wonder of the great art world for the first time stood revealed before him. He drank deep and long of the rich inspiration and felt the quickening of his own self consciousness as he gazed on the marvellous canvasses of the masters.

"*I too am a painter*," he cried and the world has vindicated the assertion. Now it is just such a quickening as this that must come to the black man in America, to stimulate his original activities. The creative instinct must be aroused by a wholesome respect for the thoughts that lie nearest. And this to my mind is the vital importance for him of the study of his own folk-lore. His songs, superstitions, customs, tales are the legacy left from the imagery of the past. These must catch and hold and work up into the pictures he paints. The poems of Homer are valued to-day chiefly because they are the simple unstudied view of the far away life of the Greeks—its homely custom and superstitions as well as its more heroic achievements and activities. The Canterbury Tales do the same thing for the England of the 14th century.

The Negro too is a painter. And he who can turn his camera on the fast receding views of this people and catch their simple truth and their sympathetic meaning before it is all too late will no less deserve the credit of having revealed a characteristic page in history and of having made an interesting study.

# 117

# The American Negro Academy

## (1898)

Cooper's article recounting the meeting of the American Negro Academy in Washington, DC, in December 1897 appeared in the *Southern Workman* in February 1898. Cooper acknowledges the academy's founder, Rev. Alexander Crummell, as well as its leading members from across the African diaspora. She notes that the academy, founded in March 1897, admitted only men, and she details the organization's values and aims, among them the promotion of African American literary, artistic, and scientific production. Cooper quotes members of the academy at length, recounts the meeting's program of speakers, and highlights calls to foster African American intellect rather than simply accept industrial training as the only fitting education for Black Americans.

SOURCE: *Southern Workman* 27, no. 2 (February 1898): 35–36.

The first annual meeting of the American Negro Academy was held in Washington, Dec. 28th and 29th, and added to the usual gayeties of the holiday season unwonted thoughtfulness and earnest discussion. Each of the public sessions drew crowds of interested outsiders, men and women from all the walks of life who showed by sympathetic applause how close to their hearts were the subjects handled.

The Negro Academy, as most readers of the WORKMAN know, was organized March 5, 1897, under the leadship of Rev. Alex. Crummell, Rector emeritus of St. Luke's P. E. Church. Its membership is confined to men. The following are its objects as set forth in their preamble: viz., The promotion of literature, science, and art; the culture of a standard of intellectual taste; the fostering of higher education; the publication of scholarly works; and the defense of the Negro against vicious assaults.

Doctor Crummell, originator of the idea and founder of the Academy, is re-elected its president for the coming year; other officers being Prof. DuBois; Rev. J. A. Johnson, Prof. Scarborough, and Prof. Crogman, vice presidents; Rev. F. J. Grimke, treasurer; and L. B. Moore and J. W. Cromwell, secretaries. To correspondent membership were elected the following eminent Negroes: Sir Samuel Lewis, of Sierra Leone; Hon. W. Blyden, of Liberia: Mr. H. O. Tanner, the artist; and Rt. Rev. J. T. Holly, Bishop of Hayti.

Among the plans under consideration is the publication of a year book of industrial, educational, and religious statistics regarding the colored people of America: and secondly, the issuing of a quarterly with the twofold object of advising colored people on lines affecting their development and improvement, and likewise of bringing the dominant race of the country to a clearer understanding and, by consequence, to a juster treatment of the Negro.

Said Dr. Grimke: "We believe that the American conscience can be touched in this matter, and not by abuse and antagonism, but by reason and the equities of the case, we are going to attempt it. Our aim is, therefore, not solely self-help, but also help of the American nation by endeavoring to educate public sentiment to a Christian conception of the Negro as a man.

"If the Negro is a man, give him a chance. If he does wrong, condemn him; if he does right, commend him. If he shows a disposition to help himself to rise, encourage him. Lend him a hand. His way at best is uphill. Don't try to make it still harder for him. Put yourself in his place, and do by him as you would be done by if you were similarly situated. If he is not just what you think he ought to be, if you find certain weaknesses cropping out here and there be patient with him, and in the spirit of Jesus try to show him the better way. Because he is down, don't put your heel upon his neck and try to keep him down. If there is anything in him, give him the opportunity of showing it. It will be a source of gratification to you in the years to come, to know that you have not been clogs in the wheels of his progress; or if he proves a failure, that you were in no way responsible for it. Treat him as you will wish you had treated him in the light of eternity and the day of Judgment. He is here by no act of his own, he was brought here against his will to minister to the wants of the white man. To the white man, therefore, he has a right to look for fair and humane treatment, yea, to expect to be treated by him with special and peculiar consideration. I submit it is not fair to bring him here, and then, because he has become a free man, to force him, by shutting all the avenues of employment against him, to die of starvation or to drift into crime as a means of subsisting. And yet such is very largely the status of the Negro. He is often stigmatized as lazy, while the simple fact is it is difficult for him to find employment even when he is able and willing to work. For this the white men are responsible. They have the money, they own the places of business, the stores and factories, the telegraph offices and railroads.

These are some of the facts that we want to bring before the American people and to keep hammering on them till we are heard."

It was decided to hold in abeyance the plan for a quarterly till an endowment can be raised for its safe launching. Dr. Crummell however has already begun singly the publication of a series of short tracts to sell for about a penny apiece, for disseminating among the colored people of the country larger ideas of thrift, economy, the acquisition of property, the building up of families, and the like.

It is well known in Washington that the idea of an Academy of colored men "to promote higher culture, encourage hesitant talent, and aid in the publication of works calculated, directly or indirectly, to help colored Americans," has for years been lying as a nidus in the mind of Dr. Crummell, and it is a matter of congratulation to his people, for whose amelioration and defense his lifelong efforts have been given, that the perfecting of his plan and the inauguration of the movement finds him at seventy-eight with brain as vigorous and pen as incisive as those of a man of twenty-five. His white hair and beard, erect frame, and resonant voice made a striking feature of the convention; and a crowded house gathered to listen to his opening address at the first public session of the Academy.

His theme was "The Attitude of the American Mind toward the Intellect of the Negro" and the rapt attention and subdued demonstrations of acquiescence accorded it, testified to the undercurrent of intense feeling existing in his audience on this subject.

After speaking of the effect of slavery and of the legislation that the slavery system made necessary, in the stamping out of intelligence among the Negroes, Dr. Crummell went on to read an indictment against the American mind even of the present day, for its attitude toward the Negro intellect. In regard to the position taken by many, that industrial education is all that the Negro needs, he said.

"You might suppose from the unanimous demand for industrialism in regard to this race of ours that the Negro had been in this land eating terrapin and indulging in champagne, going daily to dinner parties and returning home to sleep in beds of eider down, breakfasting in bed and then having his valet clothe him in purple and fine linen daily all these two hundred and fifty years: and that now at last, the American people, tired of all this Negro luxury, was imploring him for the first time in his life to blister his hands with the hoe and to learn to supply his needs by the sweat of his own brow! The fact is the Negro has been throughout his history the greatest laborer in this land. He is a laborer now and he must always be a laborer or he must die. But unfortunately for him, he has been forced into being an unthinking labor machine and this he is to-day to a large degree under freedom. *What the Negro needs is civilization.* He needs the increase of his higher wants, of his spiritual and mental necessities. And this will come to him as an individual and as a class just in proportion as the higher culture broadens and deepens in our schools and colleges and pulpits; and as the Negro learns that he is no longer to be a serf, but that he is to bare his brawny arm as a laborer not to make the white man a Croesus, *but to make himself a man!*"

Dr. Crummell closed by saying:—"Seeing that the American mind in general revolts from Negro genius, the Negro himself is duty bound to see to the cultivation and fostering of his own race capacity. This is the special purpose of this Academy. Our mission is the encouragement of genius and talent in our race. Wherever we see great ability, it is our office to light upon it, not tardily, not hesitatingly, but warmly, ungrudgingly, enthusiastically, for the honor of the race. The work we have undertaken is our special function, its noblest rewards will be the satisfaction springing from having met a great responsibility in meeting the need of a struggling race."

Dr. Johnson of the Metropolitan M. E. Church followed in an address on "The Critics of the Negro" which called forth considerable discussion.

During the forenoon of the second day papers were read by Mr. Ferris of Hartford, Ct. and by Rev. Mr. Anderson of Philadelphia. The latter reviewed the catalogue of lynchings and other obstacles in the way of the Negro's progress; but claimed that in spite of mob violence in the South, the steady unfriendliness to the Negro in the trades at the North was more destructive.

The address of the second evening was by Prof. Grisham of Kansas City, Mo. on "Aims in Negro Education." Prof. Grisham referred to the chaos of opinions on the subject; then showed that the Negro, called to exercise the highest function of American citizenship, living in the midst of the most brilliant civilization of the world, judged by its standards and tried by its codes, *needs everything.* "When we consider," said he, "the greatness of the Negro's needs by virtue of his connection with the civilization of this great Republic, we can but deprecate any narrow policy that would limit the quality of his training and preparation."

Paul Dunbar then recited most acceptably two recent sonnets of his,—"Death," and "Mortality;" after which the audience called so tumultuously for "more," that the president begged him to let "Melindy sing," and he did. After an impressive summing up on the part of the president of the many problems suggested at the sessions of the Academy, the convention closed, with resolutions of acknowledgment to the pastor and congregation of the church in which the meetings were held, to the committee of ladies who had furnished luncheon each day, and to the city press.

# 118

# Colored Women as Wage-Earners

*(1899)*

Published in the *Southern Workman* in August 1899,
Cooper begins by noting the significant number of African American women who are wage earners outside
of the home and calls for women's rights to work, education, and "fair play and all the rights of wage-earners
in general." She then argues that women who work in
the home earn and are entitled to a portion of the
wealth her work permits her husband to make outside
the home.

SOURCE: *Southern Workman* 28, no. 8 (August 28, 1899):
295–98.

I shall not take time to discuss ideal situations on the speculative
side. There may be those who think that woman has no business
to enter the struggle for existence as a wage-earner: who think
that she should be as the lilies of the field, and should toil not
except to spin and array herself in gorgeous raiment to delight
the Solomons in all their glory. The fact remains that a large percentage of the productive labor of the world is done by women;
and also another fact, recently brought out through investiga-
tions under Atlanta University, that "of 1,137 colored families
650 or 57.17 per cent, are supported wholly or in part by female
heads." So that in comparison with white, female heads of families and others contributing to family support, there is, by a
house to house enumeration, quite a large excess on the part of
colored women. Sentiment aside then, if men will not or cannot

help the conditions which force women into the struggle for bread, we have a right to claim at least that she shall have fair play and all the rights of wage-earners in general. Or, as Herbert Spencer puts it, "Justice demands that women, if they are not artificially advantaged, must not at any rate be artificially disadvantaged."

I shall have to ask first, therefore, careful attention to a few of the dry but fundamental principles of economics, to which science our subject properly belongs. Wage-earning is the complement or proper corollary to the human element in the creation of wealth. Land, labor, and capital are the factors in the production of wealth. The term land includes all natural opportunities or forces: the term labor, all human exertion: and the term capital, all wealth used to produce more wealth. The whole produce is distributed in returns to these three factors. That part which goes to land owners as payment for the use of natural opportunities is called rent; the part which constitutes the reward of human exertion is wages; and the part which constitutes the return for the use of capital is called interest. The income of an individual may be made up from any one, two, or three of these sources according to the nature of his contribution to the product. But the laborer is always worthy of his hire. Should the owner of the land and the capital have the power and the greed to disregard the claims of the man who contributed the labor, and pocket the entire product, he is manifestly a robber whether the jailors can catch him or not.

In many thousands of homes the indoor partner of the firm, who undertakes to discharge the domestic and maternal duties within is just as truly a contributor to the product gained, as the outdoor manager who conducts the business and controls the wages. The woman in the home has a right to a definite share in the wealth she produces through relieving the man of certain indoor cares and enabling him to give thereby larger effort to his special trade or calling.

But, say you, the highest services can not be measured by dollars and cents. It is sordid to talk about paying mothers to be mothers, and giving a wage to wife to be wife! True, there is a class of services transcending all rewards; but because the wife of your bosom does not take you by the throat saying, "Pay me that thou owest!" should she be made to feel like a pensioner on your bounty every time she needs a pair of gloves? The family tie is a sacred union—the most sacred on earth. It is full of mystery and God-appointed sanctity. But does it not at the same time recognize the existence of some very plain and practical rights founded on simple justice as between man and man? Two human beings have voluntarily contracted to unite their forces for mutual help and advantage. The fact that they pledged themselves to the partnership *"Till death do us part"* but adds solemnity to the duties and obligations on either side. That the partnership carries divine sanction makes all the more inviolable these duties and obligations. That the interests involved are the most precious to the state,—the building of homes and the rearing of its citizens, insures the guardianship of society over those duties and obligations.

Of this partnership, the one member goes forth in the morning, whether to dig ditches or to add figures. The world knows him as the bread winner for the firm. The silent partner toils in the home, whether to cook the dinners or direct little feet and hands. Her heart is in the work. Faithfulness and devotion are hers. At the end of her monotonous round of day's doings she prepares to welcome in the eventide the battle-scarred veteran of the outer life. She opens the door with a smile. That smile is an important part of her program. She leads him to the dinner that she has prepared; he eats with a right good relish. For he likes to be fed. Yes, she eats of the dinner too, for she has her food and her shelter and her clothes whenever she asks for them. But it never occurs to this "boarder" that his wife *earns* a definite part of the wage that he draws: and that, though she has never figured it out and presented the bill, his account is greatly in arrears for simple wages. On the other hand every right implies a duty, and woman on entering this partnership should see to it that she contributes a full increment to the stock of value.

When we pass from the home and enter the dusty arena of the world, we find women wage-earners shoulder to shoulder with men in the struggle in almost all the avenues of labor, and here it may be well to repeat, this term labor with its correlate wage-earning, in the broad economic sense, includes all the capacities in man, intellectual as well as physical and moral, which have economic significance. Moral and intellectual qualities increase the productiveness of labor. "Temperance, trustworthiness, skill, alertness, perceptions, a comprehensive mental group—all these," says an eminent writer of political economy, "and other good qualities belonging to the soul of men are of chief importance in man. The economic value of intellectual training," he continues, "is generally not sufficiently appreciated. It has been ascertained that with no exceptions, the higher in any part of the United States the per capita expenditure for schools, the higher is the average of wages, and the larger, consequently, the production of wealth." This is a fact I would like specially to emphasize for those who intend training either girls or boys for self support as laborers or wealth producers. The broadest and fullest development of all powers, though it cost a greater outlay pays the best interest in actual returns of dollars and cents. It may be hard to do without your daughter's help while she studies a few more years in preparation for her labor. But the greater productiveness of that labor will more than repay your abstinence.

And now let us apply what has been said to the special class of women mentioned in our subject. The colored woman as wage-earner must bring to her labor all the capacities, native or acquired, which are of value in the industrial equation. She must really be worth her wage, and then claim it. "Nature has made up her mind," says Emerson, "that what cannot defend itself shall not be defended," and if women enter the struggle for independent existence they should claim all the rights of advantage to men in the same positions. The world has a cold substratum on fair play and abstract justice, but it is so encrusted over with prejudices and favoritisms that the one who waits for its waters to bubble up spontaneously will die of thirst. No one deplores more than I do the "woman with elbows." Aesthetically, she pains me. But every wage-earner, man or woman, owes it to the dignity of the labor he contributes, as well as to his own self-respect, to require the rights due to the quality of service he renders, and to the element of value he contributes to the world's wealth.

As colored wage-earners, we are today under a double disadvantage destined sorely to try our fitness to survive if it does not overwhelm us in the very start. In the midst of a civilization the most brilliant on earth, in the very heydey of its ostentation and self-satisfaction, we are "let go" to start from zero—nay—from a chasm infinitely below zero, to build up our fortunes. As a consequence, the social wealth of the Negro is two hundred and fifty years behind that of the white American. You will understand what I mean by social wealth when you reflect on the many things owned by individuals which are really consumed by the society in which these individuals move. Take for example a child born in 1865 of emancipated parents. Leaving out hereditary drawbacks and losses, that child is born into a society without books, without pictures, without comforts, without homes. If he goes to school he has no dictionaries or cyclopedias to help him understand his lessons. His environment does not even furnish the language in which his books are written. Now, suppose he struggles to accumulate, secures a home, puts in it a few comforts, some books and pictures, carpets and curtains, a piano perhaps, a dictionary certainly: or he goes further and acquires orchards and lawns, a country seat and carriages:—these things are not for himself alone. All who associate with him are made the richer by such acquisitions of his, and would be to that extent impoverished should he, on dying, take them away from the society in which he had moved by bequeathing them to a white man.

Colored society is today in available social wealth in the position of a company of pioneers, or where the white American was when he conned his solitary book by the light of a pine knot, and contended with bears and Indians for the possession of his potato patch and his one-story cabin. But the white American at that stage of his social accumulation worshipped God in a log hut and his wife went to meeting in her linsey-woolsey gown and brogan shoes. The black American however, comes upon the stage when his white forerunner is becoming blasé with luxury and surfeiting. He takes the white man's standard of living just where he finds it, rears and tries to support churches as magnificent, gives presents as costly, maintains in his weddings and funerals a style as lavish and idiotic. It is as if a little harpsichord with only middle and lower gamut were keyed up to a magnificent grand piano which stands with all its eight or more octaves already at concert pitch. A terrible strain results to all the strings of the little harpsichord. Its notes are but discordant shrieks and screams, ineffectual attempts to reach the easy ringing tones of the grand: and a miracle it is if you do not hear a snap, a pop—resulting in utter rule to what might have been a very sweet instrument, had it only been allowed to keep its range.

Economically considered, the colored people in this country are a society of wage-earners, but their standards of living and their judgments of one another are as if they were a race of capitalists.

Perhaps the severest trial of all for the colored wage-earner, is the impossible height to which the standard of life is raised among us. "Standard of life" in the economic sense "is the number and character of the wants which a man considers more important than marriage and family." Now I hold that not only does the strain from keying our life to the American pitch divert into the struggle to "keep up appearances" a large part of the wage which should go to physical comforts, such as sanitary housing and feeding and clothing our bodies, but worse yet, through this artificial and hopelessly high standard of living, many young men feel that they cannot support a wife and family; and so we lose the impetus toward a higher civilization that good homes would give us.

Our children make their first bow before the public in a dazzling shimmer of costly roses and laces; and however many pinches and sweat pounds it has cost the wage-earner to afford it, we somehow feel that our child ought to appear as fine as the rest, and so it goes. Wage-earners will have to learn to discriminate between wages and interest if we are ever to bequeath to posterity a capital out of our wages. Indeed, if we are ever to start homes and families at all that in the next generation our name be not blotted from the face of the earth, it will be necessary for us to have plain living and homely virtues in honest homes, built and banded by honest earnings. For it is here, as I conceive the matter, and not, as Prof. Kelly Miller suggests in his review of Hoffman, in the "surplus" of women among us, that lies the real explanation of unnatural conditions in our large cities. Certainly the removal of the tension that comes from our effort to reach an extravagant and unattainable standard of life, by a return to simplicity of manners and naturalness of living is a more facile remedy for increasing the number of honorable marriages and pure homes than by killing off the surplus women, the only remedy apparent as Prof. Miller depicts the situation.

Surely the greatest sufferer from the strain and stress attendant upon the economic conditions noted among our people is the colored woman, and she is the one who must meet and conquer the conditions. She must be too wary to be lured on with the chaff of flattery. When her fine appearance or that of her daughter is commented upon let that be a signal for retreat. Study economy. Utilize the margins. Preach and practice plain living and high thinking. Let the wife come in as a sensible helper in building up the fortunes of the family. Let her prove that she can contribute something more than good looks and milliners' bills to the stock in trade. If her husband starts a business, let her study how she can be useful to him in it. And, shoulder to shoulder, let them plant and till, and then gather and garner the fruits of their united industry. So, by her foresight and wisdom, her calm insight and tact, her thrift and frugality, her fertility of resource and largeness of hope and faith, the colored woman can prove that a prudent marriage is the very best investment that a working man can make.

# 119

# "The Answer"

### (no date)

Cooper ponders life's questions and focuses on looking within rather than seeking outside for answers.

SOURCE: Anna Julia Cooper Papers, box 23-4, folder 44, Moorland-Spingarn Research Center, Howard University.

> Naked and alone
> My Spirit wandered
> Dreading the Unknown
> Life's Riddle we pondered:
> The Answer no night-winds could tell.
>
> Deeps o' desolation,
> Mountains of vision,
> Multitudes, multitudes,
> In vales of Decision:
> The Universe guarded it well.
>
> From planet, from comet,
> From sun, moon, or pleiad,
> No vistas consummate
> Could light give or key add
> My questioning gloom to dispel.
>
> My weary soul panted—
> The Rest that remaineth,
> The Truth that we wanted,

The Pow'er that sustaineth,
That thru, in, over, all things that dwell—

God—is not afar!
The simple may know:
The Hereafter is here;
Eternity's now;
And myself am Heaven and Hell.

# "Aunt Charlotte"

*(ca. 1906–1910)*

Cooper evokes the African American spiritual "Swing Low, Sweet Chariot"[1] as a source of hope and comfort for enslaved mothers and their children. This hope and comfort stems from heavenly acceptance and salvation despite the horrors of slavery on earth.

SOURCE: Anna Julia Cooper Papers, box 23-4, folder 45, Moorland-Spingarn Research Center, Howard University.

Swing low; sweet Chariot, swing lower,
Way down to the darkest and poorest,
From the pearly white gate where thou soarest,
To the hole of the pit where I cower.
In bondage my mother conceived me,
In bondage my first breath I uttered,
In bondage my eight babes I suckled,
The bondwoman's prayer o'er them muttered.

II

Swing low; sweet Chariot, swing lower!
My God has not left me unfriended;
Gnarled hands, broken hearts are soon mended.
The toil and the ache now are o'er.
My robe shall be radiant with morning,
My feet shod to tread pathways golden,
My little ones once more adorning
Their fond mother's breast as of olden.

### III

Swing low, sweet Chariot, swing lightly,
You'll find me all ready and outside,
A glad heart alone by the roadside,—
The Promise conned daily and nightly.
I know He will come to stand by me;
His Hand firmly holding, I hie me,
On board! Welcome Chariot, swing gently,
Come quickly to carry me home!

# "A Message"

## (ca. 1906–1910)

Cooper expresses a longing for home and reconnection that she is certain will eventually be found. As the signature reveals, this poem was written after Cooper's dismissal from M Street when she went to work as a professor at the Lincoln Institute in Missouri. It speaks to her longing for someone or something and an eventual return to home.

SOURCE: Anna Julia Cooper Papers, box 23-4, folder 50, Moorland-Spingarn Research Center, Howard University.

> As the arc moves out to the circle,
> As pole cries aloud unto pole,
> As the brook rusheth on to its ocean,
> As soul leaps aloft to its Soul
>
> So I know in the infinite spaces,
> In the infinite aeons of time,
> Somewhere my broken life traces
> The curve of its orbit sublime;
>
> Somewhere to the longing and yearning
> And hunger, fruition shall come.

Somewhere I know I shall find thee,
And my heart nestle sweetly at home.

Anna Julia Cooper
Lincoln Institute
Jefferson City, MO

# 122

# "Resurrexit, Resurgam"

### *(April 1, 1956)*

Printed on a card with a bouquet of white lilies on the cover, Cooper's poem discusses the resurrection of Jesus Christ via the imagery of a growing lily released from the earth.

SOURCE: Anna Julia Cooper Papers, box 23-4, folder 51, Moorland-Spingarn Research Center, Howard University.

> OUT of the clod
> Where earthy fetters, reeking,
> Its rootlets claim;
> Upward to God,
> Effulgent radiance seeking,
> The lily came.
>
> DEEP in the tomb,
> Rock-ribbed and sealed in blindness,
> My neighbor lies;
> Out of the gloom
> Calls Life's eternal kindness,
> All souls, arise!

SAVIOR of men!
Thy risen Pow'r, controlling,
We would obey;
Waking,—and then,
From graves unnumbered rolling
The stone away.

ANNA J. COOPER

# 123

# "Simon of Cyrene"

## *(ca. 1906–1910)*

In this three-part poem, Cooper recounts the story of Simon of Cyrene,[1] who carried Jesus Christ's cross prior to his crucifixion. Cooper emphasizes Simon's Blackness and suggests that the relationship between Black people and Christ is that of the "Burden and the Bearer."

SOURCE: Anna Julia Cooper Papers, box 23-4, folder 53, Moorland-Spingarn Research Center, Howard University.

> The human back was weary,
> The path was sharp and steep,
> A threefold load of sorrow,
> His cross of anguish deep:
> A cross of Love—rejected;—
> His own received Him not—
> "How oft would I have gathered
> Your brood of hapless lot,
> E'en as a hen her chickens,
> To save—but ye would not."
> A travail cross of service,
> The Heart that aches to give
> All of its soughing pulses
> That brother-man may live.
> And then the thorny wood-cross,
> The nails of toilsome strife
> With earth's uncouth conditions
> To give the lowly life.

And so the Cross was heavy,
Its threefold weight dragged hard;
The feet were torn and bleeding
That trod Judea's sward.

## II

Beside the road to Calvary
A swarthy figure stood
Simon of Cyrene,
Alone amid the crowd:
His brawny arms knew burdens;
His big broad shoulders, bent,
To many a loving service
A willing lift had lent.
The Man of Sorrows halted;
The man of Service saw
The look of love exalted
Triumphant over law
Of race or class proscription,
Of barriers high and low;
O'er narrowness of vision
That cannot see or know
A brother in the stranger;
O'er drowsy ears that fail
To hear the needy calling,—
The slow of heart that quail
At union in "One Father"
Or kinship in "one blood."

## III

Through all the petty nothings
That keep mankind apart
These two a look all-seeing
Shot forth from heart to heart.
Two spirits met each other
At Nature's tidal flood—
The one, a man of no caste,

The One, the Son of God!
A look, a thrill, a heartthrob
Of comprehension clear
To find in one communion
God's children far and near.
The Negro's willing shoulder
Beneath the Cross was thrust.
The Burden and the Bearer
No more shall be accurst.
"We two went up together!
And they who love the Lord
Some day shall call me brother
In mem'ry of His word."

ANNA J. COOPER
Lincoln Institute
Jefferson City, MO

# 124

# "Sterling Calhoun"

## *(ca. 1935)*

Cooper eulogizes the bravery of Sterling Calhoun,[1] a Black man who sought to rescue two drowning children heedless of their race. Underlying this poem, Cooper levels the critique that a white man might not have done the same for Black children. Cooper includes a brief note citing the story about the incident that presumably ran in *The Washington Post*.

SOURCE: Anna Julia Cooper Papers, box 23-4, folder 54, Moorland-Spingarn Research Center, Howard University.

Item: "A colored man plunged in the river to save two drowning children. He was a good swimmer, had rescued the girl & with one hand was holding her above the water when the struggling boy clamped his arms & drew him down. The three went under," An eye witness.

> Who cares what was his color!
> What matters what was theirs,
> A cry from helpless innocence
> Stirs hidden human fires.
> He sees and heeds distress signs,
> He recks not self nor cost.
> One desperate throw—he makes it!
> And who shall say he lost.
> God give us back our pity
> Smash frankensteins of pride

Set once more in our midst a Child
The least of these, our guide.

ANNA J. COOPER
201 T. St. N.W.
Washington, D.C.

# 125

## "They Also"

### *(no date)*

In this poem, Cooper reflects upon a subject who, though impoverished, is determined to make some contribution to society even as their efforts are not appreciated or recognized.

SOURCE: Anna Julia Cooper Papers, box 23-4, folder 55, Moorland-Spingarn Research Center, Howard University.

I wanted just to be useful,—
I could not express it in song,
But my heart yearned to lift in life's struggle
Some need of humanity's throng.

I had not the gold nor the silver,
Nor houses nor lands in my store;
E'en the poorest thought scorn of my pittance
And flung it unglad at my door.

So I toiled along earning my ration,
I would not repine for Earth's pelf,—
When lo, from afar, the faint whisper:
"You have lifted by being Yourself!"

# "A Bench Beside the Road"

## (1923)

Cooper recounts an unassuming bench beside the road as the site in which a singer, resting, produces divinely inspired music that elicits awe in his listeners, before moving on, leaving as his name "a friend of them that listen in." There are two versions of this poem in the Anna Julia Cooper Papers at the Moorland-Spingarn Research Center, entitled "A Bench Beside the Road 1 Poem" and "A Bench Beside the Road 2 Poem." Each poem appears to be a draft in the process of being edited by Cooper, but the former poem is more complete and organized than the latter. The version included here is "A Bench Beside the Road 1 Poem."

SOURCE: Anna Julia Cooper Papers, box 23-4, folder 46, Moorland-Spingarn Research Center, Howard University.

To Mary Europe[1] & Her Friends
Jan 1923
From any old convalescent at Dunbar

### A BENCH BESIDE THE ROAD.

No "stepping stones" lured this way.
Far were the big "halls" wide flung
   for talent proved & proving:
Here only a bench by the side of the road
Unknown, unpublished, unappraised, Chance were—

Till one hot day, a singer rested there;
Merely to mop his brow & roll a smoke, His cycle
    atilt against a tree—for far he came.
Just as a bird stays but a moment on jutting twig
Pouring forth his soul in minstrelsy for any
    or all or none as fate decrees of the passing moment.
So the singer straight from the heart of things
Seeing clear into God's eternal truth,
Sang the peace, the love, the harmony of Life:
And it seemed to those so privileged to listen in,
That the grand swell of the Universe
Shot thro' the melody of that song
And that Heaven's deepest depths,
Revealed its inmost secret springs
From that plain bench beside the road.
"Who—Who can it be? Do give your name!" We cried.
He dropt a scribbled sheet & was gone

Breathless we read:
    A friend of them that listen in.
    That was all!

# "Black Madonna"

## (no date)

Cooper celebrates the Black mother as the Black Madonna, who exhibits love, faith, and endurance despite the "hurts & back sets / of the proud pushing world." The Black Madonna figures prominently in Cooper's work, and her archive includes a collection of Black Madonna images, some of which were sent to her by Felix Klein. In reclaiming and presenting the Black woman as the sacred mother figure, Cooper counters stereotypes about Black women as sexually promiscuous or immoral by emphasizing their faith and fortitude despite their oppression and the oppression of their children.

SOURCE: Anna Julia Cooper Papers, box 23-4, folder 47, Moorland-Spingarn Research Center, Howard University.

THE BLACK MADONNA OF CHARTRES, FRANCE[1]

> I love the wonderful black Mother!
> Thro all Nature's store there's no other
> Sheds such beams of tenderness
> from the sad patient eyes,
> With the soft arms that pillow
> young life's ecstasies.
> And the wonderful heart of that Mother!
> The loving sad heart of that Mother!
> Could God grant us no other
> 'Twere proof enough, surely

His wisdom & justice, All-loving.
And the tender sweet tones of her crooning
To Heavenly music attuning
All the worries & frets
The hurts & back sets
Of the proud pushing world.
With her simple "God knows"
And her "Honey, He cares!"
Her faith, hope & love, rock buttressed
More steadfast an anchor
for storm tossed in the drift
More heartening a beacon
for fog bound and no rift
Than cathedrals & synods & masses.

                               ANNA J. COOPER

# Racial Philosophy Response to Occupational History Survey

*(1930)*

In this response to the 1930s survey of "Negro college graduates" led by sociologist and president of Fisk University Charles S. Johnson (1893–1956), Cooper provides information about her educational background, family history, and career. In her handwritten responses, Cooper's writing loops around the typed text of the questions and continues into the margins and onto the back of the pages. In answering these questions, Cooper reflects upon her own educational experiences and expresses her viewpoints on Black people's education and politics, and the activism of Black women. Her lengthy reply to question number sixty-five in the survey, "Have you a 'racial philosophy' that can be briefly stated?" is reprinted here.

SOURCE: Anna Julia Cooper Papers, box 23-4, folder 1, Moorland-Spingarn Research Center, Howard University.

My "racial philosophy" is not far removed from my general philosophy of life: that the greatest happiness comes from altruistic service and this is in reach of all of whatever race and condition. The "Service" here meant is not a pious idea of being used; any sort of exploitation whether active or passive is to my mind hateful. Nor is the "Happiness" a mere bit of Pollyanna stuff. I am as sensitive to handicaps as those who are always whining about them; and the whips and stings of prejudice, whether of color or sex, find me neither too calloused to suffer, nor too ignorant to know what is due me. Our own men as a group have not inherited traditions of chivalry (one sided as it may be among white men) and we women are generally left to do our race battling alone except for empty compliments now and then. Even so, one may make the mistake of looking at race handicaps through the wrong end of the telescope and imagining that oppression goes only with color. When I encounter brutality I need not always charge it to my race. It may be—and generally is—chargeable to the imperfections in the civilization environing me for which as a teacher and trained thinker I take my share of responsibility.

The extent, then, of the optimism in my philosophy is that (Statisticians and Social Science Research compilers to the contrary notwithstanding) the solutions of our problem will be individual and not *en masse*; and the habit of generalization and deductive logic has done its worst.

For, after all, Social Justice, the desired goal, is not to be reached through any panacea by mass production—whether Du Bois's preachment of the ballot box and intermarriage or Kelly Miller's one time suggestion of self effacement, or even Booker Washington's proposal of the solid hand and separate fingers. For human selfishness will always arise as the domineering *thumb* to over ride and keep down every finger weak enough to give up the struggle. The ballot operates just so far as dominant forces agree to respect it. Which again is reasoning in a circle to insure justice by having men become just, and the spectacle of gangster dominance among ballot holding Americans invites little hope for solution when the element of race is added to the problem. As I see it then, the patient persistence of the individual, working as Browning has it, "mouth wise and pen-wise" in whatever station and with whatever talent God has given, in truth and loyalty to serve the whole, will come as near as any other to proving worth while.

To me Life has meant a big opportunity and I am thankful

that my work has always been the sort that beckoned me on, leaving no room for *blasé* philosophizing and rebellion's resentment and with just enough opposition to give zest to the struggle, just enough hope of scoring somewhere among the winners to keep my head "unbowed though bloody."

# Acknowledgments

*The Portable Anna Julia Cooper* represents a collective effort that builds on over a century of work by bibliographers, biographers, librarians, archivists, educators, and scholars who have kept Cooper's life and writings present in the historical record as they sought to document and preserve her brilliant and timeless contributions to our country's intellectual history and literary traditions. From Gertrude E. H. Bustill Mossell, Monroe Majors, Dorothy B. Porter, Louise Hutchinson, Charles Lemert, and Esme Bhan, to Beverly Guy-Sheftall, Mary Helen Washington, Kathryn Sophia Belle, and Vivian May, this work would not be possible without their tireless efforts, groundbreaking research, and field-defining scholarship.

I am grateful for the team, Katie Warczak, Patrick Allen, Sabrina Evans, and Kevin Cedeño-Pacheco, who worked alongside me on this edition. They contributed their intellectual insights, expert research skills, and editorial and content-area knowledge in preparing headnotes, endnotes, suggestions for further reading, and the chronology, making this a truly collaborative scholarly endeavor. Many thanks go to Bill Brockman and Russ Hall at Penn State University Libraries, Curtis Small at University of Delaware Library, Kelly Woton and John Gartrell at Rubenstein Library at Duke University, Ken Grossi at Oberlin College Archives, and to David Graham Du Bois Trust and the UMass Amherst Special Collections and University Archives for preserving Cooper's papers and for assistance in tracking down documents, publications, and permissions.

A very special thank-you to Joellen ElBashir, Lopez Matthews, Makini Johnson, and Adrena Ifill and to the Moorland-Spingarn Research Center (MSRC) at Howard University for their work documenting, maintaining, processing, and digitizing Cooper's papers and for the steadfast commitment of the MSRC across the generations and decades to preserving the legacy of people of African descent for current and future generations. Many thanks also go to P. Gabrielle Foreman, Kimberly Blockett, Joycelyn Moody, Niki von Lockette, Lori Frances, and Julie Reed, who provided the encouragement, support, and intellectual community to complete this project. I also want to recognize and thank Jim Casey, Denise Burgher, Courtney Murray, D'Angelo Bridges, Eunice Toh, Justin Smith, Sabrina Evans, Wendyliz Martinez, Chris Willoughby, Heather Froelich, Racine Amos, Lauren Cooper, Brandi Locke, Anna Lacy, Kevin Winstead, Elena M'Bouroukounda, and Julia Grummitt and the entire Douglass Day–Transcribe Cooper team, the Zooniverse project, and the Center for Humanities and Information, as well as our community partners, Johncie Lancaster and Alpha Kappa Alpha, Inc. and Shelina Warren of Dunbar High School for helping to expand access to Cooper's work. Jim Casey and Justin Smith also provided transcriptions of selected writings during the preparation of this edition.

I am grateful to Henry Louis Gates, Jr. for believing in this project and encouraging me to take it forward, and to the Hutchins Center for African and African American Research at Harvard University for providing the intellectual community and support it takes to initiate a new project and launch the work. Many thanks to Elda Rotor for supporting this project, to Elizabeth Vogt for her editorial acumen and generosity in guiding this edition through to production, and to Megan Gerrity for her meticulous and thorough editing. It was a gift and a joy to work with the editorial staff for Penguin Classics every step of the way. I want to thank my partner, TJ, and daughter, Amara Julia, for waiting, reading, listening, and laughing together as this edition came to fruition. And finally, I want to give highest praise to Anna Julia Cooper for lighting the way and for sharing her words and work with us that we might "learn wisdom from experience."

# Notes

## A NOTE ON THE TEXT

1. Frances Keller published a new edition of her translation of Cooper's dissertation under the title *Slavery and the French and Haitian Revolutionists*, though Vivian May offers an alternative translation, used here, as more faithful to Cooper's original title. See Vivian M. May, *Anna Julia Cooper, Visionary Black Feminist: A Critical Introduction* (New York: Routledge, 2007), 107.

## A VOICE FROM THE SOUTH, BY A BLACK WOMAN OF THE SOUTH

1. This excerpt is taken from James Whitcomb Riley's "A Worn-Out Pencil" (1879).

## Our Raison D'être

1. Tawawa Chimney Corner was a historical house in Wilberforce, Ohio, that served as the home of two bishops in the African Methodist Episcopal (AME) Church who were also early civil rights leaders, Bishop Benjamin William Arnett and Reverdy Cassius Ransom.

## Soprano Obligato

1. Mary Ann Evans (1819–1880), English novelist, poet, and journalist, was one of the leading writers of the Victorian era and was known by her pen name, George Eliot.

## Womanhood: A Vital Element in the Regeneration and Progress of a Race

1. Ralph Waldo Emerson (1803–1882), New England essayist, poet, and philosopher known for leading the American Transcendentalist movement of the mid-nineteenth century.

2. François Pierre Guillaume Guizot (1787–1874), French historian and politician who was prominent before the revolution of 1848.

3. Henry Bidleman Bascom (1796–1850), bishop of the Methodist Episcopal Church and editor of *Southern Methodist Quarterly Review* from 1846 to 1850. He also published sermons and lectures and a volume on Methodism and slavery.

4. Cooper quotes Ecclesiastes 2:12. The full passage reads: "And I turned myself to behold wisdom, and madness, and folly: for what can the man do that cometh after the king? even that which hath been already done." She uses this as a rhetorical device for illustrating the givenness of her assertion regarding the influence of women on social progress and the degree to which it has already been stated and proven by others—in this case, she is referencing Alexander Crummell's speech "The Black Woman of the South," in which he argues that slavery was worse for Black women due to the unique violence and isolation that they experienced. She may also be stating this somewhat sarcastically, in suggesting that she is in the position of having to claim authority to speak about the Black woman, because she follows Crummell and others who have already claimed authority to speak about the Black woman on her behalf.

5. Martin Delany (1812–1885), physician, soldier, author, and editor, is known as one of the progenitors of Pan-Africanism and as a proponent of the idea that free Black people in the United States might migrate to Africa as a possible solution to slavery and the race problem.

6. Cooper quotes herself as a source and in this way underscores the value of her own position and authority as well as of the knowledge and experience of people who have repeatedly been excluded from traditional sites of learning, inquiry, and knowledge production. She likewise critically quotes Delany's formulation and inscribes herself into the text as "the BLACK WOMAN" in a way that is similar to the title and subtitle of the text *A Voice from the South, by a Black Woman of the South* to express the bottom-up privileging of the race's most vulnerable individuals in assessing the degree and quality of social progress. In doing so, she not only gestures to radical revisions that must be made to the ordinary male-centered ways that people assess social change, but also advances for her own inclusion in public discourse and thinking about the conditions for liberatory social politics. In effect, she resists her own erasure in conversations about racial progress and reform at the turn of the twentieth century.

7. Here Cooper refers to different denominations of what is colloquially referred to as "the Black church." She notes the success that the three major denominations—the African Methodist Episcopal (AME) church, the Baptists, and the Congregationalists—have had in growing parishioners in the South, and notes that the Protestant Episcopal Church, whose "colored clergy" she is addressing, have had much less success because they are not attending to the everyday needs of the larger Black community or supporting women in joining them in their missionary efforts.

## The Higher Education of Women

1. Cooper describes with sarcastic wit the kinds of irrational patriarchal fears that are captured in Marechal's text. In particular she pokes fun at the idea that with women's education will come a cessation of all their work in the domestic setting.

2. Cooper uses humor and sarcasm in calling the "experiment" to allow women to attend college "dangerous."

3. Mary Livermore (1820–1905) was a Calvinist suffragist, abolitionist, journalist, and editor of the suffragist newspaper *The Agitator*. Here and in "What Are We Worth?" Cooper notes the racist and Anglocentric attitudes and judgments that Livermore makes of nonwhite races and other groups—claiming that what Anglo-Saxons do not like about East Asian immigrants and Black people is their purported "weakness," rather than their race and racial features specifically. In both cases, Cooper rejects Livermore's opinions as illegitimate; however, in the second instance, Cooper focuses on the emotional component of racial judgments and the difficulty of altering habituated ways of feeling. Rather than excusing these attitudes and habits, however, Cooper's comments seem directed at accurately depicting the depth and difficulty of the problem of habituated racism and racial animus.

4. Edward Bellamy (1850–1898), journalist, activist, and author known primarily for writing the utopian novel *Looking Backward*.

5. Sappho (610–580 BCE), Greek lyric poet. Aspasia (ca. 470–ca. 401 BCE), written about in some accounts as the mistress or "de facto wife" of Pericles of Athens for about twenty years, from ca. 450 to his death in 429 BCE.

6. Morata (1526/7–1555) was a Ferrarese writer of Latin and Greek letters, dialogues, and poems.

7. Jane Eleanor Datcher was the first Black woman to obtain an advanced degree (BS, botany) from Cornell University in 1890.

8. Cooper relates her own experiences and struggles protesting for equal rights in education. Specifically, she recounts her experience to implore her readers and listeners to support Black girls' and women's education by making more scholarships and forms of material support available to them.

### Has America a Race Problem; If So, How Can It Best Be Solved?

1. The idea or notion of the "race problem"—specifically, the US's race problem—was often cited and discussed in Cooper's time. In mainstream white political discourse, it signified the sum of social-political conflicts and tensions between white people and newly emancipated Black people—particularly in the South. In the speeches and writings of African American abolitionists, it signifies the problem of white racial terror and lawlessness directed toward Black people.
2. Alexander Crummell (1819–1898), African American Episcopal minister, abolition philosopher, and African nationalist, known for his antislavery activism and for being one of the progenitors of Pan-Africanism.

### One Phase of American Literature

1. William Dean Howells (1837–1920), author, editor, and critic best remembered for his novel *The Rise of Silas Lapham*.
2. Albion Winegar Tourgée (1838–1905), Civil War Union soldier, lawyer for Homer Plessy in the Plessy v. Ferguson (1896) case, and author known for his activism in and literary depictions of the South during Reconstruction.
3. George Washington Cable (1844–1925), Civil War Confederate soldier, writer, and critic known for his early fictions depicting Louisiana Creoles and for his essays on civil rights, such as *The Silent South* (1885) and *The Negro Question* (1890).
4. Henry Woodfin Grady (1850–1889), journalist, orator, and co-owner of the Atlanta Constitution after the Civil War.
5. Bishop Benjamin William Arnett (1838–1906), seventeenth bishop of the African Methodist Episcopal Church, to whom Cooper inscribed *A Voice from the South*.
6. Edward Wilmot Blyden (1832–1912), West Indian scholar, diplomat, journalist, and educator who lived most of his life in Liberia and is widely known as one of the progenitors of Pan-Africanism.

7. William Sanders Scarborough (1852–1926), educator known for having been the first African American member of the Modern Language Association.

8. Joseph C. Price (1854–1893), clergyman for the AME Zion Church and educator who established Livingstone College and became its first president in 1882.

9. Timothy Thomas Fortune (1856–1928), journalist, editor, and co-founder of the New York *Globe*.

10. Maurice Thompson (1844–1901) was a writer, civil engineer, and naturalist.

11. Albery Allson Whitman (1851–1901), African American poet, orator, and clergyman who published seven collections and epic-length works of poetry that were widely read and circulated among African American readerships of his time. The works mentioned here, *Twasinta's Seminoles; or, Rape of Florida* and *Not a Man, and Yet a Man*, were published in 1885 and 1877 respectively.

12. Frances Ellen Watkins Harper (1825–1911), African American abolitionist, suffragist, poet, and educator.

## What Are We Worth?

1. Henry Ward Beecher (1813–1887), Congregationalist preacher who advocated temperance and denounced slavery. Brother of abolitionist and author Harriet Beecher Stowe (1811–1896).

2. A philippic is a fiery, bitter, or otherwise impassioned speech of denunciation—originating speeches given by Demosthenes against Philip II of Macedon. The *Philippics* is a series of fourteen speeches given by Cicero between 44 and 43 BCE, marking his reentry into politics after the assassination of Julius Caesar.

3. Selina Shirley Hastings, Countess of Huntingdon (1707–1791), an important figure in English and US Methodism who provided the funding for sixty-four chapels and the first Methodist theological college, Trevecca College (later Cheshunt College, now part of Westminster College). She was also a patroness to African American author and poet Phillis Wheatley (1753–1784).

4. Mary Edmonia Lewis, "Wildfire" (ca. 1843–1907), was an African American and indigenous sculptor of Haitian and possibly Mississauga or Ojibwa descent. The sculpture Cooper references here might be *Madonna Holding the Christ Child*, 1869.

5. The Louisiana Native Guards were some of the first all-Black regiments to fight in the Union Army during the American Civil War.

The first regiment was composed of and led by free men of color, some of whose members had served in the previous Confederate Native Guard regiment. The second regiment was purged of its Black leading officers while the first and third regiments kept their Black commanding officers.

6. Tuskegee, Alabama, is where Booker T. Washington founded and became the first president of the Tuskegee Normal and Industrial Institute (now Tuskegee University).

7. Booker T. Washington (1856–1915), African American author, orator, and political adviser who founded the Tuskegee Institute, and is famous for his "accommodationist" view of racial progress, espoused most famously in his Atlanta Compromise in 1895.

## The Gain from a Belief

1. Positivism is a philosophical and political movement inaugurated by Auguste Comte in the second half of the nineteenth century. It holds that every rationally justifiable assertion can be scientifically verified or is capable of logical or mathematical proof, and therefore rejects metaphysics and theism.

2. Herbert Spencer (1820–1903) was an English philosopher who coined the expression "survival of the fittest" and is widely regarded as a leading advocate of social Darwinism.

3. Cooper's reference here appears to be to the importance that the North Star bore for people who escaped slavery in the South and sought safe passage north.

## FROM SERVITUDE TO SERVICE: A PAGEANT

1. The "landing at Jamestown" refers to the first documented arrival of enslaved Africans in the British colonies in 1619.

2. Enslaved Africans and their descendants often sang "sorrow songs" to communicate the despair they felt due to their enslavement, and often reflected the belief that their condition mirrored the biblical story of Moses and enslaved Hebrews. The sorrow songs were later used as a form of communication, informing enslaved people of instructions on how to run away and access the Underground Railroad.

3. This episode outlines critical events and figures prior to and during the Civil War (1861–1865).

4. Cooper used *F. F. V.* as an abbreviation for *First Families of Virginia* to recognize the foundational places of Black families in the founding of the United States.

## CHRIST'S CHURCH: A TWENTIETH-CENTURY PARABLE

1. The Good Samaritan references a biblical parable in which, in seeing a traveler injured on a road, many pass by and only the Good Samaritan stops and helps.
2. This line comes from Matthew 25:43 (NIV) in the Bible and references Judgment Day, in which Jesus turns to those who did not help the less fortunate and condemns them to eternal punishment.

## "THE ETHICS OF THE NEGRO QUESTION"

1. The Quakers, or the Society of Friends, are a social justice–oriented religious group that historically took anti-slavery stances as well as often offered protection and aid to enslaved and free Blacks.
2. The Freedman's Saving Bank, also known as the Freedman's Savings and Trust Company, was created by the US government to assist in the economic development of emancipated African Americans after the Civil War, from 1865 to 1874. Due to the fraud and financial misconduct of its white board and management, the bank accrued significant debt and failed in 1874.
3. The Wilmington massacre, also known as the Wilmington insurrection of 1898, began in response to the election of Black officials in Wilmington, North Carolina. A mob of white supremacists sought to overthrow the local government and in the process violently attacked the local African American population and destroyed their businesses. This massacre was a catalyst for the overturning of many Reconstruction gains for African Americans in the South.
4. The "usual crime" that African American men were lynched for was raping white women. Using evidence from prominent white newspapers, Ida B. Wells-Barnett's anti-lynching campaign proved that the "usual crime" African American men were lynched for was in fact their aims for economic independence.
5. Jim Crow cars were the segregated railway cars that African Americans were forced to travel in and that were in no way equal to the cars assigned to whites. Oftentimes, if the train was overcrowded, African Americans would have to ride in the luggage car.

6. An excerpt from a poem entitled "Anti-Apis" by James Russell Lowell (1819–1891), an American Romantic poet and abolitionist.

## "EDUCATIONAL PROGRAMS"

1. During the Age of Revolution (1789–1848), the Lazzaroni, or Lazzari, were the poorest class in Naples, Italy.
2. Fisk University, Atlanta University, Hampton Institute, and Tuskegee Institute were all founded to help educate African Americans in the aftermath of the Civil War. While Fisk and Atlanta promoted more of a classical and liberal arts education, Hampton and Tuskegee focused predominantly on vocational and industrial training.
3. These lines are Bible verses from Acts 22:26–28 (KJV) and describes Paul's defense of his citizenship.

## "THE NEGRO'S DIALECT"

1. Paul Robeson (1898–1976) was an African American athlete, singer, and actor who was particularly active in the Civil Rights and social justice movements. Notably, he was the first Black actor to play Othello in America.
2. *Othello* is a Shakespearean play that centers on the tragic story of a Moor general in the Venetian army.
3. Amos and Andy were two characters from the *Amos 'n' Andy* show, a popular radio and television sitcom set in Harlem, New York City, which was often critiqued by the African American community for its racist stereotyping and lower-class characterizations. It featured the white actors Freeman Gosden and Charles Correll playing the titular Black characters, Amos and Andy, respectively.

## "LOSS OF SPEECH THROUGH ISOLATION"

1. In using the conventions of stage drama in the second half of the sketch, Cooper may have been drawing on the conventions of early twentieth-century anti-lynching drama, with which she was certainly familiar. As Koritha Mitchell in *Living with Lynching* asserts, anti-lynching dramas were characterized not by the spectacle of lynching, which was often conspicuously missing, but by the absences of the father or "head" of household and the focus on the consequences resulting from that absence. See Mitchell, *Living*

*with Lynching: African American Lynching Plays, Performance, and Citizenship, 1890–1930* (Champaign: University of Illinois Press, 2012).

2. Cooper uses the phrase "head bloody but unbowed" again in, her statement on racial philosophy to describe her own work in, and lifelong commitment to, education. The line is quoted from *Inviticus*, written by William Ernest Henley in 1875 and published in 1885.

## "COLLEGE EXTENSION FOR WORKING PEOPLE"

1. In this line, Cooper is referring to Howard University, founded in 1867 by General Oliver Otis Howard, who was also the commissioner of the Freedmen's Bureau at the time.

## *THE SOCIAL SETTLEMENT: WHAT IT IS, AND WHAT IT DOES*

1. Cooper is referring to "Abou Ben Adhem," a poem by English romantic poet and activist Leigh Hunt (1784–1859) in which Abou represents love for one's fellows.

## "THE TIE THAT USED TO BIND"

1. Cooper's brother Andrew J. Haywood (1848–1918) married Jane Henderson of Cumberland County, North Carolina, in 1867 and later served in the Spanish-American War (1898) (Hutchinson 26). Jane and Andrew would have been married fifty-one years at the time of his death, making this a likely referent for Cooper's story. Interestingly, Cooper's descendant, Urbane Francis Bass III, relates a similar story explaining that Cooper took care of his grandmother, Cooper's great aunt Maude Bass, after Ms. Bass's husband, Dr. Urbane Francis Bass, was killed on October 7, 1918, in France while serving in World War I. He notes that it took two years and eight months to return Dr. Bass's body, and after the burial, Ms. Bass went to stay with Cooper in Washington, DC, where Cooper helped care for her as she dealt with her traumatic loss (Personal interview, Urbane Francis Bass III, December 5, 2021). Cooper may have combined the shared similarities from these two distinct events to create a composite of a military widow struggling to cope with the repercussions of war and the loss of her husband.

### CHRISTMAS BELLS: A ONE-ACT
### PLAY FOR CHILDREN

1. "Christmas Anno Domini" translates to "Christmas in the year of our Lord," thus, when Christ was born.

### "DR. COOPER DOESN'T LIKE
### THE HUGHES POEM"

1. Hughes's poem as it appeared in Cooper's 1931–1940 scrapbook, evidently clipped from the *Washington Tribune*'s reprinting:

#### TO MIDNIGHT NAN AT LEROY'S

Strut and wiggle
Shameless gal
Wouldn't no good fellow
Be your pal.
Hear dat music—
Jungle night.
Hear dat music
And the moon was white.
Sing your Blues song,
Pretty baby.
You want lovin'
And you don't mean maybe.
Strut and wiggle,
Shameless Nan.
Wouldn't no good fellow
Be your man.

—Langston Hughes

The omitted fourth stanza reads: Jungle lover. . . . / Night black boy. . . . / Two against the moon / And the moon was joy.

### "ANOTHER APOSTLE OF RACE INTEGRITY"

1. Arthur "Alain" LeRoy Locke (1885–1954) was an African American philosopher and literary critic, and one of the progenitors of

the New Negro (Harlem) Renaissance known for publishing *The New Negro* (1925), an anthology of African American art, poetry, and literature.

2. Alexander Harvey Shannon was a chaplain at Mississippi State Penitentiary and a member of the American Anthropological Association.

3. In *The Negro in Washington: A Study in Race Amalgamation* (New York: Walter Neale, 1930), Shannon argues in favor of colonization and the creation of Black-only states as a possible solution to the "race problem" in the US.

## "SHANNON'S BOOK CONTINUED"

1. Kelly Miller (1863–1939), was an African American educator, civil rights leader, and mathematician. He was a teacher and administrator at Howard University and one of the founding members of the American Negro Academy.

## "ANNA J. COOPER MAKES COMMENT ON THE LINDBERGH KIDNAPPING AFFAIR"

1. Cooper here refers to the prominent trial and kidnapping case of Charles and Anne Morrow Lindbergh's twenty-month-old baby. The child was abducted on March 1, 1932, and discovered dead on May 12, 1932. Bruno Richard Hauptmann was convicted of first-degree murder and sentenced to death. It was considered one of the "trials of the century" by legal scholars and led Congress to pass the Federal Kidnapping Act, making it a federal offense to transport a kidnapping victim across state lines. The newspaper title, though not Cooper's article, incorrectly dropped the "h" from Lindberg. It has been corrected throughout.

## " 'A PITIFUL MOUTH' "

1. The word *tshmtn* is in the original. Reference unclear.

## "THE PROBLEM OF THE CITY CHILD"

1. *The Souls of Black Folk* (1903) by W. E. B. Du Bois is a seminal work of African American literature that uses a combination of essays and sketches to explore Du Bois's assertion that "the problem of the Twentieth Century is the problem of the color-line."

## " 'LET THE SCOTTSBORO BOYS FORGET,'
## WOMAN TELLS BILL ROBINSON"

1. Bill "Bojangles" Robinson (1878–1949), born Luther Robinson, was a famous African American tap dancer known for not only his dancing, but his philanthropy. On August 7, 1935, *The Pittsburgh Courier* reported that Robinson had offered to pay three years' tuition at a training school for Arthur Leroy "Roy" Wright, the youngest of the "Scottsboro Boys." This group of nine African American youths was falsely arrested and imprisoned for the rape of two white women in 1931. Robinson followed through with his offer and paid for Wright's education at a vocational school.

2. Samuel Leibowitz (1893–1978) was a New York attorney who defended the Scottsboro Boys pro bono during their trials in the 1930s. He also argued the related *Norris v. Alabama* (1935) case before the Supreme Court. In this case, the Supreme Court overturned one of the Scottsboro Boys' convictions on the grounds that a lack of Black jury members was unconstitutional when an African American was on trial.

## "BELLE SADGWAR"

1. Belle Manonicee Sadgwar (1912–1930) was a student of Cooper's who graduated from Dunbar High School in 1928.

## "WRITER FLAYS 'NATIVE SON';
## WOULD LIKE STORY ON VICTOR
## HUGO THEME"

1. Richard Wright (1908–1960) was an African American author, whose 1940 novel, *Native Son*, tells the story of twenty-year-old Bigger Thomas, whose life is beset by poverty and crime. The grim narrative serves as an indictment of the systemic racism in American society.

## "THE WILLKIE SMEAR"

1. Wendell Willkie (1892–1944) was an American lawyer and politician who was the Republican presidential nominee in 1940.

## "FREEDOM OF THE PRESS AND
## NEGRO PUBLIC OPINION"

1. In the *Harper's Weekly* issue of June 27, 1896, American author and literary critic William Dean Howells praised the dialect poems of African American poet Paul Laurence Dunbar (1872–1906) in his *Majors and Minors* (1895), which helped launch Dunbar's mainstream career.

## ANNA J. COOPER TO
## W. E. B. DU BOIS, SEPTEMBER 4, 1923

1. As quoted in Hutchinson, *Anna Julia Cooper*, 113.
2. As quoted in David Levering Lewis, *W. E. B. Du Bois: Biography of a Race, 1868-1919* (New York: Henry Holt, 1993), 251.
3. See Hutchinson, *Anna Julia Cooper*, 113 and Lewis, *W. E. B. Du Bois*, 249–51.

## ANNA J. COOPER TO W. E. B. DU BOIS,
## SEPTEMBER 10, 1924

1. Jean-Philippe Garran de Coulon (1748–1816) was a French lawyer and politician who was interested in Haiti and its influence on the French abolitionist movement during the French Revolution. In 1797, he wrote *Rapport sur les troubles de Saint-Domingue*, a four-volume history of Haiti.

## W. E. B. DU BOIS TO ANNA J. COOPER,
## SEPTEMBER 12, 1924

1. The NAACP was founded in 1909 as an interracial civil rights organization. Founding members included Du Bois, Mary Church Terrell, Ida B. Wells, and others.

## ANNA J. COOPER TO
## W. E. B. DU BOIS, DECEMBER 21, 1927

1. Addison Scurlock (1883–1964) was an African American photographer and businessman made famous for his photographs of the Black community in Washington, DC, referred to as "Black Washington." He took several photographs and portraits of Cooper that remain among her most iconic images.

## ANNA J. COOPER TO
## W. E. B. DU BOIS, DECEMBER 31, 1929

1. Claude Bowers (1878–1958) was a white newspaper editor, journalist, American ambassador, and author of various history books about the Southern Democratic Party.

## ANNA J. COOPER TO
## W. E. B. DU BOIS, OCTOBER 30, 1930

1. Charlotte Forten Grimké (1837–1914) was an African American antislavery activist, poet, newspaper editorialist, and educator best known for her detailed journals depicting her experiences living in the North and teaching newly emancipated African Americans in the postbellum South. She was also a lifelong friend of Cooper, whom her husband Francis Grimké charged with arranging, stewarding, and publishing her papers.
2. James Forten (1766–1842) was a successful African American sailmaker, abolitionist, and businessman who provided funds to white abolitionist William Lloyd Garrison to support the founding of *The Liberator* and who along with Richard Allen, founder of the African Methodist Episcopal (AME) Church, established the first documented Colored Convention in 1830.

## ANNA H. JONES TO ANNA J. COOPER,
## AUGUST 16, 1925

1. See note 1 for "A Note on the Text."

## GEORGE M. JONES TO
## HERMANN H. THORNTON, OCTOBER 12, 1926

1. See Katherine Shilton, "'This Scholarly and Colored Alumna': Anna Julia Cooper's Troubled Relationship with Oberlin College" (2003), https://www2.oberlin.edu/external/EOG/History322 /AnnaJuliaCooper/AnnaJuliaCooper.htm.

## JEAN DE ROUSSY DE SALES TO
## ANNA J. COOPER, OCTOBER 11, 1941

1. Possibly Loire, referencing the longest river in France.
2. French, "misunderstanding."
3. French, "to be the one we expect."

## AUTOBIOGRAPHICAL NOTE

1. Vivian May's and Louise Hutchinson's research suggests that Cooper's father was likely either Dr. Fabius J. Haywood, her mother's enslaver, or his brother George Washington Haywood, based on Cooper's own suspicions about her mother's unwillingness to discuss her paternity. See May's *Anna Julia Cooper, Visionary Black Feminist* (2007) and Hutchinson's *Anna J. Cooper: A Voice from the South* (1981).

2. Cooper's use of "second sight" references a Black folkloric tradition in which children could be gifted with the ability to foretell future events. Later, W. E. B. Du Bois uses "second sight" to describe an African American "double consciousness" in *The Souls of Black Folk* in which African Americans possess both an awareness of themselves and an awareness of how they are viewed by (white) society.

## NOTE ABOUT "COURAGEOUS REVOLT"

1. Schools were legally segregated until 1954 when Brown v. Board of Education ruled the "separate but equal" doctrine unconstitutional. This Supreme Court ruling came fifty years after Cooper waged her "courageous revolt" against a separate "colored curriculum" for her students at M Street High School.

## "DISCUSSION OF THE SAME SUBJECT BY MRS. A. J. COOPER OF WASHINGTON, D.C."

1. Anna Julia Cooper is directly responding to Fannie Barrier Williams's address at the Chicago Columbian Exposition of 1893, which was entitled "The Intellectual Progress of the Colored Women of the United States Since the Emancipation Proclamation." Williams (1855–1944) was an African American educator, lecturer, civic leader, and clubwoman who co-founded the National League of Colored Women. She was selected as a representative for the Women's Building at the 1893 Chicago World's Fair after Black women protested their exclusion from the fair's program. Williams advocated, along with many other prominent African Americans, for the achievements of African Americans to be represented at the Chicago Columbian Exposition. In her speech, Williams addressed the World's Congress of Representative Women and argued that slavery had not made Black women incapable of the same moral and intellectual development as other

(white) women. Her address was followed by this response from Cooper, a response by Fanny Jackson Coppin, and Frederick Douglass's praise of all three women's speeches.

2. Cooper is likely referencing the sexual and physical violence enslaved Black women endured from the white enslavers.

3. *Fee simple* generally refers to real estate or land ownership, in that the owner of the property has full and irrevocable ownership of the land and, in being the highest form of property ownership, the owner has freedom to do with it as they wish. In evoking this legal rhetoric, Cooper applies this complete ownership of property to the institution of slavery and its danger to enslaved Black women. Black mothers thus hope to gain the "fee simple title" to their daughters to protect them from the sexual violence of the enslaver.

4. Fanny Jackson Coppin (1837–1913) was an African American educator, missionary, and advocate for female higher education. Coppin delivered a discussion in response to Fannie Barrier Williams's speech, "The Intellectual Progress of the Colored Women of the United States Since the Emancipation Proclamation," along with several other Black women, and spoke on the future of Black womanhood. Coppin taught at and later became principal of Philadelphia's Institute for Colored Youth (ICY), fighting and succeeding at getting the school to provide an industrial education for their students after discovering that few Blacks were employed in skilled trades.

5. The Colored Women's League (1892–1896) was an African American woman's club in DC whose mission was to form a national union of African American women and improve the conditions of Black women, children, and the urban poor. The club merged with the National Association of Colored Women in 1896.

6. Josephine Yates (1859–1912) was a trained chemist and one of the first Black professors to be hired at Lincoln University and also the first Black woman to be the head of a science department. Yates was a participant in the African American women's club movement, founding and serving as the president of the Women's League of Kansas City and later serving as the second president of the National Association of Colored Women.

### "MORE LETTERS CONCERNING THE FOLKLORE MOVEMENT AT HAMPTON"

1. Alice Bacon (1858–1918), a white American writer, educator, and teacher at the Hampton Institute, sent out queries requesting support to start a society for the study of Black folklore,

ethnology, and culture among the students at the Hampton Institute.

## PAPER [TO THE HAMPTON FOLKLORISTS]
## BY MRS. ANNA JULIA COOPER

1. The Hampton Folklore Society was founded in 1893 by Alice Bacon at Hampton Institute in Virginia for the collection and study of Black folklore. See Donald Waters's *Strange Ways and Sweet Dreams: Afro-American Folklore from the Hampton Institute* (Boston: G. K. Hall, 1983) and Shirley Moody-Turner's "Recovering Folklore as a Site of Resistance: Anna Julia Cooper and the Hampton Folklore Society," in *Black Folklore and the Politics of Racial Representation* (2013).

2. Cooper maintains a sarcastic tone throughout this paragraph in response to the belief that African Americans have no cultural or artistic expressions of their own and can only imitate that of white European or American men.

3. Antonio da Correggio (1489–1534) was a famous painter during the Italian Renaissance.

## "AUNT CHARLOTTE"

1. "Swing Low, Sweet Chariot" is an African American spiritual that subversively communicated both African Americans' hope for the end of oppression in heaven and signaled information about the Underground Railroad to enslaved African Americans seeking to escape to the North. The song was later popularized by the Jubilee Singers of Fisk University during the late-nineteenth century.

## "SIMON OF CYRENE"

1. Figured as important symbol throughout Cooper's life and work. She commissioned a memorial stained-glass window at St. Augustine's College Chapel featuring Simon of Cyrene taking the cross from Christ in honor of her late husband, the Reverend George A. C. Cooper. In her poem and in the artistic commission, Simon is represented as dark skinned and "expresses power and exudes agency" (May, *Anna Julia Cooper*, 60).

## "STERLING CALHOUN"

1. The *Negro Star* newspaper's 1935 republication of these events, which speaks to the national attention he received and an effort to collect support for his surviving family: "Fund for Pauper Who Went to Hero's Grave Grows," *Negro Star* 28, no. 5 (July 26, 1935), p. 1.

## "A BENCH BESIDE THE ROAD"

1. Mary Europe (1885–1947) was an African American pianist, organist, and music educator who attended M Street High School (Dunbar High School), where Cooper taught, and later was hired there as an accompanist and music teacher.

## "BLACK MADONNA"

1. The Black Madonna in the Chartres Cathedral in France is a sixteenth-century statue of the Virgin Mary and Jesus with a black overtone resulting from environmental factors such as lead-based pigments, candle smoke, or dust and grime. In 2017, a decision was made to remove the "unsightly coating" from the statue and thus after over five hundred years of being recognized for its dark exterior, the Black Madonna of Chartres bears a white-washed, blanched visage. See Benjamin Ramm, "A Controversial Restoration That Wipes Away the Past," *New York Times*, September 1, 2017, https://www.nytimes.com/2017/09/01/arts/design/chartres-cathedral-restoration-controversial.html.

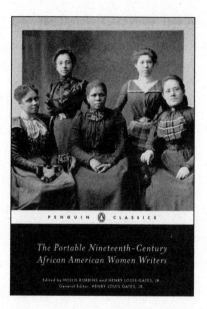

# The Light of Truth

## Writings of an Anti-Lynching Crusader

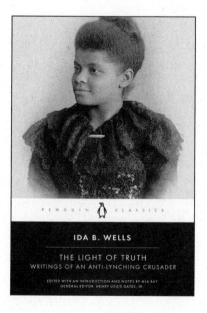

Seventy-two years before Rosa Parks's act of resistance, police dragged a young Black journalist named Ida B. Wells off a train for refusing to give up her seat. The experience shaped Wells's career, mounting an anti-lynching crusade that captured international attention. This volume covers the entire scope of Wells's career, collecting her early writings, articles, and essays. *The Light of Truth* is both an invaluable resource for study and a testament to Wells's activism.

"An enlightening read, this collection will inspire anyone who still believes that journalism can be a voice for the voiceless." –*BUST*

 PENGUIN CLASSICS